About **The Rose**

About
The
Rose

Creation and Community in Jay DeFeo's Circle

Elizabeth Ferrell

Yale University Press
New Haven and London

Published with assistance from the Nancy Batson Nisbet Rash Publication Fund.

yalebooks.com/art

Designed by Jeff Wincapaw
Set in Adobe Text Pro
Printed in Singapore

Library of Congress Control Number: 2021931875
ISBN 978-0-300-25652-9

A catalogue record for this book is available from the British Library.

This paper meets the requirements of ANSI/NISO Z39.48-1992 Permanence of Paper).

10 9 8 7 6 5 4 3 2 1

Jacket illustrations: (front) Jerry Burchard, Jay DeFeo standing in front of *Deathrose* at 2322 Fillmore Street, 1959 (detail, fig. 1); (back) Jay DeFeo, Correspondence for Wallace Berman, 1965 (detail, fig. 34).

Contents

Acknowledgments

One of this book's central findings—that creation is often social—played out in its research and writing: I am grateful for the support, guidance, and insights of many generous individuals and institutions.

The kindness, patience, and acumen of friends and colleagues nurtured me and continuously improved the manuscript. Principal among them were members of three writing groups: Karl Whittington, Christine Schick, Elizabeth Gand, Sherry Ehya, Jennifer Sakai, and Jacob Haubenreich in Berkeley; Namiko Kunimoto, Kris Paulsen, and Erica Levin in Ohio; and Delia Solomons and Linda Kim in Philadelphia. Individuals including Ken Allan, Elise Archias, Anastasia Aukeman, Sara Evans, Aaron Hyman, Tara McDowell, Bibiana Obler, Michaela Rife, and Karli Wurzelbacher similarly improved my ideas and pointed the way to completion, as did colleagues at Miami University, especially Pepper Stetler and Andrew Casper, and Arcadia University. Jill Pederson, in particular, encouraged me forward at every turn. Lastly, the book benefited greatly from the comments of the anonymous readers commissioned by Yale University Press and from the foresight and conscientious guidance of my editor, Amy Canonico.

Special thanks go to Anne M. Wagner, who first suggested that I look into DeFeo and then judiciously supervised the research and writing that laid this book's foundation. T. J. Clark, Darcy Grimaldo Grigsby, and Shannon Jackson similarly critiqued and stimulated this project early on. As the book developed, panels and symposia organized by Erika Doss, Stephen Eisenman, Catherine Spencer, and others allowed me to test ideas in public, and exchanges with anonymous reviewers and editors at *Art History,* with special thanks to Samuel Bibby and Natalie Adamson, brought the book's first chapter to life.

Funding for this project was provided by the Henry Luce Foundation/ ACLS Dissertation Fellowship in American Art; various predoctoral awards from the University of California, Berkeley; faculty development grants from Miami University and Arcadia University; Sue and Jim Ferrell; and postdoctoral fellowships from the Georgia O'Keeffe Museum Research Center and the Crystal Bridges Museum of American Art Tyson Scholars Program. Eumie Imm Stroukoff and Mindy Besaw were especially helpful during the latter two.

Many people and institutions opened their collections and recollections to my research, including the Menil Collection, the Norton Simon Museum, the Oakland Museum of California, the San Francisco Museum of Modern Art, and the Whitney Museum of American Art, where Dana Miller was especially generous and helpful. Jerry Burchard, David Carlson,

Jean Conner, Robert Conway, Lawrence Fox, Caroline Huber, Fred Martin, Michael McClure, and Rebecca Solnit shared treasured pieces of the Fillmore circle's history with me in the form of photographs, artworks, memories, and interviews. My research likewise benefited from the expert guidance of librarians and archivists, including the staff of the Bancroft Library, the Museum of Modern Art Archives, and the Archives of American Art, as well as Jeff Gunderson at the San Francisco Art Institute Archives and Jane Glover at the Katharine Hanrahan American Art Study Center at the De Young Museum. Finally, I extend my gratitude to the librarians of the various home institutions I occupied during this project, especially Adam Hess, director of the Landman Library at Arcadia University, who went to extraordinary lengths to ensure I had the materials necessary to complete my manuscript amid a pandemic.

This publication would not have been possible without the collectors, institutions, and artist estates who granted me permission to reproduce their artworks and documents, including G. B. Carson and the Estate of Wally Hedrick; the Kohn Gallery and the Estate of Wallace Berman; the Conner Family Trust; and Amy Evans McClure. I reserve special thanks for The Jay DeFeo Foundation and Leah Levy, executive director and trustee, for their years of exceptional and unflagging support.

Students, including Shelby Brisbane, Natasha Litwinow, and Hannah Weissberger, aided me through the most tedious tasks of manuscript preparation, and I am indebted to the team at Yale University Press, Raychel Rapazza in particular, for steering this book to publication.

Friends and family helped me along at every step: Santa Monica's "herd"; Berkeley's "teamo"; the Rainofs, friends who are like family; and the extended Harvey clan, friends who became family. In particular, Cathie Harvey, Rebecca Rainof-Mas, and my amazing sister, Emily, cheered me forward when my internal motivation flagged. My parents, Sue and Jim, first showed me the power of art and education and supported this project, and me, unconditionally. Finally, Edwin Harvey—partner, reader, friend. I once made him promise to finish this book if I were somehow unable. He would have, and knowing that carried me through.

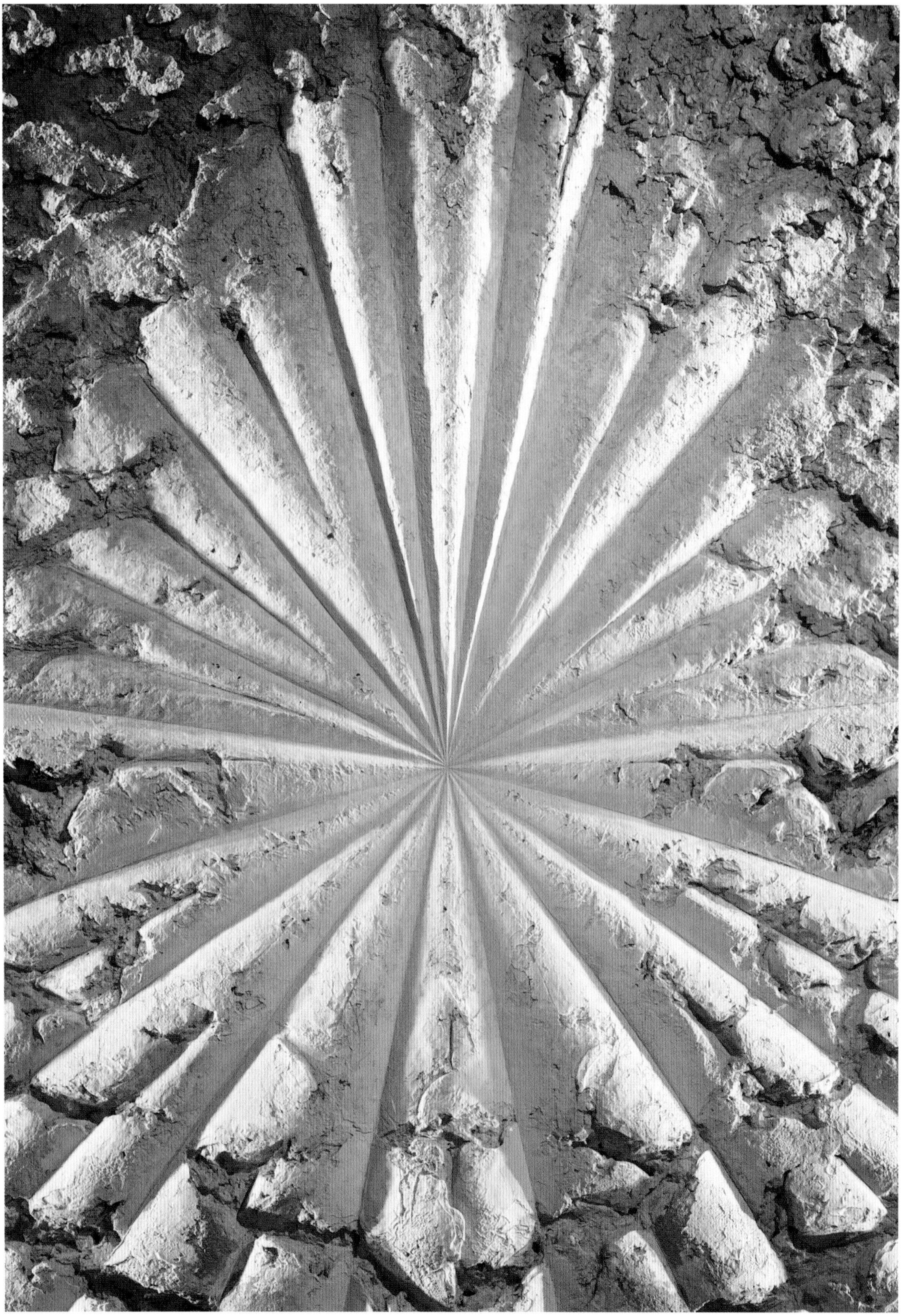

Introduction

THE BURST AND THE BODY

Two photographs taken in the same Fillmore Street apartment in San Francisco on the cusp of 1960 propose starkly divergent identities for a single work of art—namely, *The Rose,* a roughly eleven-by-eight-foot oil painting that Jay DeFeo began in that apartment in 1958 and would continue to paint there until 1965 (figs. 1, 2). In the first shot, the painting's textured surface catches sunlight streaming in through the sides of the apartment's bay window. Shimmering in the raking light, *The Rose*'s radial motif itself appears to glow, casting DeFeo as a silhouette within the rarefied air of her studio-cum-sanctuary. *The Rose* thus conforms to critic Clement Greenberg's influential period prescription for art to provide aesthetic experiences that transcend everyday life.[1] Elevating DeFeo's craft and declaring her autonomy, the photograph echoes tropes from Hans Namuth's celebratory shots of the abstract expressionist artists whom Greenberg championed (fig. 3).

The second photograph, a snapshot taken only months after the picture described above, associates *The Rose* with a different strand of postwar art. It shows the "remounting party" that DeFeo threw to facilitate *The Rose*'s transfer to a larger canvas in the winter of 1959–60, approximately one year into its production. Physically unable to complete the task alone, DeFeo invited help from some of the bevy of artists and writers who, like her, had recently moved to the Fillmore District. "There were at least twenty of us holding a part of the canvas," recalled the artist Carlos Villa. "We all were so loaded . . . it's a wonder that the painting got mounted."[2] While not all accounts of the event corroborate Villa's memory of the participants' intoxication, the damaged photograph supports his description of their teamwork: revelers hold edges of the unstretched canvas aloft as they navigate a doorway. Such fusions of artistic practice and sociability would become increasingly common in the 1960s, as evidenced by documentary shots of Happenings, Fluxus events, and the various goings-on of Andy Warhol's Factory, which camouflage artists in riots of friends, participants, collaborators, and assistants (fig. 4). The snapshot of the remounting

Detail, fig. 8

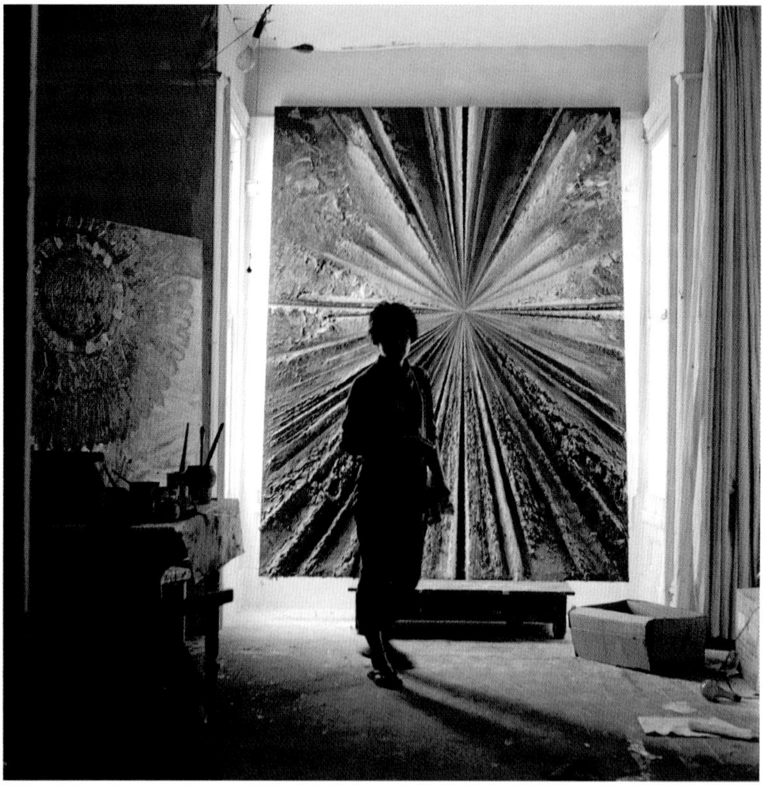

Fig. 1 Jerry Burchard, Jay DeFeo standing in front of *Deathrose* at 2322 Fillmore Street, 1959. The Estate of Jerry Burchard.

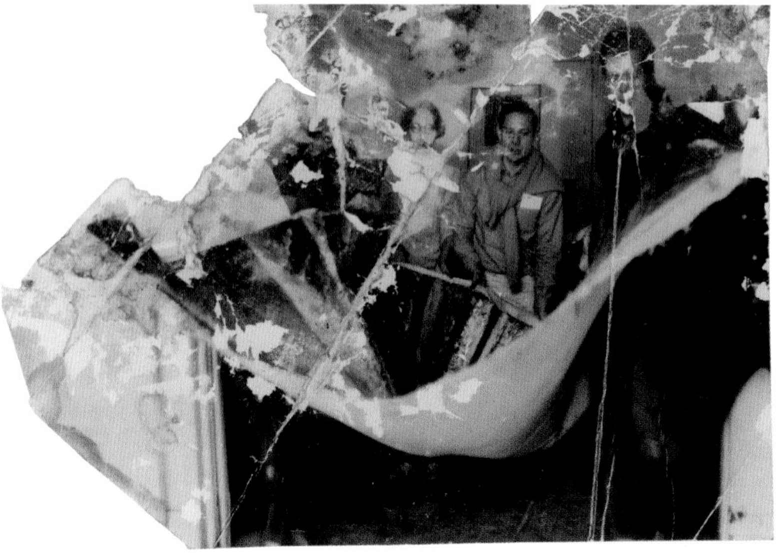

Fig. 2 Transfer of original *The Rose* (known then as *Deathrose*) canvas with Jean Conner, Craig Kauffman, and unidentified man, 1959–60. Gelatin silver copy print. Bruce Conner photograph collection, BANC PIC 1997.069, Bancroft Library, University of California, Berkeley.

party not only transforms *The Rose*'s making from a solitary activity into a highly social one; it also radically recasts the painting's form. Stripped of its gestalt, *The Rose* becomes unwieldy and vulnerable, apparent more for its base materiality than for any transcendent identity, like an anonymous corpse slumping under its own weight. This abject painting, unlike

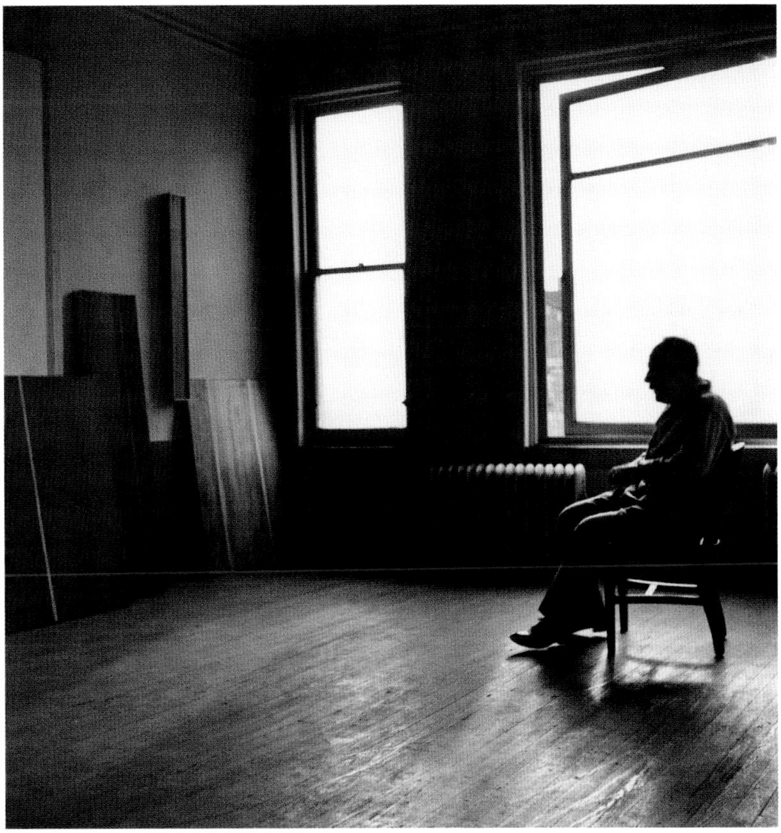

Fig. 3 Hans Namuth, *Barnett Newman, New York City,* 1951. Courtesy Center for Creative Photography, University of Arizona.

the privileged one described above, illustrates the desire to reintegrate art with mundane experience that fueled such radical cultural experiments as pop and performance.

These two photographs align *The Rose* with canonical postwar art practices that have frequently been seen as oppositional. In so doing, they pose the question: Where does *The Rose* fit within foundational discursive binaries—such as high modernism/postmodernism, individual authorship/collective labor, autonomy/heteronomy, medium specificity/intermedia, opticality/objecthood, expression/appropriation, and closed work/open text—that have historically structured dominant narratives of art made in the United States during the decades following World War II?[3] The simple answer is: *The Rose,* its making, and its consumption variously transcended, evaded, and collapsed such dichotomies. To fully understand how and why, we must work through these constructed categories, as DeFeo did, rather than simply leave them behind. For they were in use in the art practice, theory, and writing of DeFeo's time and have persisted to some extent, despite substantial critique, in historiographies of postwar art. *The Rose*'s evasion of these predominant binaries marginalized it within then-current trends and the histories that followed—a condition exacerbated by relative scholarly disinterest in the art of women, especially those who worked far from New York, the epicenter of American postwar art.

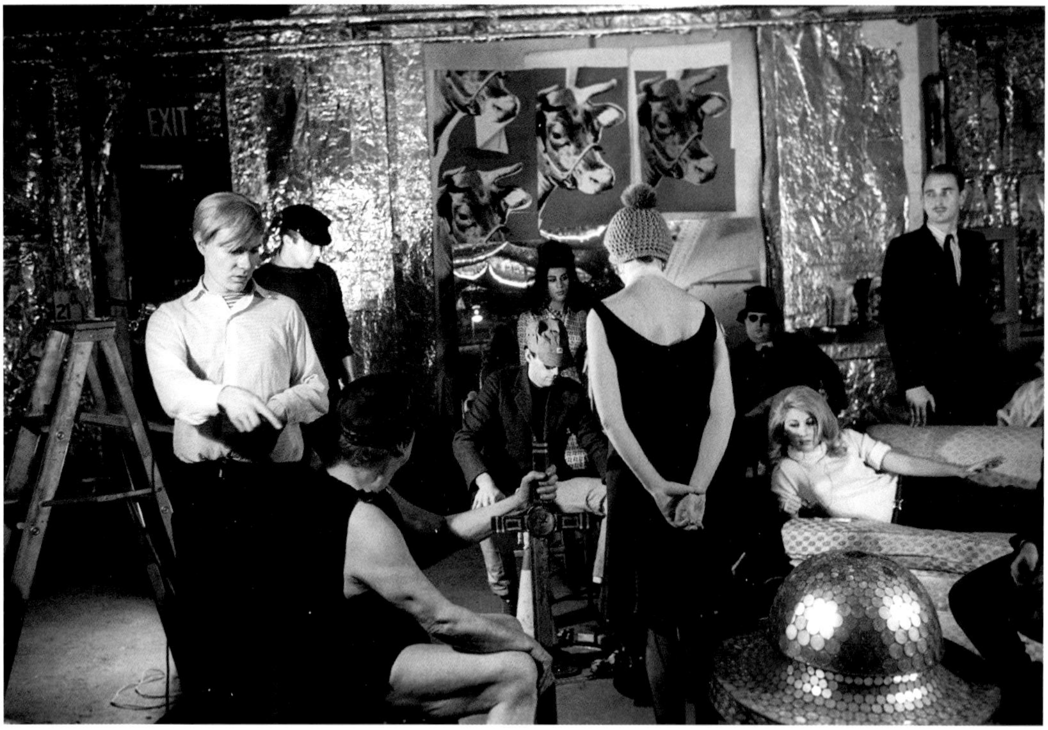

Fig. 4 The production of Andy Warhol's underground film *Camp* at the Factory, Warhol's studio in New York, 1965. Photograph by Steve Schapiro/Corbis via Getty Images.

This book reframes *The Rose*'s elusiveness by considering it together with works created in response to it. The following chapters reveal that *The Rose* served as a nexus for artistic collaboration in the Fillmore neighborhood, thereby synthesizing the seemingly incongruous artistic practices and forms of authorship presented in the two photographs described above. During *The Rose*'s long production, DeFeo's neighbors created their own works about and around it, including a series of photographs, a painting, a poem, and a film. DeFeo, in turn, responded to her friends' interpretations of her painting by recycling them into photomontages and collaged correspondence. These intertextual exchanges involved dialogical interactions between discrete works, media, and studios. They thus differed from typical models of collaboration, in which multiple artists jointly produce a single work.

To emphasize that they preserved more of each artist's individual agency, I will refer to these collaborations around *The Rose* as "interindividual." They are largely absent from previous scholarship on both DeFeo and the Fillmore District art scene of the 1950s and 1960s, despite the fact that, as we will see, close attention to these interindividual collaborations can illuminate distinctive, historically significant forms of authorship and community that DeFeo and her friends forged through her painting. The dance that these artists performed around *The Rose* between solo and group production generated a type of authorship that falls between the first photograph's image of autonomous making and the snapshot's depiction of communal creation, between the cloistered studio and the party. These exchanges had interpersonal, as well as authorial, implications because they occurred between neighbors, lovers, and friends. They became vehicles for artists to enact constellations between self and other that spoke directly to pervasive period anxieties about the relationship between individual and society, concerns that refracted through the bohemian art world of postwar San Francisco in complex ways.

In sum, the case studies featured in this book show that Fillmore artists sought ways to make art and live life together without sacrificing the identity and agency of each individual artist and subject. This was no small challenge, and I do not claim, categorically, that they succeeded. But we will see that they managed, here and there, quite remarkably, to strike fragile, momentary balances between individual and collective, personal freedom and group belonging, that bridged binary possibilities for artistic identity and subjectivity prevalent in postwar America. In doing so they discovered a sliver of middle ground between modernist autonomy and postmodernist anonymity, atomization and conformity.

This finding adds nuance to the oft-repeated but only thinly evidenced claim that the making of art and the making of community became intertwined in postwar San Francisco as the city's anemic art market encouraged artists to become one another's primary audience. Past studies have focused on either the entire Fillmore art scene or an individual artist who participated in it. My use of a single work (*The Rose*) as a lens for investigating a community of artists integrates these monographic and milieu-based approaches. The combination of focus and breadth this method provides makes the interaction between art practice and interpersonal relationships within the Fillmore neighborhood newly visible, exposing with greater clarity how the making and viewing of art affected, and was affected by, social bonds between individuals.

THE ROSE

DeFeo was born Mary Joan DeFeo in 1929 and was raised in Northern California from the time she was three. After her parents divorced in 1939, DeFeo lived primarily with her mother in San Jose, where she acquired the nickname "Jay" around the same time that her high school art teacher, Lena Emery, was encouraging her to pursue art as a career. DeFeo went on to study studio art at the University of California, Berkeley, earning both bachelor's and master's degrees by the age of twenty-two. Upon graduating from her master's program in 1951, DeFeo was awarded the university's prestigious Sigmund Martin Heller Traveling Fellowship, which she used to visit Europe, Morocco, and New York. Her travels expanded the primarily formalist training she received at Berkeley. She drew particular inspiration from prehistoric drawings catalogued at the Musée de l'Homme in Paris, from the crumbling Renaissance architecture of Florence, and from Paleolithic cave paintings in Altamira, which had only recently opened to the public. Soon after returning to Berkeley in 1953, DeFeo met fellow artist Wally Hedrick. A year later, the couple moved across the bay to San Francisco and got married. They eventually settled in the Fillmore District, which was quickly becoming one of the city's primary cultural centers. It was there, in 1958, that DeFeo began to work on *The Rose,* a monumental painting on which she labored more or less continuously until 1966.[4]

When DeFeo first started painting *The Rose,* its substantial dimensions and curious blend of exuberant paint handling and geometric composition made it typical of the style she had developed since moving to the Fillmore neighborhood. Originally titled *Deathrose, The Rose* was conceived as a pendant to *The Jewel* (1959), a narrower and more colorful canvas that echoes *The Rose*'s starburst design (fig. 5). DeFeo tended to "start things in pairs, threesomes, or sometimes foursomes, so that," she explained, "there will be a pair of images that are somewhat opposite each other." In the specific case of *Deathrose* and *The Jewel,* both paintings manifested DeFeo's initial impulse to make a work that "had a center to it," but she saw *The Jewel* as "a life symbol—positive and convex" and *Deathrose* as a "black and white concave death symbol."[5]

DeFeo had grand ambitions for this pair of paintings. She promoted them in 1959, for example, to Dorothy Miller, then a curator at the Museum of Modern Art, New York (MoMA), writing: "Frankly nothing could be more important in my whole life than the assurance that . . . the Deathrose and its color counterpart—the Jewel . . . would be in the Museum someday—that is if I can finish them to my satisfaction. . . . But it horrifies me to think the matter might be totally forgotten by the time they are complete—and of course if they *are* to be what I hope, I certainly can't rush myself."[6] Rush, she did not. Instead of the six months it typically took DeFeo to complete a painting, she worked for seven more years on *The Rose,* to the virtual exclusion of other works—and, in some ways, as we will see, to the detriment of her career.

The painting first veered off course from DeFeo's typical process in the winter of 1959–60, when she remounted it onto a larger canvas, using Elmer's glue, a staple gun, and, according to Villa's reminiscence, several inebriated friends. This enlargement made *The Rose* too big to fit through the doorway of DeFeo's studio and thus unfit for transportation to MoMA or any other public venue. It also appears to have severed *The Rose*'s dependency on its brighter, convex twin. Within months of the remounting, DeFeo quietly completed *The Jewel* and never worked on it again, whereas her work on *The Rose* would continue and intensify for years to come.

The opposition that DeFeo perceived between *The Jewel* and *The Rose* now became subsumed in a dialectic process that propelled the latter painting through a series of compositional and physical mutations. Accordingly, the painting's title changed numerous times, from *Deathrose* to *White Rose* to, ultimately, *The Rose.* DeFeo cycled between additive and subtractive techniques, using trowels to slather on layers of oil-based house

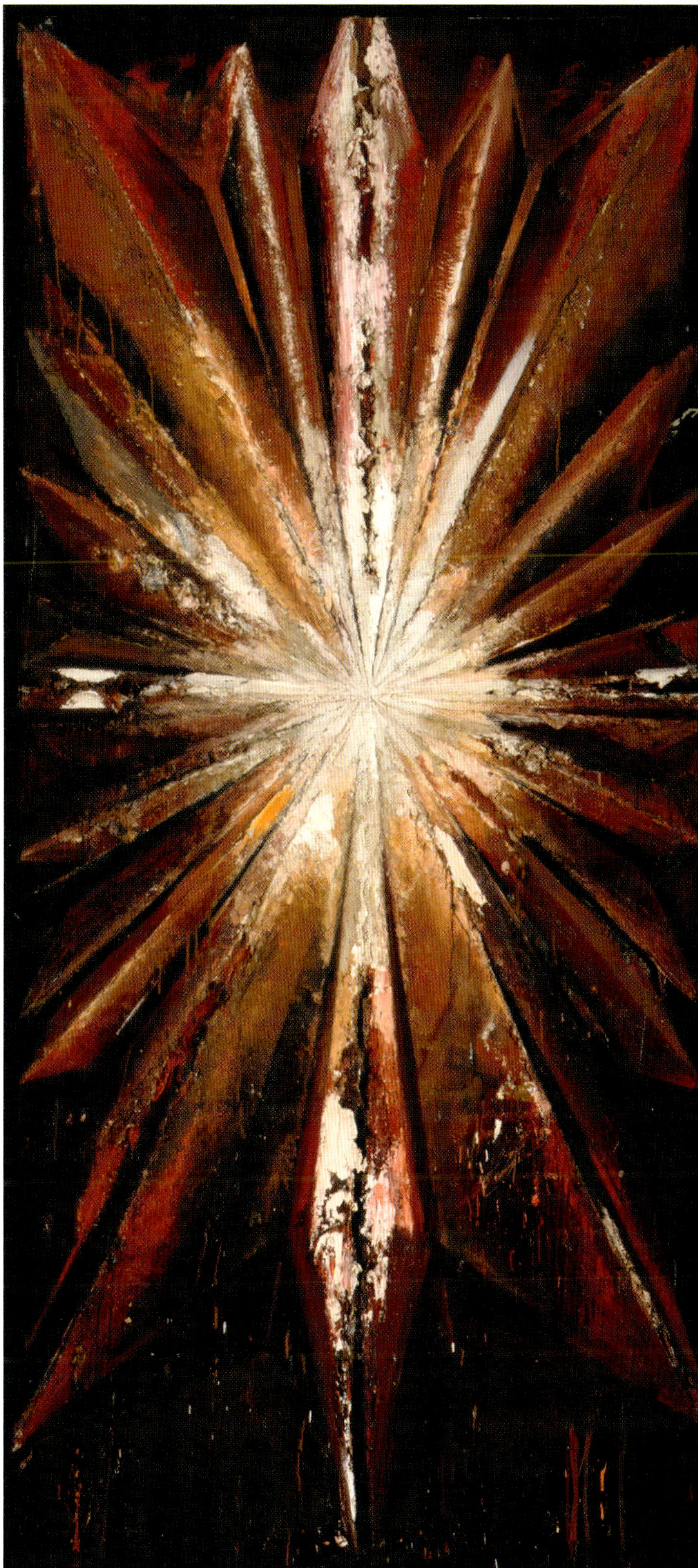

Fig. 5 Jay DeFeo, *The Jewel*, 1959. Oil on canvas, 120 × 55 in. (304.8 × 139.7 cm). Los Angeles County Museum of Art. Gift of the 1998 Collectors Committee [AC1998.47.1].

paint, mixed with mica and fast-drying agents to add heft, and then carving the hardened paint away with knives and other tools. "More than once, the whole thing was scraped down to the canvas," DeFeo recounted, "and the whole thing [then] commenced [again] from scratch." She used organic metaphors to explain the "metamorphosis" between *The Rose*'s "stages of growth," describing a transformative process she came to believe was inevitable: "I suspect that even if I had had the space to spread out these ideas on separate canvases, the work would have proceeded on a single format alone, in as much as I felt the painting had to experience its own life-span in time."[7] To DeFeo, the process of *The Rose*'s making was essential to its identity.

Studio shots trace the "stages" that the painting cycled through, as the material formation of its radial motif shifted from rigid rays into petal-like gyrations and then back again (figs. 6–8). DeFeo indulged in the manipulation of voluminous paint, begetting a motley collection of prominent brushstrokes and palette-knife trails that were eventually subsumed within a less painterly surface punctuated instead by fissures and crevasses. By

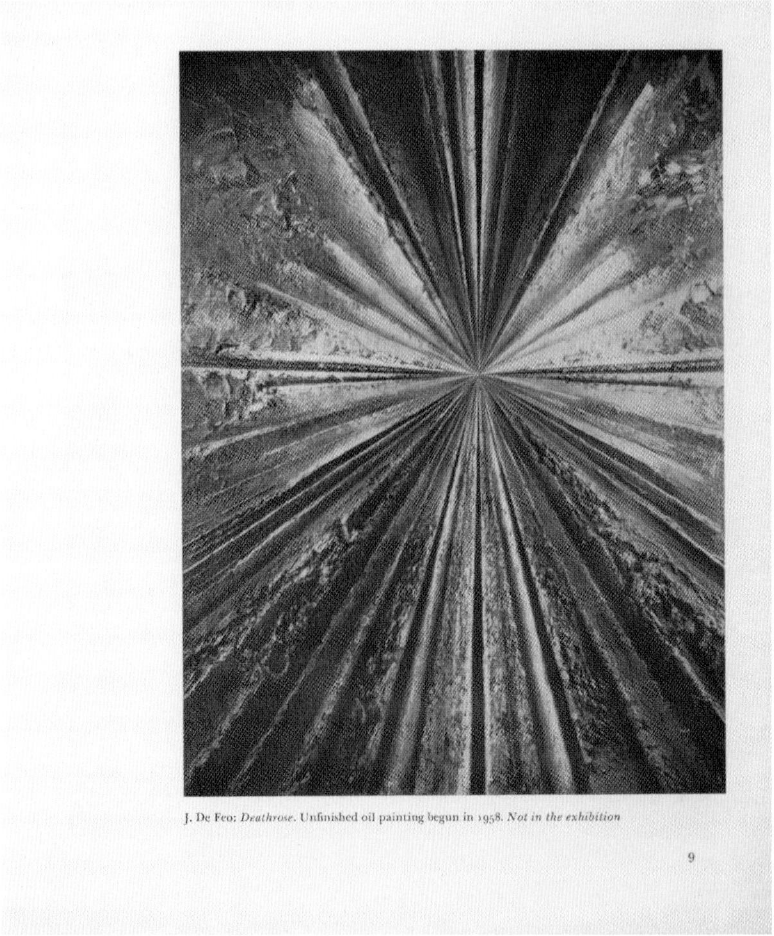

Fig. 6 *Deathrose* reproduced in the exhibition catalogue for *Sixteen Americans* (New York: Museum of Modern Art, 1959). Museum of Modern Art Library, New York.

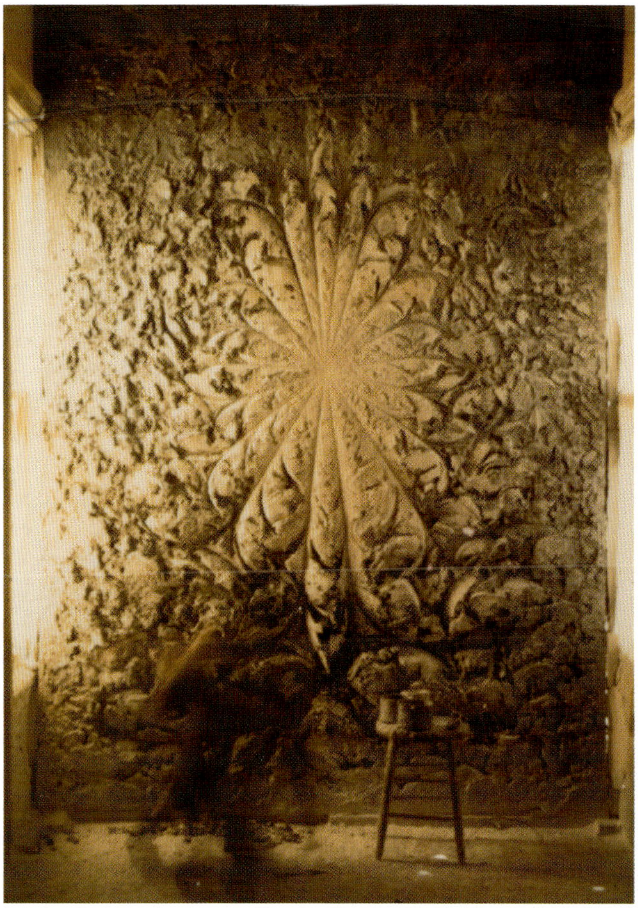

Fig. 7 *The Rose,* then referred to as *Deathrose,* "baroque" phase, with blurred figure and stool, c. 1962–63. Gelatin silver print. The Jay DeFeo Foundation, Berkeley, Calif. [JDF no. R0001].

then, *The Rose* appeared to have become hard and brittle, bearing a surface more similar to rock, crystal, or ice than to settled oil (fig. 9).

There were also moments of *The Rose*'s development, especially early on, in which it exhibited more spatial illusionism than material relief. In early photographs, smooth, dark spokes punctuate the worked paint surface as outlines rather than recesses. Later, as DeFeo heaped more and more paint onto the canvas, the illusion of a pleated surface became real, sculptural peaks and valleys that stood out in relief from the canvas—in some places by nearly a foot. Light from the bay window in which the painting stood fell obliquely across its corrugated surface, confusing tonal gradations *on* the surface with shadows cast *by* the surface. Fittingly, DeFeo described *The Rose* in 1961 as "a combination of painting and sculpture."

Despite the overtly sculptural quality of the finished work that viewers encounter today (thin scumbling at the top of the canvas swells to nearly a foot in depth just below the center), DeFeo believed that the "actual three-dimensional aspects of sculpture" never fully eclipsed the work's embrace of "the illusory nature of space," which she held to be native to painting.[8] Viewing *The Rose* with this claim in mind, one observes how the transition from brightness at the center of the canvas to darkness at the

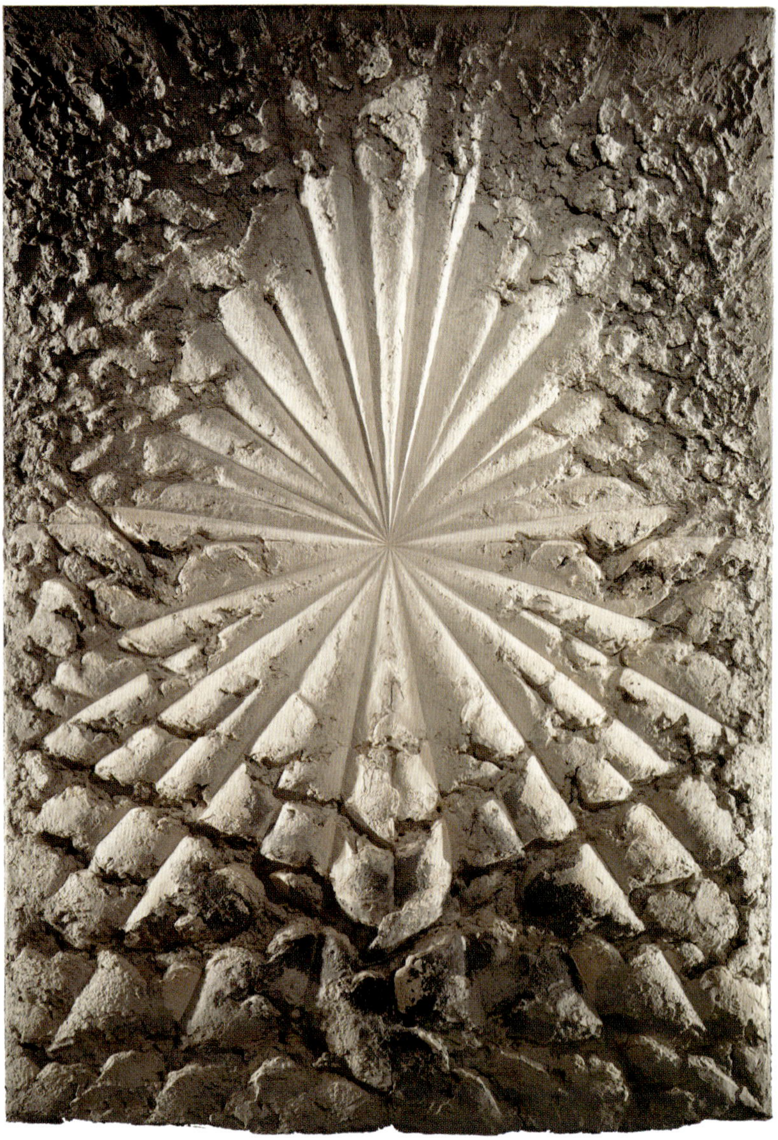

Fig. 8 Jay DeFeo, *The Rose*, 1958–66. Oil with wood and mica on canvas, 128⅞ × 92¼ × 11 in. (327.3 × 234.3 × 27.9 cm). Whitney Museum of American Art, New York. Gift of The Jay DeFeo Foundation and purchase, with funds from the Contemporary Painting and Sculpture Committee and the Judith Rothschild Foundation [Inv. N.: 95.170].

periphery is produced by changes in both tone and texture: crisply honed corrugation at the center of the composition cedes to a lumpy tumult of grays and blacks at the edges. DeFeo flecked the work with other colors of paint and sparkling chips of mica. The thick paint surface harbors other materials as well: upon acknowledging that her experiments were pushing the medium of oil paint toward its structural limits, DeFeo began to embed wooden dowels within the paint strata and stuffed newspapers into the cracks that opened up when those attempts at shoring up the thick surface proved insufficient (fig. 10).[9]

In 1965 DeFeo's long production of *The Rose* was halted when the rent for her and Hedrick's apartment dramatically increased, effectively evicting them. By that time, the painting weighed nearly a ton and required a team

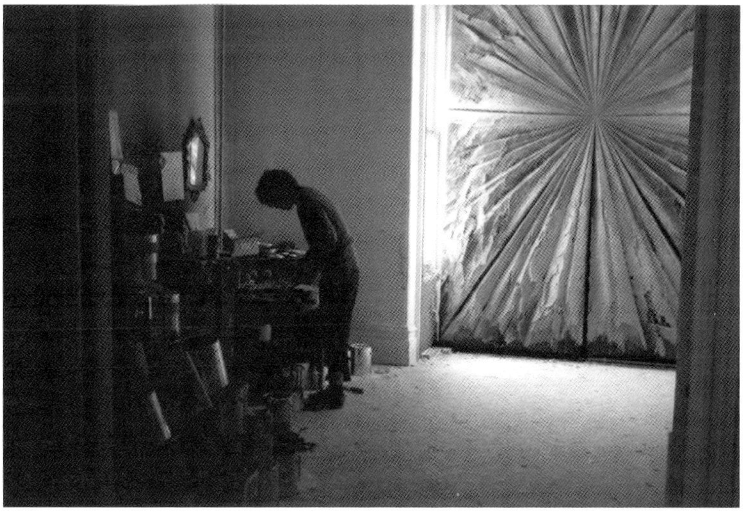

Fig. 9 Jay DeFeo working on an early version of *The Rose* (known then as *The White Rose*) at 2322 Fillmore Street, 1960–61. Digital file from negative. The Jay DeFeo Foundation, Berkeley, Calif. [JDF no. R0353].

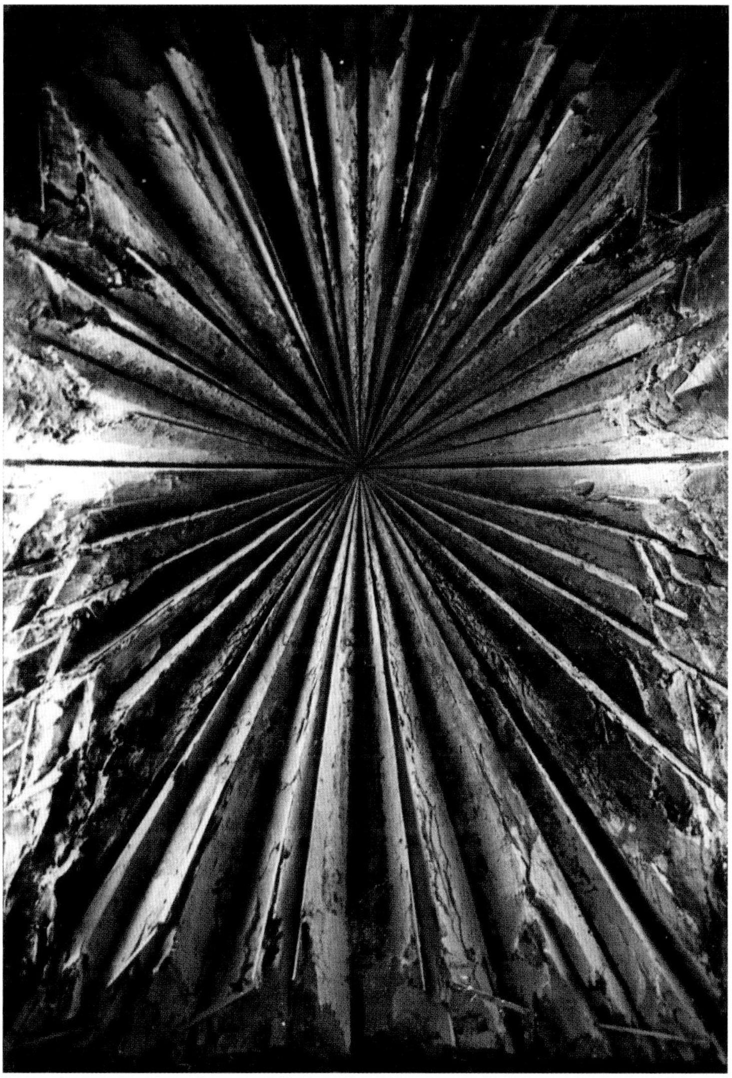

Fig. 10 Early version of *The Rose* with wooden dowels at 2322 Fillmore Street, 1960s. Gelatin silver print. The Jay DeFeo Foundation, Berkeley, Calif. [JDF no. R0650].

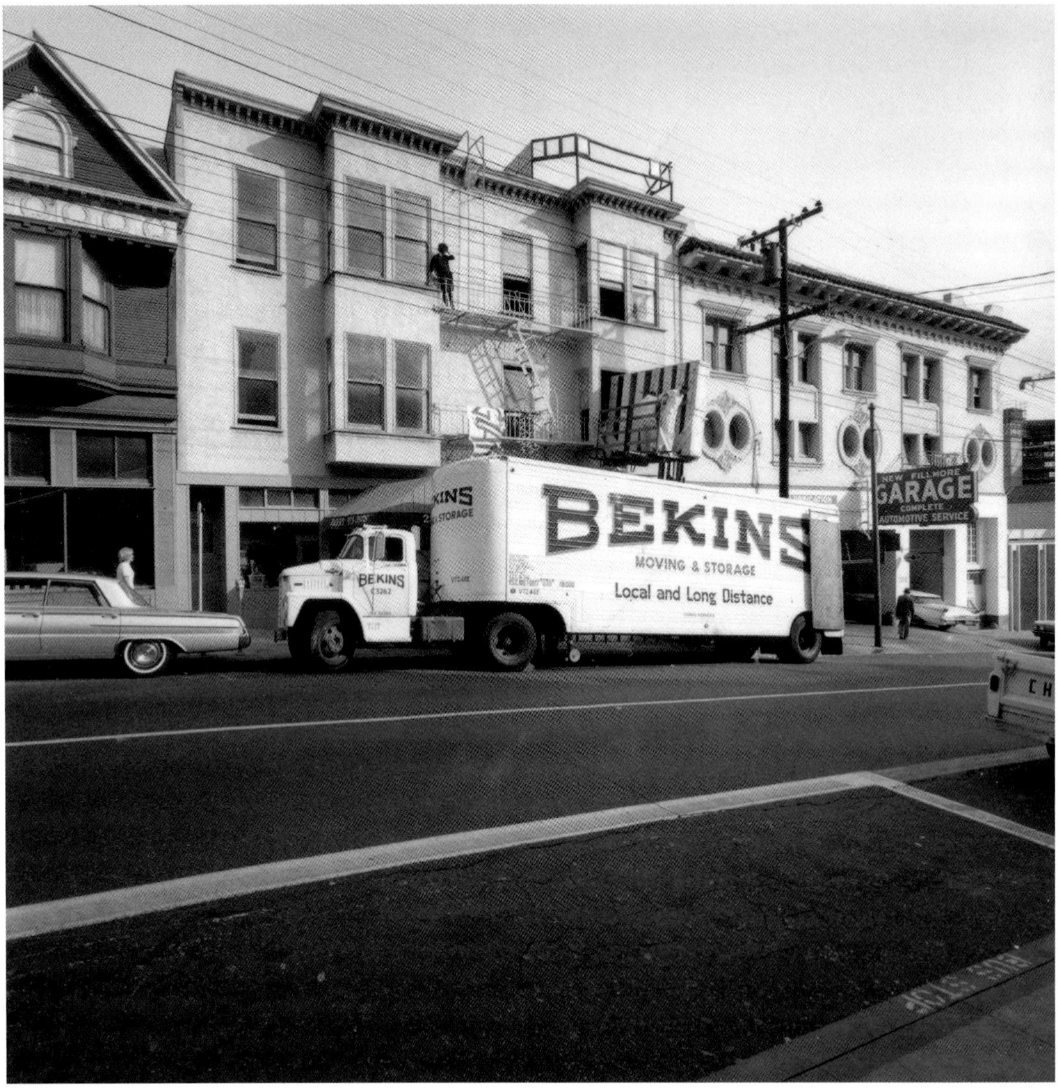

Fig. 11 Removal of *The Rose* from 2322 Fillmore Street. *The Rose,* packed and crated, is lowered by forklift while Jay DeFeo looks on from the fire escape above, November 9, 1965. Digital scan from 120mm negative. The Jay DeFeo Foundation, Berkeley, Calif. [JDF no. R6833].

of professional movers to cut through the studio's exterior wall and then use a hydraulic lift to lower the work safely to the street (fig. 11). DeFeo often wavered when discussing *The Rose*'s completion, indicating the significance that the process of making the work acquired. She claimed in 1972, for example, that the painting reached the telos toward which it was always tending, if in a somewhat meandering fashion: "The final version of the painting is definitely the one I was working toward all those years." But she immediately walked back this initially conclusive statement, adding: "Still the final details and refinement of the surface qualities . . . all that had to remain undone. . . . It has even crossed my mind to recommence the concept completely." DeFeo hedged similarly against *The Rose*'s finality in 1975: "I suppose [*The Rose*] was only 'finished' because we were evicted from our studio."[10]

After *The Rose* was removed from DeFeo's studio in November 1965, it was taken to the Pasadena Art Museum (PAM). PAM's director at the time was Walter Hopps, who had previously run the Ferus Gallery in Los Angeles, which represented DeFeo's work for many years and, at times, helped support her with a monthly allowance. DeFeo felt obligated to Hopps, as well as to a few other California-based gallerists who had championed her, and she therefore committed to debuting the work on the West Coast.[11] DeFeo spent the early months of 1966 in a makeshift studio at PAM, laboring over the painting's finishing touches while living in Pasadena, apart from Hedrick, from whom she had separated and would eventually divorce. She then returned to the Bay Area, settling in the town of Ross. Three years later, in February 1969, the painting was finally shown—first at PAM, for only a month, then for two months at the San Francisco Museum of Art (SFMA, now the San Francisco Museum of Modern Art), and finally for two additional months at the San Francisco Art Institute (SFAI).[12]

These three brief exhibitions unfortunately marked the end of institutional attention to *The Rose,* at least during DeFeo's lifetime—though not for lack of interest earlier in the painting's life. The prominent collector J. Patrick Lannan had expressed interest in acquiring *The Rose* in 1959, and Miller, who was introduced to DeFeo and her work on a scouting trip to the Bay Area that same year, wanted to include it in *Sixteen Americans,* the showcase of works by up-and-coming artists that she was curating at MoMA.[13] But DeFeo was unready, at that time, to part with her still-in-progress work for Lannan, and she likewise denied Miller's request on the grounds that *The Rose* was unfinished. She did, however, permit the painting to be reproduced in the *Sixteen Americans* catalogue as a work in progress (see fig. 6). Thanks, in part, to the promotional efforts of Miller and Hopps, other photographic reproductions of *The Rose*—sometimes shown with DeFeo working on it—appeared prominently elsewhere in the early 1960s, including in the magazines *Art in America, Holiday,* and *Look,* and in the government-sponsored book *Creative America.*[14] These publications variously represented *The Rose* as an emblem of DeFeo's oeuvre, of

San Francisco's picturesque bohemia, and of America's creative ingenuity.

By 1969 the interest that curators and collectors had shown in purchasing the painting a decade earlier had evaporated. DeFeo was unable to secure a buyer for *The Rose,* despite extensive efforts, and a SFAI conference room that was supposed to be a temporary stopover became the painting's indefinite home. Fearing for the *The Rose*'s safety in the early 1970s, DeFeo initiated an attempt to address its structural instability: she hired conservator Tony Rockwell to encase the fragile painting in a protective coating, composed primarily of plaster, in the hopes of safely transporting it to SFMA's conservation lab. However, a dearth of funds and an abundance of logistical obstacles prevented *The Rose* from leaving the SFAI conference room. Eventually, drywall was placed in front of the already-shrouded work; one could have looked directly at it in situ and not known it was there.[15]

The Rose remained thusly immured at SFAI until 1995—six years after DeFeo died from lung cancer at the age of sixty—when the trust formed through her will partnered with the Whitney Museum of American Art to restore the work, both physically and to the canon of postwar American art. Since then the conserved painting has appeared in several major exhibitions at the Whitney, including *Jay DeFeo: A Retrospective* (2012–13), greatly raising the profile of both artist and painting.[16]

The Whitney's DeFeo retrospective culminated a monographic approach to interpreting *The Rose* that had been both prevalent and productive since the painting's return to public view. This approach (which entails contextualizing the work within the chronological arc of DeFeo's biography and the formal progression of her oeuvre) has helped, in particular, to normalize the painting's seeming eccentricities by situating them within the artist's lifetime of work. Such studies have often been framed as correctives: by mustering facts about DeFeo's life and *The Rose*'s facture, monographic methods are seen to counter the many "myths" that her friends from the Fillmore neighborhood and later critics told about the work, especially the series of romanticized tales of martyrdom, obsession, madness, and futility that visual and verbal representations of *The Rose* perpetuated during the painting's long absence from public view.[17] One of the challenges (and, I hope, contributions) of this book is to revisit these myths and recover some of their value without dismissing the gains of the foundational monographs that preceded it.

THE FILLMORE-UNION MONTPARNASSE

The Rose's restoration in the 1990s was part of a rising tide of interest in the art of postwar California that has continued to swell ever since. Rebecca Solnit's *Secret Exhibition* (1990) and Richard Cándida Smith's *Utopia and Dissent* (1995) paved the way for more focused books and exhibitions about art in midcentury San Francisco, such as Anastasia Aukeman's *Welcome to*

Painterland (2016), which surveys the Fillmore community that DeFeo belonged to during her production of *The Rose.*[18] This body of scholarship represents a second significant approach to studying *The Rose.* By situating it within the art world of postwar San Francisco, rather than within DeFeo's career, such studies have painted an increasingly detailed picture of art practice in the Bay Area during the decades following World War II. The broad strokes of that picture are as follows.

The apartment at 2322 Fillmore Street that DeFeo and Hedrick moved to in 1955 was on the second floor of a nondescript building on the border between two traditionally distinct neighborhoods—the working-class Fillmore District and affluent Pacific Heights. The Fillmore was, at the time, undergoing a massive, government-funded "urban renewal," which was designed, as other scholars have shown, to displace its predominantly Black population in order to make room for wealthy white residents like those residing in Pacific Heights. The intermediary zone where DeFeo and Hedrick lived was sometimes referred to as Upper Fillmore, Cow Hollow, or Union.[19]

Soon after they moved in, their building became a hub for the mostly white, middle-class artists and writers who were moving into the neighborhood, attracted by the low rents and bebop clubs that lined lower Fillmore Street. "There was kind of a network of people—friends of friends of friends of friends, and it just sort of centered there," DeFeo later recalled of the building. "The Fillmore Street address kind of drew everybody together from divergent places and connections." The building may even have acquired the nickname "Painterland," affirming its cultural significance.[20]

While the artists who lived in the Fillmore District from the mid-1950s to the mid-1960s did not constitute a cohesive artistic movement (with a codified philosophy, aesthetic strictures, and official institutions), they did experience a sense of social belonging and shared identity. "We were a we," declared the artist Joan Brown, whose first-person plurality included DeFeo, Hedrick, Wallace and Shirley Berman, Bruce and Jean Conner, Michael and Joanna McClure, Manuel Neri, Sonia Gechtoff, and James Kelly. The group socialized, including at DeFeo and Hedrick's frequent raucous parties, and founded galleries and exhibition collectives that catered more to local artists than to the city's scarce collectors. These activities led Alfred Frankenstein, the art editor for the *San Francisco Chronicle,* to dub the area "the Fillmore-Union Montparnasse," conjuring a bohemian enclave distinct from, though affiliated with, the better-known and more literary-minded Beats of North Beach.[21] The terms "community," "circle," "coterie," and "group" all aptly describe the social structures these artists established while living and working in the Fillmore District, for each captures aspects of the mix of cohesion and looseness that characterized the milieu's social dynamic.[22]

The Fillmore community was also a node within a larger network of cultural circles that were scattered throughout the Bay Area in the decades following World War II—groups of artists, gallerists, writers, publishers, dancers, filmmakers, and playwrights who, collectively, were responsible for the flourishing of avant-garde activity that came to be known as the San Francisco Renaissance. Their diverse output was united by a willingness to defy formal conventions and traditional boundaries between media. This aesthetic deviance went hand in hand with an embrace of traditions and lifestyles that fell outside of, and could be seen to challenge, the narrow norms of mainstream American society.

Helping to foster the city's postwar renaissance was San Francisco's reputation as a tolerant place, its history of political radicalism, and its non-commercial cultural landscape.[23] Compared to many other locations in the United States, San Francisco was therefore, on the whole, more accepting of those who transgressed hegemonic prescriptions, and it afforded a greater degree of anonymity for cultural producers who feared censorship. The stakes were high: even in the Bay Area, artists and writers sometimes faced harsh consequences for making their alternative values and behaviors (their experimentation with narcotics, sexuality, and esoteric spirituality, for instance) the content of their work, as demonstrated most famously by the 1957 obscenity trial over Allen Ginsberg's "Howl." Such instances of outright legal censure, as well as the media's sensationalized stereotyping of San Francisco's bohemian denizens as "beatniks," encouraged many artists to keep their work largely underground.[24]

Unlike New York, the Bay Area had few commercial galleries in the 1940s through the mid-1960s, especially ones that would show experimental work. So, artists mainly relied on public-sector institutions and artist-run spaces for support and recognition. Important institutions included SFMA, the second museum in the United States dedicated exclusively to modern art, and the San Francisco Art Association (SFAA), the city's long-standing professional organization of visual artists. The latter hosted an annual juried exhibition, in which DeFeo and other Fillmore artists frequently participated. SFAA also founded an offshoot organization, the Art Bank, to promote local artists nationally.

Another key player in the formation of San Francisco's distinctive cultural landscape was the California School of Fine Arts (CSFA, now SFAI) in the Russian Hill neighborhood, approximately two miles from the Fillmore District. The school rose to prominence soon after World War II under the directorship of Douglas MacAgy, when it boasted prominent abstract expressionists Clyfford Still and Mark Rothko as instructors and attracted returning veterans who enrolled on the G. I. Bill. For a brief period in the late 1940s, CSFA cultivated a nonhierarchical, freewheeling atmosphere, promoting the idea that art is a tool for personal exploration rather than commercial gain. This independent spirit was subsequently fostered within the bohemian circles of artists and writers that thrived in the city during the 1950s and 1960s. Many Fillmore artists had ties to CSFA as former students, teachers, or both. Given the city's dearth of commercial opportunities, teaching provided area artists with a way to make a living. Some found teaching to be not only a necessary alternative to gallery representation but also a preferable alternative, as it allowed them to remain untethered from market demands.[25]

Artists supplemented these official institutions by creating their own. Between 1952 and 1960, a number of galleries (including the King Ubu, Six, East and West, Spatsa, Dilexi, and Batman) sprang up along Fillmore Street and its tributaries. While sales were scanty, the venues—most of which were run by local artists or their acquaintances—exposed neighborhood artists to local newspaper critics and, occasionally, to a nationally known gallerist, collector, or curator passing through the Bay Area. However, the primary audience for these galleries was the artists themselves. Co-ops such as the Six Gallery (which was founded by the poet Jack Spicer and five of his students from CSFA, including Hedrick) were concerned less with launching their members' careers and more with experimentation, as is evident in the Six Gallery's closing notice: "The gallery has been a very valuable impetus to many . . . concerned not only with painting, but with music, dance, experimental photography and sound, and poetry. It has afforded all of us the space and freedom to experiment."[26] The openness of these spaces to intermedial exchange was particularly apparent in the events they frequently hosted, such as theatrical performances and poetry readings, the most famous of which was the group reading at the Six Gallery in 1955 at which Ginsberg debuted "Howl."

In sum, the largely non-commercial cultural landscape of midcentury San Francisco has been presented in previous scholarship as a primary driver of the artistic creeds and practices of "the Fillmore-Union Montparnasse," which were distinct from, if not dialectically opposed to, the creeds and practices developing in the hothouse of New York's postwar art market. The insularity of the Bay Area art world, so the argument goes, replaced New York's modernist medium specificity, market-driven styles, and competitive environment with approaches to art-making that were experimental, personal, and communal.[27]

Regarding experimentation, the commonly accepted claim today is that the creation of art primarily for an audience of peers encouraged artists in San Francisco to take bold risks with form and content. With little hope of profits or posterity, they were free to experiment with unconventional techniques and materials—such as debris scavenged from the demolitions taking place in the Fillmore District. Their art could be hybrid, ephemeral, process-driven, and interwoven with the stuff, routines, and relationships of their daily lives. It could also be a forum for expressing beliefs—such as anger at the consumerism, militarism, and conformity of American society—and exploring topics that public audiences would likely have found taboo. The artists' experimental approaches thus yielded works that challenged both prevailing definitions of art and mainstream values.

In terms of Bay Area art being more personal, conventional wisdom holds that artists' reliance on nonprofit and artist-run institutions nurtured the idea that creative activity is, in Cándida Smith's words, a pursuit of "personal meaning-finding in opposition to established authority."[28] Cándida Smith has traced this ethos to early twentieth-century California, arguing that San Francisco's Beat generation artists and writers played a key role in molding it into the broader antiestablishment fury that powered the counterculture of the late 1960s and 1970s. The belief that genuine art-making derives from the interrogation of one's personal experience meant that Fillmore artists were often, though not uniformly, suspicious of professional success, as traditionally defined. They tended to react ambivalently to gallery representation, press coverage, and inclusion in prominent shows, seeing such accolades as potentially ensnaring their autonomous creative pursuits in market-determined demands.

The alienation that San Francisco artists experienced from both the larger art world and mainstream American society was, scholars have argued, cushioned by the camaraderie of the coterie—a claim that highlights the communal nature of art-making in the Fillmore. Isolated by geography and, to varying degrees, by choice from the conformist pressures of censorship and the market, they formed communities of likeminded individuals who saw beauty where others saw blasphemy. The close proximity of the home studios and galleries in which the artists of the Fillmore District lived, worked, and exhibited bred solidarity and sociability. As they viewed one another's works at parties, casual gatherings, and festive openings, their artistic activity acquired a social valence—the making of art and the making of community became intertwined.

Studies of San Francisco's midcentury art world typically present *The Rose* as exemplifying these tendencies toward the experimental, the personal, and the communal. For example, the way DeFeo's manipulation of oil paint tested the material and conventional limits of the medium—yielding a work that arguably hybridized painting with sculpture, process art, and site-specific installation—is described as quintessentially experimental insofar as it emblematizes the radical directions artists were free to pursue when sheltered from the market imperative to produce sellable objects. Likewise, the seeming ambivalence with which DeFeo greeted her early success (evident, for example, in her refusal to include *The Rose* in *Sixteen Americans*) is made to epitomize the personal, West Coast artistic ethos of prioritizing private vision over worldly success.[29] And DeFeo's choice to isolate herself from the larger art world in order to focus on *The Rose* is interpreted, somewhat ironically, as communal insofar as the artist's continual withholding of her magnum opus from public exhibition was, as Cándida Smith articulated, "sustained by a select group of friends convinced that she was indeed creating something extraordinary." Artists in the Fillmore neighborhood, the story goes, saw the painting as a manifestation of and symbol for their bohemian commitment to art as a personal, independent pursuit. "Her heroic effort rallied her friends around her and allowed a sense of community to cohere," Cándida Smith explained of *The Rose,* going so far as to interpret the painting's "inner center" as an attempt to "symbolically materialize" her "community." Furthermore, commentators have framed *The Rose*'s removal from DeFeo's apartment in 1965 as punctuating the end of the community of artists who had made the Fillmore neighborhood their home for a decade—as if the sundering of work from studio dissipated the lively, collective energy generated by the painting's festive remounting seven years earlier.[30]

The Rose, then, is no longer seen as emblematic solely of DeFeo's oeuvre; it has also come to represent the communal, dynamic art practice that developed within the Fillmore neighborhood, as artists bonded together to support one another in their mutual alienation. Evidence presented throughout the rest of this book opens a new avenue for investigating and deepening that latter claim by revealing that DeFeo's painting was a nexus not only for her friends' support and admiration, but also for their creative activity, which, while entwined with DeFeo's, also remained, like her own, powerfully individual.

MERGING MONOGRAPH AND MILIEU

Over *The Rose*'s long production, it was the subject of a series of photographs by Wallace Berman, a painting by Hedrick, a poem by Michael McClure, and a film by Bruce Conner, each of which is the focus of one of this book's chapters. DeFeo likewise responded to her friends' creative interpretations of her painting, often by producing collages that she gifted to them. While literature exists on Berman's photographs and Conner's film, it does not recognize that these works were part of a larger pattern of dialogue among Fillmore artists that was mediated by *The Rose.* The exchanges that DeFeo and her neighbors engaged in around *The Rose* provide insight into the relationship between art practice and community formation in the Fillmore coterie for two reasons: first, because they offer concrete examples of instances when the creative practices of individuals within the group intersected; and second, because the artists' intimate relationships not only formed the immediate context for their aesthetic dialogues but were inextricable from them. The artists' friendships and love affairs helped motivate and sustain their creative interchanges that, in turn, framed and affected their relationships.

To provide a detailed account of the interaction between the artistic and the social as it played out around *The Rose,* each chapter of this book focuses in on one of the works that DeFeo's friends produced about the painting, and her response to it. Each case mobilizes archival evidence and visual analysis to reconstruct the interpersonal dynamics of the exchange, as well as the network of artists, processes, and works it yielded. Reading across the web of elements that ramified from *The Rose* reveals both how they interacted and the relationships—the authorial and interpersonal constellations—those interactions produced. The chapters thus examine discrete moments when DeFeo's artistic practice and identity intersected with those of her neighbors in order to articulate the relationships between self and other they generated.

Homing in on specific exchanges that took place around *The Rose* allows us to combine the two main methodological lenses (discussed in the preceding sections) through which *The Rose* has been viewed in the past. While both approaches have yielded valuable insights, neither is designed to probe connections between art practice and community formation.[31] On the one hand, by restricting attention to an individual artist, monographic studies (such as the Whitney's retrospective) preclude in-depth examination of the ways an artist's creative practice connected him or her to others. On the other hand, the expansive scope of social historical studies that take the entire Fillmore art scene as an object of investigation (such as Aukeman's book) encourage movement from one artist to the next in a more or less serial fashion, yielding a successive analysis of works created in proximity to one another, but with little attention to the messy micro-histories and sub-contexts of how those works specifically interacted with and relate to one another. In contrast, the method applied here combines the in-depth looking of monography with the relational thinking of milieu studies in order to ameliorate the structural restrictions of each, using a single work as a gateway through which to examine a complex series of relationships between particular pairs of artists. The drawback, of course, is that the subject addressed here is, in some senses, narrower than, say, "DeFeo's oeuvre" or "the art of postwar San Francisco." But if we are to clarify something as complex as art's ability to shape interpersonal bonds, or otherwise to substantiate and elaborate the foundational claims asserted in previous studies about the relationship between art and community that developed in the Fillmore neighborhood, then narrow is necessary.

This study thus uses *The Rose* like a zoom lens to focus in on specific instances in which the making of art and the making of social bonds between individual artists in the Fillmore District affected each other. In doing so, it tackles persistent questions in the literature on postwar art in San Francisco: Within the intimate confines of the Fillmore neighborhood, did the making and viewing of art become a tool for shaping interpersonal relationships between artists? If so, what did it look like for artistic practice to acquire social agency? What kinds of community (of relationships between self and other) did the artists propose and enact through their creative activity?

While distinct from previous approaches to *The Rose,* the line of inquiry pursued here was encouraged by a growing number of studies that, over the past ten years, have examined how the interpersonal dynamics of artist circles helped form the authorial stances, signature techniques, and goals of modernism and postmodernism.[32] In particular, this book draws inspiration from a body of interdisciplinary scholarship that focuses on the network of mostly queer male artists, composers, and poets—including Robert Rauschenberg, Morton Feldman, and Frank O'Hara—that formed in New York during the same decades as the Fillmore circle. This group developed private practices and modes of address, which Paul Goodman famously dubbed "occasional," that rhetorically proposed and literally enacted forms of community that diverged from the strict heteronormativity of the public sphere.[33]

My method draws its general shape from these studies. Some of them strike a similar balance between the monograph and the milieu by treating a central artist as I treat *The Rose*—to quote Branden Joseph, "less as the monographic subject of this book than as the Orpheus guiding" an exploration of "the contiguous networks and connections" that formed through it.[34] In other words, they tend to consider "not (or not only) the production of singular art objects," as Tirza True Latimer explained, "but (also) the creation of social contexts—including reading and viewing communities—in which acts of art could be freely exercised and integrated." Thus, while monographic studies of DeFeo often reject her friends' interpretations of the painting as so many myths, this book embraces them as evidence. Crafting a thorough understanding of *The Rose* necessitates viewing it not only in the context of DeFeo's oeuvre but also, returning to Joseph, "through the situations and dialogues, the networks and interconnections, of which it was a part"—in other words, interpreting the painting in relation to the verbal and material responses it engendered.[35]

This approach takes up a challenge posed by Andrew Epstein, a scholar of O'Hara's coterie: "We need to be more aware of how aesthetic and cultural forms cannot be fully understood through the study of individual authors in isolation or solely as manifestations of external sociopolitical conditions, but rather should be seen as a product of densely interwoven cultural, intertextual, interpersonal spaces."[36] Though written in the context of literary studies, Epstein's words equally apply to art history. They speak to long-standing biases in the discipline toward the monographic and against art that engages the social on a primarily interpersonal, rather than political, level.

Answering Epstein's call from a neighboring discipline, this project attempts to foster a more comprehensive understanding of art's social agency—one that considers art's ability to shape relationships between individuals at an interpersonal level through the material procedures of its production and reception, as well as its ability to affect the social at a political level through the ideas it communicates. Past studies of the Fillmore community have illuminated the latter by asserting that the unconventional ideologies and lifestyles the artists cultivated influenced countercultural and liberation movements of the 1960s and 1970s.[37] This study amends a complementary storyline to this narrative of the community's significance within the contentious social landscape of postwar America. While attentive to the mutually constitutive relationship between the private sphere and the public sphere, the interpersonal and the ideological, I focus primarily on the relationships between self and other that the artists experimented with in the privacy of their coterie—largely leaving to the side how the alternative collectivities yielded by their experiments may have influenced the radical proposals for society that erupted into the public sphere in the following decades.

The method modeled in this book—which embeds the traditional skills of close looking and biographical reading within an intertextual framework—was developed, above all, in relation to *The Rose,* a particular and rather idiosyncratic work of art that repeatedly rebuffed my many previous, more conventional attempts to describe it. Admittedly, the resulting method is, itself, particular and idiosyncratic.[38] Nevertheless, I hope it may prove useful to ongoing efforts to expand our still-nascent understanding of the roles that the internal, interpersonal dynamics of artists' circles played in the development of twentieth-century art and society.

THE RING AROUND *THE ROSE*

Applying the method described above to exchanges that DeFeo and her neighbors engaged in around *The Rose* reveals that they yielded an unusual type of collaboration that I call "interindividual." Their exchanges resist typical definitions of collaboration, in which two or more artists come together to jointly produce a single work. DeFeo and other Fillmore artists deviated from such precedents by merging their practices in ways that retained more of their autonomy as individual artists. As DeFeo's neighbors took up *The Rose* as the basis for new works that she, in turn, used as the foundation for yet other works of her own, they established a dialogue—an iterative give-and-take between discrete artists, works, processes, and studios—rather than a simultaneous, seamless cooperation. Their interactions were intertextual calls and responses that blurred production and reception into a kind of creative recycling that spun out from, but always pointed back to, *The Rose.*

Because these exchanges navigated between individual creative sovereignty and more open, collective modes of making, I have chosen to qualify "collaboration" with the term "interindividual" when describing them. By combining the relational signifier "inter-" with "individual," the label captures the distinctive mix of connection and separation that characterizes the collaborations analyzed in this book. Such collaborations were not all joyful marvels of collective-yet-independent creativity; often they were burdened by or borne of anxiety, insecurity, conflict, or ambivalence. In short, these interindividual collaborations were frequently both as awkward and necessary as my neologism itself.

The exchanges around *The Rose* indicate, among other things, that artists used the combination of independence and interaction that interindividual collaboration affords to enact types of authorship and community in which individual identity and agency were preserved, and even strengthened, through contact with the collective. Evidence also reveals, however, that this ideal balance between, on the one hand, artistic autonomy and personal freedom and, on the other, communal creativity and group belonging was rarely achieved. The artists' attempts to forge harmonious relationships between individual and community spoke both to the particular conditions of San Francisco's midcentury art world and to larger period anxieties about the relationship between self and society. Specifically, the nuanced, though often fraught, relationships between individualism and collectivity that DeFeo and her friends performed through *The Rose* established a middle ground between the period's dominant, binary models of artistic identity and subjectivity.

Of course, those binary models have since been critiqued and deconstructed many times over.[39] As cultural constructs, they mapped only imperfectly, and often poorly, onto lived experience, relationships, and art practice. Yet we need to keep them in mind to understand the discursive context of the collaborations around *The Rose*. One can hardly deny that emergent binaries such as modernism/postmodernism, and more firmly entrenched polarities such as individualism/collectivity and male/female, framed mainstream perceptions of American culture and society in the 1950s and 1960s or that such dominant frameworks were experienced and taken up, in particular ways, within the Fillmore community. The call-and-response exchanges around *The Rose* suggest that the relative insularity of the coterie encouraged DeFeo and her friends to experiment with constellations of authorship and being that bridged the binaries through which "the artist" and "the social" were popularly, if reductively, framed. Bridged, transgressed, played with, but not fully dismantled or superseded, these binary frameworks continued, to some degree, to structure histories of later twentieth-century art in the United States decades after the Fillmore community disbanded. Thus, detailing how seemingly contradictory authorial identities, artistic practices, and aesthetic ideologies collided and conflated around *The Rose* helps clarify the Fillmore coterie's relationship to its historical moment and explain the uneasy, peripheral position of both that coterie and DeFeo's painting within dominant narratives of postwar American art.

Collaborations around *The Rose* blurred the hard line that was frequently drawn in the postwar period, and that still persists to some extent in art-historical discourse today, between what would come to be known as high modernist and postmodernist authorship—positions that are figured, respectively, in the two photographs that open this book. The former was most commonly associated with abstract expressionism and thus with the Romantic ideal of creation ex nihilo often attributed to it, for example, in Harold Rosenberg's canonical "The American Action Painters" (1952). Meanwhile, postmodernist authorship—which began to be articulated in the late 1950s and was codified in criticism of the 1980s—was seen to reject this introspective stance and the emphasis it places on the individual artist's autonomy and authority by embracing collaboration and appropriation. The postmodern artist is, to borrow Allan Kaprow's gendered phrase, "a man of the world" who draws together already-extant images, materials, ideas, participants, and co-creators—resulting in works that are radically open, in terms of attribution, form, and meaning.[40] Such practices cede the individual artist's authority (to varying degrees) to the viewer and/or the anonymous collective. It has been commonplace for general narratives of postwar American art to describe how intergenerational struggles in the 1950s New York art world pitted these prevailing models of authorship against each other, such as in Robert Rauschenberg's oedipal erasure of Willem de Kooning's gesture.[41] Often this contest is presented as precipitating, in the early 1960s, a transition from, among other things, the heroic individualism of the abstract expressionist artist to the anonymous collectivity of Fluxus, from autonomous mark-making to appropriative assemblage, from authorial intention to interpretive indeterminacy, from neo-Romanticism to neo-avant-gardism—or, so the story goes, from modernism to postmodernism.[42]

The interindividual collaborations that played out around *The Rose* complicate this familiar and, as many have observed, facile story of postwar American art. With its mix of solo and collective making, interindividual collaboration in the Fillmore District ostensibly preserved each artist's sovereignty over his or her individual practice even as it opened the works that resulted to appropriation. This combination ideally allowed for interpretation without jeopardizing authorial intent and put the artist in touch with the world while maintaining space for introspection. In this way, Fillmore artists negotiated between the extremes of authorial autonomy and authorial dissolution (into the collective and into the processes of signification) that were supposedly battling in New York, brokering a fragile rapprochement between abstract expressionism's lonely genius and Kaprow's embedded impresario.

The simultaneously authorial and interpersonal relationships that DeFeo and her friends staged around *The Rose* transgressed binaries that structured not only the art world of postwar America, but also its social imaginary.[43] Beginning in the late 1930s, fascism's murderous vision of nation as total belonging and Joseph Stalin's rise to power sparked widespread suspicion of collectivism—defined as the suppression of difference and individual will. As the Cold War set in, popular sociological texts, films, and novels—such as *The Lonely Crowd* (1950), *The Man in the Gray Flannel Suit* (1955), and *The Organization Man* (1956)—also blamed American consumer and corporate culture for fueling conformity under the cloak of capitalist individualism, which reduced free will to consumer choice.[44] While artists and subcultural figures, such as the Beats, were sometimes heralded as rare exemplars of nonconformity, they were also dismissed as poseurs who molded themselves to rebellious, rather than "square," stereotypes for the sake of media attention and financial gain. Considered together, these representations of conformity, social atomization, and self-alienation expressed profound period uncertainty about the possibility of experiencing genuine selfhood and non-oppressive interconnectedness, especially in combination.

Interindividual collaboration potentially resolved such doubts about the compatibility between self and society by bringing the individual and collective together in ways that allowed autonomy and belonging to be mutually constitutive, rather than mutually inhibiting. Through their exchanges, DeFeo and her friends thus negotiated a third option to the devil's choice, frequently presented in the period, between atomized individualism and oppressive conformity. The resonance between postwar social discourses and the relationships that played out around *The Rose* suggests that the former shaped and lent urgency to the latter. On the one hand, this dialogue between the interpersonal and the ideological highlights the Fillmore coterie's embeddedness within the broader sociopolitical landscape of postwar America. On the other hand, it indicates that San Francisco's largely underground art world sheltered artists from the public sphere enough that they felt comfortable experimenting with alternative forms of collectivity. While such experimentation was certainly more of a choice for the predominantly heterosexual artists of the Fillmore circle than it was for their queer counterparts, they still had reason to fear the policing of non-hegemonic identities and ideologies, as evidenced by the instances of censorship discussed above. The intimacy and obscurity of the Fillmore art scene, in sum, appears to have fostered a relatively free and forgiving environment for artists to explore ways to each be themselves within and through a community of others—to balance the social imperatives of individualism and collectivity, independence and belonging, that had become calcified in opposition within the dominant culture.

The social formations that took shape through *The Rose* indicate that this balance was difficult, if not impossible, to strike—even within the relatively amenable conditions of the coterie. One complicating factor, which is highlighted throughout this study, was gender difference. The "ring" that formed around *The Rose* was unusual in that a woman artist constituted the center of a circle of men. This dynamic was particularly notable in the 1950s and 1960s given the rampant sexism of the American art world, and most other sectors of American society, prior to the women's liberation movement. The case studies in this book show that *The Rose* served as a site for the construction of gender identity: the interpretations that DeFeo's male friends crafted for *The Rose* proposed scripts for her heterosexual femininity—identities that her responses amplified, rejected, and otherwise manipulated. *The Rose* thus became a vehicle for DeFeo and men close to her to negotiate how to inhabit the intersecting gender and sexual identities available to them in ways that sometimes subverted and other times replicated the rigid gender norms, hierarchies, and sexual strictures of 1950s America. This finding nuances the claim that the relative lack of commercial competition in San Francisco's art world all but negated gender inequity among Fillmore artists.[45] The exchanges around *The Rose* suggest, in fact, that the greater parity between male and female artists in San Francisco (as compared to New York and Los Angeles) did not preclude gender difference and its attendant power dynamics from factoring into how they perceived their artistic identities and experienced their relationships with one another.

The findings summarized above unfold over the following four chapters, each of which takes up a different exchange that occurred around *The Rose.* Replicating the dynamics of these collaborations, each chapter strikes a different balance between discussing DeFeo and discussing her collaborator. The case studies are arranged chronologically so that the book tracks *The Rose*'s production and reception through time, even as this linear structure branches out within each chapter to chart a different constellation of artists, works, and processes. Each instance of interindividual collaboration is examined to determine the kinds of authorship and community it proposed and enacted, as well as how those relationships were refracted through the specific interpersonal dynamics and interests of the artists involved. As we will see, DeFeo and her friends conceptualized their nontraditional collaborations, as well as the alternative authorial and social structures they constituted, through such diverse frameworks as esoteric hermeneutics, domestic partnership, the body, memory, and make-believe play. In this way, *The Rose* functioned as a forum for DeFeo and her neighbors to experiment with artistic identity and subjectivity, while also engaging in dialogues about sexuality, death, embodiment, gender, domesticity, mysticism, and other ideas essential to the countercultural philosophies of the West Coast's postwar underground.

Chapter 1, "Model Artist," examines an untitled series of photographs from 1959 that Wallace Berman took of DeFeo posing in her studio, including in front of *The Rose,* that frame making the photographs as an act of esoteric interpretation akin to the practice of Kabbalah. The second chapter, "Making Home," takes up the painting *Life Game* (1959) by DeFeo's husband, Wally Hedrick, which positions *The Rose* as an essential part of the couple's domestic existence. Chapter 3, "Body Language," analyzes a poem composed by DeFeo's upstairs neighbor Michael McClure in 1965. Using words he spontaneously generated while watching DeFeo make *The Rose,* the poem describes the confluence of painterly and poetic processes that generated it as evidence of the creative power of the libidinal body. The fourth chapter, "Afterlives," examines artistic collaborations around *The Rose* that happened after its ostensible moment of completion, focusing, in particular, on a 1967 film by Bruce Conner that uses footage he shot of *The Rose*'s removal from DeFeo's apartment. The chapter explores the ideas of death, memory, and make-believe that Conner and DeFeo employed to frame their decade-long interindividual collaboration, which began with his film. Finally, a coda draws together the chapters' analyses of the gender dynamics of the collaborations that circled *The Rose,* teasing out how these findings affect our understanding of the roles that gender played within the Fillmore community.

THE CONSTELLATION FROM THE CARD

In late 1960, about two years after she began *The Rose,* DeFeo gathered chunks of paint that had come loose from the work's constantly transforming surface, mounted them to card stock, and sent them through the mail as holiday greetings (fig. 12). The glittering nuggets of paint that DeFeo attached to the cards speak to *The Rose*'s elusive liminality: to the way it brings together apparent opposites such as painting and sculpture, object and action, unity and fragmentation. The cards exemplify Goodman's definition of "occasional" art, further demonstrating how *The Rose*'s constant mutation within DeFeo's studio cultivated a particular type of collectivity. By recycling pieces of *The Rose* into holiday cards, DeFeo used the painting's material dissolution and dissemination to reinforce and mold her personal social network.

The other works explored in this book similarly recycled *The Rose*—though they usually took up its image rather than its substance—to form a galaxy of works and artists that pinwheeled out from DeFeo's painting. Produced by DeFeo alone in her studio but sent as gifts to friends, the cards performed the dialectic between isolation and connection, distance and proximity, individual and community, that characterized the interindividual collaborations catalyzed by *The Rose.* The painting's radiating composition figures this push and pull between center and network, consolidation and dispersal.

DeFeo sent the unconventional holiday cards to her neighbors in the Fillmore District and to acquaintances farther afield. The card she mailed to MoMA's Miller articulates the tension between private and public, the coterie and the professional realm, that DeFeo and so many of her neighbors felt. In it, DeFeo reflected on her decision to withhold *The Rose* from *Sixteen Americans* and attempted to justify its continued confinement to her studio. "Its [*sic*] such a beautiful idea—it will be so hard for me to give it up," she confessed. "I know this sounds corney [*sic*] but even though its [*sic*] always going to be a part of me somehow—I don't know—just giving up this material object will be unbearable."[46] She describes herself as caught in the painting's gravitational field, the mystical yet material force that kept so many artworks and members of the Fillmore community orbiting around it. Though DeFeo felt the pull of the public sphere, *The Rose* was, for the time being, the more powerful draw.

Perhaps DeFeo suspected that Miller, viewing the situation from her remote perspective, would see only the way *The Rose*'s confinement to

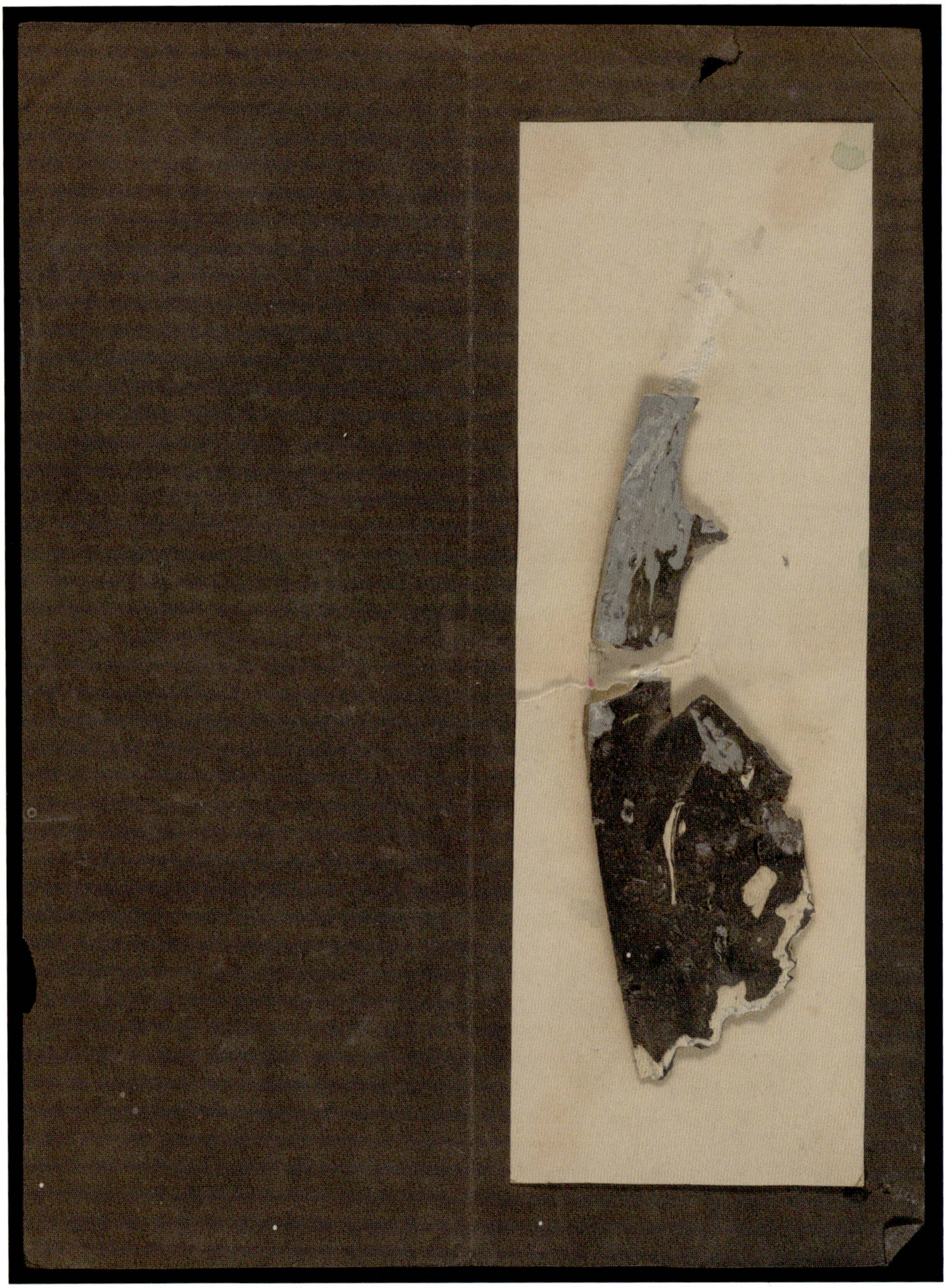

Fig. 12 Jay DeFeo, Holiday card featuring a piece of *The Rose*, 1960. Jay DeFeo papers, Archives of American Art, Smithsonian Institution, Washington, D.C.

DeFeo's studio was secluding her from the larger art world, not the community it was congealing around her. The fragment of *The Rose* that DeFeo included in Miller's holiday card can be read as a talisman against this partial perception, which this book also attempts to correct. Isolated against a sheet of off-white paper pasted on a large black card, the sparkling, sculptural chip radiates a strange alien presence. It is a relic, a part-object, and an astral fragment—proof of life beyond the solar system of the New York art world. With this small token, DeFeo included Miller within the growing constellation of relationships—explored over the following chapters—that *The Rose* held aloft, luring her to its distant center.

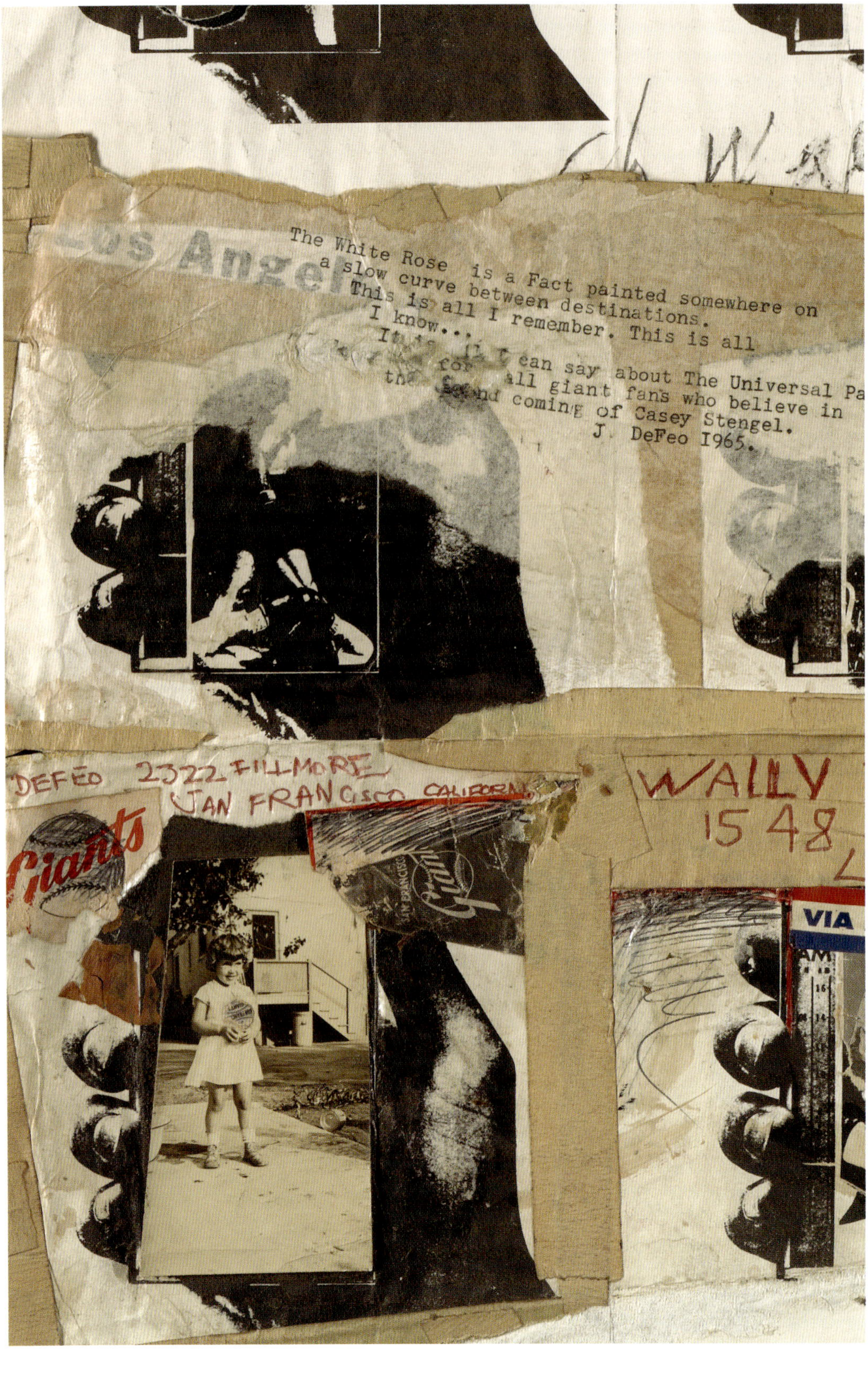
Los Angel
The White Rose is a Fact painted somewhere on
a slow curve between destinations.
This is all I remember. This is all
I know...
can say about The Universal Pa
all giant fans who believe in
coming of Casey Stengel.
J. DeFeo 1965.
DEFEO 2322 FILLMORE
SAN FRANCISCO CALIFORN
WALLY
1548
Giants
VIA

CHAPTER 1

Model Artist

TRICKSTER PHOTOGRAPHS

In October 1959, approximately one year into her production of *The Rose,* Jay DeFeo mailed a set of photographic portraits of herself to Dorothy Miller, a curator at the Museum of Modern Art (MoMA). The portraits were candidates for reproduction in the catalogue for Miller's imminent exhibition of up-and-coming artists, *Sixteen Americans,* which also featured works by Jasper Johns, Ellsworth Kelly, Robert Rauschenberg, and Frank Stella. Inclusion in this exhibition elevated DeFeo's art to national prominence, exposing her to an audience beyond her immediate artistic community in San Francisco's Fillmore District. Though the record of DeFeo and Miller's exchange does not identify the specific images DeFeo mailed, it does reveal that they were taken by two different photographers—DeFeo's husband, Wally Hedrick (who was also featured in *Sixteen Americans*), and their close friend and fellow artist Wallace Berman. "I'd like to state my preference for Wally Berman's picture," DeFeo wrote in the letter that accompanied the photographs, "but if you think any one of the others better, use it."[1]

The Berman photograph was most likely drawn from a series taken in DeFeo and Hedrick's apartment the previous spring (figs. 13–20), all of which are very unlike the conventional "artist's portrait" photo by Hedrick.[2] The latter photograph—in which a smoking, turtleneck-wearing DeFeo gazes musingly off to the side—was the result of a portrait session the couple hurriedly convened after receiving a phone call from Miller requesting materials for the *Sixteen Americans* catalogue (fig. 21).[3] In Berman's photographs, which evade period norms for publicly representing artists, DeFeo's performative poses and Berman's obvious manipulation of the prints (which included projecting the negatives through a patterned transparency during the developing process) give the images an enigmatic, self-consciously artistic character.[4] Even the most portrait-like shot—a three-quarter close-up of DeFeo, and the most likely candidate for the image she sent Miller—is uncommonly dark, reducing DeFeo's face to mask-like contours (see fig. 15).

Detail, fig. 34

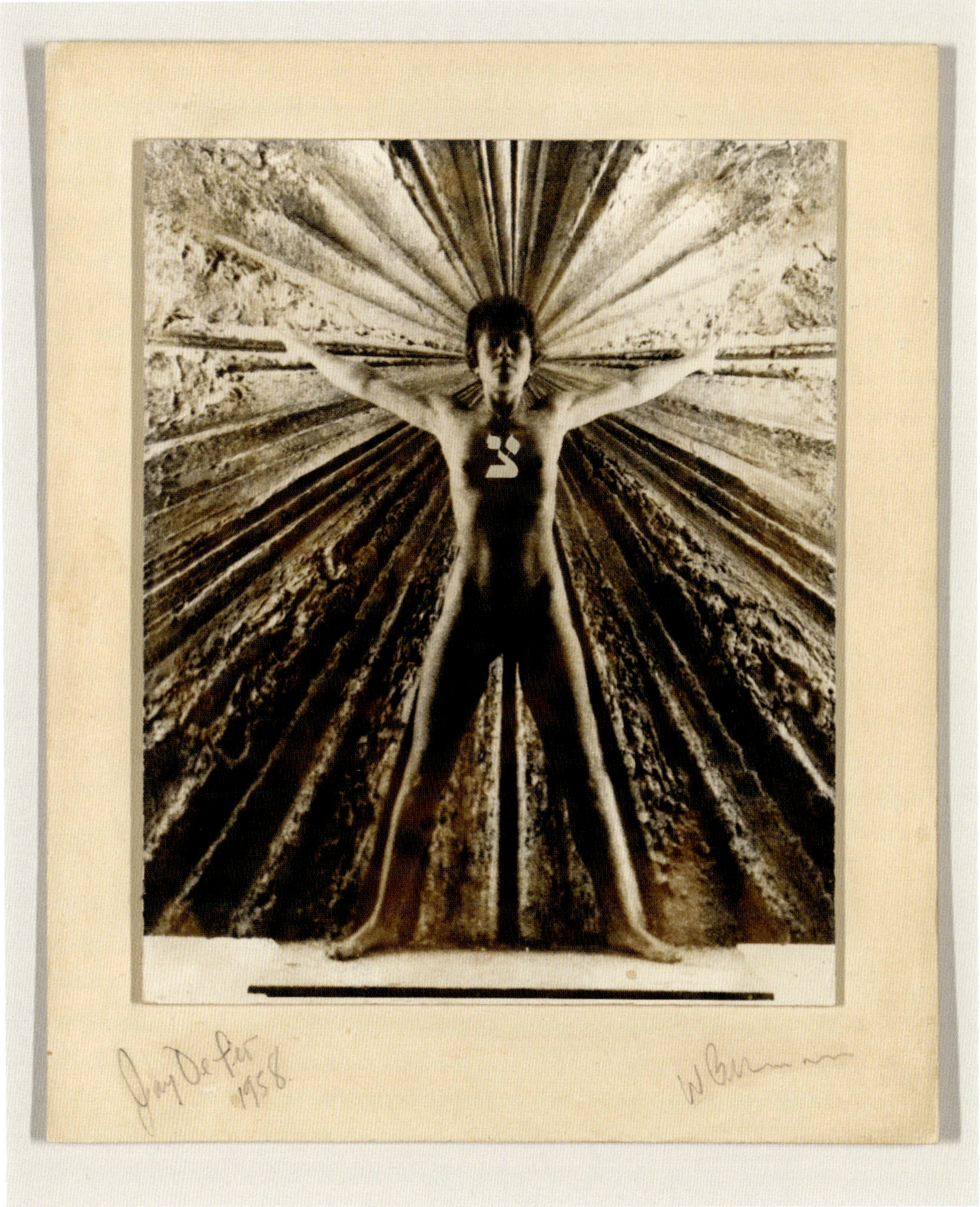

Fig. 13 Wallace Berman, *Jay DeFeo*, 1959. Toned gelatin silver print with transfer type, 7⅛ × 5⅞ in. (18.1 × 14.9 cm). Whitney Museum of American Art, New York. Gift of the Lannan Foundation [Inv.: 96.243.9].

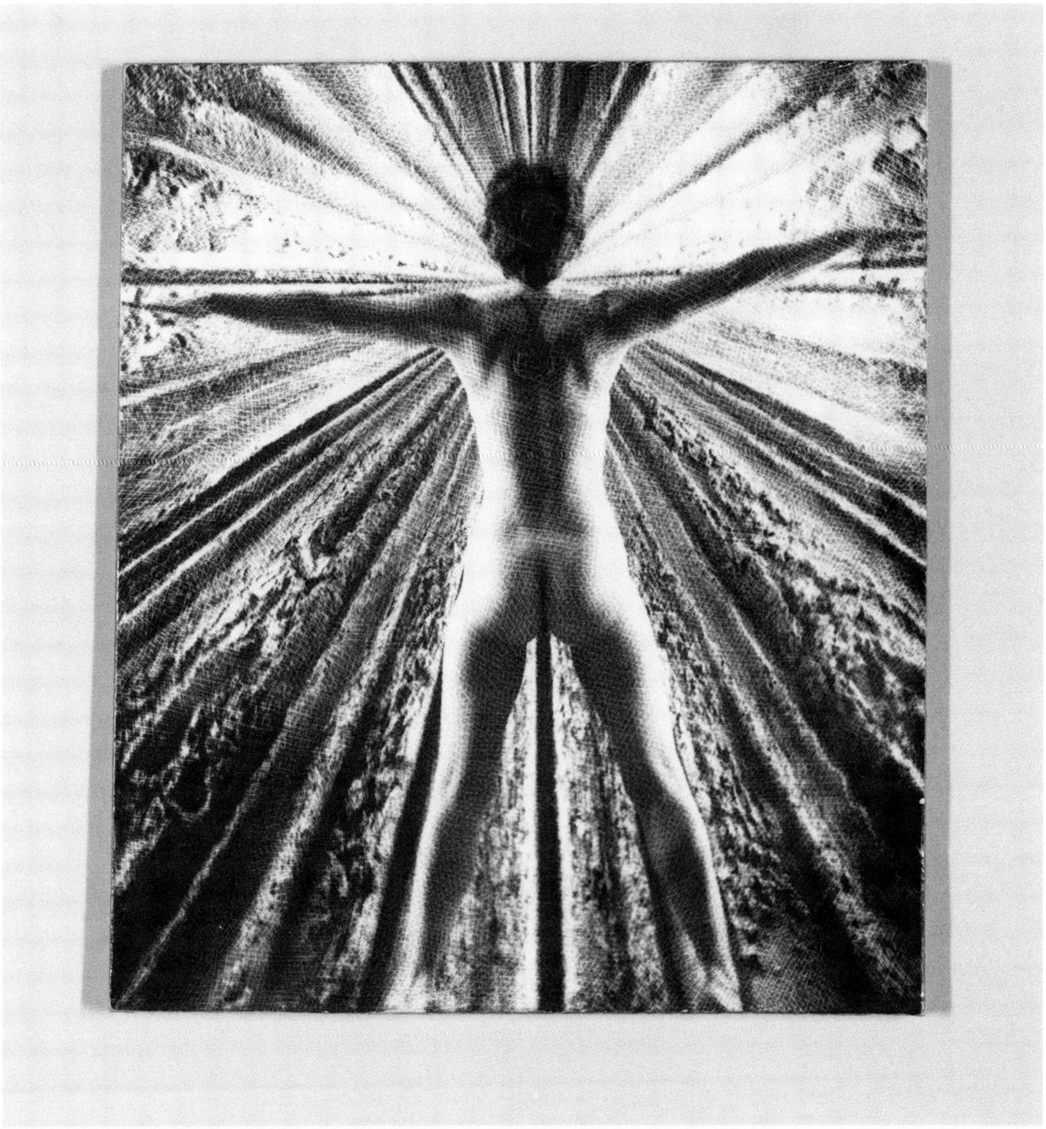

Fig. 14 Wallace Berman, *Jay DeFeo*, 1959. Gelatin silver print, 5⅛ × 4¾ in. (13 × 12.1 cm). Whitney Museum of American Art, New York. Gift of the Lannan Foundation [Inv.: 96.243.8].

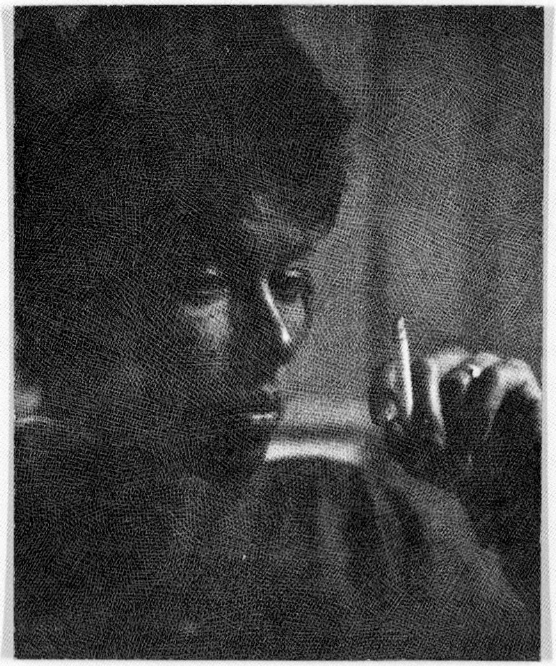

Fig. 15 Wallace Berman, *Jay DeFeo*, 1959. Gelatin silver print mounted on board, 5¼ × 4⅜ in. (13.3 × 11.1 cm). Whitney Museum of American Art, New York. Gift of the Lannan Foundation [Inv.: 96.243.1].

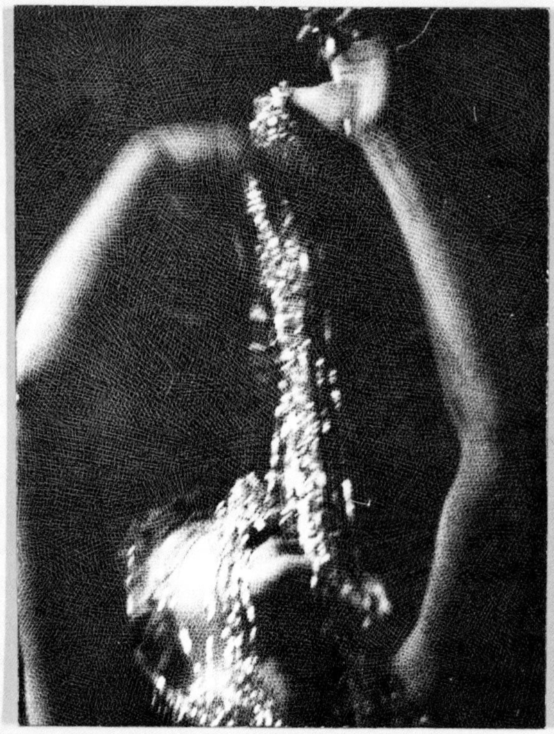

Fig. 16 Wallace Berman, *Jay DeFeo*, 1959. Gelatin silver print, 5½ × 4⅛ in. (14 × 10.5 cm). Whitney Museum of American Art, New York. Gift of the Lannan Foundation [Inv.: 96.243.7].

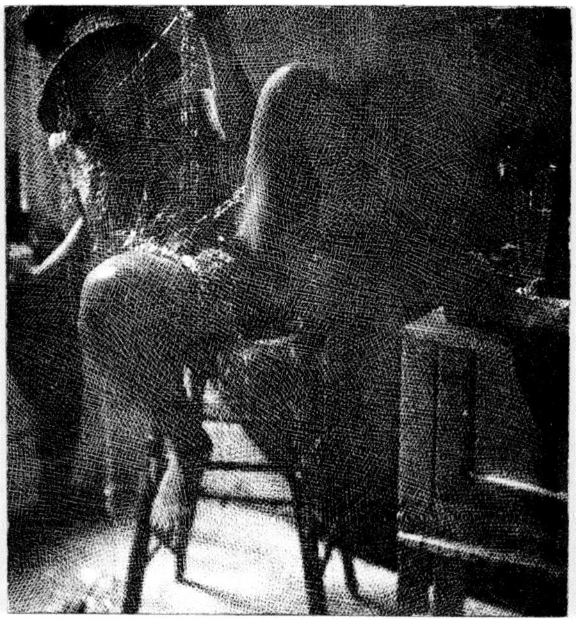

Fig. 17 Wallace Berman, *Jay DeFeo*, 1959. Gelatin silver print, 4¾ × 4½ in. (12.1 × 11.4 cm). Whitney Museum of American Art, New York. Gift of the Lannan Foundation [Inv.: 96.243.4].

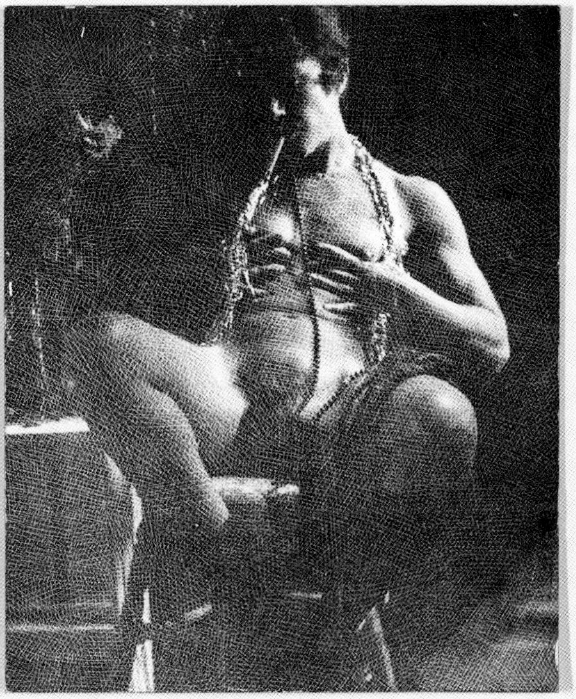

Fig. 18 Wallace Berman, *Jay DeFeo*, 1959. Gelatin silver print, 4⅞ × 4 in. (12.4 × 10.2 cm). Whitney Museum of American Art, New York. Gift of the Lannan Foundation [Inv.: 96.243.5].

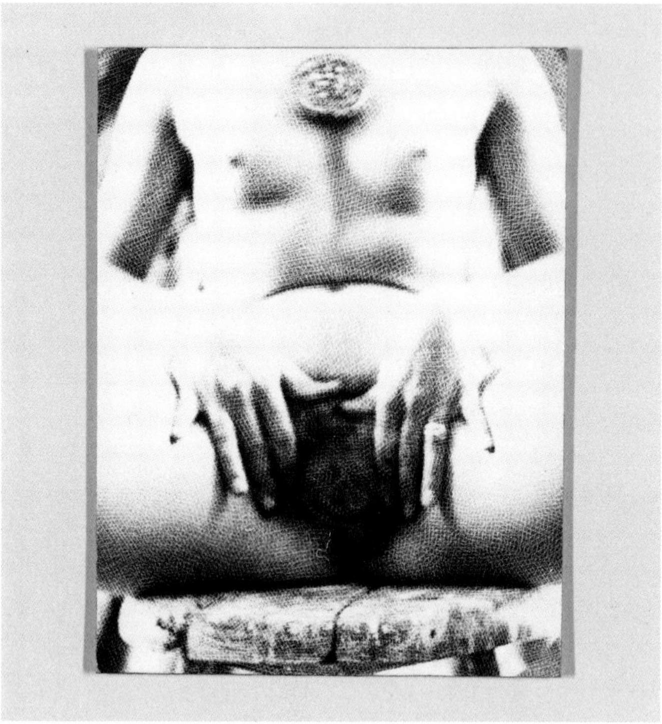

Fig. 19 Wallace Berman, *Jay DeFeo,* 1959. Gelatin silver print, 4¾ × 3⅝ in. (12.1 × 9.2 cm). Whitney Museum of American Art, New York. Gift of the Lannan Foundation [Inv.: 96.243.6].

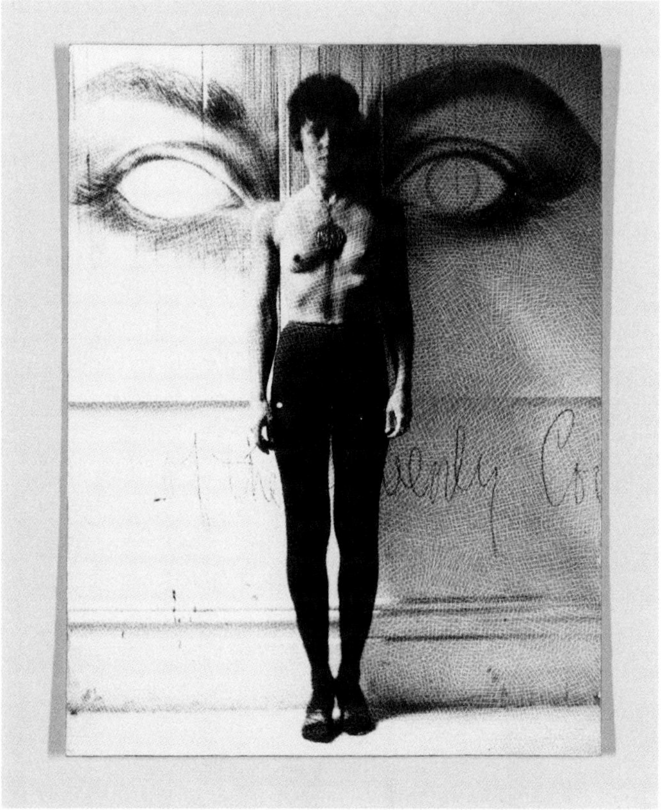

Fig. 20 Wallace Berman, *Jay DeFeo,* 1959. Gelatin silver print, 5¼ × 4⅛ in. (14 × 10.5 cm). Whitney Museum of American Art, New York. Gift of the Lannan Foundation [Inv.: 96.243.2].

FACING PAGE

Fig. 21 Wally Hedrick, Photograph of Jay DeFeo, 1959. Reproduced in *Sixteen Americans* (New York: Museum of Modern Art, 1959). Museum of Modern Art Library, New York.

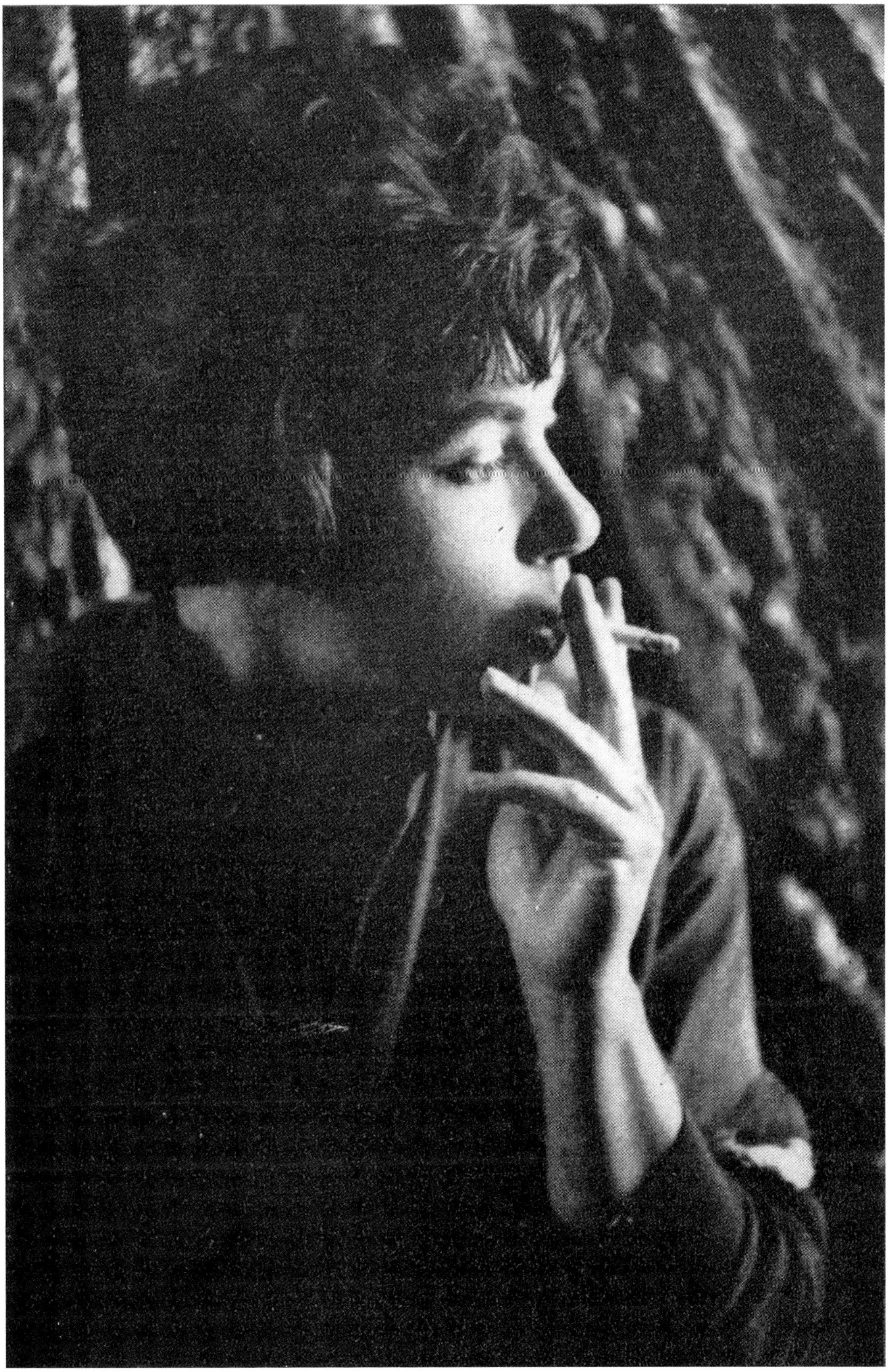

These photographs by Berman variously exceed and undermine portraiture's imperative to convey likeness. Moreover, all but two of the shots depict DeFeo naked or partially undressed, flagrantly violating conventions governing artists' portraits in the United States during the 1950s. Berman exhibited the series in a one-day show at his home, where they were seen only by invited mutual friends, thereby reinforcing the photographs' private nature.[5] In the end, Miller's decision sealed the photographs' fate as private images: the curator went against DeFeo's preference and chose to publish one of Hedrick's shots on the grounds that "Wally Berman's trick photograph won't reproduce."[6] Thereafter, reception of the Berman series remained confined to DeFeo and Berman's circle until the 1970s.

Berman and DeFeo's photo session occurred at a pivotal moment in each artist's career. Berman had moved to San Francisco from Los Angeles two years earlier. He had begun his artistic career in the late 1940s drawing surrealist-inspired album covers for Dial Records. The son of Russian Jewish immigrants, Berman felt alienated by the materialism and militarism he perceived in the conservative culture of postwar Los Angeles, but he

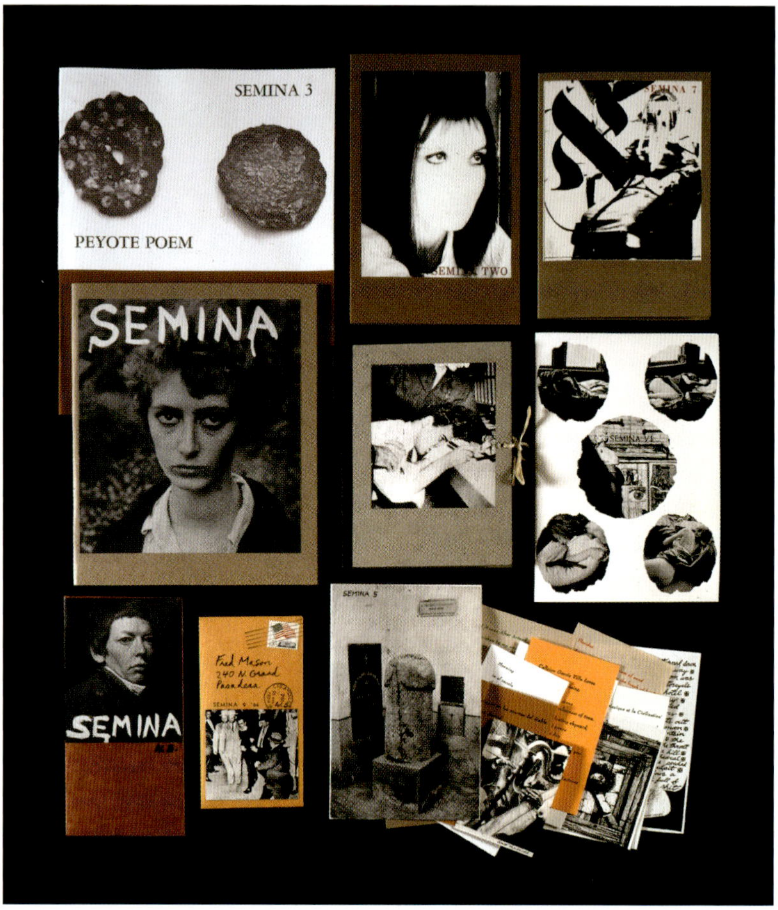

Fig. 22 *Semina* (editions 1–9), conceived and edited by Wallace Berman with various contributors, 1955–64. Mixed-media limited edition artist's publication. The Estate of Wallace Berman and Kohn Gallery, Los Angeles.

empathized (like so many of the Beat generation) with the bebop musicians represented by Dial who played the South-Central Los Angeles nightclubs he frequented. Inspired by the subcultural community he found there, Berman sought to foster a similar collectivity for the city's marginalized writers and artists, especially those associated with the burgeoning assemblage movement. In the early 1950s, he held informal salons in his home in Beverly Glen canyon and produced an underground journal, *Semina,* that connected likeminded individuals across the sprawling metropolis (fig. 22). Friends and family also frequently appeared in his photographs, collages, assemblages, and film, *Aleph* (1956–66), beside a diverse array of found images cannibalized from the mass media, interwar avant-gardes, esoteric traditions, and pornography.[7]

Berman was spurred north by his criminal conviction for including sexually explicit material in his one-man show at the Ferus Gallery—Los Angeles's premier venue for avant-garde art—in 1957.[8] The incident echoed higher-profile obscenity charges leveled at Beat literature in the period, including the trial, in the same year as Berman's conviction, over the publication and distribution of Allen Ginsberg's poem "Howl," which ended in acquittal. Such instances of censorship manifested the postwar public's hostility toward even white, straight, and male artists such as Berman, for whom marginalization was more of a choice than it was for his Black, brown, queer, and female counterparts. Berman's conviction confirmed his perception of mainstream America as brutally conformist, bent on violently persecuting difference—a view shared by many artists and writers who made San Francisco their home in the decades following World War II. Like Berman, they saw an opportunity for freedom in the anonymity that the city's non-commercial, largely underground art world could grant them.

Upon moving to the Bay Area, Berman settled, with his wife, Shirley, and son, Tosh, into a large Victorian house on Scott Street near Alamo Square, less than two miles from Hedrick and DeFeo's apartment on Fillmore Street. He continued to take photographs and to produce *Semina* from his new northern home, which (like the apartment building where DeFeo lived) quickly became a hub for the city's filmmakers, writers, and artists, including those in the Fillmore District. Berman is often remembered as a nonchalant impresario who nurtured creativity in others while embodying hipster cool. "Berman was one of the most supportive people to me, without any kind of overt encouragement," recalled the artist Joan Brown, who was DeFeo's next-door neighbor when Berman was living in San Francisco. "I was tremendously influenced by Wally Berman. But by him as a person, not by his work. He just stood, for me, for the whole idea of the individual."[9] DeFeo and Berman, as will become clear, developed a similar relationship. The photographs he took of DeFeo and his private exhibition of them show that his dedication to cultivating coteries continued in San Francisco, as did his wariness of the public. Shirley Berman recalled that he hid the prints from his photo shoot with DeFeo in a phone book while transporting them home from the public darkroom in which he had developed them, suggesting that he was hyperaware that they could have been construed as obscene.[10]

DeFeo was on the precipice of a similar transition when the friends convened their photo session. Nineteen fifty-nine would prove the most professionally successful year of her early career. She showed in three exhibitions, including *Sixteen Americans* and a solo show at the Dilexi Gallery in San Francisco that Miller saw during a scouting trip to the West Coast. DeFeo's correspondence from this period indicates that she experienced these successes with a mixture of excitement and anxiety.[11] She began to perceive tensions between her art practice and the art world's demands that manifested, for example, in her decision to not send *The Rose* to *Sixteen Americans* because she considered the work unfinished. As the introduction to this book details, she continued to labor over *The Rose* for six more years, to the virtual exclusion of other works. This choice isolated her from the larger art world that *Sixteen Americans* opened to her, but it also embedded her more strongly within her local art community. By the early 1960s, *The Rose* had become a potent, multivalent symbol for artists and poets living in the Fillmore District, as well as a nexus for creative exchange as her friends produced works of art about the painting. Berman's series represents an especially rich example of these projects.

Given both artists' struggles with the public reception of their work, it is tempting to see a greater significance in the failure of Berman's photograph to materially register in the *Sixteen Americans* catalogue. One reading, informed by previous scholarship about postwar art on the West Coast, could see this incident as an allegory of the incongruity between the art worlds of San Francisco and New York in the late 1950s. In this interpretation, the photograph represents the Fillmore neighborhood's reclusive, communal art practice, which MoMA's institutional frame—emphasizing individual artistic autonomy and originality—is literally unable to register.[12] The photograph's manipulated surface, the source of its irreproducibility, is a fail-safe against publicity, a material mechanism preserving the aura of DeFeo, her studio, works, and community. Interpreted this way, the "trick photograph" becomes a trickster photograph, a recalcitrant object mischievously eluding the mainstream art world. The photograph thus emerges as a surrogate for Berman, DeFeo, and the anti-institutionalism generally attributed to West Coast artists. DeFeo requested to Miller that the photographs "be returned eventually" because they "were little gifts, sort of, from the people that took them," a demand that supports this explanation of the anecdote.[13] Her identification of the photographs as "gifts" foregrounds the entwinement of artistic production and reception with the performance of intimate relationships in DeFeo and Berman's circle—an affective, interpersonal dynamic generally represented as peripheral, at best, to New York's institutionalized, market-driven, and individualistic art scene.

DeFeo's choice to not send *The Rose* to *Sixteen Americans,* as well as her and Hedrick's decision to not attend the opening, has similarly been seen as indicative of bohemian attitudes prevalent in postwar California, in particular an understanding of art "as personal ritual and spiritual commitment" that was "unfettered by outside concerns like publicity or financial success," as Rebecca Solnit and Rebecca Schoenthal articulated, respectively. DeFeo's correspondence, however, tells a more complicated and conflicted story. As Dana Miller discovered, her letters point to a more mundane reason for the couple's absence from the opening: they could not afford to travel to the East Coast.[14]

How accurate, then, is this speculative interpretation of what was, if Dorothy Miller is to be believed, merely a technical mismatch between Berman's photograph and the *Sixteen Americans* catalogue? If the series offers an alternative model of authorship to the artistic individualism championed in postwar America's dominant art discourses and exhibition practices, what is it? The photographs do not readily divulge answers to these questions. Indeed, the diverse images craft seemingly contradictory representations of DeFeo. Standing before *The Rose,* she plays the role of divine creator. The combination of high-contrast side lighting and the alignment of her splayed body with the canvas's radial composition creates the illusion that the painting emanates, halo-like, from her commanding form. By rehearsing the well-worn association between radiating light and creation ex nihilo (think William Blake's *The Ancient of Days,* 1794), the photographs enact a Romantic equation between artist and God. Berman's addition of the Hebrew letter צ (*tsade*) on DeFeo's chest adds to the image's Old Testament overtones.[15] No doubt Carter Ratcliff had these particular photographs in mind when he concluded, in 2002, that the series is "well-calculated to promote the cult of genius."[16]

Other photographs from the series, however, cast DeFeo in the role of the artist's model instead of the divine artist. In several images that depict her posing on a stool, her body is a receptive surface for light, embodied by the tinsel that she drips across her skin, rather than the source emitting it (see figs. 16–18). The broad-brimmed hat and long string of beads she sports were likely accessories she used when modeling (clothed) at the California School of Fine Arts.[17] In one photograph, DeFeo grabs and lifts her breasts, presenting them to the lens. This blunt gesture leaves little doubt that her body is on display for the viewer's delectation (see fig. 18). She performs the fantasy of the promiscuous life model, whose availability to artistic representation is inseparable from her sexual availability.

The two sequences, in sum, offer conflicting accounts of artistic production: the image of autonomous, visionary creation staged with *The Rose* contrasts with the representational procedures implied by the artist's model. In the former, the studio is a site of isolation; in the latter, it is a site of encounter. They also cast DeFeo in opposite roles within the familiar, sexist drama of the studio. Standing before *The Rose,* she is the omnipotent agent of creation whose imposing, yet ethereal, form radiates generative power. Posing on the stool, she is the object of creation, the gaze, and the artist's amorous advances—the artwork's content rather than its cause. The sequences also differently gender her body in accordance with the binary positions traditionally assigned men and women in the creative process. The high-contrast *Rose* shots androgenize DeFeo's lean form by blackening out her telling torso. Her commanding pose—the rigidity of which is amplified by the painting's strict geometries—gives her form a masculine connotation. In the model photographs, by contrast, DeFeo assumes languid and suggestive poses, some of which foreground her sexual difference and blatantly refer to pornographic conventions. Given these contrasts, the two sequences could be read, respectively, as personifications (even caricatures) of abstract expressionism and Bay Area figuration, the dominant painting styles practiced in San Francisco at the time.

The photographs' authorship is as slippery as their portrayal of the artist. At question is the nature of DeFeo's contribution to the series. Did she participate with Berman in the aesthetic and conceptual decision-making that shaped the photographs, or was she simply a tool through which Berman realized his autonomous vision? The evidence is contradictory. DeFeo's description of the series, nearly twenty years later, as a "collaboration between two artist friends," suggests that they created it together. Later interpreters, such as Michael Duncan and John Bowles, have reiterated this interpretation by reading the series, respectively, as "clearly a kind of collaboration" and as evidence of "the artist as integral to a close-knit community."[18]

However, in a letter written just months after DeFeo referred to the photographs as a "collaboration," she portrayed her participation in their creation in a way that counters the idea of mutual making: "I am not entirely happy with Wallace's portraits, but seldom have models been altogether happy with artists' conceptions of them. I did not feel it was appropriate to intervene and edit Wallace's 'series portrait' as it was his vision, his interpretation. . . . My consent to all this was out of respect to Wallace as an artist, and I wanted him to have his portrait as he saw it. I was the model only and not the artist in this situation." Dana Miller has used this statement to conclude that "Berman was the sole author" of the photographs.[19]

In these two passages, however, DeFeo's characterization of her contribution to the series vacillates between the seemingly incongruous roles she plays in the photographs: she imagines herself as, alternately, artist and model, co-creator and mere content. Jason Goldman, in the only previous in-depth analysis of the series, has read these contradictions as evidence that DeFeo struggled to codify the photographs' authorship once they were made public in the mid-1970s because, up until that point, the images' private nature allowed for the roles played by Berman and DeFeo to remain ambiguous and largely unarticulated.[20]

This chapter elaborates that ambiguity to see what it discloses about the kinds of authorship that emerged within the subcultural conditions of San Francisco's postwar art world. It takes as its starting point the confounding contradictions that give the photo series its tricky character. Looking at the photographs together—as both Berman and DeFeo appear to have intended—means taking seriously the challenges the series poses to established categories of representation, gender, and authorship.[21] The following pages articulate the kind of artistic identity and creativity the series proposes by examining its perverse play with the binary oppositions (between artist and model, creator and content, expressionism and naturalism, individual and collective, and male and female) that typically structure interpretations of artists as social and creative beings, and that had particular currency in the United States circa 1960. My guiding questions for these examinations have been: What accounts for the series' construction of opposing identities for DeFeo? What model of creativity do the photographs provide through both their representation of DeFeo and the hints they divulge of their own facture?

One thing this chapter does not do, and which Dana Miller has already done, is attempt to determine the photographs' authorship in a traditional art-historical sense. While this chapter speaks more about Berman's contributions to the series than DeFeo's, it does not strive to settle the debate over whether the photographs should be considered a collaboration or be attributed to Berman alone. The focus here is rather on describing some of the ways in which these tricky images purposefully evade and problematize the black-and-white notion of authorship that this debate supports.

A close reading of the series and the postcard that Berman likely sent DeFeo to set up their photo session reveals that the photographs are not documents of the artist or her process, but rather allegories that frame both in esoteric terms. Specifically, they recontextualize DeFeo and her practice within Kabbalah, a mystical Jewish tradition that posits the interdependence of autonomous creation and communal interpretation. In this way, the series imagines an ideal mode of artistic creation that integrates solitary action with collaboration, but it also hints at the ways Berman and DeFeo's partnership fell short of achieving a mutually constitutive relationship between individual and collective modes of art-making. This model of authorship, and the frictions it generated, resonated with the practices of Berman and DeFeo's Fillmore circle, in which artists maintained individual studios but also appropriated one another's works through informal creative exchanges—a dynamic that would come to be exemplified by artistic activity about and around *The Rose.* It thus provides insight into the ways that the underground nature of San Francisco's art scene opened space for artists to experiment with alternatives to the hegemonic and, from the artists' perspective, oppressive social formations and authorial modes of postwar America and its art world.

Berman and DeFeo's photographs of *The Rose* with its artist were circulating privately at the same time that other artists' photographs of DeFeo with *The Rose* were circulating publicly.[22] Comparison between these public, mainstream representations and the Berman series confirms the novelty of the latter's representation of creativity and artistic identity.

Working in association with Magnum Photos in 1960, Burt Glinn took the most widely distributed photographs of *The Rose,* which were reproduced in several magazines and a coffee-table book, *Creative America*—a standard specimen of Cold War cultural propaganda that was published jointly by Ridge Press and the U.S. government in 1962 to raise funds for the National Cultural Center in Washington, D.C. The book combines *Life*-like montages of other Magnum photographs with essays by politicians and cultural luminaries (including James Baldwin, Dwight D. Eisenhower, Robert Frost, John F. Kennedy, and Harry S. Truman) to argue that "individuality and humanity" are affirmed through creative activities and the reception thereof.[23] A cropped version of one of Glinn's shots appears in the final section, "Aspirations," which is the only area in which photographs appear uncaptioned, suggesting that they were intended to function more as metaphors than illustrations. The spread situates DeFeo across from a dramatic image of a silhouetted cowboy riding through the desert—the work of Glinn's fellow Magnum photographer Ernst Haas, who (unsurprisingly) also shot ad campaigns for Marlboro cigarettes (fig. 23).

This juxtaposition of an anonymous artist with an equally unnamed cowboy invites analogies—at once clichéd and strained—between the two images. Glinn's film gives *The Rose*'s cool grays a hot cast, suggesting a consonance between the painting's craggy ridges and the desolate panorama to its right. The infinite projection of the painting's radial composition reinforces its resemblance to the sublime expanse. Both figures turn away from the viewer and toward the terrain before them. Through these formal echoes, the montage analogizes DeFeo's creative activity to a cowboy traversing the wilderness. The spread thus represents painting as a risky adventure that necessitates courage, perseverance, and self-reliance. Creativity, the montage asserts, is a solitary activity—a heroic exercise of independence. The layout thus rehearses the metaphors articulated in Harold Rosenberg's influential essay "The American Action Painters" (1952), in which he likens the abstract expressionist artist to archetypes of the American West to champion their spontaneous, gestural process as one of existential risk and freedom.[24] Given the strongly masculine coding of the heroic persona that DeFeo is made to embody, it is unsurprising that the photograph conceals her gender.

Berman's photographs of DeFeo with *The Rose* share important compositional features with Glinn's in *Creative America*. Notably, both restrict the photograph's field of view within the painting's borders, unmooring the

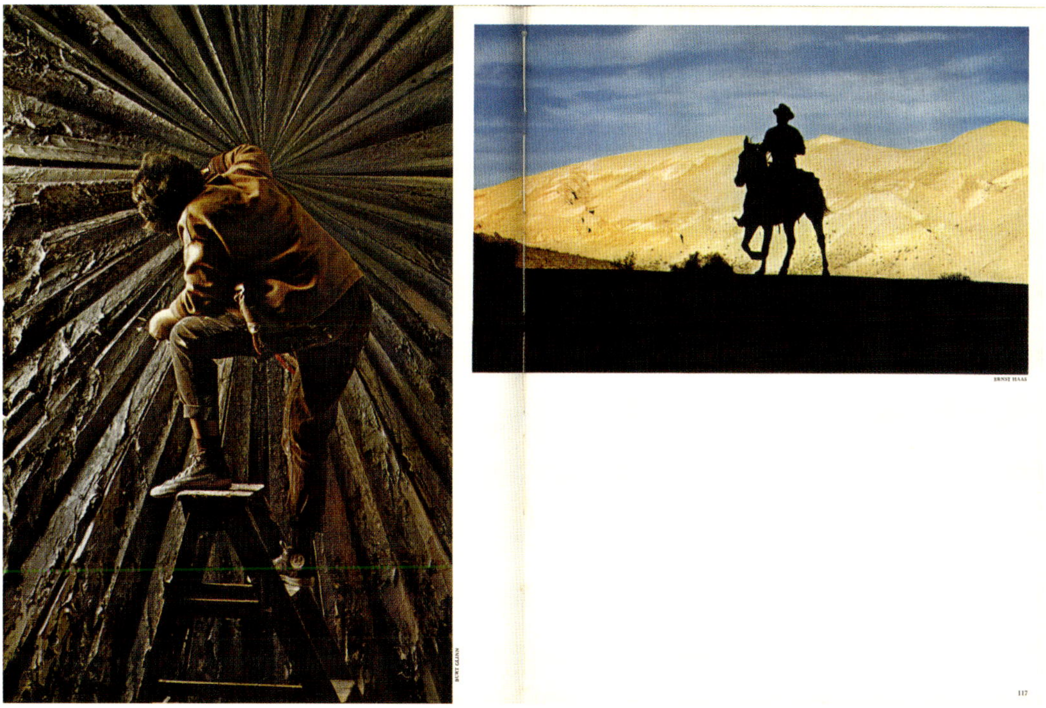

work from its surrounds and pressing the canvas's surface together with the picture plane of the photograph. This narrow field of view highlights qualities that make *The Rose* an ideal photographic subject: namely, its frontality and rectilinearity, as well as the crossed lines at its center, all of which make the painting appear to have been designed with a camera's viewfinder in mind. Moreover, the painting's radiating orthogonals mimic linear-perspectival constructions of illusionistic depth. The photographs thus help us (and, indeed, encourage us) to see that, by drawing upon photographic techniques for translating three-dimensional space into two dimensions, DeFeo enhanced the painting's play between real and illusory space. In each image, the combination of this decontextualizing cropping and the prominence of the artist's body gives her a strong and autonomous authorial presence. Each photograph focuses this image of the commanding, independent creator through a different (but, by 1960, equally shopworn) mythological lens: while the *Creative America* spread draws on imagery of the American West to represent the artist as an adventurer, Berman borrows from the Romantic tradition to represent the artist as God.

Fig. 23 Spread in *Creative America* (New York: Ridge, 1962) featuring a photograph by Ernst Haas and a photograph by Burt Glinn of Jay DeFeo working on *The Rose* in 1960. Photograph by Ernst Haas/Ernst Haas via Getty Images. Photograph by Burt Glinn/Magnum Photos.

Notably, Berman and DeFeo's photographs represent the expressionist model of creativity in a curious way—by abstaining from the depiction of DeFeo's actual painting process. Their flattened images completely extrude the studio space and its telling trappings (brushes, palette knives, paint cans, and so on). Fragmented and blanched, *The Rose* barely reads as a material object, let alone as a painting. Moreover, DeFeo's closed eyes and static pose establish a relationship between her body and the canvas that defies

Fig. 24 From the pages of *Life* (May 13, 1957): The opening spread of "Women Artists in Ascendance," featuring photographs of Helen Frankenthaler and Grace Hartigan by Gordon Parks. Photographs by Gordon Parks/The LIFE Picture Collection via Getty Images. LIFE and the LIFE logo are registered trademarks of TI Gotham Inc. used under license.

Fig. 25 From the pages of *Life* (May 13, 1957): The closing spread of "Women Artists in Ascendance," featuring photographs of Jane Wilson and Nell Blaine by Gordon Parks and of Joan Mitchell by Dean Loomis. Photographs by Gordon Parks/The LIFE Picture Collection via Getty Images. Photograph by Loomis Dean/The LIFE Picture Collection via Getty Images. LIFE and the LIFE logo are registered trademarks of TI Gotham Inc. used under license.

the interaction, the contact through vision and touch, between painter and painting. As both intimately bodily and seemingly metaphysical, her naked communion with *The Rose* looks nothing like the many actions (the drawing, mixing, brushing, daubing, plastering, chiseling, scraping, and sanding, for instance) she used to produce the work.

Rather than picturing the scene of production, as Glinn does, Berman deploys artist and work in a symbolic staging of creation ex nihilo. His photographs read as allegories of creativity, not as documents of it. While Glinn's photograph positions the viewer as a witness to artistic action, Berman's photographs ask to be decoded. And like all respectable allegories, Berman's use the nude female figure. Other formal aspects of the photographs reinforce their emblematic character. The images' flatness, symmetry, and geometric linearity give them an iconic, diagrammatic feel. In addition, DeFeo's hieratic pose and the high-contrast printing render her schematic, abstracting her body (her specific, material form) into a symbol (a generalized, intangible figure). Indeed, many commentators have noted the striking resemblance between *The Rose* photographs and Leonardo da Vinci's famous diagrammatic drawing of the *Vitruvian Man* (c. 1490).[25] The front-facing shot's inclusion of a literal symbol (tsade) reinforces its representation of the body as a code.

Not all the photographs in the series impersonate symbols. The sequence that depicts DeFeo as an artist's model overturns the geometric flatness that gives *The Rose* shots their diagrammatic look. Though still highly performative, her poses are now languid. The light follows DeFeo's lead as the flinty, arrow-like rays melt into showers of tinsel. Her reclining postures also give the photographs depth. The prints' dramatic tenebrism adds to this sense of space, as highlights carve out swells of flesh from the darkness. While *The Rose* photographs collapse and cement DeFeo's form into an immediately graspable shape, the model photographs emphasize the malleability and materiality of her body, which they present in so many glimpses.

Like *The Rose* photographs, however, the model shots had counterparts in the popular visual culture of postwar America. They resonated with contemporary representations of American female artists such as "Women Artists in Ascendance" (1957), a now-notorious *Life* magazine article featuring five of DeFeo's contemporaries from New York—including the second-generation abstract expressionists Grace Hartigan, Joan Mitchell, and Helen Frankenthaler (figs. 24, 25). Though surrounded by their works, none of the artists represented in *Life* is shown at work. All assume relaxed, mostly sitting, postures that range from self-enfolding to supine. Their limp inertness sharply contrasts with the dynamic image of the "American Action Painter." As Anne M. Wagner observed, the artists' paintings are displayed as decoration rather than as works in progress. They hang framed and off the easel or masquerade as décor. Frankenthaler sits on her unstretched painting as if it were a living room rug. Like their paintings,

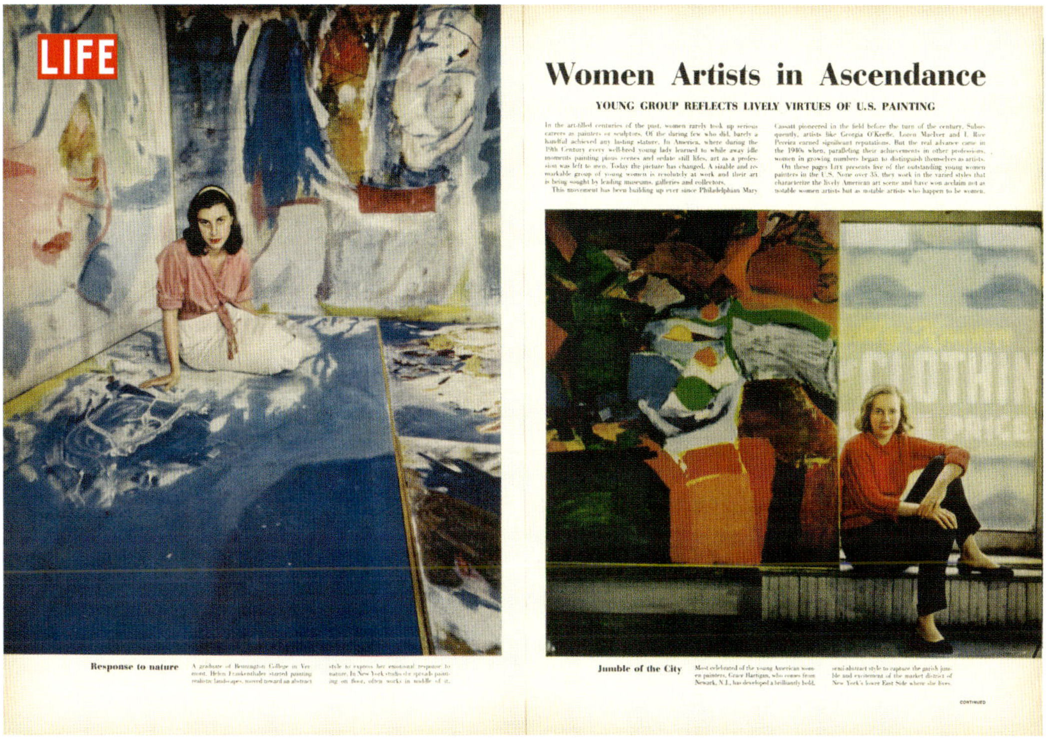

LIFE

Women Artists in Ascendance

YOUNG GROUP REFLECTS LIVELY VIRTUES OF U.S. PAINTING

In the art-filled centuries of the past, women rarely took up serious careers as painters or sculptors. Of the daring few who did, barely a handful achieved any lasting stature. In America, where during the 19th Century every well-bred young lady learned to while away idle moments painting pious scenes and sedate still lifes, art as a profession was left to men. Today the picture has changed. A sizable and remarkable group of young women is resolutely at work and their art is being sought by leading museums, galleries and collectors.

This movement has been building up ever since Philadelphian Mary Cassatt pioneered in the field before the turn of the century. Subsequently, artists like Georgia O'Keeffe, Loren MacIver and I. Rice Pereira earned significant reputations. But the real advance came in the 1940s when, paralleling their achievements in other professions, women in growing numbers began to distinguish themselves as artists.

On these pages LIFE presents five of the outstanding young women painters in the U.S. None over 35, they work in the varied styles that characterize the lively American art scene and have won acclaim not as notable women artists but as notable artists who happen to be women.

Response to nature A graduate of Bennington College in Vermont, Helen Frankenthaler started painting realistic landscapes, moved toward an abstract style to express her emotional response to nature. In New York studio she spreads painting on floor, often works in middle of it.

Jumble of the City Most celebrated of the young American women painters, Grace Hartigan, who comes from Newark, N.J., has developed a brilliantly bold, semi-abstract style to capture the garish jumble and excitement of the market district of New York's lower East Side where she lives.

CONTINUED

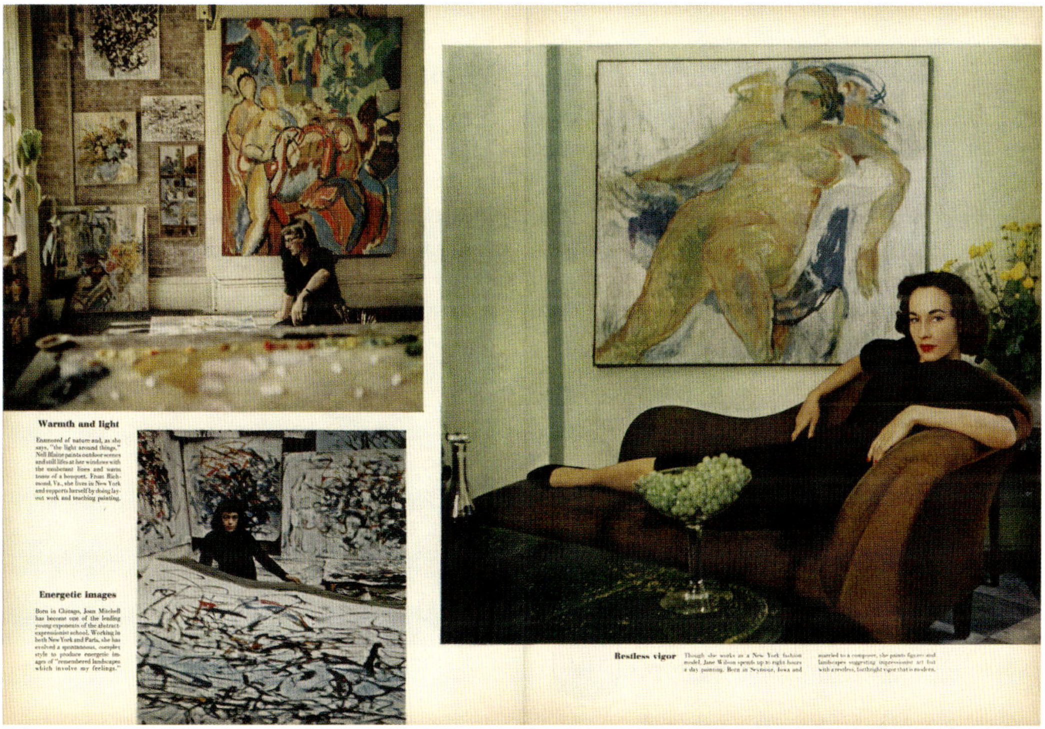

Warmth and light

Enamored of nature and, as she says, "the light around things," Nell Blaine paints outdoor scenes and still lifes at her windows with the exuberant lines and warm tones of a bouquet. From Richmond, Va., she lives in New York and supports herself by doing layout work and teaching painting.

Energetic images

Born in Chicago, Joan Mitchell has become one of the leading young exponents of the abstract-expressionist school. Working in both New York and Paris, she has evolved a spontaneous, complex style to produce energetic images of "remembered landscapes which involve my feelings."

Restless vigor Though she works as a New York fashion model, Jane Wilson spends up to eight hours a day painting. Born in Seymour, Iowa and married to a composer, she paints figures and landscapes suggesting impressionist art but with a restless, forthright vigor that is modern.

the artists are consciously on display. With one exception, the women meet the camera's gaze, and they have clearly dressed for media attention; they are painted instead of painting. Unlike male abstract expressionists, who are almost always depicted absorbed in the act of painting or lost in introspective reverie, the female artists blatantly assume the role of object viewed.[26]

The article's subliminal identification of female artists with artist models becomes explicit in the large photograph of Jane Wilson that concludes the spread (see fig. 25). Wilson, who the accompanying text notes is not only a devoted painter but also "a New York fashion model," reclines on a chaise lounge under an impressionistic painting (presumably her own) of a voluptuous nude in a blue chair. Her luxuriating pose offers her body up to the viewer, likening that body to the glass of grapes on the table in front of her. The composition also compares the artist's body to the model's body in the painting behind her and, in doing so, positions the viewer in the artist's shoes.

DeFeo clearly takes up the role of model differently than do her peers in *Life.* Instead of dressing up for the camera, she disrobes, exaggerating self-display and seductiveness through explicitly lascivious poses. These modifications bring the subtext of *Life*'s representation to the surface: DeFeo blatantly assumes the part of the artist's model and the expectations of sexual availability that come with it. The series' flagrant sexuality attests to its private nature—to the fact that, unlike *Life,* Berman's photographs were not intended for mass circulation. This is not to say, as Richard Cándida Smith has, that this series of photographs was intended to parody, and otherwise respond defiantly to, prevailing period conventions for representing women artists.[27] There are, I agree, connections to be made between the series and contemporary, misogynistic representations of women artists, but I read the photographs less as stably satirical and more as elusive, as will become clear. Either way, clarifying how DeFeo performed the role of artist's model does not fully elucidate why she performed it. Thus, the question remains: What motivated Berman's and/or DeFeo's curious decision to represent this particular artist as an artist's model?

This decision seems slightly less odd if the series is viewed in the context of Berman's larger photographic and artistic practice. According to Kristine McKenna, Berman shot approximately 2,300 negatives from the early 1950s until his death in 1976.[28] He photographed friends and family almost exclusively and only showed his prints privately, in constantly rearranged vignettes in his home and sent as postcards. While some shots have a candid, almost snapshot-like appearance, many share the staged, theatrical quality of DeFeo's photographs. Moreover, a fair proportion of his photographs of female acquaintances depict them partially unclothed or naked and, often, in sexually suggestive poses. The fact that many of these images recycle pornographic tropes raises the specter of objectification and exploitation. However, as McKenna and other commentators have noted, other aspects of the photographs—such as their small scale and murky

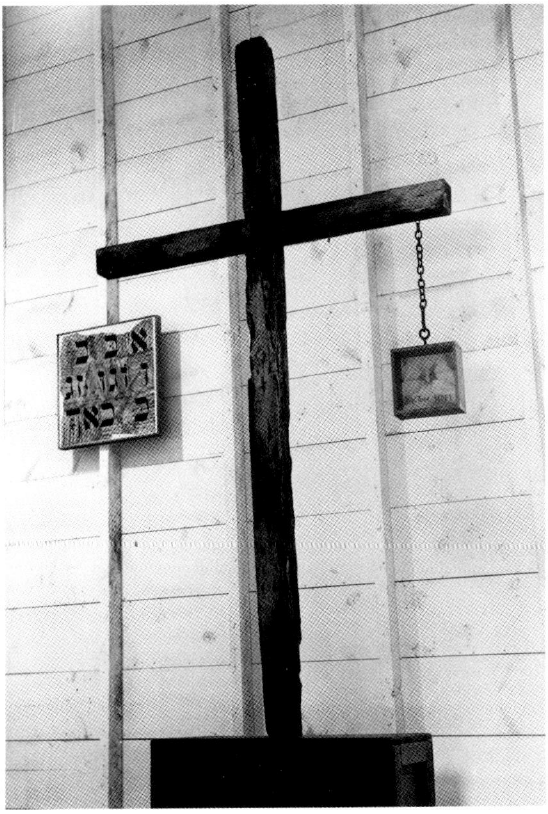

Fig. 26 Charles Brittin, Photograph of Wallace Berman's *Cross*, Ferus Gallery, c. 1957. Charles Brittin papers, Getty Research Institute, Los Angeles [2005.M.11]. © J. Paul Getty Trust.

tones—contradict these assumptions by conveying an intimate atmosphere that testifies to a high degree of trust across the lens.[29]

The perplexing mixture of tenderness and brazen explicitness that distinguishes many of Berman's photographs of women, including those of DeFeo as a model, makes more sense if the images are seen as part of Berman's countercultural championing of sex and the body. Many of his collage and assemblage works, such as the construction *Cross* (1957, which likely prompted the anonymous complaint that led to the closure of his Ferus show), combine religious and pornographic imagery (fig. 26). *Cross* brings together a weather-beaten crucifix and painted Hebrew letters with a photograph of heterosexual coitus. The shock value of the photograph may not immediately be perceived, however, as the close-up image resembles, on first glance, a mandala, and it bears the handwritten Latin inscription "*factum fidei*," which translates to "act of faith." By likening the carnal to the transcendental in his art, Berman sought to redeem sexual experience from its demonization in repressive postwar culture. Mixing the sacred and the profane was a characteristic strategy of cultural rebellion—a way of asserting individual freedom against the limits imposed on expression and identity by mainstream culture—for many of the Beat writers with whom Berman associated. A friend, the poet David Meltzer, described this approach as "turning the world upside-down[;] it was redemptive to affirm

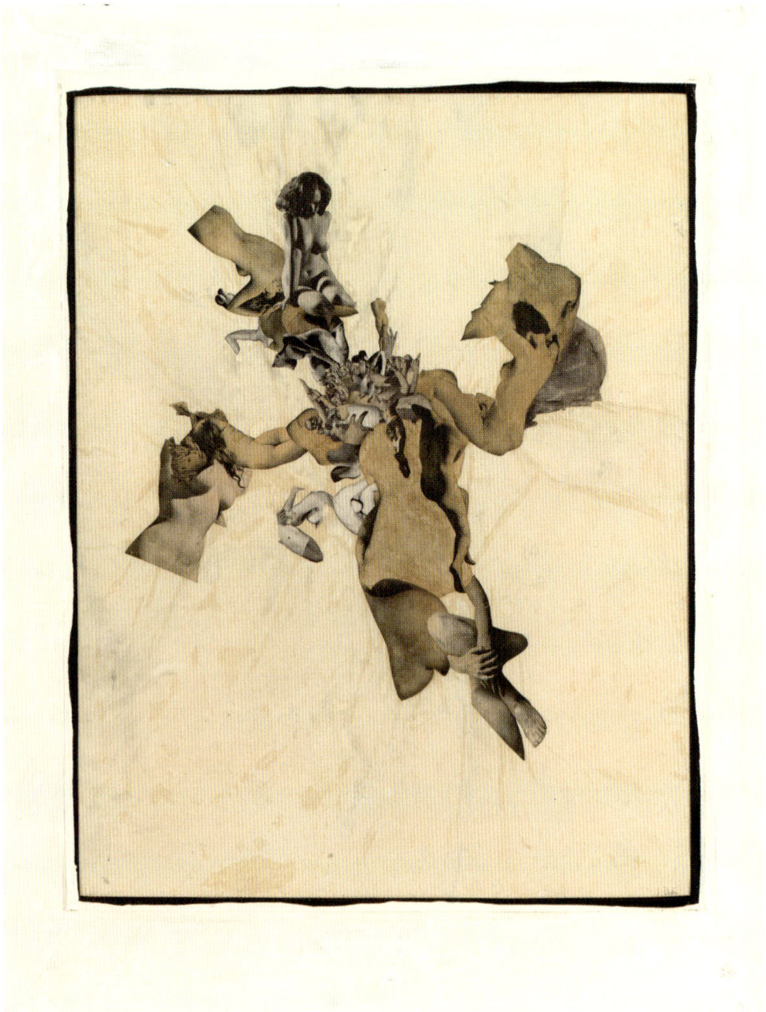

Fig. 27 Jay DeFeo, *Blossom*, 1958. Collage of photomechanical reproductions with paint and tape on paper mounted on painted canvas, 43⅛ × 33⅞ in. (109.5 × 86 cm). Museum of Modern Art, New York. The Fellows of Photography Fund and The Family of Man Fund.

the illicit, to iconize the fallen and lionize the lowly." Jack Kerouac famously asserted that the term "Beat" possesses such a dual connotation, signifying both "down and out" and beatific. Ginsberg's "angelheaded hipsters," in the opening lines of "Howl," exemplify this trope.[30] The model shots, with their fusion of ethereal lighting and sexually graphic content, also fit this template.

As Goldman has noted, DeFeo also experimented with incorporating erotic images into her art in the 1950s. A year before her photo session with Berman, she made two collages, *Blossom* and *Applaud the Black Fact,* using photographs of naked, mostly female bodies likely culled from art and soft-pornography magazines (fig. 27).[31] She arranged the cut-out bodies to form amalgamated silhouettes that appear to unfurl within the negative space of the blank page. The collages show that DeFeo shared Berman's interest in combining figuration and abstraction, even if her engagement with eroticized bodies was more fleeting and formalist—lacking the overt spiritual symbolism that characterizes many of Berman's works.

A negative that Berman exposed but likely never printed (given its different scale and treatment from the rest of the series) suggests that one way their photo series attempted to revalue the sexualized female body was to revise its role in the creative process (fig. 28). The photograph combines aspects of the model sequence with characteristics of the artist sequence; it reads as a long shot to the close-up presented in figure 19. DeFeo sits on a stool in front of *The Rose*. Though she is seated, her body is tense. While the photograph is explicit, it is not erotic. She spreads her labia, but her rigidity, as well as the dark shadow between her legs, renders the gesture unexpectedly chaste. Her open mouth, pendant necklace (which she made), and vulva visually rhyme with one another and with the center of the painting, merging the pornographic with the iconographic, as in Berman's *Cross*. The adamant quality of her pose and the camera's monumentalizing angle of view give her a powerful presence. She throws back her head and opens her mouth as if emitting a song or yell. The painted rays converging above her synesthetically evoke the sound waves that she appears to bellow forth, adding to the vision of her as a commanding creator.

By analogizing DeFeo's sexed form with her painting's form, the shot seems to claim her body as the source of her work. The image suggests two possible readings of this relationship. First, *The Rose*'s iconography could be inspired by her anatomy, à la Judy Chicago's "central core" imagery of the

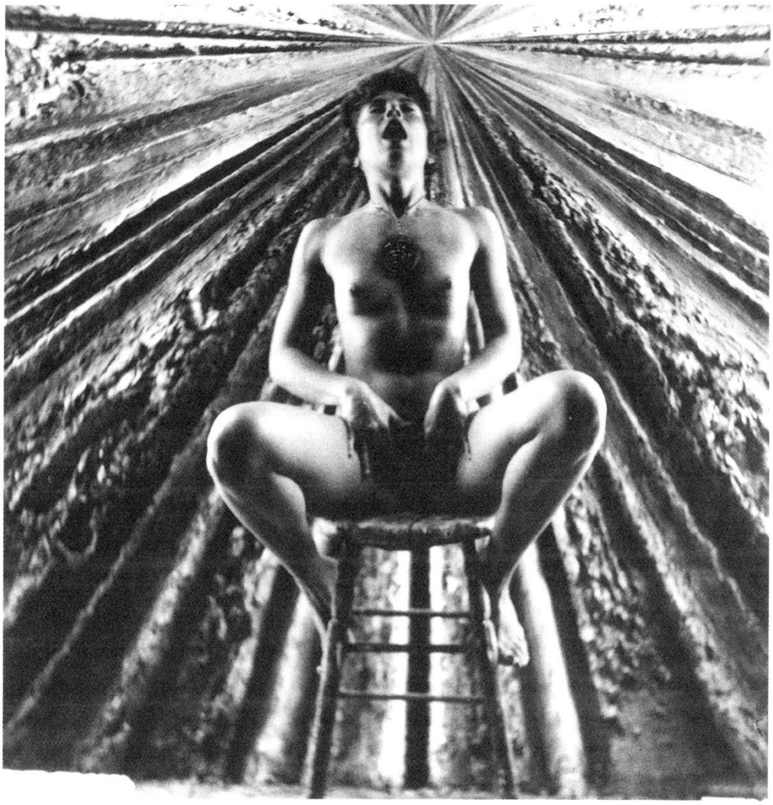

Fig. 28 Wallace Berman, Untitled portrait of Jay DeFeo in front of *The Rose*, San Francisco, 1959. Gelatin silver print, 20 × 26 in. (50.8 × 66 cm). The Estate of Wallace Berman and Kohn Gallery, Los Angeles.

1970s.[32] Second, the photograph could be seen to offer an even more radical revision of the female body's traditional role in the creative process: rather than serving as a model for her work, DeFeo could be viewed as directly generating it. By likening the artist's bodily orifices to her painting's radiating center, that is, the photograph seems to strive toward a female version of expressionism, in which creative emanation is represented as giving birth rather than as ejaculating (as in Jackson Pollock's drip-painting process). The expansive unfurling of erotically coded female forms in DeFeo's *Blossom* could be read as similarly asserting the generative power of women's bodies.

However, in the photograph, DeFeo's gesture of exposure is ultimately ambiguous: it represents her body as simultaneously generative (as giving "birth" to the radiating forms around her) and receptive (as holes to be penetrated). The shots that show DeFeo standing in front of *The Rose* also contain this uncertainty: the lower, central ray of the painting's starburst design could be read as either projecting from or penetrating DeFeo's vagina. In this way, the images amplify a perceptual irresolution inherent in the painting's composition: like all perspective constructions, the orthogonals seem to both radiate out from and vanish into its center point. All three photographs thus mobilize a long-standing tradition in Western art of arranging a one-point perspective representation of space such that the vanishing point is concentric with a female figure's vagina. This mapping, which is most famously represented in Albrecht Dürer's illustration of a perspective machine in *The Painter's Manual* (1525), confirms the patriarchal basis of Western illusionism. "As a means of adding knowledge to visual experience," Kelly Dennis explained, "perspective enacts the desire to know the woman's body and its vanishing point."[33]

The fact that Berman chose not to print the negative suggests that he found its account of the woman artist or, more specifically, of the creative female body unsatisfactory. Perhaps he realized that its account of gendered artistic production was potentially essentializing, as was the case with so many attempts by Beat generation artists and writers to elevate marginalized identities. DeFeo may also have objected to the photograph's blatant gendering of her artistic identity. As both Lucy Lippard and Goldman have discussed, DeFeo, like many female artists of her generation, bristled at the label "woman artist," having experienced the ways this marked category limited the reception of her art.[34] DeFeo similarly refuted later commentators' assertions that she consciously designed *The Rose* to evoke vaginal imagery. "Just an additional note here about subject matter from the women's movement's point of view," she explained in 1978. "Although I recognize some reference to this kind of imagery in the finished work, I am no way motivated toward sexual symbolism in my work on any conscious level. . . . I certainly have never felt any inclination or responsibility to raise 'social consciousnesses' in this area. This attitude has been something of a disappointment to some interviewers, but that's the way I feel."[35]

Despite DeFeo's objections to reading sexual imagery in her art, she speculated (somewhat obliquely) in 1978 that Berman photographed her in part to make such a claim: "I believe Wallace's intent was to present a broad spectrum of mood as well as to present all parts of the body as having aesthetic validity. . . . It occurred to me that Wallace . . . was reflecting on some of the recurrent images . . . of an abstract nature, that reoccur in my own painting."[36] Whatever the reason, the decision to omit the shot left the remaining photographs and the identities they construct for DeFeo divided into two discrete sequences that reiterate the stereotypical, binary gender roles of the studio—those of the male creator and the female model.

Berman and DeFeo explicitly play these roles in a photograph that was likely exhibited with the original series but survives only as a posthumous print (fig. 29).[37] The shot captures the pair posing in a mirror. The tinsel that drapes around DeFeo's shoulders and falls over her exposed right breast

Fig. 29 Wallace Berman, Untitled (Jay DeFeo and Wallace Berman in DeFeo's San Francisco studio), c. late 1950s. Contemporary gelatin silver print, 10 × 8 in. (25.4 × 20.3 cm). The Estate of Wallace Berman and Kohn Gallery, Los Angeles.

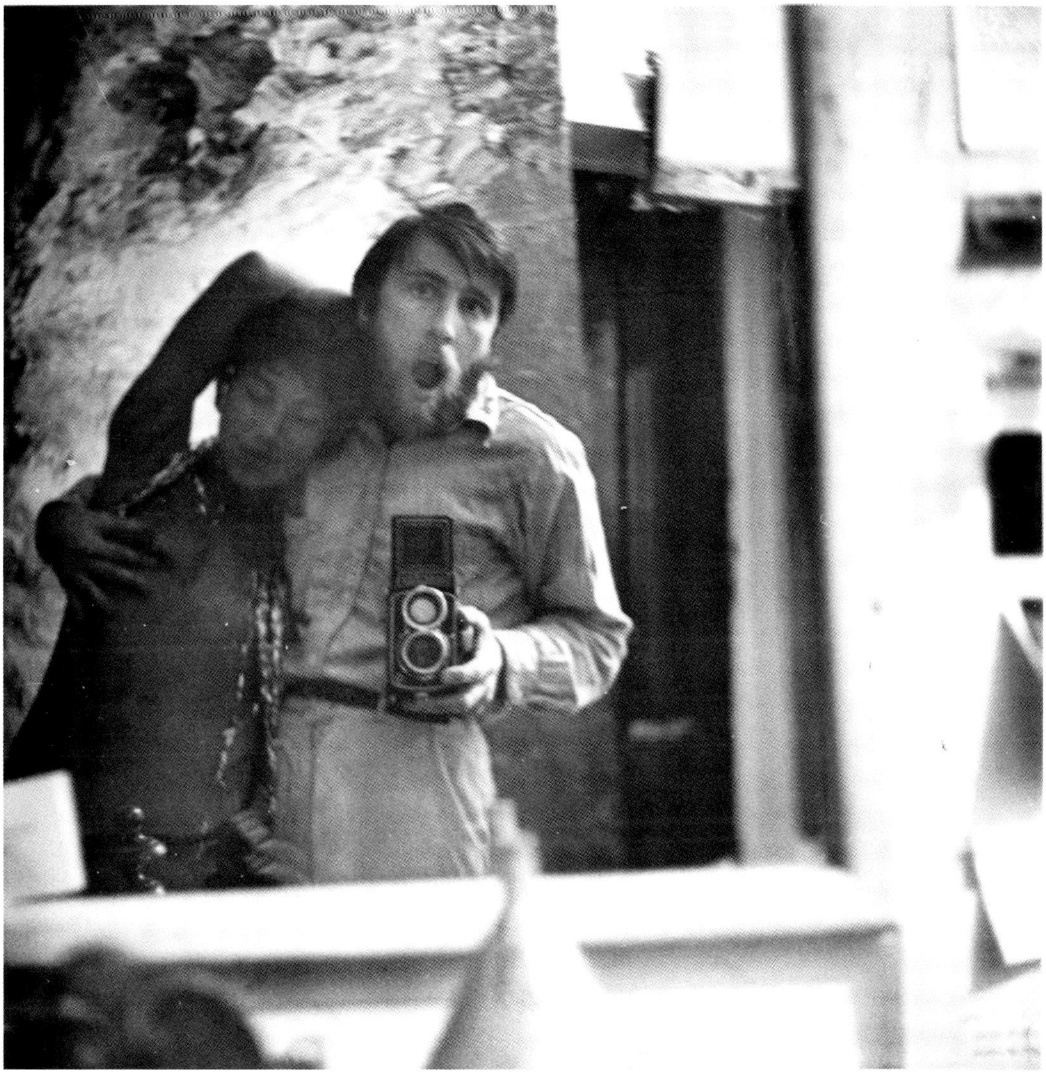

links the photograph to those of her posing on the stool. The manifestation of Berman and his camera in front of the lens gives the image a "behind the scenes" feel, as if it pulls back the curtain to reveal the conditions of the series' production—specifically, the relationship between photographer and model. The photograph presents a stereotypical account of that relationship: DeFeo embodies the objectified model, and Berman epitomizes the virile artist. She is naked, while he is clothed. She closes her eyes, while he stares directly at the viewer. His erect body supports her drooping form, as she acquiesces to his groping right hand. Now it is Berman's turn to enact, in exaggerated terms, the fantasy associated with his role: he performs the artist's unmediated access to the model's body by grabbing her breast. His gesture crudely equates the camera and DeFeo's breast and, thus, conflates sex and artistic creation, a concept that is foundational to the sexist mythology of the modernist studio.[38] Here, Berman is in control of vision, the female body, and the creative act, and DeFeo is the material he possesses, both perceptually and physically. The shot, in short, contradicts DeFeo's later assertion that the series was "an objective collaboration between artist friends" by deliberately performing the opposite extreme: the sexualized and hierarchical relationship between artist and model.

Berman's slack-jawed expression, however, unsettles the authenticity of the pair's embodiment of artist and model, pushing the representation from stereotype to caricature. His papers at the Smithsonian Institution's Archives of American Art contain several snapshots in which he sports similar looks of exaggerated astonishment. Usually the expressions signal his playful reaction to kitsch items that sensationalize subcultural activities, such as a poster about the dangers of marijuana. In these photographs, Berman lampoons the mainstream's priggish response to his bohemian lifestyle. Mobilized in the context of Berman and DeFeo's photo shoot, the expression seems to predict and parody reductive interpretations of the series as titillating and scandalous (as, in other words, evidence of a sexual relationship between the friends). By poking fun at an imagined public, for whom the photographs were never intended, the shot confirms the series' private nature. Those who viewed the suite at Berman's home would likely have gotten the joke, and their laughter would have confirmed their insider status. It is less clear, however, if DeFeo was in on the punch line; her serene expression and gentle lean into Berman's body lack his playful performativity and read, instead, as a sincere manifestation of intimacy.

Berman's and DeFeo's mismatched expressions point to the trickster quality of the model shots. They self-consciously play with representational conventions from pornography and studio mythology, complicating the way such images usually objectify women's bodies. In doing so, they suggest a new relationship between artist, model, and viewer—one that allows for intimacy and a revaluation of sexuality. This transformation, however, is fragile and was likely legible only within the context of DeFeo and Berman's circle, as his sarcastic expression in the mirror seems to admit. The images' purposeful evasiveness manifests in their unplaceable tone, which shuttles between the parodic, the erotic, and the surreal. The murky quality of the prints gives formal expression to their mystery: the photographs' veiled surfaces contradict both their content (DeFeo's exposure of her body) and their facture (Berman's exposure of the film). While their subject matter conveys the viewer's proximity to DeFeo's body, their obscurity distances the viewer from her both perceptually and psychically. By manifesting the images' mediated nature, in sum, the scrim-like surface of each photograph counters the illusion of direct access to the model's body, a pretense that underwrites pornography and most images of the artist's model.

Goldman has argued that the darkroom effects transform the explicit shots from pornographic images (which, according to Dennis's definition, inspire a "physical breach of the presumed boundary between image and beholder") into erotic ones (which give rise to viewing experiences that do not violate "disinterested pleasure").[39] Indeed, the play between revelation and concealment in the photographs could be seen to freeze the titillating dynamic of the peep show into a static image. Moreover, the printing techniques obscure the details of DeFeo's body, giving the representations a distant, aestheticized look; in most of the images she appears more nude than naked.[40] I would argue, however, that the photographs' structuring dialectic never fully resolves into the erotic. In the images where DeFeo reveals her body explicitly, even aggressively, through the printed veil, the contradictions between display and disguise, presence and absence, content and form, remain pointed and perplexing.

PHOTOGRAPHER AS CHIROMANCER

Berman sent a postcard to DeFeo on April 14, 1959, most likely to set up the photo session that yielded the series (figs. 30, 31).[41] The card provides insight into Berman's conception of the act of photographing his friend and, in doing so, helps make sense of the series' many contradictions. The collaged postcard juxtaposes two seemingly unrelated images: a self-portrait and a palmistry diagram. The latter is an illustration in at least two publications to which Berman could have had access: *Amulets and Superstitions* (1930), British Egyptologist E. A. Wallis Budge's catalogue of talismans and other ritual objects from the ancient Mediterranean and Middle East, and *The Mirror of Magic: A History of Magic in the Western World* (1948), an occult primer by the Swiss-American surrealist Kurt Seligmann, who was an acquaintance of Berman's friend Philip Lamantia.[42] In both texts, the diagram illustrates descriptions of chiromancy (or palm reading), specifically, in Budge, as practiced within Kabbalah. Berman printed the photograph atop the diagram so that the index finger and the thumb of the splayed, schematically rendered hand extend into the photograph, violating the otherwise abrupt border between them. The photograph displays Berman's typical darkroom manipulations. Shadow practically blots out his body and

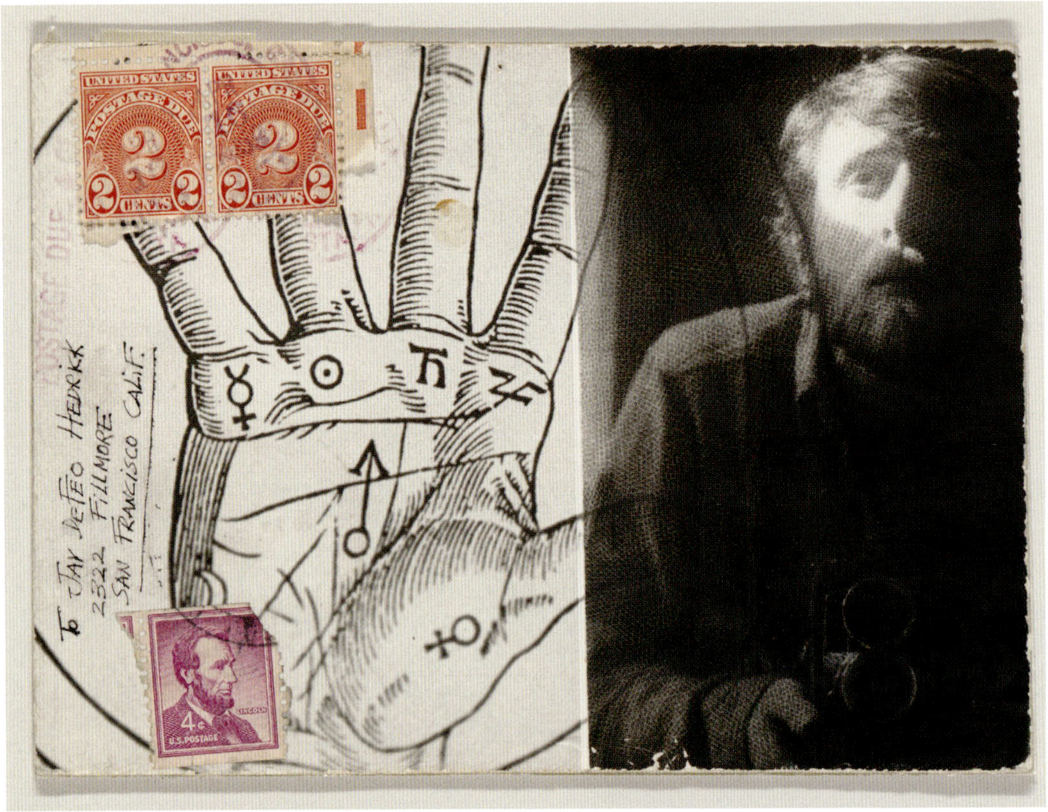

Fig. 30 Wallace Berman, Untitled, 1959 (recto). Photomontage, ink, and collage on board, $4\frac{1}{2} \times 6\frac{5}{16}$ in. (11.4 × 16 cm). Whitney Museum of American Art, New York. Gift of the Lannan Foundation [Inv.: 96.242.1].

the camera he holds at his waist. A dramatic splash of light illuminates his right eye, giving it a celestial glow. An elliptical, cryptic note scrawled on the back of the card reads: "Am ready for shooting—let me know the rite day." Berman's substitution of "right" with its homonym "rite" is typical of his zeal for wordplay. There is a countercultural mischief to his toying with standards of communication. The card's palimpsest of postmarks registers bureaucratic disapproval or, at least, bewilderment at Berman's attempt to carve out a creative space in the most mundane of missive forms.

Read together, the two images suggest a palm-reading scenario. With his camera obscured and his dramatically illumined right eye trained toward the diagram, Berman assumes the role of chiromancer. The viewer's gaze automatically shuttles between the white paper of the illustration and Berman's brightly lit eye, establishing a connection between them. Like his photographs of DeFeo with *The Rose,* the collage elides Berman's physical labor as a photographer (pressing the shutter) with the fortune-teller's metaphysical labor (that of divination). By using an image of himself as a photographer to represent himself as a diviner, Berman analogizes the two activities. The message on the back of the card reinforces this metaphor by playfully referring to their photo session as a ritual. Furthermore, the palmistry diagram bears a notable resemblance to the photographs that

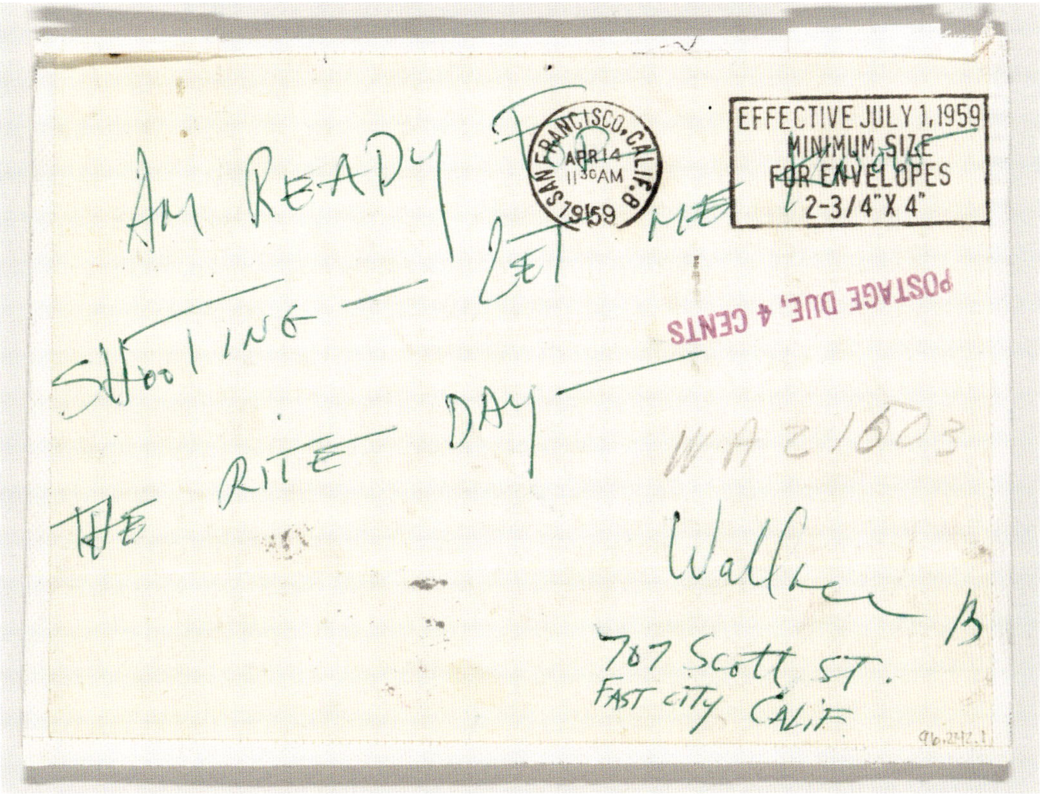

Fig. 31 Wallace Berman, Untitled, 1959 (verso). Photomontage, ink, and collage on board, 4½ × 6⁵⁄₁₆ in. (11.4 × 16 cm). Whitney Museum of American Art, New York. Gift of the Lannan Foundation [Inv.: 96.242.1].

Berman would soon take of DeFeo in front of *The Rose*. Her outstretched limbs echo the spread fingers, and the photographs' edges tightly circumscribe her body (especially in the back-facing shot) like the circular border around the hand. In both the print and the photographs, the combination of splayed figure and tight framing has a flattening, emblematizing effect on the represented bodies. The astrological symbols inscribed on the open palm likewise predict Berman's collaged branding of DeFeo's chest with the Hebrew letter. *The Rose* photographs, in other words, are as much esoteric emblems as the diagram itself, and they thus recall other, better-known examples of esoteric emblematic images such as Leonardo's *Vitruvian Man*. Other examples include illustrations of Kabbalistic concepts, such as "The Perfect Man" and "The Wheel," found in *Amulets and Superstitions*. All of these images, including *The Rose* photographs, inscribe, regiment, and measure the human body within geometric forms and text.

The postcard, I am arguing, offers a metaphorical account of the photo session that Berman sent the card to set up. The juxtaposed images stage, across the card, the confrontation, across the lens, between Berman and DeFeo. On the postcard, Berman reimagines the photographic scenario as one of ritual divination in which he, aided by the camera eye, is the "seer," and the composite form of DeFeo and her painting is the object of his esoteric interpretation. What is to be made of Berman's bizarre reimagining of the studio scenario? What bearing does it have on the model of creativity that the series both figures and performed through its production?

Though the postcard's occult references would have been hopelessly obscure to most Americans in 1959, they were a vital component of the visual culture of Berman and DeFeo's circle. The influence of esoteric philosophy and ritual on artists and writers in California during the mid-twentieth century is well documented. Esotericism, as it is generally conceived, understands both sacred texts and things in the world symbolically: scripture and the objects of empirical experience are hints pointing to the true, hidden nature of creation. Revealing and, often, communing with this secret, divine realm is the goal of occult practices and mystical traditions, including Kabbalah, chiromancy, tarot, astrology, alchemy, and numerous others enumerated in Budge's and Seligmann's texts. According to literary scholar Stephen Fredman, these clandestine magical traditions spoke to a generation of young artists and writers on the West Coast who, like Berman, felt alienated by the conformity and materialism of postwar society.[43]

Surrealism was a primary conduit to the mystical and occult for members of California's artistic underground. For example, Meltzer and some of Berman's other poet friends, including Stuart Z. Perkoff and Jack Hirschman, described their work in the 1970s as "kabbalah surrealism." Though spiritual in origin, esotericism's cryptologic account of the universe deeply informed Romantic strands of modernism. The symbolists and the surrealists, for example, both attempted to counter the deadening rationality of modern life by reinfusing it with a beyond. Some surrealists, such as Antonin Artaud, ventured past Sigmund Freud's unconscious to discover the "beyond" through mystical practices, such as Kabbalah, and drug use. Grove Press had published the first English translation of Artaud's *The Theater and Its Double*—in which Artaud defines ritual as a performative means to violently transcend bodily experience—not long before Berman wrote his postcard to DeFeo. Berman, thus, may have had Artaud's esoteric definition of ritual in mind when he referred to their photo session as such. Either way, the regularity with which Artaud's name, writings, and image appear in *Semina* helps to show that Berman—like many artists and writers of his generation, especially those in California's bohemian undergrounds—fancied himself an heir to this vein of renegade surrealism.[44] Visual evidence also supports this connection insofar as Berman's shots of DeFeo bear hallmarks of surrealist photography such as distorting and defamiliarizing the nude female body through framing and printing techniques.[45]

Like Artaud, Berman and many of the Beat poets he associated with regarded psychotropic drugs (such as marijuana, peyote, and heroin) as esoteric aids that could help uncover hidden levels of experience. Many contemporary literary works by Berman's companions made this claim through ecstatic verse. Michael McClure's "Peyote Poem" (1958), for example, chronicled the poet's first time taking peyote, emphasizing his revelation that the everyday world is intimately connected to the cosmos. Berman facilitated the poet's revelatory experience and its dissemination by giving the peyote to McClure and publishing the resultant poem as the third edition of *Semina*. Philip Lamantia's 1959 anthology *Narcotica* similarly analogized pharmaceutical and religious experience. The photographs Berman took for the first edition illustrate Lamantia's conflation of Catholic transcendence and the effects of heroin by depicting the author shooting up before a cross. Berman suggested that similar mind-expanding effects could be induced by viewing the photograph of DeFeo facing *The Rose* when, in an undated note to DeFeo, he described "having a universal trip of yr [*sic*] body in relation to 'rose.'"[46]

The postcard he sent to DeFeo makes a similar claim by analogizing photography and divination, the camera's eye and the seer's supernatural gaze. This metaphor is as old as photography itself. Chiromancy supposedly allows one to decipher the imperceptible (the interior, metaphysical, future, and cosmological) from the perceptible (the exterior, physical, present, and specific). Throughout its history, photography has popularly been thought to possess the same ability to miraculously augment vision. From its highly problematic use by physiognomists to lay bare the souls of criminals and madmen to its use by the surrealists to reveal the unconscious mind's coding of our everyday experience, the camera's mechanical "eye" has been positioned as a revealer of hidden forms and meanings.[47]

The postcard attests to a connection between esotericism and Berman's photography that adds to current interpretations of the references to Kabbalah that he included in assemblages, collages, paintings, and film. Although Berman could not read Hebrew, his library contained several English-language publications on Kabbalah, indicating that he possessed at least some degree of knowledge about the tradition's general principles. Taking that assumption as a point of departure, past readings of Berman's references to Kabbalah have mainly focused on his use of the tradition as a framework for producing appropriative, multivalent artworks.[48] These qualities are native to esoteric hermeneutics—the practice of meaning production within mystical traditions such as Kabbalah. As mentioned above, these traditions see scripture and nature as encrypted with divine knowledge. It is the exegete's job to decode God's secrets from sacred texts and the outward appearance of the world. Such a belief that the world is divinely encrypted has two main hermeneutic effects of relevance to Berman's art: first, it restricts understanding to a small group of initiates who have at least some understanding of where to begin their search; and second, it casts perennial doubt upon all links between signifier and signified. Because hints are inherently unstable communicators, that is, the meanings they offer are highly elusive. As the philosopher Moshe Halbertal explains, "The addition of an esoteric level expands the text's 'receptive capacity to meaning' to almost infinite dimensions. What can be read into it becomes far more varied and extreme." Indeed, esoteric practices such as Kabbalah encourage their exegetes to propose radical, novel interpretations to even the most studied sacred texts, creating an environment in which, Halbertal notes, the "most guarded [knowledge] is the most open ended."[49]

Meltzer appears to have had this aspect of esotericism in mind when he asserted, in 1992, that Berman took the Kabbalists' imaginative "rite of reading" as the model for his artistic activity. Just as Kabbalists suss out multiple, secret meanings in scripture by "allowing a word or phrase to bridge out and into a lit-up network of connections and associations," Meltzer argued, Berman "scanned a continuously unrolling text" of postwar mass culture, "decoding and recoding constantly, appropriating messages without images, the image a surface concealing clues to larger shifting meanings." Other scholars have since supported this association between Berman's appropriation and montage techniques and the activities of any esoteric exegete who "continuously interprets and reinterprets, endlessly combining and recombining."[50] Ken D. Allan, for example, has convincingly argued that Berman was one of many artists of his generation who turned to premodern traditions, such as Kabbalah, as the basis for their postmodernist response "to the increasing importance of information and technology in the postwar world."[51] Many of these interpretations have noted that Berman's montage juxtapositions foster open-ended viewing—a mode of reception commonly associated with postmodernism—by prompting viewers to make idiosyncratic associations across disparate found images and glyphs, thereby passing on the Kabbalists' "rite of reading" to the viewer.

The accord between Berman's practice and the Kabbalistic idea that the world is a text open to the interpreter's revealing rearrangements is readily apparent, as many commentators have noted, in Berman's *Radio Aether* series of prints from the 1960s and 1970s. Using a Verifax machine, an early form of photocopy technology, he collaged found images onto the photograph of a handheld transistor radio, which he lifted from a Sony advertisement.[52] *Bouquet,* a Verifax collage from 1964 that Berman reproduced as a poster for the Los Angeles Film-Makers Festival and sent to DeFeo, is characteristic of the series in that it uses a gridded scaffolding of repeated radios to combine a variety of incongruous image fragments, including representations of a boxing match, manacled hands, Artaud, a corpse, and various indeterminate scenes (fig. 32). One also finds the Hebrew letter *aleph* in the lower-right corner. Unknown to uninitiated viewers in terms of meaning, the letter is nonetheless intuitively recognizable as a deliberately distinct, and thus in some way symbolic, communicative form. As an exegete makes wild associations within sacred texts to reveal secret significances, so Berman draws together seemingly random snippets from the image continuum of postwar society to endow them with novel meaning. The organizing logic of the grid implies an underlying structure of reason and thus that there is, in fact, meaning to be made from this odd

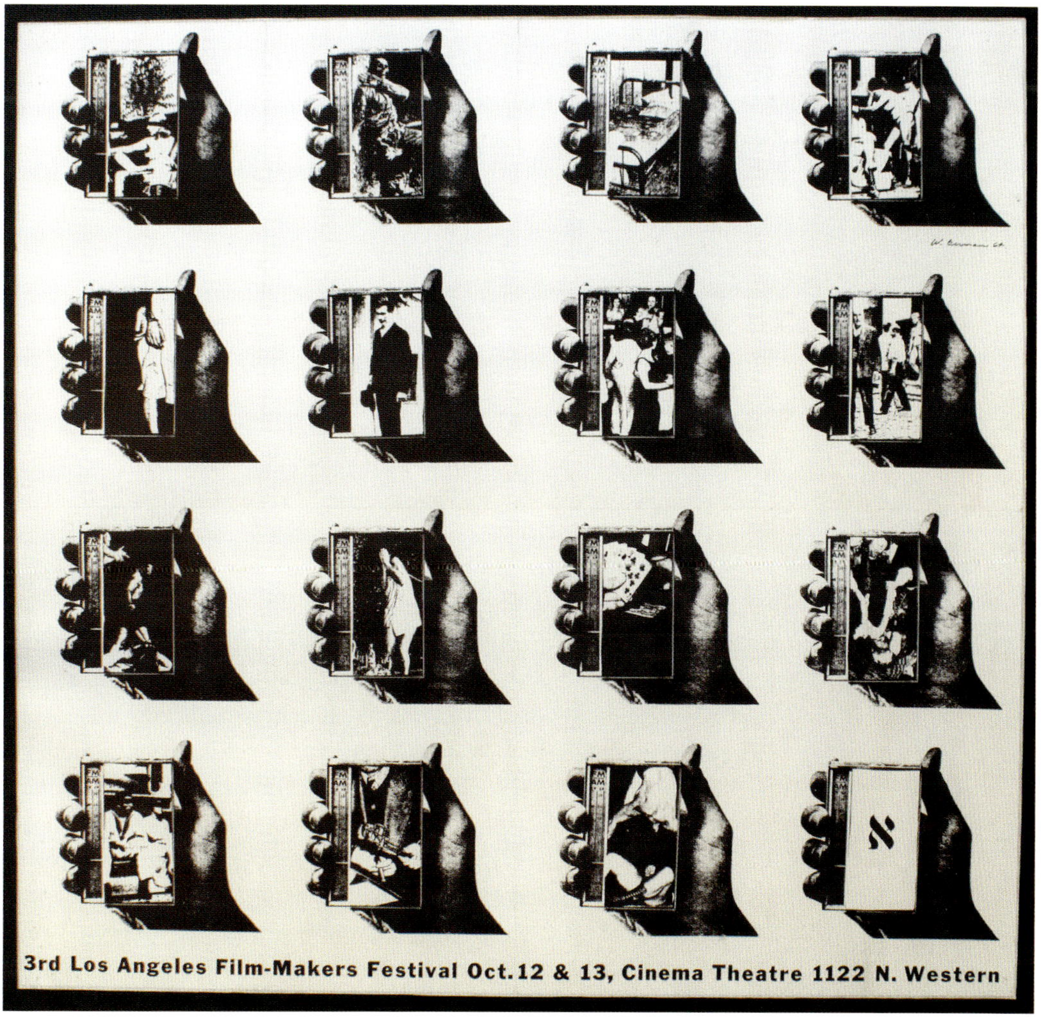

Fig. 32 Wallace Berman, Poster for the 3rd Los Angeles Film-Makers Festival, 1964. Offset lithograph of a Verifax collage. MSS 294, the Charles Henri Ford archive relating to Om Krishna II, Special Collections, University of Delaware Library, Museums and Press, Newark.

association of found things, goading the viewer to reveal it—or, at least, to interpret it. The print thus claims that the act of appropriation that made it and the active reception it prompts are each a Kabbalistic rite of reading.

Those who recognize the meaning of aleph, the first letter of the Hebrew alphabet, have found it to be an appropriate emblem for this model of artistic practice insofar as it represents, as Allan explains, "the breath before speaking, the medium through which all knowledge is transmitted."[53] As such, aleph gestures to the authorial model that Berman shared with both the prototypical postmodernist and the Kabbalist—creation as the selective, interpretive reception of transmissions from postwar culture and beyond. It is little wonder, then, that Berman adopted aleph as a kind of signature symbol, inscribing it on many of his works.

The postcard that Berman sent to DeFeo supports the idea that he adopted Kabbalah as a model for art-making—and specifically, for our purposes here, as a model for photography. Taking the photographs of DeFeo into account, however, highlights the way in which Kabbalah preserves individual creative authority, even as it opens the work to infinite interpretation. Indeed, as is not the case with post-structuralist deconstruction, esotericism's radical opening of the text and empowerment of the reader do not spell the "death of the author." For it is precisely the author's (that is, God's) infinity that creates the text's infinite capacity to mean. Within Kabbalah's mystical logic, literary theorist Betty Rojtman notes, "indeterminacy" proceeds from the "absolute" without contradiction.[54] Esotericism, in short, posits a relationship between author, text, and reader that defies earthbound models of meaning production. It combines the seemingly mutually exclusive models of meaning-making that became commonly associated with modernism and postmodernism in the latter half of the twentieth century: its empowerment of the reader's infinite interpretive capacity resembles postmodernist reception theory, while its preservation of absolute authorial intent echoes modernist values. Rabbinical scholar Moshe Idel articulates this apparent contradiction: "Paradoxically, the kabbalistic identification of text and author and the infinity acquired by the text make it possible to extract from the text an infinity of meanings, a process that creates a strong reader."[55] Kabbalah, in sum, necessitates both a strong author and a strong reader, while avoiding the violence of both the author's totalitarian control and his death.

Esotericism also makes meaning unplaceable by provocatively confusing the superimposed and the revealed. As Harold Bloom observed, Kabbalah requires the interpreter to take a "double stance: on the one hand, he will insert or super-impose depths of meanings into the narrative line of the text; on the other hand, he will claim to bring them to the surface."[56] The initiate's activity thus blurs reception and creation. It is, according to Jewish studies scholar Elliot Wolfson, "simultaneously interpretive and visionary," and the product it yields is a hybrid "between text and commentary."[57]

Viewing the photographic series through Kabbalah's mystical hermeneutics—as Berman's postcard asks—helps square its authorial contradictions. According to esotericism, DeFeo could be simultaneously the revered source of all meaning and an object of interpretation, a catalyst for the creative processes of others. She could be, in other words, both Godhead and model. As simultaneously generative and receptive, DeFeo's female form embodied this paradox, as the posthumous print of her sitting in front of *The Rose* asserts. Likewise, in Kabbalah, creation both issues from a single creator in an instantaneous act of divine emanation and accrues over generations of interpretation. In this way, it combines the contrasting models of artistic production depicted in the photo series—the creation ex nihilo staged in *The Rose* shots and the representational procedures implied by the model sequence. In both esotericism and the photographs, creation is not only autonomous but also relational; it is both an individual act and one that occurs through encounter, appropriation, and interpretation. As discussed, Berman and DeFeo's particular encounter occurred across lines of gender difference, and their interpretation of those differences self-consciously played with society's codes for representing them.

In addition, the curious play that Berman's obscuring printing techniques produce between exposure (of DeFeo's body, the studio sanctuary, and the film) and concealment also structures esoteric inquiry. Because of its encrypted nature, the object of the mystic's study simultaneously reveals and veils God. Many Kabbalistic commentaries acknowledge the erotic relationship that this dialectic establishes between text and initiate. As Halbertal has noted, "The deeper layers of Torah [are understood] as God's own body uncovered in the interpretative act. The multi-layered text that both reveals and conceals is conceived in terms of the erotic subtle movement of intimacy and alienation."[58] Berman's 1959 prints of DeFeo manifest this metaphor pictorially. Like God seen through the veil of text, she appears through the veiled surface of the photograph as, to borrow a phrase from one of Berman's Kabbalistic volumes, simultaneously "knowable and unknowable."[59] By highlighting the print's mediated nature and giving the images a spectral quality, Berman's unconventional printing techniques foreground the loss that underwrites photographic representation in general. The images thus emphasize the poignant play between absence and presence that characterizes both photography and esoteric hermeneutics.

In sum, reading the series through the lens of esotericism cannot resolve the conflict among the multiple artistic identities DeFeo occupies in the series. On the contrary, and for the better, it compels us to leave that multiplicity intact and to find art-historical value within it—namely, the visual expression of a period-specific model of making that bridged autonomous creation and collective production. The series also shows that the particular concept of Kabbalah that structured Berman's art practice is more complex than what has previously been explained in regard to his nonphotographic works. The photographs he made with DeFeo suggest that esoteric exegesis was a desirable template for his communal art practice not only because it opened every artwork to appropriation, but also because it preserved individual artistic authority, intent, and originality within that interpretative free-for-all.[60]

Berman recognized (and, likely, relished) the similarity between Kabbalah and the types of informal, appropriative art practices that were developing in Los Angeles and San Francisco in the 1950s and 1960s, where artists maintained separate studios but were also in frequent contact—viewing one another's works in homes, studios, and neighborhood galleries. Their encounters often generated new works as they recycled their friends' works, through either representation or material appropriation—a process exemplified by exchanges about and around *The Rose.* Mystical hermeneutics similarly embeds the independent creator within an interpretative community, confounding traditional definitions of authorship and producing liminal objects that are simultaneously independent works and interpretations of others. Berman and DeFeo's photo series exemplifies these ambiguities. In this way, the series supports one of the main claims of this book—that the coterie conditions of the Fillmore neighborhood enabled, and even encouraged, artists to act on their desires to produce new forms of community and authorship as alternatives to the oppressive conformity and reductive individualism they perceived within the public sphere and art institutions of postwar America.

Such an interpretation of the authorial model that Berman drew from Kabbalah also expands our understanding of Berman's other works that reference the tradition, such as the *Radio Aether* series discussed above. Berman, I believe, appreciated the authorial ambiguity that esoteric hermeneutics possesses because that style of exegesis (like other touchstones for his creative practice such as Romantic inspiration, the artist-model relationship, surrealist shock, and postmodernist appropriation) is fundamentally relational. The Kabbalist exegete/artist is both passive and active, both a humble vessel for transmissions from outside (from God, a muse, the unconscious, or existing sources) and an exalted agent transforming, or even imposing, received meanings. This space of intersubjective creation makes precise attribution impossible and, thus, opens up the possibility of experimenting with different kinds of shared authorship.

The combination of submission and agency that Berman appears to have attributed to Kabbalah also helps explain the odd mix of mystery and subversion he attributes to it in *Bouquet*. The print likens the act of appropriation to divine inspiration, suggesting that images leap out at the artist in the same miraculous way that the word of God and radio transmissions manifest from the ether. Yet, even as *Bouquet* positions the artist as a passive receiver of the deluge of media images, it asserts his agency. The collage fragments and randomizes the spectacle's monolithic flow, a disruption that allows for new, personal meanings to emerge. Berman's "rite of reading" is thus akin to postwar practices, such as the Situationist International's *détournement* and Michel de Certeau's tactics, that harness the act of consumption to preserve personal freedom and critical thought within a society increasingly dominated and hegemonized by consumer capitalism and its attendant media spectacle.[61]

Berman's underground art and literary journal, *Semina,* indicates that many of the collaborations he fostered were characterized by esotericism's defining contradictions (see fig. 22). With *Semina,* as with his photographs of DeFeo, Berman assumed the role of the transistor/medium/exegete by transmitting the works of others. To produce an issue, he collected poems, drawings, and photographs from his friends (those who lived both near and far), reprinted them on a variety of small cards, gathered these "pages" into envelopes or folders, and mailed them back to his friends. Unlike a page bound to a spine, each card retains its physical identity as a discrete work; they coalesce to produce a whole that is tenuous at best. McClure once described the magazine as perched "on the lip of entropy—it's about to fall apart." *Semina*'s loose-leaf structure instantiates the independence of each author and act, reflecting both the dispersed nature of the publication's production and the loose-knit community it represents.[62]

While the magazine's unbound nature safeguards authorial supremacy by segregating each work, the format also has the opposite effect: it fosters a strong reader. As many commentators have noted, the issues' sturdy, palm-sized "pages" invite readers to rearrange them into sequences or constellations, thereby discovering their own, idiosyncratic correspondences through study or chance.[63] Torn, folded, and taped, DeFeo's surviving copies of *Semina* in the Archives of American Art index instances in which the publication's format succeeded in initiating precisely such interactive consumption. Berman's photo series also bears witness to DeFeo's creative uptake of the journal. The photograph of DeFeo standing before her large-scale drawing *The Eyes* (1958)—the titular forms unfurling like wings from her shoulders—reveals that she scrawled beneath it lines from an untitled poem by Lamantia that first appeared in *Semina* in 1959 (see fig. 20).[64] While both drawing and poem evoke visionary experience and thus conjure Romantic notions of solitary creation, this detail shows that DeFeo nourished her art practice with the work of another distributed via *Semina*—an intertextual cycle that Berman's photograph both documents and continues.

Through participatory engagement like DeFeo's, each reader ideally contributes to *Semina*'s form and meaning; reception continues the production process, muddying authorship. Like esoteric hermeneutics, *Semina* enacts a complex relationship between individual and collective authorship. The dialectic it performs between the autonomous act and communal production is generative, just as Kabbalah's preservation of God's authority is the basis of the exegete's inexhaustible interpretive powers.

The photo series depicts *The Rose* as a similarly generative work. By portraying the painting as an occult symbol, the photographs imply that it will serve as a catalyst for creativity among initiates (the artist's circle), since hermetic signs require interpretation. Framing the painting as a symbol to be decoded, in short, opened it to further appropriation by DeFeo and Berman's community—an invitation that, as this book charts, bore out over the additional six years the painting remained in her studio. *The Rose* photographs not only mimic hermetic symbols; they (and the rest of the suite) also performed one of the primary functions of occult cultural production: they forged subcultural identity. By encrypting texts and restricting their circulation, Kabbalists transform the activity of interpretation into an affirmation of the exegete's membership to their exclusive group.[65] Berman treated both *Semina* and the photo series as esoteric objects by tightly circumscribing their audiences. Moreover, the photographs' revealing content, which would have scandalized the general public, reinforced the privileged intimacy of the invitees who viewed them in Berman's home. In this way, the act of viewing the series marked the beholder as part of DeFeo and Berman's inner circle, bringing into being a kind of order of *The Rose* that demarcated and reinforced community ties.

Semina likewise reflected an image of Berman's dispersed community back to itself. The reciprocal nature of the magazine's production and reception—that its creators were also its audience—meant that it enacted the ever-shifting boundaries of Berman's coterie. McClure described the journal's power to generate social cohesion: "*Semina*s are a form of love structure that Wallace made, drawing friends together. Friends are drawn together into the assemblage of the magazine, but the magazine is also sent to acquaintances who are drawn into the circle of friends, so it expands and becomes a larger event."[66] The journal's private distribution meant that the act of receiving it marked one as a member of Berman's subcultural circle. The magazine thus possessed social agency, the ability to generate belonging. In this way, Berman's extended, underground community fit Michael Warner's definition of a counter-public—a group of individuals bound together in opposition to the mainstream through the circulation of texts.[67] At the same time, however, both *Semina*'s autonomous pages and the photographs' play of revelation and concealment signaled that separation was crucial to the kind of belonging their reception enacted. The dance of intimacy and alienation that the images stage between the viewer and DeFeo mimicked the loose collectivity that developed among the artists living in the Fillmore District—the dialectic between the isolation of the studio and the togetherness of the neighborhood, between individual and communal authorship.

It may appear that DeFeo's more traditional studio practice precluded her from the model of authorship that the photographs of her construct. As Glinn's photograph indicates, most representations, whether pictorial, verbal, or written, of *The Rose*'s production invoke tropes of artistic individualism to depict it as a solitary, even isolating, activity. However, in the years following the photo shoot, *The Rose* was a primary site through which individual making and artistic exchange coalesced in the Fillmore community, as DeFeo's (male) friends made works about the painting to which she, in turn, responded creatively. Hereafter, I shall refer to such intertextual dialogues that spun out from *The Rose* as "interindividual collaborations" in order to emphasize the fact that, while they brought artists into contact, they nonetheless preserved, to some degree, each artist's autonomy.

The photo series, I am arguing, figured and, ideally, enacted through its production this distinctive mix of individual and collective production, independence and connection. In an interview toward the end of her life, DeFeo described her relationships with Berman and the artist Bruce Conner (who is the focus of Chapter 4) in terms that resonate with the kind of relational practice modeled in the photographs:

> Through nobody's fault but my own, I pretty much maintained a solitary existence, but Wallace [Berman] was probably closer to me

than anybody. . . . I never really got *that* close to him, but theoretically Wallace and I were very, very close. . . . Like Bruce [Conner], in many ways, I had kind of an identification; let's say as a soulmate kind of thing with both of them in different ways, but sort of at a distance you know. I guess maybe an old hackneyed term would be kind of like a muse, maybe. They both kind of fed my imagination. I'd get a little something in the mail from Wallace or something quirky from Bruce and I would creatively respond to it, in either some funky way or else in a larger way as far as my work was concerned.[68]

Her portrayal of these relationships accords with the mixture of distance and communion, solitude and contact, characterized by both esoteric exegesis and artistic practice within the Fillmore community. It is notable that DeFeo struggles to label her simultaneously interpersonal and creative relationships with the men, settling on the terms "soulmate" and "muse." By identifying male artists as her muses, DeFeo reverses the word's typical gender and complicates the notion that the roles of artist and model were ever clear-cut within her circle.

Given that Fillmore artists were familiar with *Semina* and with other works by Berman that mobilize Kabbalah, it is likely that the select interpretive community DeFeo and Berman invited to view the photographs would already have been clued in to how to engage them. Archival evidence cannot tell us with certainty the extent to which the photo series influenced either their friends' later representations of *The Rose,* many of which are explored in the following chapters, or DeFeo's continued production of the painting itself. Perhaps their photographs invented the painting's occult identity, or perhaps they simply reflected an account of the work that already pervaded their circle, steeped as it was in esotericism. The 1959 photographs may have been a self-fulfilling prophecy; they may, that is, have encouraged DeFeo's extended production process by framing her creativity in esoteric terms, thus positing the private practice of making as meaningful in and of itself. A short time after the photo shoot, DeFeo made two decisions that signaled her commitment to a lengthy production process with *The Rose:* in the winter of 1959–60, she chose to continue working on the painting rather than send it to *Sixteen Americans,* and to remount it to dimensions that all but required it to remain in her studio.

In any case, the text that DeFeo's old friend and fellow artist Fred Martin wrote for the brochure that accompanied *The Rose*'s debut exhibition at the Pasadena Art Museum in 1969 shows that members of her coterie continued to frame the painting in esoteric terms. Martin's flowery ode brands *The Rose* as occult to stress the work's privacy:

There was a notion, common in that age, that it was a flower which knew the secret; and it was known among the initiates that Jay was

> that flower. Her eyes had seen the wings of angels; in the dark crevasse of highest mountains had lain her woman's sign; and then, in the penultimate year, had begun to burn the nova star of the bindu point, the shining rays of the center of her head. . . .
>
> Time came and the ultimate year. The flower of the initiates was ravished into public spectacle, sales item, prestige pitch. (The flower was two: the death rose of an angel's brain, and a dreaming girl.) Time passed, the carousel sweep missed the silver ring (now ivory and white, waning), a diamond-petal in a period of zircons. The rose aged on an abandoned strand; and the girl, lost and numbed among doors closing and the rush of moving planes, was forlorn.[69]

The passage conflates DeFeo and her painting ("Jay was that flower") and describes this amalgam as a keeper of "secret" knowledge for "initiates."

Martin's conception of *The Rose* as an esoteric entity belonging to DeFeo's circle resonates with the 1959 photo series, as does some of his imagery—for example, his conflation of artist and work, and his description of "shining rays of the center of her head." The mystical lens through which Martin interprets *The Rose* helps account for both the ode's riddle-like prose and its solemn tone, which is decidedly strange for a debut. In a 2009 interview, Martin confessed that he made the text intentionally cryptic, that he loaded it with insider references—in his words, "little inside things . . . little group things"—that only those close to DeFeo could understand.[70] In effect, he converted the exhibition brochure into a hermetic commentary. As a text that is encrypted to reserve its content for a select few despite its wide circulation, Martin's statement qualifies as instrumental esotericism.[71] The passage's convoluted language and reliance on metaphor evidence his desire to retain *The Rose* for the Fillmore coterie that witnessed its creation, even at its public unveiling.

In the final paragraph, Martin makes his hostility toward the exhibition more overt, writing: "The flower of the initiates was ravished into public spectacle, sales item, prestige pitch." He equates making the painting public with soiling a sacred object and casts DeFeo as the tragic Romantic artist. Like Honoré de Balzac's Frenhofer from *The Unknown Masterpiece* (1831), the exposure of her masterwork leaves her "lost," "numbed," and "forlorn." Martin's statement indicates that the painting's long production process confirmed its esoteric nature, which Berman's photographs asserted years before, by essentially reserving it for a private audience. It also demonstrates that DeFeo's seemingly perpetual painting process played into stereotypes of the bohemian artist sacrificing worldly gain in a principled (if somewhat irrational) exercise of art for art's sake. DeFeo appears to have been uneasy with the Romantic lens that Martin, like so many commentators after him, applied to her production of *The Rose.* "I'm sure it was well intended," DeFeo wrote in 1973, expressing discomfort with, if not altogether rejecting, Martin's lyrical, melancholic portrayal of *The Rose,* "but I was a little surprised and embarrassed."[72]

Martin's ode, in sum, describes *The Rose* as paradoxical in the same way as esoteric knowledge. In his definition of the latter, Halbertal wrote: "The hidden sphere allows a great degree of freedom, being unrestricted by constraints and friction of the outside rigid world. . . . Yet such space and freedom is purchased at the price of the ethereal nature of the esoteric and its marginality."[73] According to Martin, I am suggesting, DeFeo's *The Rose* could similarly be or generate anything within her circle of friends, but at the risk of being nothing to those outside the circle's small circumference.

Berman may have viewed his artistic activity in similar terms, as indicated by his description of his cultural practice as "swinging in the shadows."[74] "Swinging" conjures, among other things, an image of unrestrained movement; "shadows" evokes obscurity. Moreover, "shadows" may have held an Artaudian connotation for Berman, given that, in *The Theater and Its Double,* shadows are a prominent metaphor for our flitting spiritual doubles. Berman's "swinging in the shadows" thus likens the marginal space of his subculture to the hidden, higher plane of existence posited in esoteric thought. The phrase indicates that Berman saw his creative work as enacting the values of esotericism—specifically, the mix of freedom and marginality that *The Rose* came to exemplify for many in DeFeo's community and, consequently, that made the work emblematic of the community's outsider stance—even if this reading failed to capture the complexity of DeFeo's thoughts and feelings toward publicity and the mainstream art world. The 1959 photo series implies, at the very least, that Berman found esotericism to be an apt metaphor for the cultural underground to which he and DeFeo belonged. Within the hermetic circle of their coterie, as within the hermetic circle of esoteric practice, a mix of privacy, intimacy, and freedom allowed for relationships between self and other that were disallowed within the predominant culture that lay beyond its borders.

COMMUNITY THROUGH CORRESPONDENCE

A photographic self-portrait taken by Berman in 1960 figures the type of community that, this chapter has argued, he hoped his esoteric-inspired collaborations would construct (fig. 33). The shot depicts a display of Berman's photographs arranged in his home on Scott Street. The arrangement may resemble his exhibition of DeFeo's series, given its similarity in time and location. A handful of small prints are clustered haphazardly on the wall and are crookedly propped atop a line of books that snakes along the bottom of the frame. The hanging photographs depict Berman's friends and were mostly taken in the Bay Area the previous year, contemporary with the DeFeo series.[75] The domestic display appears to represent Berman's

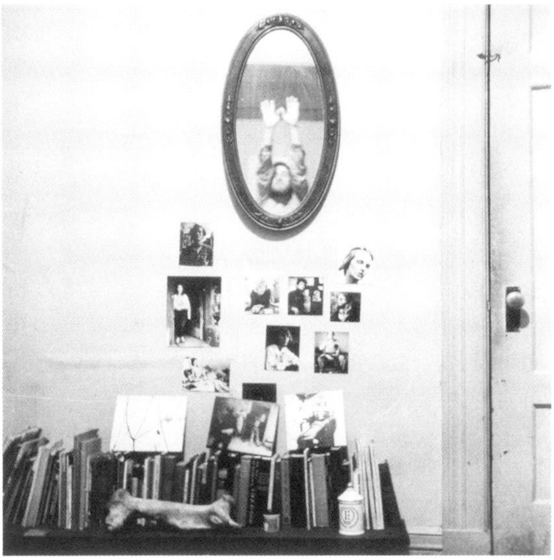

Fig. 33 Wallace Berman, Self-portrait, Scott Street, San Francisco, taken in 1960, printed in 1999. Unique gelatin silver print, 11 × 14 in. (28 × 35.5 cm). The Estate of Wallace Berman and Kohn Gallery, Los Angeles.

underground community and his position in it. The fact that he displayed this arrangement and others like it in his home, where his family and friends were apt to see them, suggests that he wanted his photographs to function as *Semina* did—as a mirror reflecting back to viewers an image of their social and cultural connectedness. Berman models this self-reflexive viewing dynamic in his self-portrait, which literalizes the equation between photograph and mirror. An oval mirror reflecting Berman's bearded visage crowns the display of images like a head on a body. The blurry and miniaturized quality of the reflection assimilates it with the surrounding images, while the mirror's scale, roundness, and apex position distinguish his likeness from the rest. Berman raises his arms—palms open, thumbs touching—in a deliberate but enigmatic gesture. His pose makes the viewer question how he took the photograph, augmenting its mystery.

The photograph crafts a specific understanding of community by marrying photography and montage. More "readymade collage" than photomontage, the shot generates a perceptual strain between unity and multiplicity, similar to that created by *Semina*'s loose-leaf format and by the randomized grids of Berman's Verifax collages. The photograph's smooth surface prompts the viewer to perceive it as a cohesive scene, while the discrete images jostling within the photograph's frame invite the viewer to trace the play of similarity and difference between them, a relational mode of looking normally reserved for composite representations. The photographic postcards that Berman mailed to his friends—the other way he gave his prints social agency—enacted the relationships illustrated (or imagined) by the constellation of photographs hanging in his apartment. The missives performed the dance between connection and separation figured in the display by bridging the physical and social distance between sender and recipient even as they codified it. Once again like his Verifax collages, Berman's photo displays and postcards operated on the principle of correspondence between discrete entities. Through their references to Kabbalah, his Verifax collages allude to the esoteric iteration of this principle—to the idea that things in the world "correspond" to ethereal entities in the spiritual plane.

The self-portrait, in short, stages a collective that is characterized by an irresolvable tension between whole and part, group and individual, belonging and difference. In this way, it speaks to Jean-Luc Nancy's inoperative community, which resists both collective totality and atomized individualism in favor of "being-in-common."[76] According to Nancy, community exists in the liminal space between "interdependency and independence," "dependency and autonomy," and "intimacy and estrangement."[77] The uneasy pull between the unifying frame of Berman's photograph and the discrete images it contains mimics this liminality, as does the play of revelation and concealment in his photographs of DeFeo.

Moreover, the portraits' irregular arrangement and the ample wall space around them give the display an improvised, temporary character. The photograph of the installation thus performs a transformation into collective being that is fluid, contingent, and provisional—qualities that, for Nancy, inoculated the inoperative community against the social diseases that plague authoritarianism (oppressing the individual in the name of the collective) and liberalism (sacrificing the greater good in the name of individual autonomy). These parallels between the French philosopher's and the California artist's concepts of ideal community are compelling in part because both were, to some extent, intellectual responses to widespread concerns about the failure of modernity's primary forms of collectivism following World War II (as discussed in the introduction to this book). Such skepticism prompted many philosophers, writers, and artists—including, this book asserts, those in the Fillmore District—to radically rethink democracy and community.

The DeFeo series suggests that Berman saw this type of community, and the style of collaboration it fostered (and that fostered it), as a way of preserving individual authorial freedom without the isolationism of autonomy, as represented by contemporary caricatures of American artists such as the one DeFeo played in *Creative America*. The photographs indicate that esotericism offered a way for Berman to frame his belief that appropriation is an act of reverence, not a violent dispossession. This is all to say that the generous, reciprocal relationship esotericism posits between individual and collective production embodied Berman's ideal vision of art practice in the Fillmore community and in his larger underground network of artists and writers. Many artists in California's West Coast underground felt this ideal was foreclosed by the conformity and reductive individualism within American society in general and the New York art world in particular. Kabbalah thus provided a framework in which the ambiguities of authorship that arose from collaborations like his photo shoot with DeFeo could be a source of pleasure rather than concern.

While Berman's self-portrait signals a desire to balance individualism and collectivity, it also seems to acknowledge that the unconventional collaborations he engaged in could be interpreted in ways that went against his ideals. As noted above, the photograph establishes a relationship between Berman and the pictorially assembled community before him that is provocatively equivocal. Does he lift his arms like a worshipper venerating his idol, or like a maestro conducting his orchestra? The action makes his figure seem precarious and liminal, as if he were about to swan dive out of the mirror's frame. However, it also reads as an assertion of presence: he appears to stretch up in order to join the virtual gathering via photography staged before him—his physical effort registering a desire to belong or perhaps to claim; the zigzag of his abutting hands could be interpreted as a "W" for "Wallace." On the one hand, then, his gesture could be read as humble and reverential—an interpretation that accords with the view that manipulating his friends' works to make pieces such as *Semina* and his photographs of *The Rose* enacted respect and generosity. On the other hand, his gesture could be read as an expression of ownership or control, suggesting that his appropriative practices amount to domination. Berman, ever the trickster, left the image open to both meanings.

Some aspects of the DeFeo photo series, I think, also acknowledge the tensions and challenges that necessarily arose when Berman applied Kabbalah's otherworldly model of production to his flesh and blood community. They hint at the ways in which personality, ego, difference, and power made enacting the esoteric ideal in an interpersonal context a messy affair. The most telling photograph in this regard is the one in which Berman appears with DeFeo (see fig. 29). His mock shock could simply be poking fun at the postwar public's prudishness, but the expression also seems self-conscious. The series suggests that Berman wanted his collaboration with DeFeo to make the artist-model relationship truly intersubjective by playing up the unplaceability of meaning inherent to it. The pair's caricature of the objectifying artist-model dynamic conveys their desire to transcend it. At the same time, however, the caricature admits to the similarities between their working relationship and the stereotype they perform. In this way, the image acknowledges that, in photographing DeFeo, in using her body and works as the basis for his art, Berman risked objectifying and even exploiting her.

The context in which DeFeo made the comments on the series quoted at the beginning of this chapter evidences the hazards she faced in collaborating with Berman. Her reflections derive from correspondence regarding her lawsuit against *Artforum* in 1978 over its unauthorized publication of one of the photographs in an article about Berman, who had died two years before (see fig. 18). Following the advice of her dealer, Paule Anglim, and the director of the San Francisco Museum of Art, Henry Hopkins, DeFeo eventually dropped the charges.[78] The suit, which charged the magazine with libel and gross invasion of privacy, demonstrates that the photographs' ambiguous authorship became a problem for DeFeo when they were unexpectedly made public, because it effectively meant that she was no longer in control of her professional image.[79] DeFeo was especially afraid that *Artforum*'s publication of the risqué photograph would jeopardize her current teaching position at California State University, Sonoma.

As she explained to her lawyer and the magazine, the private context in which the series was originally shown tempered this alienation because the audience's intimate knowledge of Berman and DeFeo minimized the probability that they would misunderstand the works.[80] The feelings of shame and humiliation that she claimed to have experienced upon seeing herself naked in *Artforum* indicate that the exposure ideally experienced as intimacy within the artists' circle was experienced as a violation outside of it. Such variation across contexts is an essential feature of esotericism, according to Halbertal: "An exposure that might be perceived in relation to another subject as the violation of individuation and transgression of boundaries is experienced in a proper intimate context as an evocation of presence, a way out of isolation. The desire to disappear which accompanies that sense of violation of boundaries is replaced by an acute sense of being, though hesitant."[81] DeFeo's gender meant that her authorial validity was always more vulnerable than it was for the male friends she engaged through *The Rose*. This incident confirms the risk she took in participating in those interindividual collaborations.

While DeFeo's reaction to the photograph's publication in *Artforum* demonstrates her awareness that, in partnering with Berman, she chanced being misrepresented, it also reveals her deep understanding of the value and reciprocity of their alliance. The passage quoted in the first section of this chapter, in which she describes herself as a model, crystallizes this complexity:

> I am not entirely happy with Wallace's portraits, but seldom have models been altogether happy with artists' conceptions of them. I did not feel it was appropriate to intervene and edit Wallace's 'series portrait' as it was his vision, his interpretation. . . . My consent to all this was out of respect to Wallace as an artist, and I wanted him to have his portrait as he saw it. I was the model only and not the artist in this situation. He, in turn, demonstrated his gratitude for this freedom of expression by protecting me from public scrutiny and misrepresentation. For this reason the only early showing was one for friends of us both by invitation only.[82]

As previously noted, this statement seems to flatly contradict the notion that the photographs were produced collaboratively. According to her, Berman was the sole conceiver and executer of the work, and she was merely the means (part muse, part material) with which he did so.

While her characterization of their working relationship opposes typical notions of collaboration as joint mental and/or physical labor, it nevertheless conjures the loose, dialectical style of collaboration described in this chapter. She characterizes their partnership as an exchange of favors: "out of respect," she allowed him to appropriate her body and works, and he, in turn, expressed his "gratitude" by "protecting" her "from public scrutiny." Her statement makes clear that, although Berman conceived the works, she secured the "freedom of expression" that made them possible. In this way, her account reframes autonomy, a quality usually associated with isolation, as a function of relationship. As she describes it, the photographs' production was profoundly intersubjective—conditioned on esteem, generosity, trust, vulnerability, and the privacy of the studio and the coterie. The "*Artforum* incident" indicates how fragile and fleeting this space was.

Perhaps DeFeo's fraught feelings toward the series prompted her, years after the photo shoot, to propose an alternative metaphor for their collaboration—one that set aside both the studio and the cabal. In 1965, during the hectic months leading up to her and Hedrick's eviction from Fillmore Street and her forced completion of *The Rose,* she sent a collaged letter to Berman, who had since moved back to Los Angeles (fig. 34). Despite this distance, the artists would continue to correspond and make art in response to each other's works until Berman's death in a car accident in 1976. Several of their exchanges reiterated themes (such as gender and Kabbalah) present in their 1959 series, and mentions of *The Rose* frequently appear in their correspondence from the 1960s, indicating that the work continued to loom large in their relationship.[83] Indeed, the collaged letter from 1965 invites Berman and his family to witness *The Rose*'s removal. While her note indicates that she was struggling with the painting's imminent departure (she compares waiting for its removal to "being on death row"), it also expresses her desire that the work finally escape the hermetic circle that had nurtured and interpreted it over the past seven years. "I want you & Shirley & Tosh . . . here so bad . . . when *The Rose* goes," she confessed. "I want this for *The Rose* [and] the few that are responsible for it."[84] She appears to have reached out to Berman, then, not only for emotional support during this difficult time, but also because she felt him in some way "responsible" for the painting.

Echoing his appropriation of her work six years before, DeFeo composed the note on the poster for the Los Angeles Film-Makers Festival, featuring *Bouquet,* that Berman had designed and mailed to her. The collage's aleph colophon recalls the tsade he branded, via montage, onto her chest in *The Rose* shot. She encased the aleph in a graphite heart, transforming Berman's authorial sign into an emblem of relationship and thus signaling her transformation of his work. She likewise treated *Bouquet*'s reiterative radios as so many frames to fill, covering some of the appropriated images Berman chose with her own selections. After amending Berman's poster, she folded it in quarters and bound the edges with masking tape to form a kind of postcard-pouch, which she then mailed. Her alterations to *Bouquet* work both with and against its formal and semantic structure: her

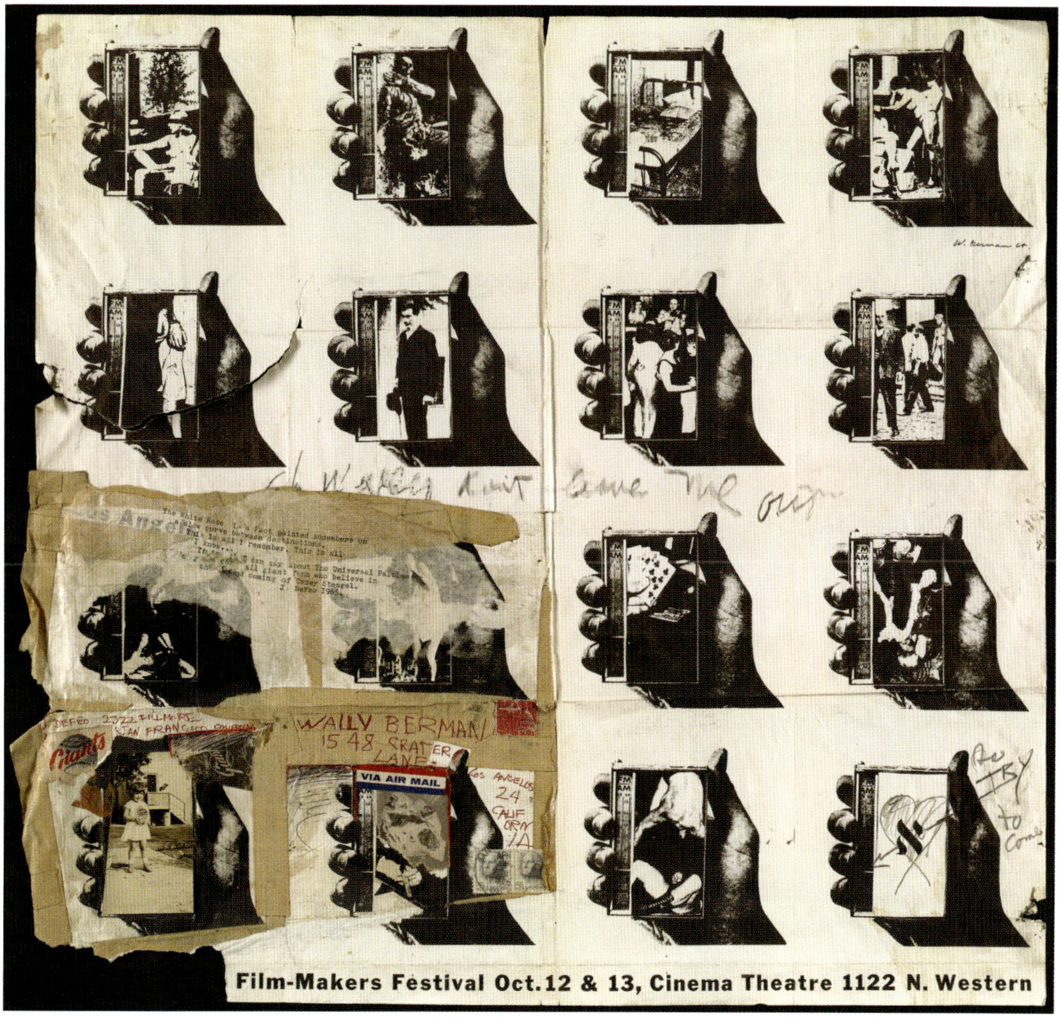

Fig. 34 Jay DeFeo, Correspondence for Wallace Berman, 1965. Writing and collage elements on a poster for the 3rd Los Angeles Film-Makers Festival. Wallace Berman papers, Archives of American Art, Smithsonian Institution, Washington, D.C.

vigorous folding and sloppy collage additions interrupt the poster's seamless flatness and repetition, but this distortion amplifies the viewer's ability to read *Bouquet*'s images relationally, a latent potential previously muffled by the rigorous compartmentalization of its organizing grid. DeFeo's epistolary appropriation creates a conflicted interdependence between the two works: each work articulates its full range of meaning only through dialogue with the other, but their dialogue is marked by dissonance as much as resonance, a pushing against as much as an opening toward.

In the corner containing her address, DeFeo nestled a snapshot of herself as a child, over which she glued two baseballs (emblazoned with the logo of the San Francisco Giants)—one in the upper-left corner, the other in her cupped hands. She portrays herself not as a model or an esoteric symbol but as a sandlot slugger. She humorously acknowledges the ambiguity of her dynamic collaboration with Berman by likening it to a baseball game. Through montage, she takes the mound and Berman the plate; passing the ball/work back and forth, they play both with and against each other.

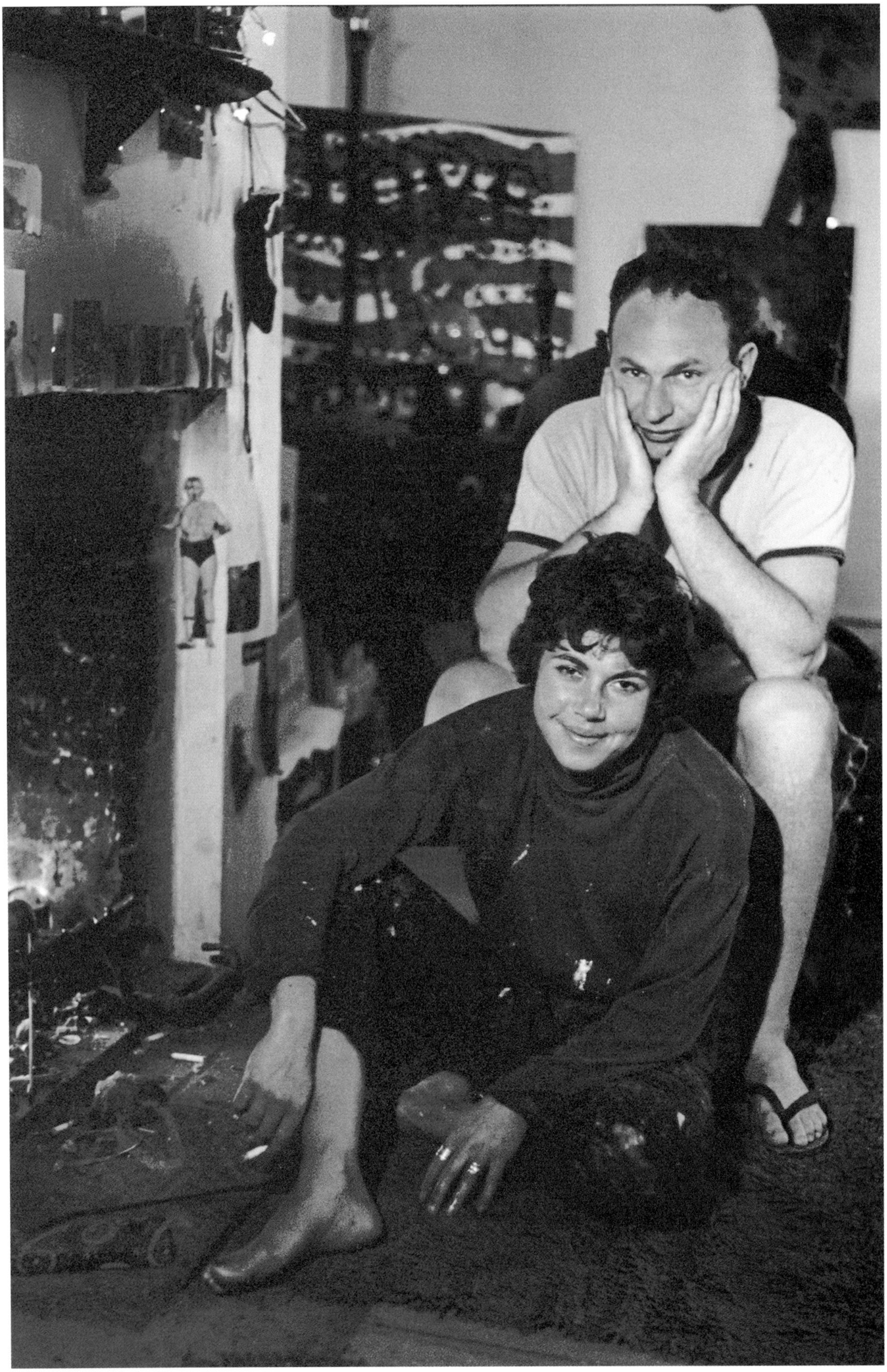

CHAPTER 2

Making Home

THE GAME OF ART AND LIFE

Eight arms fan out from the center of a circle, creating a series of wedge shapes that parse a ring of words (fig. 35). A corresponding symbol nestles in the wedge below each word: "X" for gin, "heart" for love, "whip" for sex, "flower" for rose, and so on. Arcing trails of high-toned paint sweep from the tip of each spoke, creating an impression of counterclockwise spin. Caught between diagram and depicted object, the seemingly tangible symbol courts multiple associations. It has been described as a roulette wheel and an alchemist's star, but it also recalls the medieval wheel of fortune, the compass rose, and the spinner for a board game—an association supported by the painting's title, *Life Game.* Given its comet-like tails, the form in this now-lost painting also resembles the satellites that were slowly filling the night sky when Wally Hedrick, Jay DeFeo's husband, created the work in 1959. Hedrick, however, associated the emblem with an earthlier referent: "This was like a color wheel to me," he explained, "except it had to do with my living. The primaries might be love, art and spirit. If you add love and art together, you get rose, which refers back to that painting of Jay's; sex and spirit makes feel; art and spirit makes me. Those would be the secondaries. Love and rose is gin, which had to do with openings."[1] The painting thus charted Hedrick's life: it mapped the relationships between the activities, objects, and subjective states that constituted his daily experience. Notably, *The Rose* featured prominently in his existential inventory.

Life Game's reference to *The Rose* is jarring given the stark aesthetic differences between the two works. With its symbols, words, and rudimentary illusionism, *Life Game* deploys representational systems that *The Rose*'s raw materiality and resolute abstractness seem determined to circumvent, if not vanquish. The works that were selected to represent each artist in *Sixteen Americans*—an exhibition discussed in the previous chapter that opened at the Museum of Modern Art, New York, the same year Hedrick painted *Life Game*—codified this division. DeFeo's large, gestural canvases followed closely on the heels of abstract expressionism (as critics noted with a

Detail, fig. 45

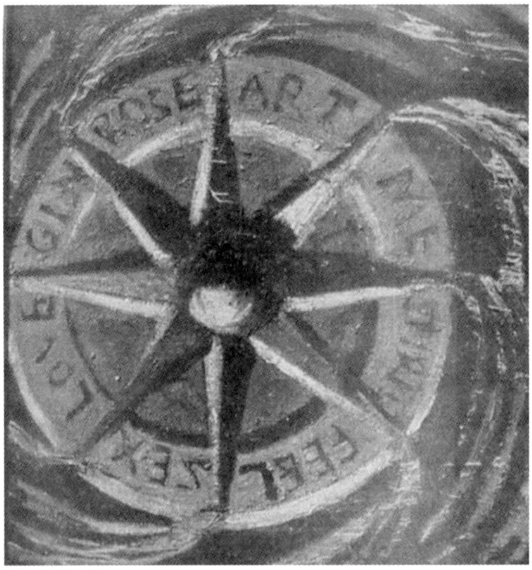

Fig. 35 Wally Hedrick, *Life Game*, 1959 (no longer extant). The Estate of Wally Hedrick.

shrug), while Hedrick's paintings played with convention and appropriated symbols, presaging practices that would come to be seen as postmodern critique. Hedrick's *For Service Rendered* (1959) and *Heroic Image* (1959/90), for example, digest the ornate metalwork and jeweled surfaces of treasures from Russia's monarchical past into an abstract vocabulary of crosses, spheres, and curlicues (fig. 36).[2] While his heavy, occasionally dripping paint-handling signals abstract expressionism, when applied to his intricately patterned compositions the visible marks look more like careless craftsmanship than indicators of emotional authenticity. The paintings literalize the dismissive equation of abstract art and decoration to take aim at the perceived pomposity of abstract expressionism. Pried free from chalices, orbs, and crowns (ceremonial objects that already signal a toppled regime), the ornamentation becomes absurd—a monstrous multiplication of signs of power and glory divorced from a context that would give their authority meaning. Hedrick's wry comment that he created such works to award himself "recognition as a hero artist" suggests that he intended them to parody postwar America's apotheosis of the action painter.[3]

DeFeo and Hedrick confirmed the distinction between their approaches in the *Sixteen Americans* catalogue. Labeling herself "an expressionist as well as a symbolist," DeFeo described her art practice as a perilous journey of self-discovery, a voyage to the transcendental within. "Only by chancing the ridiculous," she wrote, "can I hope for the sublime. Only by discovering that which is true within myself, can I hope to be understood by others." Hedrick, by contrast, roundly rejected the broadly high modernist rhetoric, subject position, and aesthetic philosophy that animate DeFeo's characterization of her art. "I have tried to arrange things so that I can do what I want," he declared. It was a sentiment he had previously expounded in another exhibition catalogue: "I do not 'suffer' when I paint, nor approach a new canvas in the spirit of entering upon a battlefield. There is, no doubt, an element of hedonistic selfishness in the act of my painting, for I enjoy it. I *like* to paint."[4] By depicting art-making as an enjoyable activity rather than a tortured, existential struggle, Hedrick intentionally deflated the ponderous rhetoric around action painting—echoing similarly irreverent declarations by *Sixteen Americans* artists that would come to be seen as indicative of the "postmodern turn," such as Frank Stella's infamous "What you see is what you see."[5]

Scholars since have reiterated the idea that DeFeo and Hedrick occupied distinct positions within the transitional field of American art circa 1960. While noting some convergences between the artists' formal and thematic vocabularies—such as a predilection for wing-like forms, references to mountain climbing, and the mandalic compositions evident in both *Life Game* and *The Rose*—most analyses emphasize their differences. "Yet, while bearing similarities," Michael Duncan concluded in a typical assessment, "the works of DeFeo and Hedrick evidence fundamentally different beliefs about the nature of art. . . . Hedrick wanted to demystify art at the same time that DeFeo had embarked on a painting with unparalleled mythic ambitions." In this highly gendered account, as DeFeo drew out the last breaths of Romanticism with *The Rose,* Hedrick, to quote Rebecca Solnit, was "ahead of his time," a "maverick" making works that predicted pop art and other pivotal developments of the 1960s.[6]

Notwithstanding *Life Game*'s foregrounding of some of the differences between DeFeo's and Hedrick's art, it also reveals common ground between them. As an autobiographical work that represents *The Rose* as an essential feature of Hedrick's existence, *Life Game* asserts that the couple's distinct

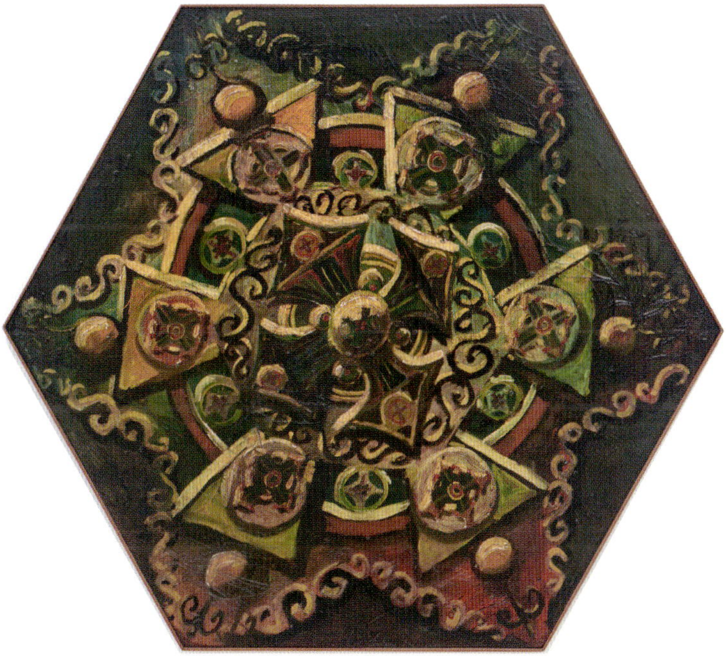

Fig. 36 Wally Hedrick, *Heroic Image*, 1959/90. Oil on shaped canvas over panel, 62½ × 71½ in. (158.8 × 181.6 cm). Private collection, courtesy Brian Gross Fine Art.

art practices became enmeshed with their shared life, catalyzing convergences between their works, such as *Life Game*'s reference to *The Rose.* The merger of art and life, representation and experience, is a common theme in the literature on each artist. Hedrick's paintings and assemblages of the late 1950s and early 1960s—which often cite his personal relationships and domestic environs—have been read as a means of making "life, and . . . know[ing] the life he lived," as the couple's close friend, curator Fred Martin, asserted in 1967. Several decades later Rebecca Schoenthal similarly concluded, "*The Rose* is the most telling example of the interrelatedness of art making with daily life as represented by the breakdown between home and work among the subculture discussed here."[7]

As her comment suggests, the integration of art and everyday life evident in the couple's works is often framed as a telling manifestation of the significance that the domestic sphere (defined by Hannah Arendt as the private realm of "household and family" and activities "related to the maintenance of life") assumed within the Fillmore community and other bohemian circles in postwar California, largely because public indifference and animosity to their work forced artists to take their practices underground. Richard Cándida Smith, who has given the most thorough accounting of this phenomenon, coined the term "domestic utopia" to describe the belief held by many of the state's midcentury artists and writers that familial relationships and the home offer a protective space within which to create alternative identities, communities, and artistic practices—a belief that held up a dark mirror to mainstream America's conformist and materialistic cult of domesticity.[8]

Life Game thus asks that the two main arguments about DeFeo and Hedrick (that they occupied dichotomous positions within the field of postwar art and that their art practices merged with their domestic lives) be read together. In doing so, it hints at a dimension of authorship unrepresented in both *Sixteen Americans* and the literature on art in postwar California. *Life Game* prompts viewers to ask: What happened to DeFeo's autonomous expressionism when it became embedded, through making *The Rose,* within the daily routines and spaces she shared with Hedrick? Likewise, while *Life Game* uses a visual vocabulary similar to Hedrick's other paintings of the period, it cites *The Rose* in order to pay homage to, rather than to ironize, DeFeo's painting, suggesting that Hedrick's postmodern proclivities, too, mutated within the domestic environment.

Taking its cue from *Life Game,* this chapter recovers the rules for "the game of art and life" that DeFeo and Hedrick endeavored to play by examining how those rules materialized in *The Rose.* It builds on Cándida Smith's idea of "domestic utopia" and Anastasia Aukeman's observation that the perennial question of art's relation to life was widespread in the late 1950s and early 1960s. Indeed, within months of Hedrick painting *Life Game,* Allan Kaprow declared that artists "must become preoccupied with and even dazzled by the space and objects of our everyday life," and

Robert Rauschenberg proclaimed his intent to "act in that gap between" art and life.[9] What follows is a more specific demonstration than previous accounts have given of how the popular question of art's relation to life was answered within the Fillmore community, as well as the implications that answer had for authorship. Pushing beyond the established notion that domesticity loomed large in the identities and practices of Fillmore artists, we will consider some of the ways in which DeFeo merged the material procedures of making *The Rose* with her everyday life—succinctly defined by Rita Felski as "the essential, taken-for-granted continuum of mundane activities," of which home life is a particularly indicative part.[10] We will find that, contrary to the beliefs of most of their contemporaries on the East Coast, DeFeo and her friends believed that the domestic environment principally protected (rather than liquidated) the possibility for autonomy and transcendence by providing a rare space of creative freedom. This expansion of the self into the private sphere preserved the artist's sovereignty, but in a modified form: while the stuff, intimate relationships, and routines of everyday life became the raw materials for the artist's creative expression, they also exerted their own agency. Thus, the account of authorship that this "domesticized high modernism" yielded evaded the neat divisions between autonomy and heteronomy, expression and appropriation, transcendence and demystification, that were, so the standard story goes, beginning to calcify in the New York art world circa 1960 and that came to define DeFeo's and Hedrick's respective legacies.

Combining profound and ethereal aspects of Hedrick's existence (love, spirit, feel) with concrete, even profane ones (gin, sex, rose), *Life Game* is indicative of the specific proposal for the relationship between artistic practice and domesticity that developed in Hedrick and DeFeo's circle. This chapter proposes that *The Rose* too manifested the belief that the mundane could serve as the ground for transcendence, even as it demonstrated the tensions and contradictions that inevitably arose when attempting to bridge the everyday and the sublime. DeFeo and those around her believed that her daily practice of making *The Rose* was a means of transforming the space and time of domestic experience, rather than a means of escaping from or capitulating to that experience—the relationships between art and life typically attributed to high modernism and postmodernism, respectively. To enact this transformation, DeFeo made *The Rose* in a way that merged the spheres (private and public) and types of action (labor and work) traditionally associated with women and men. Distinct from later feminist artists' engagements with the domestic, DeFeo's play with gender norms demonstrated both the potential and limits that the bohemian conditions of the Fillmore community provided for destabilizing mainstream America's rigid cult of domesticity.

Hedrick's and DeFeo's comments about *The Rose* and their life together indicate that, in their experience, the painting exacerbated the antipathy between art and life as much as, if not more than, it integrated them into a transformative synthesis. Likewise, the authorial structure enacted by *The Rose*—the way it embedded visionary genius within the web of personal and object relations that make up the domestic sphere—generated friction between each artist's desire for creative freedom and the commitment to intimacy and dependency symbolized by their marriage. One of the central claims this chapter makes is that these tensions are unsurprising, given that DeFeo's desire to transform her everyday life through the painting appears to have been motivated by her discontent with being a "housewife" as much as by her acceptance of the domestic sphere as a fertile site for self-fulfillment and expression. Simultaneously schematic and sloppy, static and spinning, *Life Game* suggests both the ideal of integrating art and life that Hedrick and DeFeo nurtured and the messiness of their attempts to realize that ideal within their household.

MAKE YOURSELF AT HOME

Hedrick and DeFeo met in 1953 in Berkeley, California. She had recently returned from a yearlong travel fellowship in Europe, which she won after completing her master's degree in art at the University of California, Berkeley. Hedrick, a native of Southern California, moved to the East Bay in 1952 to attend the California College of Arts and Crafts on the G.I. Bill after completing a year of active military service in Korea. In 1954 the couple moved to a basement apartment on Bay Street in San Francisco near the California School of Fine Arts (CSFA), where Hedrick had transferred, and got married (in part, it seems, to increase Hedrick's monthly military pension). In Berkeley, DeFeo's practice included large-scale paintings, sculpture, and jewelry. After moving to San Francisco with Hedrick, she focused almost exclusively on jewelry-making, as it better suited the couple's modest living space and income.

Within a year, they outgrew their charming but cramped flat and began to look for an apartment large enough to accommodate both their studio needs. A friend was vacating 2322 Fillmore Street and alerted them to its availability. This new apartment was dilapidated but spacious—a deep warren of tall-ceilinged rooms that occupied an entire side of the building's second floor. "I walked into this place and I was just overcome," DeFeo recalled. "It was just an enormous flat, really huge. It just seemed to go on and on." The couple leased the apartment for fifty dollars a month and also began to rent the space directly above them when Michael and Joanna McClure vacated it several years later.

From the early 1950s to the mid-1960s, the apartment building hosted a rotating cast of creative tenants (including Craig Kauffman, Sonia Gechtoff, James Kelly, Bill Brown, Joan Brown, Manuel Neri, and the McClures), by some accounts earning it the nickname "Painterland." As Aukeman details in *Welcome to Painterland,* DeFeo and Hedrick's arrival helped solidify the residence's reputation as a local cultural and social hot spot.[11] The couple became fast friends with their neighbors and may have even knocked a hole in the wall that separated their apartment from the Browns' to facilitate passage between their households. They also hosted raucous Christmas parties fueled by Hedrick's bathtub-brewed beer and music by the CSFA-affiliated Studio 13 Jass Band, which featured Hedrick on banjo.

In the first five years of their marriage, the couple cobbled together a living from Hedrick's military pension, DeFeo's jewelry-making, and various part-time jobs. DeFeo (as the previous chapter explains) likely moonlighted at CSFA as a life-drawing model, and for a time, she received a monthly stipend from the Ferus Gallery, which represented her, to help "pay paint bills." Hedrick began teaching full-time at CSFA soon after earning a master's degree from San Francisco State University in 1958, making him the household's primary breadwinner.[12] DeFeo did not hold a full-time job outside the home for most of their marriage and appears, instead, to have performed most of the housework. This arrangement was in part born of necessity as, according to DeFeo, a conviction for shoplifting a can of paint in 1953 effectively barred her from teaching until the mid-1960s.[13]

While the division of labor within DeFeo and Hedrick's marriage conformed to gender expectations for heterosexual couples in the 1950s, the fact that they did not have children defied the postwar "baby boom."[14] The dynamics of their household also distinguished DeFeo and Hedrick from most heterosexual couples in the Fillmore community, who had one child and the female partner worked outside the home in addition to or instead of the male partner. The high frequency of women in the workforce signaled the community's progressive nature by violating the period's strict and, as second-wave feminists would soon contend, oppressive "separate spheres" doctrine. At times, however, it also shored up the patriarchal status quo, as Cándida Smith observed, by casting wives in the role of monetarily supporting their husbands' creative practices, often to the detriment of their own.[15]

Hedrick and DeFeo's new home had an obvious impact on their art. In response to the capacious interiors, DeFeo abandoned jewelry-making and returned to painting. "My environments have always determined what I do as far as my work is concerned," she explained. As her works expanded to touch the soaring ceilings, the apartment environs began to permeate Hedrick's works. He appropriated the stuff of their home—their fire escape, television set, and beer cans drained during their parties—as content and material for his paintings and sculptures (figs. 37–39). While the domestic setting shaped their art, the couple in turn fashioned the space, transforming the ramshackle apartment into an aestheticized realm. Works in various stages of completion leaked from their studios into contiguous living spaces, flooding hallways and bursting forth into the building's communal stairwell (figs. 40, 41). DeFeo scrawled reminders to perform domestic chores (such as "Water the plants!") on her studio walls along with excerpts from poems by local writers that inspired her work.[16]

Fig. 37 Wally Hedrick, *Fred's TV*, 1955. Oil on canvas, 127 × 78 in. (322.5 × 198 cm). Collection of David R. Packard and M. Bernadette Castor.

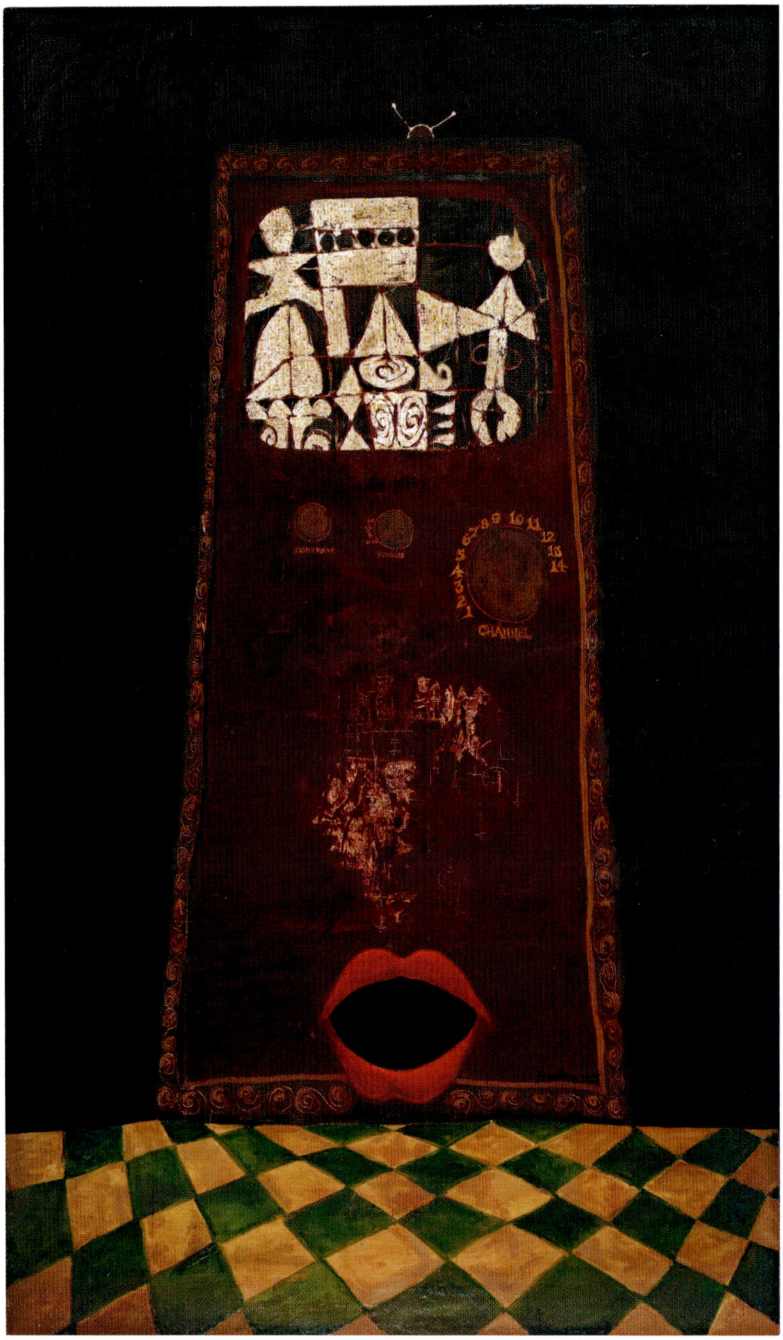

This fluidity between the stuff of art and the stuff of mundane existence meant that their apartment—like most artists' homes in the Fillmore neighborhood—became an important space for the reception, as well as the production, of art. As elaborated in the introduction to this book, the lack of a robust commercial infrastructure and public audience for art in postwar San Francisco meant that viewing art in the Fillmore neighborhood was often an informal, convivial experience as artists encountered one

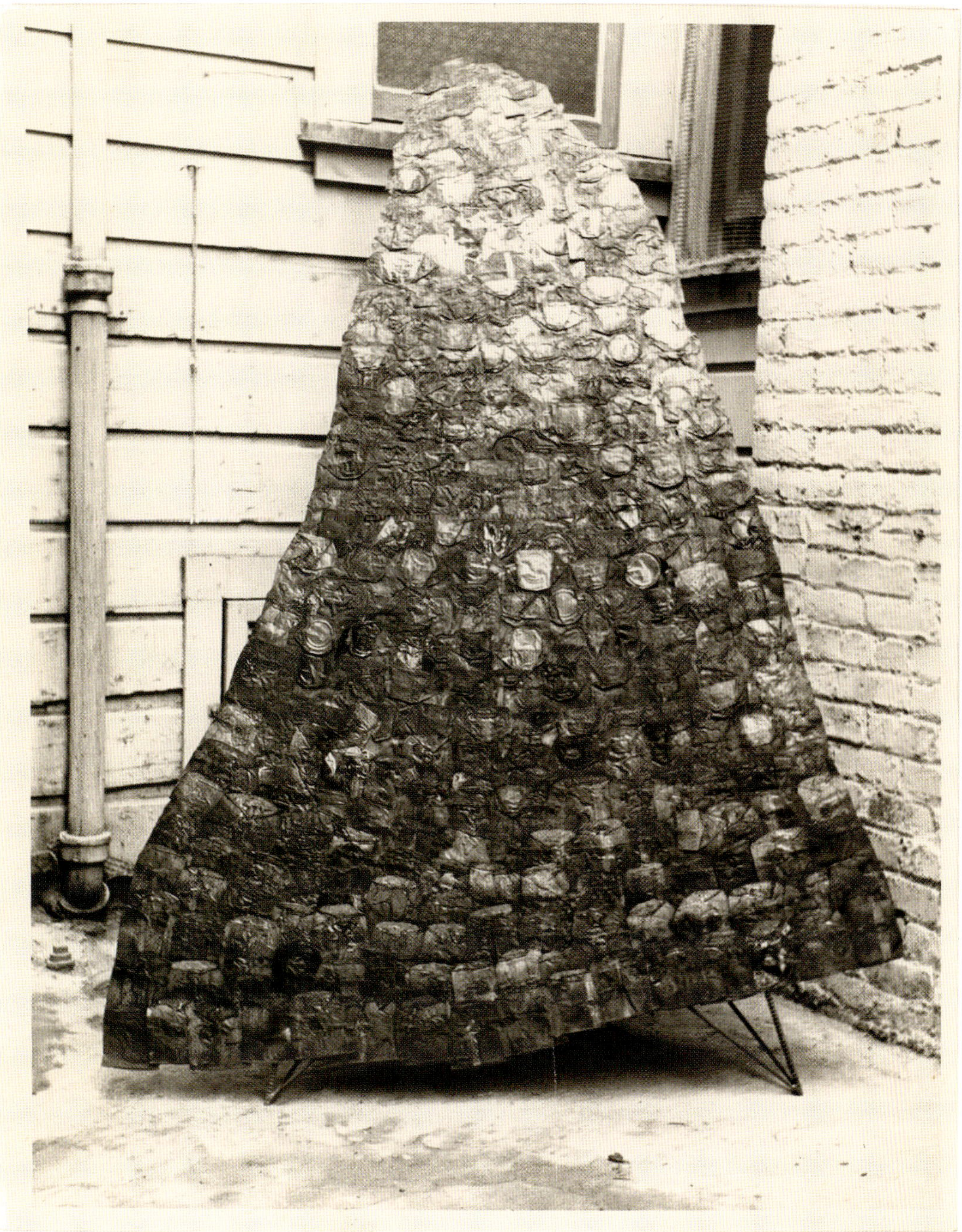

Fig. 38 Wally Hedrick, *It Can Be Done!*, c. 1959–68. Gelatin silver print, $9^{15}/_{16} \times 8^{1}/_{16}$ in. (25.2 × 20.5 cm). Dorothy C. Miller Papers, I.15.k, Museum of Modern Art Archives, New York.

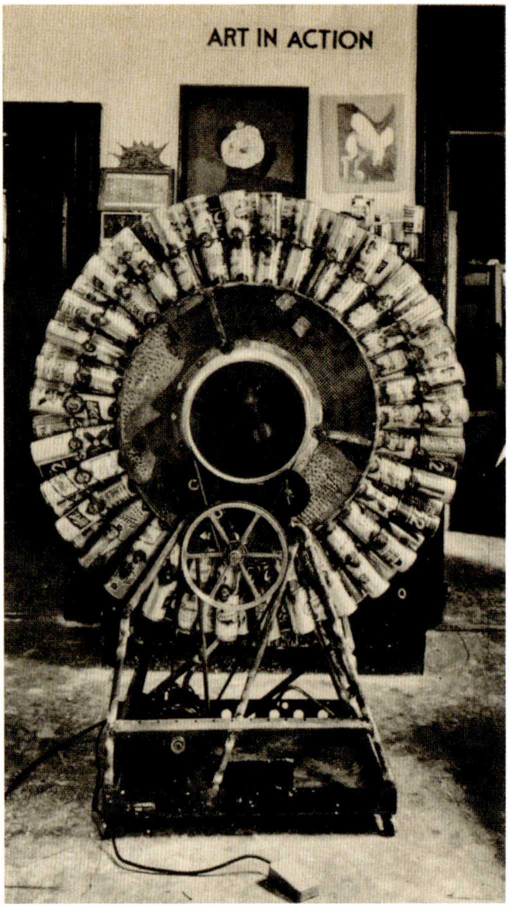

Fig. 39 Wally Hedrick, *Soul Thing,* 1960 (no longer extant). Mixed-media assemblage. Reproduced in *Artforum* (October 1962).

another's works in domestic settings during parties and social calls just as often as, if not more than, they did in local galleries.

Four years after their move, DeFeo, Hedrick, and 2322 Fillmore Street were featured in a traveling group exhibition titled *The Individual and His World,* which was curated by Fred Martin on behalf of the San Francisco Art Bank. Recognizing the city's lack of a developed critic-dealer system, CSFA and the San Francisco Art Association founded the Art Bank and hired Martin to run it. His job was to get works by participating local artists into museum exhibitions, onto collectors' walls, and into dealers' inventory books by curating traveling shows and acting as a guide for curators, critics, museum directors, and collectors who were visiting San Francisco.[17] Nearly half the artists selected for *The Individual and His World* (DeFeo, Hedrick, Bruce Conner, and David Simpson) lived in the Fillmore neighborhood, and several others (notably, Jeremy Anderson and Seymour Locks) regularly exhibited there.

Martin lived in Oakland, but he frequently showed his own art at Fillmore venues, most famously at the Six Gallery the night Allen Ginsberg debuted "Howl." He had known DeFeo, in particular, since the 1940s, when the two were undergraduates together at Berkeley. In the decades that

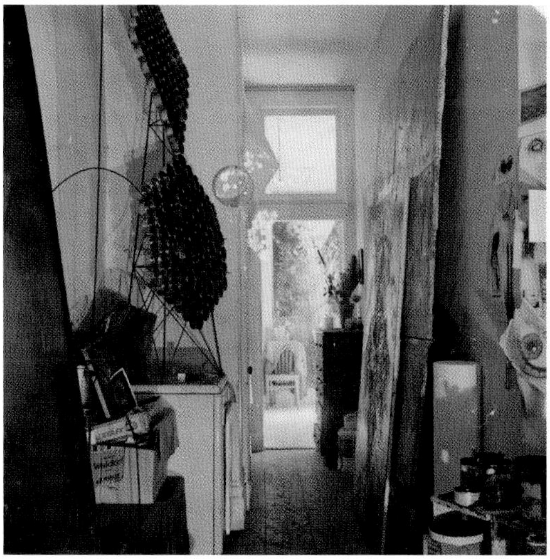

Fig. 40 2322 Fillmore Street hallway looking into a studio at the end of a hallway with an unidentified DeFeo painting (later destroyed). Hedrick sculpture and paintings visible in the hallway, c. 1959. Gelatin silver print. The Jay DeFeo Foundation, Berkeley, Calif. [JDF no. R0408].

Fig. 41 2322 Fillmore Street apartment interior with unidentified painting (later destroyed) and *Peace* (1953) by Wally Hedrick, c. 1957. Gelatin silver print. The Jay DeFeo Foundation, Berkeley, Calif. [JDF no. R0347].

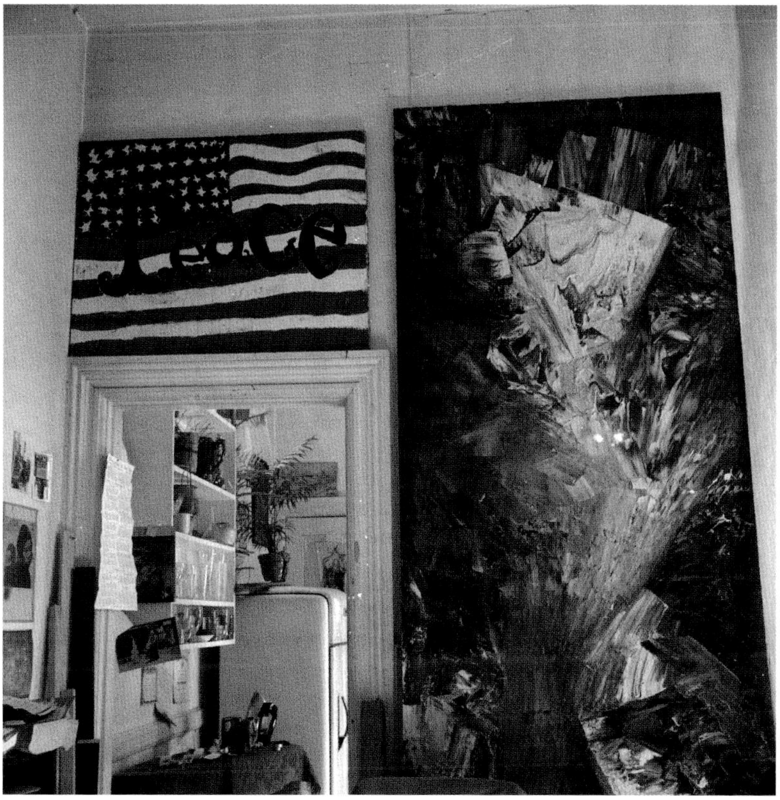

followed, he responded willingly to DeFeo's periodic calls to write about her work for museum shows—a fact that attests not only to the friendship between them, but also to the success each garnered playing respective roles in the San Francisco art world: DeFeo as a showing artist, and Martin as a theorist-impresario of the local scene.[18]

Opened in the same year Hedrick painted *Life Game, The Individual and His World* proposed a similar relationship between artistic practice and domesticity, suggesting that it codified the relationship between art and life that was developing in the Fillmore community as homes became prime sites for making and viewing art. "All artists are individuals," Martin declared at the beginning of the exhibition's press release, before laying out the show's premise: "Some, however, find themselves as individuals in a more lonely place, and seem to discover themselves to be more often upon those peaks in Darien which the rest of us view through them with only the wildest surmise. This exhibition includes painting and sculpture by ten individuals of unusual and remarkable direction. The work of each is accompanied by several photographs of the artist in his world. The photographs help to make clear the natural and logical development of the art from the artist's personal environment and his reaction to it."[19] He borrows John Keats's spatial and imperialist image of Romantic genius (Hernán Cortés surveying the Pacific from the "peaks in Darien") to describe the artists' sublime subject position—an elevated stance that makes their works inscrutable, objects of the viewer's "wildest surmise."

In the final lines, however, each artist's "world," the private realm his art manifests, morphs from a sublime interior vista into the concrete and mundane space of his "personal environment." As in *Life Game,* the supposedly transcendent domain of the artist's psyche collides and conflates with the domestic sphere. Creation, likewise, transforms from an unfathomable visionary phenomenon into a "natural and logical" process laid bare by photography—specifically, shots taken and arranged on panels by the San Francisco photographer Jerry Burchard of each artist's home and studio (figs. 42–44).

By rooting the artist's genius—his unique and sublime subjectivity—in the home, *The Individual and His World* negotiated a middle ground between the authorial models typically associated with high modernism and postmodernism. It preserved modernist autonomy but expanded the defensive boundary between artist and world beyond the artist's subjective interior to encompass his domestic interior as well. In this way, Martin's artists resembled neo-dada, pop, neo-realist, and other contemporary artists who were integrating artistic practice with mundane existence, instead of using art to transcend the everyday. However, while these artists, who are often viewed as early postmodernists, collapsed art with postwar consumer capitalism (by appropriating its advertising images, commodities, and techniques of mass production and consumption), the artists in *The Individual and His World,* the exhibition asserted, allowed their art to mix with a much more circumscribed aspect of life—the private sphere contained within the walls of their homes. The incorporation of art and life represented in *The Individual and His World* was thus supposed to shore up the artist's individuality, creativity, and subjective plenitude, instead of liquidating them through exposure to the mindless, conformity-inducing consumption of the public sphere. By acting as a liminal zone between self and world, the household (much like the "esoteric circle" discussed in the previous chapter) was supposed to broker an intermediary authorial identity between the aloof, introspective artist associated with high modernism and the contingent, porous artist associated with postmodernism—an authorial position obscured by binary readings of DeFeo's and Hedrick's art.

The specific relationship between art and life that *The Individual and His World* proposed—which I will refer to as "domesticized high modernism"—relied on an ideology of domesticity that was foreign to most postwar art discourses.[20] Photographs from the period tended to represent the artist's autonomous, transcendent selfhood by quarantining him from, rather than immersing him in, the domestic environment. Hans Namuth's famous photographs of abstract expressionists from earlier in the decade, for example, almost always depict the artist secluded in an austere studio (see fig. 3). Like the "white cube" of the modernist art gallery, the studio is presented as a neutral, passive container for creative agency, contemplation, and subjective plenitude.[21]

This trope reflected the idea, often repeated in modern accounts of everyday life, that domesticity is inimical to individual selfhood. The routinized nature of everyday life has been seen to stymie creation, invention, and progress.[22] This clash is generally presented in gendered terms: while the household's cyclical rhythms of biological reproduction and capitalist consumption are read as female, independence and self-determination are coded as male. As a masculine assertion of individuality and pure avant-garde rupture, abstract expressionist mark-making could easily be seen as an existential escape hatch from the familial obligations and prosaic eternal return of domestic life. This understanding of domesticity gained renewed relevance in the United States during the postwar housing boom. With their monotonous design and lack of privacy, new suburban developments, pundits argued, routinized experience and reduced self-expression to consumerism, turning their inhabitants into "other-directed" zombies. As one critic sardonically concluded in 1957: "Mass produced dwellings produce mass dwellers."[23]

The convention of representing an artist's practice apart from that artist's life began to change on the East Coast in the 1960s. At that time, photographers began to regularly depict artists' daily routines and social lives in order to illustrate a new version of artistic subjectivity and production (which would come to be labeled "postmodernist," among other things) consistent with the view that art is continuous with, rather than elevated above, the materialist landscape of consumer society.[24] But in 1959, Martin's exhibition was still very much against the grain insofar as it conflated artists' homes with their transcendent selfhoods. Indeed, his presentation of art practice contained within it an alternative ideology of domesticity—one reflected in both mainstream America's cult of domesticity and bohemian America's "domestic utopia."

While some have viewed the home as a site of oppression, others have perceived it as a safe haven from the alienation of urban modernity. The

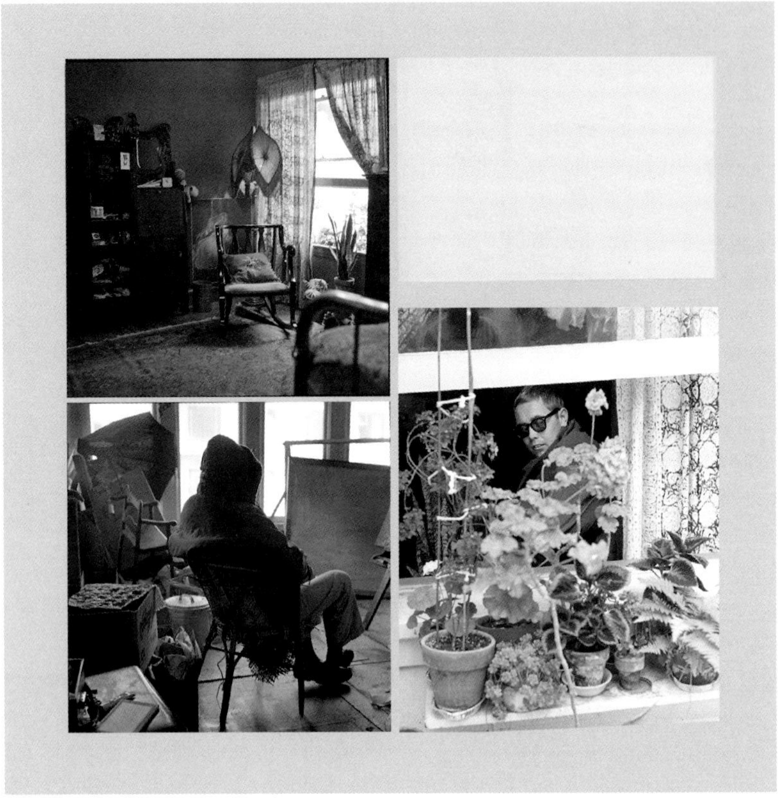

Fig. 42 Jerry Burchard, Photo panel to accompany Bruce Conner's works in *The Individual and His World*, 1959. Gelatin silver prints mounted on board, 24 × 20 in. (60.9 × 50.8 cm). Reconstructed by Dennis Hearne. The Estate of Jerry Burchard.

bourgeois home, not unlike the work of art, has been seen as a privileged site for self-definition, expression, and authentic experience.[25] *The Individual and His World* asserted that the bohemian home possessed similar powers. It portrayed the household as a protected space in which opening the autonomy of the individual artist, in a limited way, to the intimate object and interpersonal relations that constitute "the artist's personal environment" could nurture, rather than compromise, the artist's independent identity and creative freedom.

Years later, Martin described DeFeo and Hedrick's apartment in terms that echoed his exhibition's portrayal of the domestic sphere as an incubator for individual creativity: "In those days I used to be the director of CSFA exhibitions and one of my jobs was to take visiting curators, critics, directors around, and I would always take them to Jay and Wally's place—for lunch preferably, because the setting would just make their eyes pop. The way the rooms were, the height of their rooms, the way Jay's big *Rose* painting was at the end of these rooms, the way there were Jay's and Wally's things everywhere, the way Jay would do her lunch with a hundred little bits of things; it was like a Chinese lunch. It was by far the most arty. . . . I guess it was fifties bohemia."[26] He portrays the couple's eccentric apartment as the opposite of Levittown's homogenous Cape Cods, with their prefab furniture and equally plastic inhabitants. The materials and results of art-making erupt, to chaotic effect, within the domestic interior. Even

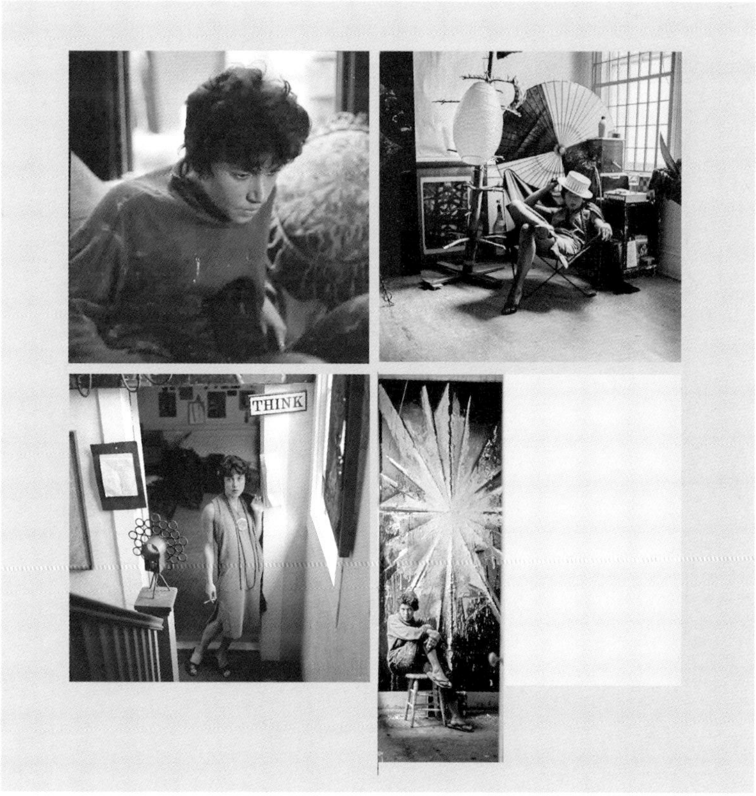

Fig. 43 Jerry Burchard, Photo panel to accompany Jay DeFeo's works in *The Individual and His World,* 1959. Gelatin silver prints mounted on board, 24 × 20 in. (60.9 × 50.8 cm). Reconstructed by Dennis Hearne. The Estate of Jerry Burchard.

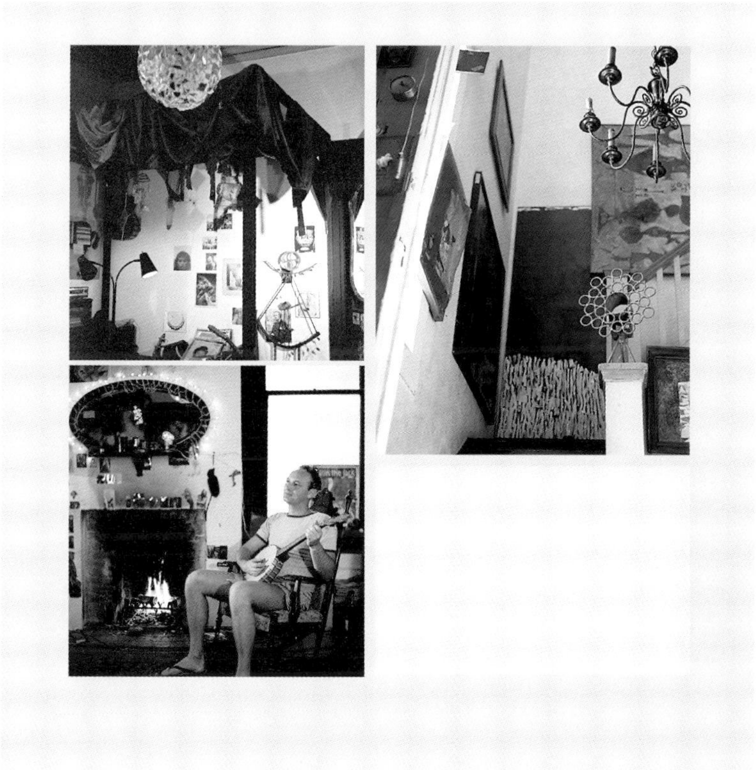

Fig. 44 Jerry Burchard, Photo panel to accompany Wally Hedrick's works in *The Individual and His World,* 1959. Gelatin silver prints mounted on board, 24 × 20 in. (60.9 × 50.8 cm). Reconstructed by Dennis Hearne. The Estate of Jerry Burchard.

the mundane task of eating becomes a vehicle for the artists to express their uniqueness, as well as the eye-popping exoticism and artiness of "fifties bohemia." Notably, though, as in Levittown, it is still the wife's responsibility to cook lunch.

The photo panels that Burchard made for *The Individual and His World* are published here for the first time, indicating that they have previously been paid little attention, despite their counter-conventional representation of home as a protective container for self-definition and expression.[27] Burchard's close-cropped images tightly delimit the spaces they picture. He often shot through windows and doorways (as evident in the lower photographs on DeFeo's panel), creating liminal points of view that make viewers self-conscious of their imminent intrusion into the artist's private space (see fig. 43). The panels thus treat each artist's home as a hermetic habitat—segregated and isolated like the "lonely" artists themselves. They further exaggerate the separateness of each artist's private "world" by representing it (through montage) as a labyrinth of enclosed, often dark, spaces rather than the single airy chamber of the abstract expressionist studio. Burchard's arrangements also convey Martin's claim that these sheltered spaces foster personal expression by staging a promiscuousness between the spaces of art and domesticity that popular representations of the abstract expressionist studio strictly forbade. The vertical juxtaposition of Hedrick's canopied workbench with his hearth, for example, posits a fluid exchange, a migration of objects and aesthetic influences, between the two spaces (see fig. 44). In these brimming interiors, paintings and sculptures overflow crowded studios and spill onto living-room walls and mantels, where they mingle with knickknacks, houseplants, and lace curtains. Contrary to the East Coast's neutral, self-effacing lofts, these profuse and decorative interiors exude personality, conveying the idea that a home expresses and even helps to nurture the identity of its inhabitant.

However, discrepancies between Martin's press release and Burchard's photographs reveal that the exhibition's attempt to knit together modernist autonomy and postmodernist heteronomy was far from seamless. The sublimity that Martin, using Keats's figure of the surveying conqueror, ascribed to the artist's autonomy rarely translates into Burchard's crowded interiors. Glimpsed through doorways or from behind, the artists seem like individuals more in the antisocial mode of the hermit than the intrepid mode of the adventurer. By portraying independence as a function of retreat into the private sphere, the panels give the impression that each artist's sovereignty is fragile and limited, rather than secure and expansive. The panels' representation of privacy as misanthropic withdrawal likely contributed to the *Oakland Tribune* critic Miriam Dungan Cross's reading of the show's artists as Beat provocateurs, out to deliberately shock the audience.[28] Home, in Cross's reductive interpretation, becomes a cipher for the subculture—an underground cultural space sheltered from the public sphere that permits unbridled personal expression.

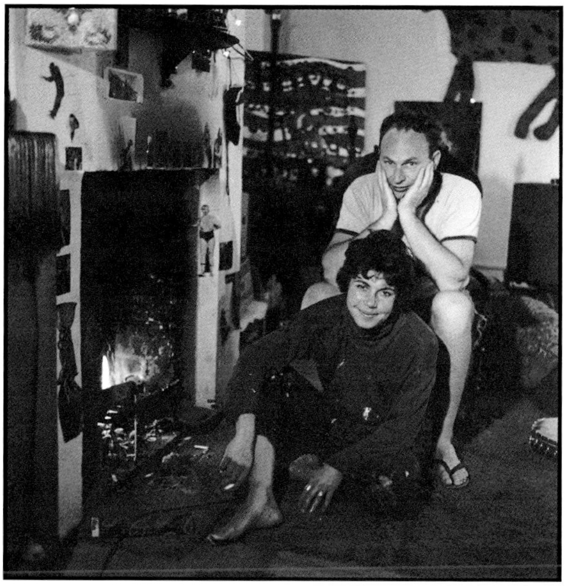

Fig. 45 Jerry Burchard, Jay DeFeo and Wally Hedrick at 2322 Fillmore Street, 1959. The Estate of Jerry Burchard.

The photographs also demonstrate how conflating the artists' subjective and domestic interiors complicates authorship by muddling the locus of agency. While Namuth's bare studios provide a blank slate for the creative act, leaving no doubt that the artist is solely responsible for the resulting work and existential position, Burchard's teeming interiors snag the artist in a net of object relations. His photographs often give the stuff of home and studio an animate quality. On Conner's panel, for example, rowdy piles appear to behave according to their own laws of accumulation and entropy as they encroach, swarm-like, upon the artist (see fig. 42). Burchard's depictions of the artists' homes often simulate the experience that literary theorist Bill Brown describes as "thingness"—the startling awareness one gets of an object's unruly materiality when one encounters it outside its habituated context of use.[29] Arrested by Burchard's lens, artists likewise assume the immobile, mute quality of things and, unlike Jackson Pollock, are rarely caught in the act of making. Some shots further the confusion between subject and object by using shadow to dissolve the artist's body into the surrounding décor. Sunken into a butterfly chair, DeFeo is barely discernable within the jumbled assortment of objects depicted on the upper right of her panel. The photo panels, in sum, portray home and artist as mutually constitutive. The creative act is thus shown to originate neither within the artist (as with abstract expressionist creation ex nihilo) nor within the environment (as with postmodernist appropriation), but somewhere within the tangle between the two.

Burchard's emphasis on the home's object relations also highlights his neglect of its interpersonal relations. Proof sheets from Burchard's photo shoots show that he systematically edited out images of artists interacting with others, including shots of Hedrick and DeFeo posing together in their living room (fig. 45). The omissions suggest that Burchard and

Martin struggled to reconcile the exhibition's thesis—that home is a vessel for the individual artist's unhampered expression and self-fulfillment, an idea encouraged by the spatial confluence of art and life in the Fillmore neighborhood—with the fact that for most artists in the show, "home" was a shared space. To preserve the autonomous, masculine character of the artist as visionary genius while embedding him in the household, they erased the collectivity and femininity traditionally associated with the domestic sphere. The family's world became the individual's world; theirs became his.

MALLORY'S ROSE

In an unpublished essay likely written around the same time as *The Individual and His World,* Martin clarified how he perceived the rapprochement between art and life playing out in Hedrick's and DeFeo's works. According to Martin, abstract expressionism's emphasis on autonomy led, ironically, to a revival of realism in San Francisco. This return to the real manifested, in contrasting ways, in the representational paintings of the Bay Area figurative movement and in works by some Fillmore artists, including Hedrick and DeFeo. While Bay Area figurative painters depicted the "ordinary home," Hedrick and DeFeo focused their depictions on aspects of existence akin to Cortés's "peaks in Darien," as Martin conjured them in the previously quoted press release for *The Individual and His World.* Martin's DeFeo turns away from the "middle-class sphere" to "concern herself with ultimates," creating through her art "an avalanche, a safe place in the ice, an adventure on a glacier and a chain of very high mountains." While courting the sublime, her art, in Martin's view, diverges from abstract expressionism by refusing to provide introspective escape; her paintings speak "clearly and simply of what is important in the world" despite their abstractness. Martin asserts, furthermore, that the realism provided by DeFeo's "concrete art" is more profound than the realism of the Bay Area figurative movement: the latter imitates mundane appearances, whereas DeFeo's art distills the existential quality of extreme experiences and sublime states to create works that exceed the aesthetic. The resultant works, Martin concludes, are "not art but an adventure in the heights of the world."[30] His characterization of DeFeo's art thus anticipated Alex Potts's 2004 description of 1960s assemblage as conveying "the last glimmer of . . . the idea that art presents its audience with a material reality where affectively charged possibilities are intimated that the actual world denies."[31]

The mountaineering metaphors in Martin's essay allude to DeFeo and Hedrick's interest in George Mallory's ill-fated attempt to scale Mount Everest in 1924, an incident with which they became fascinated leading up to Sir Edmund Hillary's successful expedition in 1953. As Martin's essay suggests, mountain climbing became a framework for the couple's conversations about art and life, especially regarding the relationship they saw *The*

Rose brokering between the goals of high modernist art and their domestic existence. In the 1950s, both artists made works that referenced mountain climbing, including abstract paintings that DeFeo dubbed her "mountain series." She painted *The Rose* over an unfinished canvas from the series and later connected the two works conceptually by acknowledging that the couple's fascination with climbing "influenced *The Rose* a bit."[32]

In statements following *The Rose*'s completion, both artists used the metaphor of mountain climbing to portray DeFeo's production of the painting as a Romantic attempt to exceed the everyday. Hedrick repeatedly connected the work to Mallory's tragic climb:

> The famous quote about climbing a mountain because it's there was [Mallory's] answer to a journalist who asked him why. *The Rose* was exactly the same. Mallory had tenure at his school, a nice family, everything, then one day . . . he and a young friend were struggling up a ridge. . . . It was four in the afternoon, clouds were forming, there obviously was going to be a storm. They had to either turn around . . . , or go on to the top, and die. That was the last time anyone saw Mallory. They knew what they were doing. Jay knew what she was doing. She decided to go for the top.[33]

By equating DeFeo with Mallory, Hedrick characterizes *The Rose* as exemplary of the avant-garde idea of art-making as risk-taking, adventure, testing limits, and chasing dreams despite the substantial sacrifices it incurs. Like Mallory's doomed ascent, the painting represents an escape from the attachments, routines, and responsibilities (as well as the comfort and safety) of quotidian existence.

The mountaineer provides a distinctly masculine metaphor for the artist. The agonistic athleticism of man versus mountain, as well as the hubristic scope of the climber's ambition (which could be read as a selfish disregard for family), fit with the conventionally masculine fantasy of exceeding both the stifling, female-controlled domestic sphere and the limits of artistic convention—desires also evident in contemporary accounts of action painting. Despite the incongruity between the mountaineer's assumed gender and her own, DeFeo confirmed the association. She stated that "images of mountains, to me, symbolize striving" and that climbing "lent itself to the abstract expressionist movement." For both DeFeo and Hedrick, then, mountaineering stood for art-making as a heroic, but tortured (even fatalistic) existential journey like she described in the *Sixteen Americans* catalogue. "We were very romantic about our associations in those days," she reflected in 1979, "likening the struggle of mountain climbing to the struggle of the artist."[34]

Other statements DeFeo made about mountain climbing, however, suggest a more nuanced view of its and, by extension, *The Rose*'s relationship to everyday life—one more in keeping with the rapprochement represented in *Life Game* and *The Individual and His World.* "Obviously, there is the idea of challenge there," she explained toward the end of her life, "to do the best you can each step of the way."[35] By characterizing climbing as a "challenge," she continues to associate it with the high modernist goal of pushing beyond mundane reality. However, her description of ascending as a gradual, cumulative process (in which you "do the best you can each step of the way") echoes the durational, repetitive quality of routinized experience. In what ways might *The Rose* have been seen to integrate the striving of the male-connoted visionary artist toward transcendence, sublimity, risk, and freedom with its apparent opposite—the concrete, delimited, routinized, and communal reality of the female-connoted domestic sphere?

For some artists in the Fillmore neighborhood, *The Rose*'s unusual temporal structure ground the work in DeFeo's everyday life. "The room had no electricity," Conner recalled of DeFeo's studio. "When the sun came up, the room was illuminated, she worked on the painting. . . . The light went away, she left the room."[36] According to Conner, DeFeo took the temporal pattern of daily existence—the sun's rhythmic rise and set—as the template for her art-making. Like the collection of old, withered Christmas trees she steadily amassed in her studio, the materiality of *The Rose* indexes the gradualness and recursion of mundane experience: its encrusted surface signals steady accrual, reflecting the plodding passage of time—the regular accretion of minutes into hours into days into months into years—that characterizes monotonous, humdrum existence. "When people ask me how something was done, I simply can't remember," DeFeo confessed of *The Rose* in 1988. "It's trial and error, laying and layering, like my life, it's additive and subtractive, a constructive and destructive process." For DeFeo, making *The Rose* assumed the pervasive yet elusive quality of everyday life—the way, as Felski observed, the everyday rests like a "blurred speck at the edge of one's vision that disappears when looked at directly."[37] Indeed, the tellurian and geological metaphors that critics frequently use to describe *The Rose*'s paint surface evoke the gradualness of the painting's production, which made DeFeo's labor difficult to perceive, like the slow churning of Earth's crust.[38]

DeFeo's practice of regularly scraping the canvas bare and building it up again likewise mimicked the cyclical quality of routine, as well as the Sisyphean quality of household chores. As with repetitive, quickly consumed tasks like cleaning and cooking, the results of most of DeFeo's efforts were rapidly erased—either buried under subsequent layers of paint or chipped onto the studio floor by her merciless palette knife. *The Rose*'s production thus approximated the structure of what Arendt (writing the same year DeFeo began *The Rose*) called "labor"—the cyclical, largely unseen effort required to maintain bodies, families, and households that generally falls to women.[39] In this way, DeFeo incorporated aspects of domestic existence into her art practice that the high modernist tradition largely sought to counter—a contrast evident in the fact that her gradual, recursive, and virtually imperceptible process essentially inverted the spontaneous, decisive, and dramatic gesture associated with action painting.

DeFeo and Hedrick's comparisons of *The Rose* to mountain climbing, however, indicate that they did not see the work as simply reproducing the temporality and labor of their household; instead, they saw DeFeo's process as stubbornly shaping the experiential structure of everyday life into its opposite. *The Rose* "passed through several stages," DeFeo noted in a typical statement. "There was a kind of archaic version at six months, then followed a very developed geometric version which gradually transformed itself into a much more organic expression. Curiously, this stage got thoroughly out of hand at one point (baroque), and I managed to pull it all the way back to the final 'classic' Rose."[40] Her description of *The Rose*'s development echoes the terminology and structure of the Swiss art historian Heinrich Wölfflin's history of style, which DeFeo most likely encountered in her art history courses at Berkeley. In Wölfflin's historical model, form both perpetually cycles between opposing poles (the dialectic, for example, between the geometric and the organic) and develops in a linear, progressive way toward a telos.[41] DeFeo's implicit allusion to Wölfflin suggests that she saw *The Rose* as similarly synthesizing cyclicality and change. Through the recursive process of applying paint to the canvas and scraping it away, DeFeo gave the work's development a transformative trajectory akin to the successive stages of Western art. By merging repetition and transformation, the mountaineer's plodding steps and the extraordinary ascent they accomplish, *The Rose* could be seen to mold mundane experience into the meaningful sweep of history.

Making *The Rose* thus merged labor, as defined by Arendt, with what the philosopher called "work"—the transformative, individuating, and world-making activities generally reserved for men and exemplified by heroic acts such as Mallory's climb. DeFeo's process also combined reproduction, as described by Julia Kristeva as the cyclical time of biological generation and domestic maintenance, with production, "time as project, teleology, linear and prospective unfolding . . . in other words, the time of history."[42] By fusing "repetition and linearity, recurrence with forward movement," DeFeo's production of *The Rose* troubled the gendered binaries through which art and everyday life were generally viewed in the postwar period, demonstrating Felski's conclusion that "acts of innovation and creativity are not opposed to, but rather made possible by, the mundane cycles of the quotidian."[43] Unlike the abstract expressionist act, DeFeo's art practice accepted domesticity as a formative reality, even as it sought to shape mundane existence to accommodate traits conventionally associated with men and the public sphere, such as challenge, achievement, and risk.

DeFeo and her friends recognized that *The Rose* not only transformed the time but also the space of her daily existence. "Myself and tree—later studio for Rose," DeFeo noted on the back of a holiday snapshot depicting the space in 2322 Fillmore Street that she and Hedrick originally used

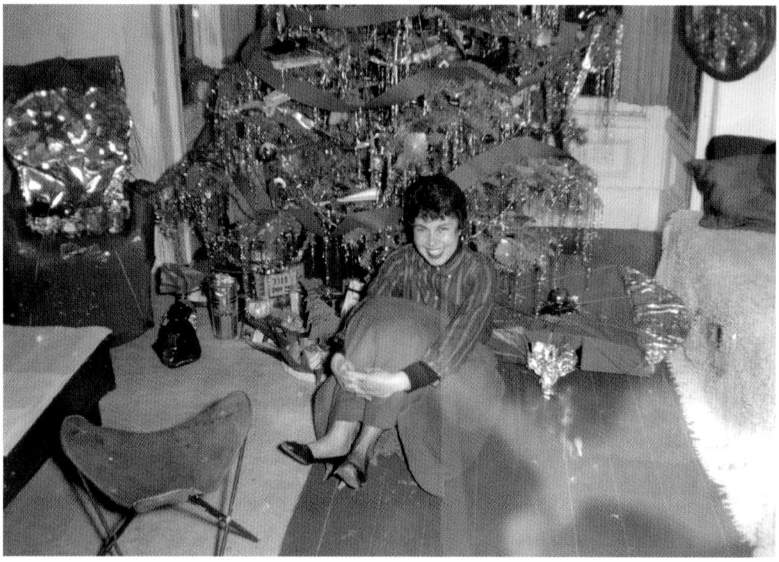

Fig. 46 Jay DeFeo with a Christmas tree in bay window at 2322 Fillmore Street, c. 1957. Gelatin silver print. The Jay DeFeo Foundation, Berkeley, Calif. [JDF no. R0577].

as a living room (fig. 46). Her production of *The Rose* soon converted the cozy domestic space into a paint-splattered cavern dominated by the work's radiating presence, a state that Burchard captured during the photo shoot for *The Individual and His World* (see fig. 1). Through the use of backlighting, Burchard's photograph depicts the studio as a dark, hushed, and mysterious chamber. *The Rose* rises altar-like behind DeFeo's ethereal silhouette, its starburst pattern emitting an otherworldly glow. Conner described DeFeo's studio in similarly mystical terms: "The room became a temple and the ritual object of the footstool raised Jay to greater spiritual heights. I have always considered it an artwork in itself."[44] Making *The Rose,* Conner claims, converted the mundane living area into a temple—a liminal space where the concrete, earthly realm touches the spiritual and transcendent. The medial environment elevated ordinary, functional objects (such as the step stool that DeFeo used to reach the top of the canvas) into art, and DeFeo's repetitive, physical process into a solitary ritual of transcendence, propelling her ascent "to greater spiritual heights."

Other photographs from Burchard's shoot at 2322 Fillmore Street show Hedrick painting in the same studio as *The Rose.* While the couple's shared studio space was most likely staged for the camera, the paintings that Hedrick is shown to have created next to *The Rose*—*Virgin and Child* (1959) and *Transenna* (1959, a mandala-like painting visible to the viewer's left of *The Rose* in figure 1)—acknowledge the studio's sacred atmosphere through their religious subject matter.[45] A transenna is a protective screen for a shrine and exactly the kind of sacred, threshold-marking object into which Burchard's photography transforms *The Rose.*

In situ, *The Rose* fostered the perception that it acted as a portal between mundane and sublime space by performing an incongruous relationship between matter and image. As DeFeo made the cyclical rhythms of her domestic life the pattern for *The Rose*'s production, so she made the walls of her living room the physical frame for the painting by remounting the canvas to fill the entire height and breadth of the bay window—an act that, as DeFeo knew, made the work too large to fit through the room's doorway.[46] She indicated that the painting's physical attachment to the space was not simply circumstantial but held conceptual significance by stating, following *The Rose*'s completion, that she wished the finished canvas would be exhibited in a way that simulated "the original setting and lighting" of her studio.[47] DeFeo compounded the work's entrapment by loading the massive canvas with layers of paint, the weight of which (at some points reaching nearly a ton) literally anchored *The Rose* to the floor. By effectively walling in the studio, the painting's placement in front of the window signaled the retreat enacted by grounding the work within the private, domestic space of 2322 Fillmore Street.

The Rose's starburst composition counteracted this cloistering effect by mimicking infinite space. Like the orthogonals of linear perspective, the painting's radiating spokes exploded the wall of DeFeo's studio through the illusion of expansiveness. In 1995 Carlos Villa, an artist and close friend of Hedrick and DeFeo, recalled how this "optical illusion" made *The Rose* seem both "real and unreal"—perceived simultaneously as a tangible feature of the material fabric of DeFeo's apartment and as opening up that delimited, physical reality to a transcendent beyond.[48] DeFeo indeed appears to have associated *The Rose*'s starburst design with the sublime sight of the visionary artist; she represented a similar cluster of diagonal lines radiating from the right pupil of her monumental drawing *The Eyes* (1958), which hung in her studio as she was beginning *The Rose* (fig. 47). As Dana Miller noted, DeFeo retroactively identified the drawing as "the aperture through which . . . she was able to envision . . . *The Rose*."[49] The interplay that *The Rose* enacted

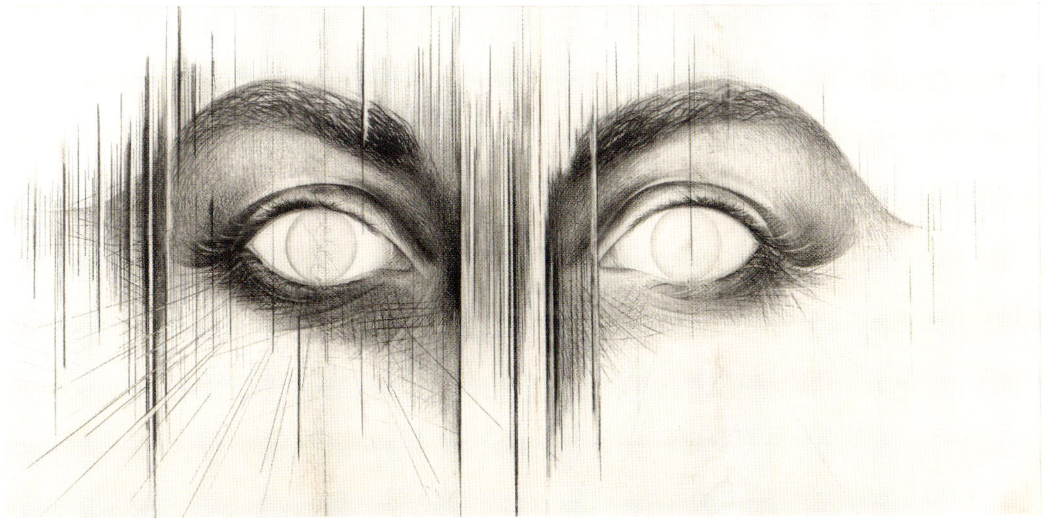

Fig. 47 Jay DeFeo, *The Eyes*, 1958. Graphite pencil on paper, 42 × 84¾ in. (106.7 × 215.3 cm). Whitney Museum of American Art, New York. Gift of the Lannan Foundation [Inv. N.: 96.242.3].

between matter and image, physical reality and optical illusion, could thus be seen to broker a relationship between the concrete cloister of the artist's domestic interior and the ethereal elsewhere of her subjective interior, akin to *The Individual and His World*'s conflation of home and inhabitant.

The Rose's placement in DeFeo and Hedrick's apartment also created the surprising impression that domestic space fosters transcendent experience. Burchard's photograph makes it easy to imagine how the labyrinth of dark, disordered rooms through which visitors had to travel before entering DeFeo's studio would have made the painting's monumental starburst appear all the more striking and otherworldly. Another description that Martin gave of 2322 Fillmore Street confirms this interplay between apartment and work. "The whole place had it as the fixed focus," he stated of *The Rose,* "which is why it was so dramatic when you went there. It was like a little cathedral. You came into this room, with very high ceilings, long and narrow, with this sublime number at the end, where the window would have been."[50] Martin may have had such encounters with *The Rose* in mind when he wrote, in the essay discussed earlier, that DeFeo's art provides otherworldly experiences that possess a powerful realism. The familiar, intimate setting likely augmented the abstract work's powerful presence not only by providing contrast, but also by endowing the painting's ethereality with a forceful immediacy. The interaction between 2322 Fillmore Street and *The Rose* thus performed the notion, codified in *The Individual and His World,* that the domestic sphere makes possible (acts as a precondition for) the experience of sublimity that high modernist art ideally provides.

Like the color wheel that Hedrick made of his life, *The Rose* blended the concrete, mundane, and objective with the ethereal, transcendent, and subjective in a particular way. It performed a dialectical dance between the postmodern impulse to accept everyday life—specifically, in this case, domestic existence—as the grounds for artistic practice and the Romantic desire to exceed it. The relationship between art and life it enacted was thus marked by transformation rather than by either capitulation or escape, immanence or transcendence, heteronomy or autonomy. Even as DeFeo integrated *The Rose* with the temporality, labor, and space of her life at 2322 Fillmore Street, she used the work to radically alter those aspects of her domestic existence—shaping the imperceptible recursions of routine experience into the legible, linear form of historical progress and opening the confines of the household to an infinite beyond. DeFeo's fusion of the housewife's chores and domestic spaces with, respectively, the adventures and sublime vistas of the Romantic artist/mountaineer manifested her community's belief that the protection provided by the domestic sphere preserved a potential for self-fulfillment, expression, and transcendence that the postwar American public sphere denied. Thus, the home, for DeFeo and her coterie of Fillmore artists, was an ideal site for artistic practice—a belief that embraced, albeit unconventionally, the postwar cult of domesticity.

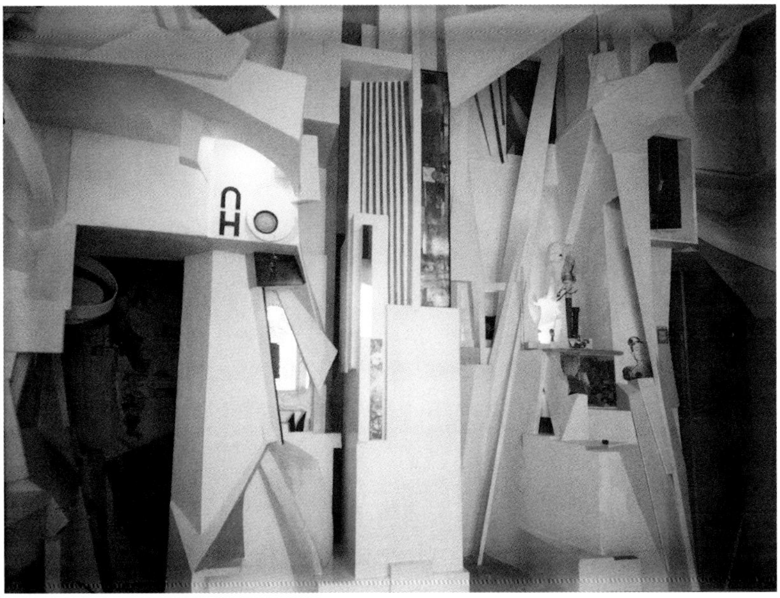

Fig. 48 Kurt Schwitters, The *Merzbau* in Hanover (entrance from the stairwell). Installation, destroyed in 1943. Paper, cardboard, gesso, glass, mirror, metal, wood, stone, paint, various materials, and electric lighting, 154⁷⁄₁₀ × 228³⁄₁₀ × 181¹⁄₁₀ in. (393 × 580 × 460 cm). Photographed by Wilhelm Redemann in 1933. Positive photograph from glass negative, 9²⁄₅ × 7 in. (24 × 18 cm). Sprengel Museum, Hanover [Inv. KSA 2008, 14].

Perhaps not surprisingly, given their concept of the home as a site well suited to artistic creation, both DeFeo and Hedrick admired the eccentric, German dadaist Kurt Schwitters, whose *Merzbau* (1923–37) had previously explored the relationship between art and life (fig. 48). Hedrick identified Schwitters as an important touchstone for his assemblages of the 1950s, explaining in 1974: "Kurt Schwitters would walk around all day picking up junk and then he'd take it home and build this monster thing he was working on. . . . Thirty years later I started doing the same thing." More whimsically, but perhaps no less significantly, DeFeo acknowledged Schwitters's influence by naming one of her dogs "Merz."[51]

Like *The Rose,* Schwitters's environmental assemblage radically integrated art-making with the space and time of domesticity to transformative effect. As he incorporated items scavenged from the streets of Hanover into his home, Schwitters converted its conventional bourgeois interior into a bizarre, ever-evolving creative sanctuary that evidenced his belief—which the Fillmore community would later share—that the private sphere is a productive site for artistic expression. While Schwitters opened his art to the stuff, spaces, and contingent experiences of his daily existence, he believed that his creative process transformed those base elements into works of art that existed separately and above everyday life.[52] He thus attempted to broker an alchemical relationship between heteronomy and autonomy similar to that enacted by *The Rose.*

Hedrick described his assemblage process as performing a similar metaphysical conversion: "If I can take something useless . . . and if I can make it into something that has status, the elevated status of art . . . well, that's even better than God."[53] I read this statement, like most of Hedrick's, as partly tongue-in-cheek.[54] However, the spiritual allusions that he incorporated into the titles and forms of many of his beer can assemblages of the 1950s and 1960s—including *American Everest* (1956–57), *Ceiling Wings of Brew '52* (1958), and *Soul Thing* (1960)—suggest that he subscribed, at least in part, to the Romantic equation of artistic and divine creation. According to Hedrick's statement, his assemblages demonstrate that equation by transmuting empty cans, "something useless," into works of art, something with "elevated status." While many "junk artists" of Hedrick's generation produced chaotic assemblages that appeared to passively index consumer culture (for example, Arman's messy *Poubelles* and Rauschenberg's "random order" combines), Hedrick followed Schwitters in shaping the discarded commodities he salvaged into symbolic gestalts, creating a perceptual tension between material flux and pictorial form, the detritus of everyday life and the work of art, heteronomy and autonomy.[55]

Hedrick's sculpture *American Everest* (also known as *It Can Be Done!*), for example, resembles a jagged, asymmetrical peak mounted on spindly metal legs (see fig. 38). Instead of layers of earth, however, the crag contains layers of flattened cans welded together into a sheet that curves slightly at the base and summit. While somewhat ungainly under bright light, the sculpture acquires an ethereal quality when the lights dim and darkness cloaks the thin legs, creating an illusion that the sculpture hovers above the floor. Light flickers over the puckered surface of the crushed cans, dissolving the steel into a shimmering field that gradually fades as the plane curves away, augmenting the illusion of levitation.

A second assemblage, *Soul Thing,* reflects Hedrick and DeFeo's penchant for mandalic forms, rather than their infatuation with mountaineering (see fig. 39). It consists of a wheel of vertically stacked cans, two thick and two deep, mounted on a washing-machine motor. When plugged in, the visible gears and belts snap into motion, spinning the cans with a rattling whir. The motley labels of the sculpture's cans evoke individual consumers, while the shape the cans form is cohesive and whole in its simple circularity. This coming together is not staid or static; it is energetic. The individual cans swirl in unison like dancers aroused by beer, jazz, and conversation at one of DeFeo and Hedrick's legendary bashes. At once mandala-like and shabby, the sculpture suggests that for Hedrick the "soul" represented by *Soul Thing* was both mystical, akin to the transcendent effects of art and religion, and funky, akin to the animating spirit of jazz and inebriation that transforms a gathering of individual invitees into a party.

A similar tension can be perceived in many of Kaprow's Happenings from the same moment. Of the many proposals circa 1960 to put art back in contact with the everyday, Kaprow's Happenings—which redeployed familiar things and habituated activities in novel combinations—resonate strongly with *The Rose* and Hedrick's assemblages. Kaprow intended his ritual-like performances to re-enchant everyday life, which consumer capitalism had thoroughly colonized, thereby "bringing into focus those things one ordinarily does every day without paying attention—like brushing one's teeth."[56] In this way, Happenings, like *The Rose,* preserved some version of high modernism's desire for transcendence, even as they followed postmodernism's turn toward the everyday.

These transhistorical and trans-coastal comparisons delineate an approach to mixing art and life that differs from the "shock effect" most commonly associated with the interwar avant-gardes and those who followed in their footsteps. As both Walter Benjamin and Peter Bürger influentially argued, dada, surrealist, and other interwar artists used montage and readymades to sublate the sphere of art into that of everyday life with the intent to shock viewers—an effect that Bürger saw neo-avant-garde artists ineffectually attempting to repeat in the 1960s.[57] This sensory disorientation and addling of the rational mind was supposed to jolt viewers out of their habituated perception of the world, ideally spurring them to revolutionary action. By contrast, DeFeo and Schwitters, as well as Hedrick and Kaprow, to some extent, mingled art and life within the circumscribed realm of the home to preserve rather than liquidate autonomy (including notions of artistic genius, expressive creativity, and transcendent viewing) in modified form. The changes they catalyzed by merging their artistic practices with the spaces, routines, and identities of their domestic lives were thus more gradual and limited than those prompted by shock—circumscribed within the private sphere and, therefore, experienced primarily by the artists and their friends and family. While less dramatic and political, the transformations their approach generated were more concrete: instead of depending on viewers to act on their modified consciousnesses, the artists directly altered the tangible realm of the home, its rooms and routines, as they converted their private lives into an artistic medium.

Situating *The Rose* within this alternative tradition of the avant-garde sublation of art and life (which manifested in postwar San Francisco due to the significance the home assumed as a site for artistic practice) helps make sense of some of the work's apparent incongruities, which are often presented as evidence of either DeFeo's irrationality or her bohemian rejection of the commercial art world.[58] This tradition posits the home as a site, perhaps the only site, where the grand ambitions of Romanticism are still potentially achievable in the twentieth century. If DeFeo was thinking along these lines, then she would have seen integrating *The Rose* with the rhythm and space of life in her apartment as a productive, even necessary, path to creating a masterpiece in the high modernist tradition, even if this approach kept the work both out of the public eye and out of sync with the art market. Viewed through the lens of "domesticized high modernism," *The Rose* looks less like an aberrant exception within the history of twentieth-century art and more like one iteration, striking as it may be, of that century's continual and varied experimentation with the relationship between art and life.

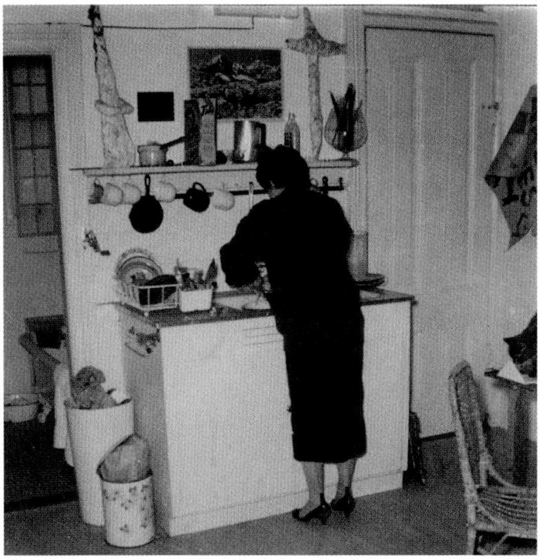

Fig. 49 Jay DeFeo at kitchen sink with two of her plaster sculptures on the shelf above, c. 1955. Gelatin silver print. The Jay DeFeo Foundation, Berkeley, Calif. [JDF no. R0574A].

EVEREST OF THE KITCHEN SINK

A snapshot, likely taken around the time DeFeo began *The Rose,* suggests the complex relationship between artistic practice and everyday life that the painting performed (fig. 49). The photograph shows DeFeo scrubbing dishes in the kitchen of 2322 Fillmore Street. Two wood-and-plaster sculptures she made in the early 1950s perch on the narrow shelf above her, keeping company with a saucepan, coffeepot, box of detergent, and bottle of liquid soap. The assortment attests to the porous physical boundaries between the stuff of art and the stuff of quotidian existence in the couple's home. Hanging directly above the sink, where one might expect a window, is a poster of Mount Everest—the splendor of its majestic ridgeline mocking the row of lowly household items in front of it. The poster both is physically integrated into the mundane setting of DeFeo's domestic chore and promises escape from it, into the sublime realm of nature and adventure. The photograph thus figures the transformative dialectic between integration and opposition that characterized the ideal relationship between art and life that, as this chapter has described, developed in DeFeo and Hedrick's household and community.

In keeping with this ideology of "domestic utopia," Hedrick viewed romantic partnership as a vital foundation for his art-making. "There have been several people in my life. Jay was one of them," he confessed in a late interview. "These people helped me. If you don't have some sort of support, it's hard to do stuff." He recognized, as DeFeo did with *The Rose,* that the domestic sphere enables, rather than prevents, innovation and individuation. "Domestic utopia" thus emerges as one of the frameworks that Fillmore artists developed to integrate individual and collective subjectivity, as well as authorship. Other times, however, Hedrick espoused an opposing view of domesticity. "I decided a long time ago that I can't be

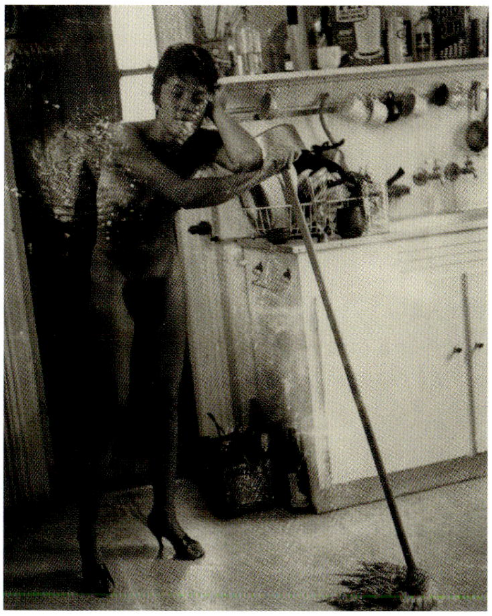

Fig. 50 Jay DeFeo with kitchen mop in Fillmore Street kitchen, c. 1959. Gelatin silver print. The Jay DeFeo Foundation, Berkeley, Calif. [JDF no. R0575B].

a nice, middle-class American and do what I want to do," he admitted in 1985. "Can we understand that to be free, we have to watch it? The chains are coming from every direction, and sometimes they're camouflaged. . . . You have to be really egocentric and think of yourself first. Kids, wives, mothers—all of that has to be set aside."[59] In keeping with his description of Mallory's fatalistic flight from patriarchal obligation, Hedrick portrays familial relationships as oppressive "chains," rather than supportive foundations, that prevent the artist from pursuing the "egocentric" activity of making art and self.

DeFeo also at times represented her home life as a burdensome infringement. "Wally never took me anywhere in the whole time we were married where there wasn't some kind of a thing where he could perform," she lamented to an interviewer in the mid-1970s. "You're getting the irate housewife." Echoing Betty Friedan's portrait of the entrapped, disgruntled homemaker in the *Feminine Mystique* (which was published during *The Rose*'s production), DeFeo characterized her domestic life and her husband's reluctance to liberate her from it as stifling.[60] Another photograph of DeFeo in the kitchen of 2322 Fillmore Street seems to express resentment toward the household chores she was expected to perform as a wife (fig. 50). The undated image shows DeFeo stark naked except for high heels, leaning on a mop and closing her eyes out of weariness or boredom. Donna Reed she is not. DeFeo's discontent with her wifely role may have sprung in part from her perception that her domestic duties competed with her artistic activities for her time and energy. "I've been painting so frantically lately," DeFeo confessed while making *The Rose,* "I hardly find time to sweep the floor."[61]

The statements reveal that DeFeo's and Hedrick's experiences of and attitudes about their domestic life were more conflicted than *Life Game* and *The Rose* suggest. Both found it difficult to navigate the dual—sometimes complementary, sometimes contradictory—roles of artist and spouse, and they experienced their artistic practices and everyday lives clashing as much as, if not more than, they experienced them seamlessly combining. Their recollections thus lend credence to Cándida Smith's assertion that the ideal of "domestic utopia" cultivated within California's postwar artistic undergrounds was difficult to achieve.[62] Given this revelation, it seems likely that *The Rose* was born not only from DeFeo's belief in the compatibility of domesticity and creativity, as I have argued thus far, but also from the incompatibility she experienced between them—that the discontent she felt as an "irate housewife" also encouraged her to attempt to shape her domestic existence into a more satisfying form.

While DeFeo's production of *The Rose* may have been propelled in part by her dissatisfaction with traditional gender expectations, the work largely diverges from the feminist art movement that developed approximately a decade after she began the painting. *The Rose* acknowledges that the private sphere and its gendered roles are unavoidable conditions that necessarily shape artistic practice and subjectivity. In the 1970s, works by feminist artists such as Mierle Laderman Ukeles similarly revealed that maintenance—the generally invisible labor performed by women and the working class—makes possible the creative, innovative, and esteemed work generally performed by affluent men in the public sphere.[63] Similar to avant-garde shock, this ideological revelation was supposed to lead to the revaluation of women's contributions and greater gender equality by sparking political activism. *The Rose* also transformed the experience of maintenance, but it did so in a very different way—by collapsing the temporal and spatial structures associated with the recursive, imperceptible labor of the domestic sphere and the inventive, noteworthy work of the public sphere. This approach allowed DeFeo to directly mold the experience of domesticity into a form that she felt was more meaningful (instead of relying on viewers to initiate change), but it also confined that modification to the artist's private experience (instead of allowing change to ripple through society).

The differences between *The Rose* and later feminist works suggest that, like most women prior to the women's liberation movement, DeFeo experienced her dissatisfaction with the gendered roles she was expected to play as personal, rather than political. According to Lucy Lippard, DeFeo resembled most of her female peers in being "intellectually uncomfortable with the notion of being singled out as a woman artist while men remained the generic artists." DeFeo's valuation of and identification with traditionally masculine activities, such as Mallory's voyage up Everest, were thus typical of prefeminist-generation artists.[64] Second-wave feminists would most likely have deemed retrogressive DeFeo's adoption of masculine metaphors to characterize her identity and artistic practice; however, her

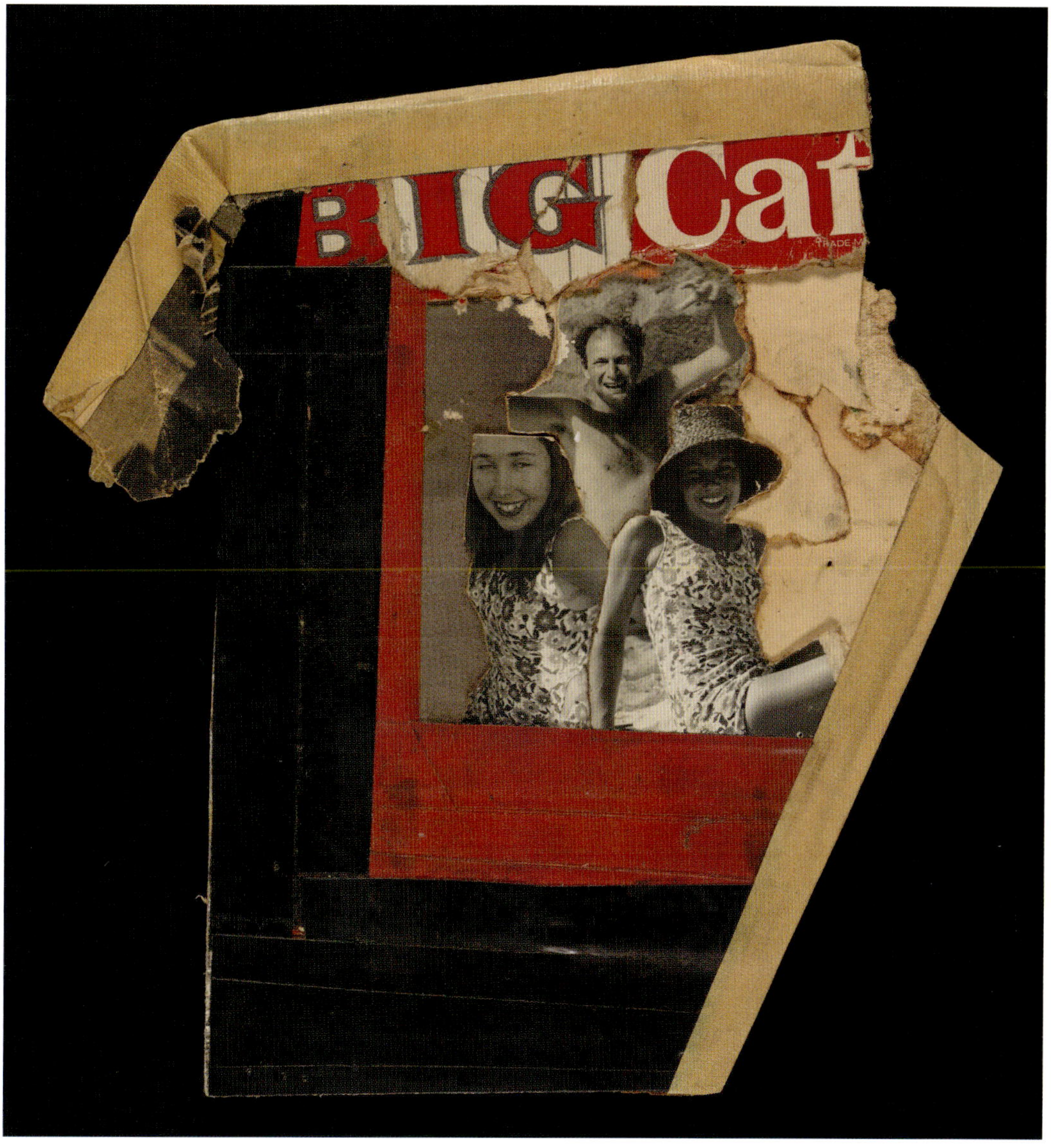

attempt to hybridize "the masculine" with traditionally feminine attributes and activities nevertheless enacted a transgressive elision of the binaries that structure conventional gender identity.

A number of the collages that DeFeo created during her production of *The Rose* play similarly with gender. "I was always making joke collages and giving them away," DeFeo stated of these playful works, many of which combine personal snapshots with found images to foreground gender stereotypes.[65] For example, DeFeo used the bacchanal, or some such scenario of sexualized pursuit, as a template to represent beach outings she and Hedrick regularly took with their Fillmore neighbors, converting herself and Joan Brown into nymphs pursued by a whimsically threatening Hedrick-fawn (fig. 51). Other times, DeFeo—like Hannah Höch before

Fig. 51 Jay DeFeo, Untitled collage, c. 1960. Photographs, paper, card stock, and tape. Jay DeFeo papers, Archives of American Art, Smithsonian Institution, Washington, D.C.

her—used montage juxtaposition to invert gender expectations, as when she replaced her own head with Hedrick's in one of Burchard's photographs (fig. 52). The jarring combination of her coy pose with Hedrick's beaming, bearded visage is humorous—a result one might expect from works she labeled "joke collages."

Some of the works, however, manipulate gender representation in ways that exceed jocularity and seem to point to DeFeo's dissatisfaction with her role as a "housewife." In 1964 she pasted an unflattering cutout of Hedrick's face on the cover of a program for the San Francisco Giants (fig. 53). She then inverted the masculine connotations of both by appending the voluptuous torso of a *Playboy* centerfold (that extends below the bottom edge of the illustration seen here) to act as Hedrick's body. The model she selected wears nothing but a gauzy apron, a costume that fetishizes women's traditional role as domestic caretakers. DeFeo's further addition of the double entendre "foul balls" across Hedrick's chest hints that her frustration with

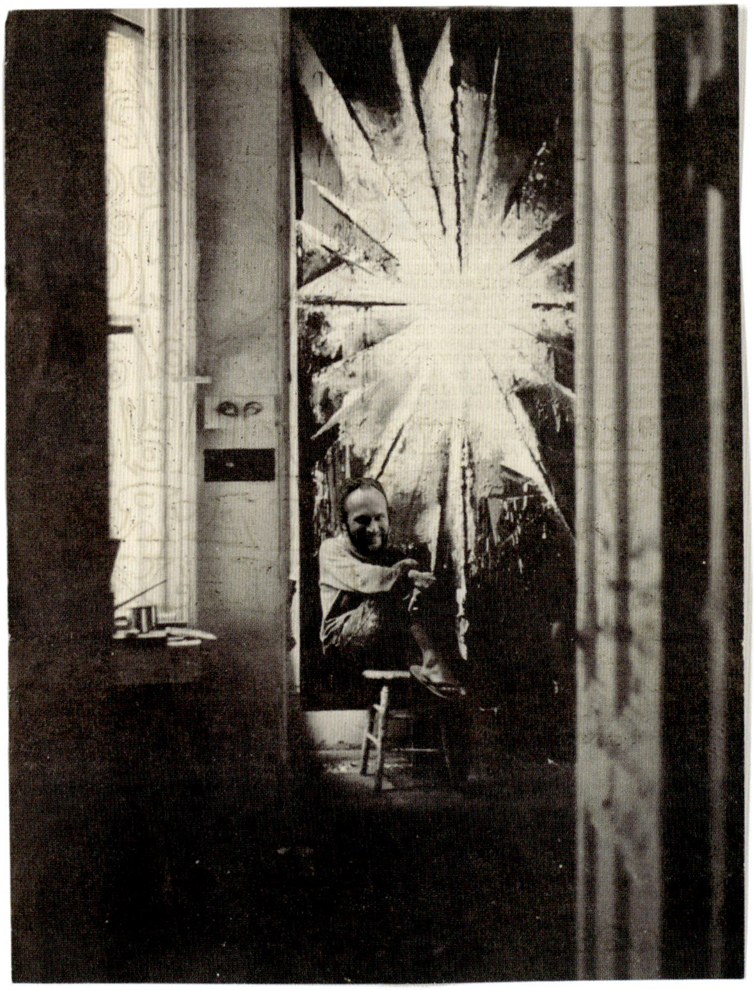

Fig. 52 Christmas card from Jay DeFeo and Wally Hedrick to Dorothy C. Miller, 1959 (verso). Offset, printed in black with applied glitter and cutouts, 11 × 8½ in. (27.9 × 21.6 cm). Dorothy C. Miller Papers, I.15.k, Museum of Modern Art Archives, New York.

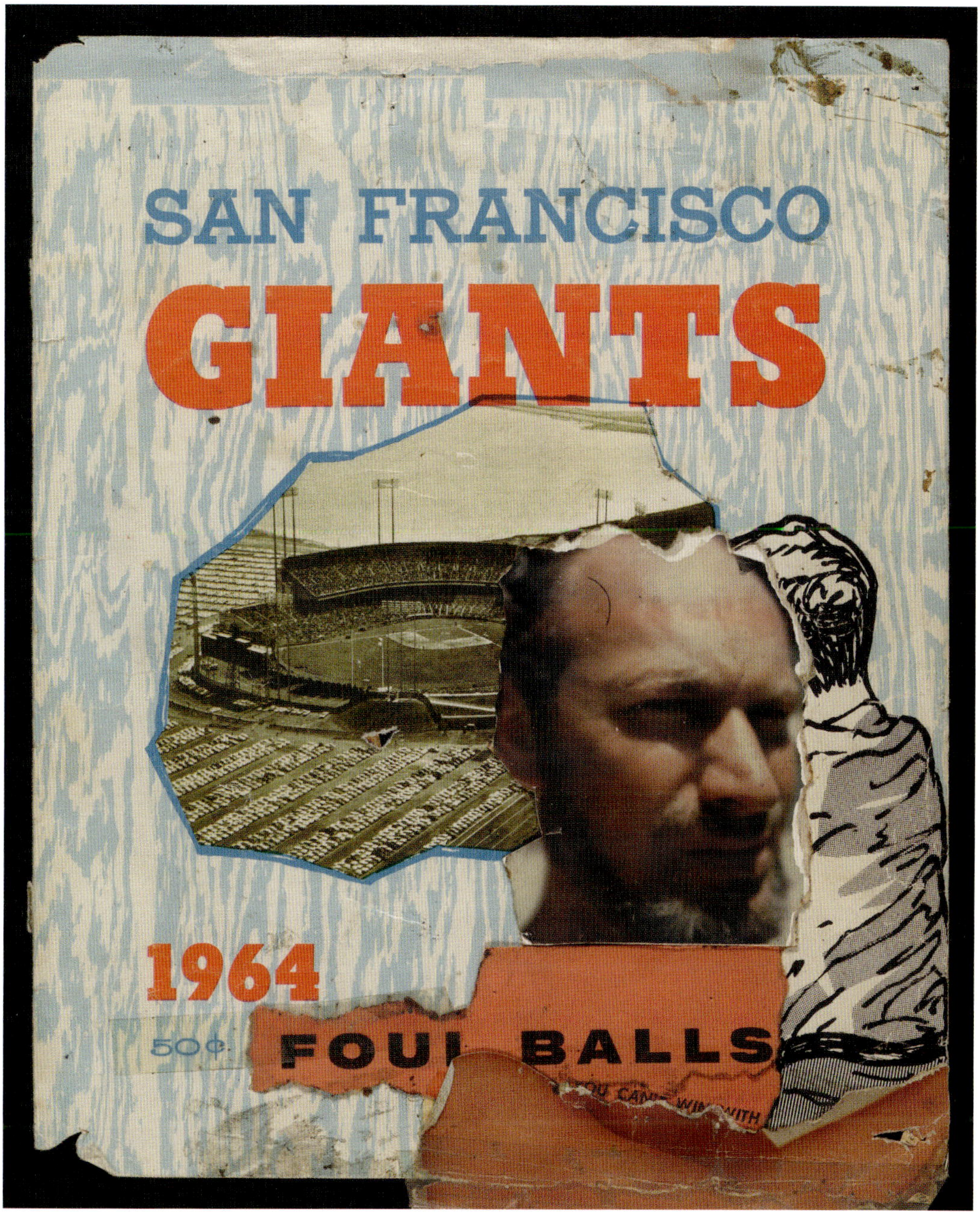

Fig. 53 Jay DeFeo, Untitled collage, c. 1965. Photomechanical reproductions and cover of the 1964 season program for the San Francisco Giants. Jay DeFeo papers, Archives of American Art, Smithsonian Institution, Washington, D.C.

their marriage and the expectations it placed on her to perform the conventional role of wife motivated the collage's subversive scrambling of masculine and feminine. The collage demonstrates that DeFeo exploited the relative freedom that the bohemian atmosphere of the Fillmore community provided from the strict gender expectations of 1950s America, even as she acutely felt the limitations of that freedom.

DeFeo's and Hedrick's assessments of *The Rose* reflected their conflicted view of the relationship between their domestic life and artistic practices. While they lauded the work as a symbol of Romantic striving, they also conceded that it burdened their life and relationship. In 1965 the couple received word that their rent was increasing drastically, forcing them to leave 2322 Fillmore Street. The move precipitated the termination of both *The Rose* and their marriage.[66] The couple had originally planned to move together to a rented house in Ross, a small town approximately fifteen miles north of San Francisco. However, when DeFeo returned from a several-month stint at the Pasadena Art Museum, where she was attempting to finish *The Rose,* she moved into the house in Ross by herself. Their divorce was finalized in 1969. In later interviews, DeFeo partially blamed *The Rose,* as well as Hedrick's extramarital affairs, for the failure of their relationship. "He always had been something of a womanizer anyway," DeFeo explained in 1988, "but at any rate all of that activity, plus my own intensity over my work, was not doing either one of us any good, and although we are friends now, it was coming to an end."[67] The statement echoed DeFeo's claim from 1975 that *The Rose* "had a great deal to do with the eventual collapse of my marriage." She similarly characterized the work as a detrimental strain on her existence and person, claiming that "my personal life as well as my psyche" required repair "after the heavy experience that the painting of *The Rose* was" and, furthermore, that there were many "disappointments and changes in my life for which *The Rose* was directly or indirectly responsible."[68]

Hedrick gave a more specific account of the havoc *The Rose* wreaked on their household. "I was living with her [DeFeo] when she painted *The Rose,*" he recalled in 2009, before expounding his experience of the work's production:

> I built the stretcher bars that it's on. . . . I used to carry [the gallons of paint] up the stairs for her. She used Pro white, which means it was a mixture of titanium, lead, white and flake white. . . . She used to smoke two or three cigarettes at once and with all that lead paint all over her hands it went into her lungs. . . . When she finished painting that was the end of us. We had to tear off the front of the building to remove it. The landlord went bananas. As soon as he saw the condition of her studio—there was paint a half foot deep on the floor—he raised our rent by a factor of ten. And we couldn't afford that. And so we had to leave after the building was ripped up. . . . To

me the painting was just a white elephant. It practically destroyed my life.[69]

He frames *The Rose,* in no uncertain terms, as responsible for ruining DeFeo's health, the couple's living arrangement, their relationship, and, ultimately, his life.

According to these statements, instead of elevating the everyday, DeFeo's merger of high modernism's model of art-making as epic adventure with domesticity highlighted their incompatibility by placing undue practical burdens on the latter. The astounding accrual of paint on the canvas and the floor of DeFeo's studio may have transformed their apartment into a temple, but it also made their apartment uninhabitable—at least in their landlord's eyes. Likewise, DeFeo's protracted painting process may have honed the cyclical pattern of domestic labor into the evolutionary form of pioneering work, but it also added to Hedrick's list of household chores, as he assisted with the many maintenance tasks (such as building stretcher bars and carrying buckets of paint) required to sustain the massive work. He appears to have grown dissatisfied with playing supportive roles, which historically women have more often assumed in heterosexual creative couples.[70]

The Rose "was sort of like our baby," Hedrick further explained. "The only thing holding us together was that monster painting. And it was moved out in '64 or '65. So it gave me a vision of how it would be to do what I—well, my whole main concern was not to have any strings attached to me."[71] The painting, from Hedrick's perspective, essentially nullified the couple's nonnormative childlessness, necessitating that he reassert the masculinist freedom from domestic responsibility required, in his eyes, to create art. In other words, by likening DeFeo's creative production to the quintessential domestic task of biological reproduction, he once again represents *The Rose* as an onerous household duty, a stifling familial relationship from which he, à la Mallory, needed to flee.

In sum, DeFeo's and Hedrick's recollections reveal that the bridge she attempted to build via *The Rose* between kitchen and Everest, dishwashing and mountain climbing, was shaky at best. Like Schwitters's *Merzbau,* the painting combined heteronomy and autonomy—openness to life and transcendence above it—in a way that underscored the unresolved tension between them. By detailing how *The Rose*'s transformation of the everyday resulted in destruction as well as exaltation, their comments frame the painting as exemplary of the relationship—the mix of harmony and discord—that they perceived between their homemaking and art-making more generally. DeFeo's attempt, through *The Rose,* to manifest the ideal synthesis of art and life figured in *The Individual and His World* within the complex reality of her marriage, apartment, and daily routine thus exposed the challenge, if not the impossibility, of realizing the Fillmore community's ideal of "domesticized high modernism" in practice.

The Rose also revealed the ambiguities and contradictions inherent in the model of authorship that this ideal prescribed—complexities to which the incongruencies and occlusions in *The Individual and His World* likewise pointed. Burchard's photographs show that embedding Romanticism's visionary genius within the home's intimate object and familial relations obfuscates the source of creative agency. A similar authorial ambiguity pervades many of DeFeo's statements about *The Rose*. "I knew there was an image somewhere so I nursed it along," she recollected. "If the image happens too soon, it can be stillborn. It is there but it doesn't have a substance, any life. . . . Am I going to let this image live?"[72] Although her terminology suggests that she, like Hedrick, saw herself as *The Rose*'s parent, she stops short of characterizing herself as the work's origin. She describes herself instead as nurturing an already-existent, though nascent, image along its predestined developmental path. DeFeo's statement recalls Pollock's declaration that because "the painting has a life of its own, I try to let it live."[73] The idea expressed in both quotations, that creativity is partially propelled by forces beyond an author's conscious control, can be traced to Romantic notions of divine inspiration, which filtered into abstract expressionism via surrealism's desire to create from the unconscious.

DeFeo, though, was more willing than Pollock to accept the compromised or, at least, composite authorial agency posited by this model of creative practice. Pollock famously rejected suspicions that his drip-painting technique undermined his complete (masculine) control over the production of his works by proclaiming, "I deny the accident."[74] DeFeo may have been more comfortable with the authorial ambiguity inherent in the Romantic tradition in part because siting her artistic practice in the home exacted similar compromises by increasing the external factors that could potentially impose on the artist's free will and conscious intent. In addition to divine inspiration and unconscious impulses, the work of art could be shaped by the contingencies of daily life—by the dimensions of existing architecture, the rhythms of bodily necessity, and the influences of a spouse. The fact that DeFeo compared the dance between control and determinism in her creative process to child-rearing suggests that the external forces she saw shaping her art were mundane, as well as mystical.

Hedrick's and DeFeo's conflicted accounts of their marriage's impact on their art indicate that opening their creative processes to the interpersonal relationships of their home proved particularly challenging. According to "domestic utopia," the intimate collectivity of familial relations fosters, rather than threatens, the artist's individual creative authority. In theory, *The Rose* could thus exemplify the lonely striving of the Romantic artist even as it physically depended upon the architecture of DeFeo's apartment and the maintenance labor of her husband. The couple's reflections, however, reveal that they often experienced the relationships of the domestic sphere as suppressing, rather than fostering, their individual creativity. Like Burchard's erasure of DeFeo and Hedrick's relationship from their panels in *The Individual and His World,* their recollections suggest that the dance between sovereignty and reliance, independence and intimacy, required to embed high modernism's visionary genius within the shared space of the home proved difficult to choreograph.

The friction within the relationship that DeFeo and Hedrick built around *The Rose* points up the fact that they achieved a lesser degree of interindividual collaboration than DeFeo did with the other artists described in this book. Hedrick created *Life Game* (see fig. 35) in response to *The Rose,* but DeFeo does not appear to have replied directly and creatively to his painting. Hedrick was also more inclined than the other artists featured in this book to see *The Rose* as a joint effort, to some extent, between DeFeo and himself, the result of a collaboration that sacrificed, or at least compromised, the two artists' individual identities. These discrepancies speak to the fundamental difference between DeFeo's relationship with Hedrick and her relationships with the other Fillmore artists who responded to *The Rose.* They suggest that the bonds of marriage and household disallowed the interpersonal and literal distances required for the kinds of call-and-response exchanges that developed between DeFeo and some of her male friends. Their domestic partnership, in other words, exacerbated the strain between independence and intimacy that suffused the Fillmore community by emphasizing the latter. Whitney Chadwick and Isabelle de Courtivron see this strain as a hallmark of creative coupledom generally: "If the dominant belief about art and literature is that they are produced by solitary individuals, but the dominant social structures are concerned with familial, matrimonial, and heterosexual arrangements, how do two creative people escape or not the constraints of this framework and construct an alternative story?" Hedrick's and DeFeo's struggles to reconcile their artistic and domestic identities thus attested to tensions pervasive not only within the Fillmore community, but also among heterosexual artist couples working within the framework of modernism, as Anne M. Wagner, Bibiana Obler, and others have explored.[75]

Life Game largely leaves out the disharmonious results of DeFeo's and Hedrick's attempts to mix their art and life. Four years earlier, however, Hedrick alluded to the tensions discussed here in *J. Me et Cat* (fig. 54). Painted the year the couple married, it reads as a subversive "family portrait" that substitutes a cat, the mascot of bohemia, for the obligatory offspring of the heterosexual nuclear family.[76] The work depicts the eponymous figures in styles reminiscent of their art, foreshadowing how *Sixteen Americans* would reduce DeFeo and Hedrick to ciphers for high modernism and postmodernism, respectively, while obscuring the gray area that "domesticized high modernism" proposes between them. DeFeo is represented by a dripping, black oval and mustard stripe that loosely correspond with the gestural abstractions she was painting at the time. Hedrick denotes himself with an etched, rectilinear column of interlocking geometries that recalls both his Klee-esque painting style and welded wire sculptures of the

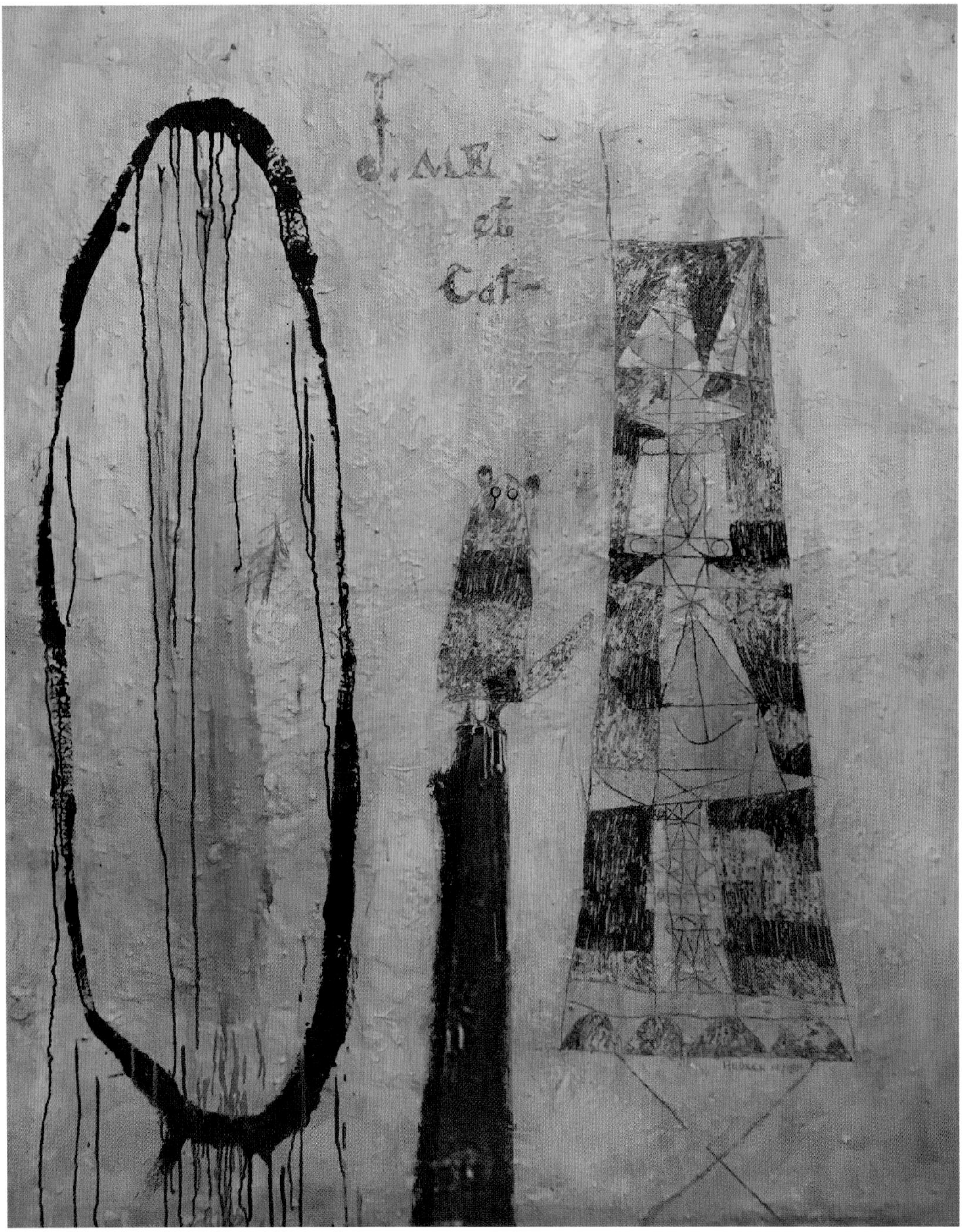

Fig. 54 Wally Hedrick, *J. Me et Cat*, 1954. Oil on canvas, 47 × 57 in. (119.4 × 144.8 cm). Collection of Lawrence Fox.

mid-1950s. The couple's cat perches, like a cartoonish sculpture, on a plinth between them. Except for the basic column on which the cat sits, Hedrick makes no effort to describe the brimming, private environment that he and DeFeo would soon build together. The painting support is the most rudimentary cipher for "home." The figures, that is, are utterly decontextualized, as if to ward off any specters of environmental influence. The peach background, whimsical font, playful use of French, and childlike way the figures line up along the bottom of the support give the painting the warm, lighthearted tone expected for a depiction of newlyweds.

The irresolvable stylistic differences between the figures strains this cheeriness, however. The characters queue up along the edge of the canvas, but the serial composition refuses to subsume them into a cohesive whole. Instead, their juxtaposition underscores their distinctiveness. Next to the spritely decoration of Hedrick's emblem, the yawning muteness of DeFeo's rudimentary avatar looks utterly alien. Hedrick's interpretation of the painting, written in 1956, fittingly emphasizes difference: "On the right is myself, or rather how I see the form of my world. On the left is my wife, or how she sees the form of our life. . . . It's a logical portrait containing the paradox of the ridiculousness of the situation together with the frightening revelation that self-delusion haunts all the days of our lives."[77] Hedrick's switch from "my world" to "our life" in the passage is telling of the strain between autonomy and relationship described in this chapter. The artists' disparate styles, he explains, represent their disparate worldviews—subjective visions so fundamentally divergent that the prospect of unifying them, of constituting a shared perspective, is both "frightening" and "ridiculous." He implies that achieving the social cohesion and collective identity that constitutes a family requires "self-delusion." The awkwardness of the painting—the way it juxtaposes but never synthesizes incongruent styles—can thus be seen to perform the strain between unity and independence that DeFeo and Hedrick felt as their identities as spouses and artists entwined within their household. *J. Me et Cat* suggests that marriage made Hedrick acutely aware of the dangers and limits of intimacy and, in doing so, propelled his quest for individuation. Nearly a decade later, *The Rose* helped prompt this conflicted interpersonal dynamic to once again surface in the couple's relationship, this time to end it.

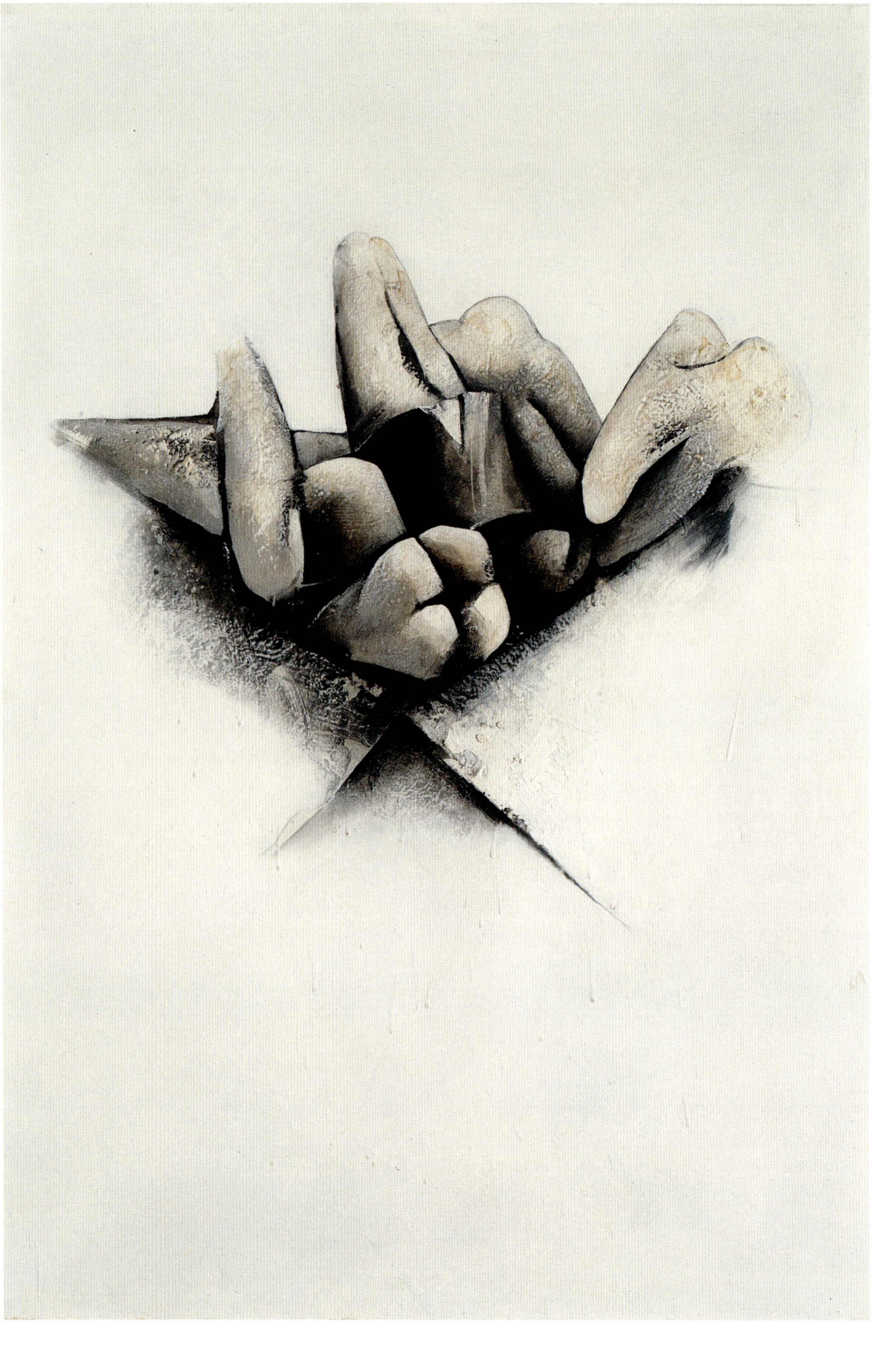

CHAPTER 3

Body Language

EXCEEDING EKPHRASIS

In the stressful tumult leading up to *The Rose*'s removal from her studio, Jay DeFeo solicited her friend Michael McClure to write a text for the painting's debut exhibition at the Pasadena Art Museum.[1] Her request echoed the appeal she had made to McClure six years earlier to write about her art for the *Sixteen Americans* catalogue. This pair of invitations, which bracketed DeFeo's protracted production of *The Rose,* suggests that she saw McClure as an insightful and sustained witness to the painting's creation. DeFeo met McClure in 1956, when he moved with his first wife, the poet Joanna McClure, and their daughter into the apartment above DeFeo and Wally Hedrick on Fillmore Street. "Her studio was right below our [living room]," McClure recalled. "It was like my daughter's bare feet were only eight or ten feet from the top of Jay's head."[2]

This physical proximity catalyzed a relationship between the neighbors that was both social and creative. "I got friendly with Mike and his wife," DeFeo explained. "Mike was very interested in painting and he liked my stuff a lot." However, McClure's notebooks from the period suggest that the neighbors' relationship was not always harmonious. "Wally was a pain," McClure recollected in 2012. "But Jay I was in love with. Everybody was. She was beautiful." A playful note that he wrote DeFeo on her thirty-second birthday testifies to their affectionate relationship: "Jay DeFeo you're a brown-eyed deer an Eagle on a Lily's trunk. I saw you look into the crevice of tenderness and secretly pluck the shamrocks on GOOD FRIDAY!"[3]

When McClure met DeFeo, he already had a long-standing interest in visual art. He moved to San Francisco in 1954 to study "gestural expressionism" with Clyfford Still and Mark Rothko at the California School of Fine Arts (CSFA)—wanting, he explained, "to bring their use of material and thought into my own art."[4] Finding that both painters had returned to New York, he instead enrolled in Robert Duncan's poetry workshop at San Francisco State University. McClure began writing poetry and, later, plays, becoming a prominent figure in San Francisco's literary renaissance of the

Detail, fig. 63

1950s and 1960s. He moved fluidly between the city's various coteries, including Duncan's circle and the Beat writers of North Beach—as indicated by his participation in the famous Six Gallery reading of 1955 at which Allen Ginsberg debuted "Howl" and his central appearance (between Ginsberg and David Meltzer) in Larry Keenan's much-reproduced photograph of Beat writers assembled outside City Lights bookstore in 1965 (fig. 55).

McClure also maintained close ties to the city's visual art scene. "More than any single figure," Steven Watson observed, "McClure provided a bridge between the worlds of art, theater, and poetry that so enlivened the San Francisco Renaissance years."[5] Between 1956 and 1962, the years he lived on Fillmore Street, McClure was intimately involved in the neighborhood's artistic community. He was a founding member of the Rat Bastard Protective Association, a group of local artists established by Bruce Conner, who had been friends with McClure since they met in Kansas as adolescents. McClure not only regularly attended openings at local galleries but also gave readings, staged performances, exhibited artworks, and even found employment at them. He showed paintings from his *Visionary Heads* series at the Spatsa Gallery in 1961 and worked as a desk attendant and press writer for the Batman Gallery in the early 1960s.[6] He sometimes wrote about his friends' works—motivated by either the artists' requests for statements or his desire to understand and respond to their art.

Given McClure's nodal position within San Francisco's cultural underground, it is little wonder his oeuvre reflects the convergence of poetry, theater, and visual art that occurred there. This hybridization resulted, in part, from the non-commercial nature of the scene. Freed from the pressure to market to collectors, the city's relatively scarce and informal art venues instead served multiple cultural communities. As previous scholars have noted, co-op galleries in the Fillmore neighborhood, such as the King Ubu and the Six, were jointly founded and run by artists and poets, and they served as popular sites for not only art exhibitions, but also poetry readings, music concerts, and theatrical performances.[7] McClure was attuned to these intersections. His accounts of the 1955 Six Gallery reading almost always include descriptions of the sculptures by Fred Martin that were on display at the time. "The Six Gallery [was] another instance of the connections between the poets and the painters," he recalled. "The sculptures probably were exactly right and appropriate to be the setting for the six of us at the Six Gallery."[8]

The oracular quality of much San Francisco Renaissance poetry, including McClure's, reflected the intermediality fostered by these conditions.[9] By giving primacy to poetry in its spoken form over its printed form, writers drew poetry closer to other forms of embodied cultural practice, such as theater and action painting. Duncan took this cross-pollination further by staging a reading of his masque *Faust Foutu* (1953) at the King Ubu Gallery in 1955. McClure played "A Boy" in the performance and deemed the event "a marker for everyone." For him, it was not only the setting, but also the

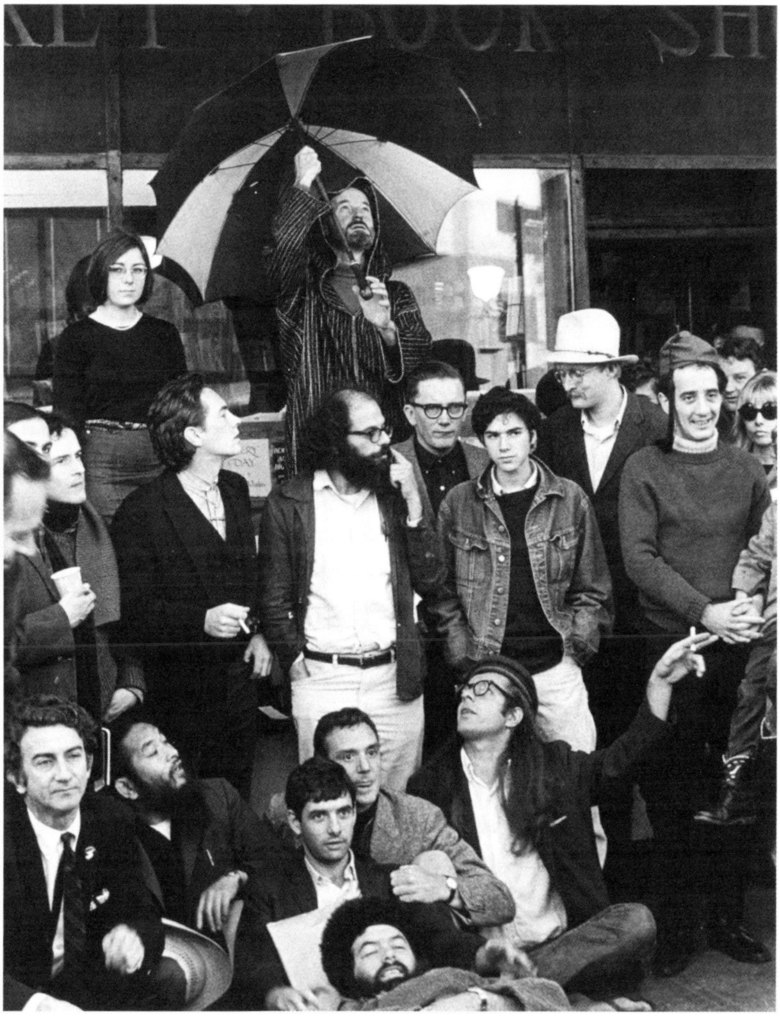

Fig. 55 Larry Keenan, *The Last Gathering of Poets and Artists of the Beat Generation, City Lights Books, North Beach, San Francisco,* 1965. Photographic print, 8⅗ × 7 in. (22 × 18 cm). Photographs of San Francisco artists/Larry Keenan, Jr., 1965–66, Archives of American Art, Smithsonian Institution, Washington, D.C. © Larry Keenan.

diversity of the participants that cultivated an atmosphere of avant-garde possibility. "There was a magic quality about our event . . . because of the people doing it," he asserted, "filmmakers, poets, painters, composers."[10]

In the late 1950s, as DeFeo was starting *The Rose,* McClure began training his oracular poetry in the direction of performance. Following Duncan, he developed the intermedial configurations that resulted (both accidentally and purposefully) from the local practice of holding poetry readings in art galleries into a new performative art form. Commencing with the debut production of *!The Feast!* at the Batman Gallery in 1960, he organized performances of his masque-like plays in local galleries and theaters that deliberately blurred distinctions traditionally drawn between poetry, drama, and visual art (fig. 56). With minimal costumes and staging, these early plays resembled group poetry readings as much as they did traditional theatrical productions.

Works by local artists unwittingly served as mise-en-scènes. *!The Feast!,* for example, consisted of thirteen of McClure's friends wearing

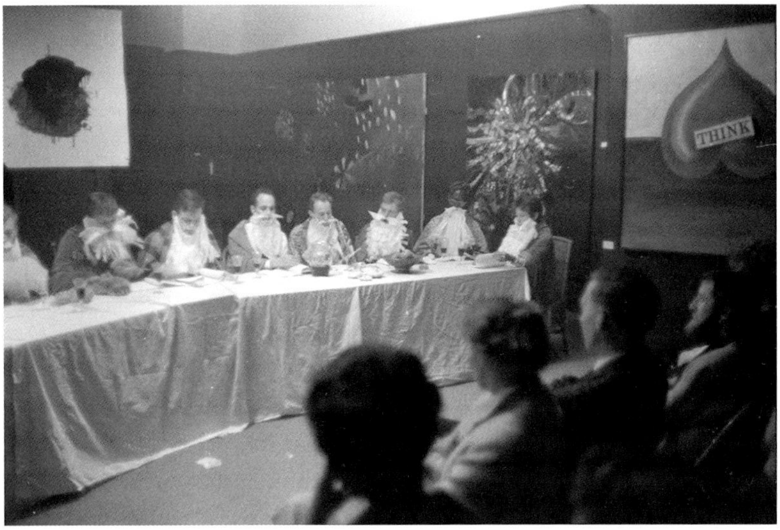

Fig. 56 James Oliver Mitchell, *!The Feast!* by Michael McClure performed at the Batman Gallery, 1960. Digital scan from a photographic negative. Collection of James Oliver Mitchell.

paper beards and reading the script around a table surrounded by an exhibition of abstract paintings that constituted the scene's motley backdrop. McClure continued to cultivate this confluence between the arts when his plays moved out of local galleries and into auditoriums. He commissioned George Herms, an assemblage artist and friend, to design the set for his play *The Blossom, or Billy the Kid* (1964) and incorporated several of Herms's works into early performances of his most famous play, *The Beard* (1965).[11] In the second half of the 1960s, the innovative form and, in many cases, sexually explicit content of these works—especially *The Beard*—helped make McClure a succès de scandale and artistic luminary of the countercultural movement. His performance at the Human Be-In in Golden Gate Park in 1967 and selection as the guide to San Francisco's hippie scene for the television documentary *The Maze: Haight/Ashbury* (1967) testified to his stature as a countercultural figure.[12]

McClure appears to have initially responded to DeFeo's request for a piece about *The Rose* by writing a short poem evincing his current experimentation with performance. The poem assumes the voice of DeFeo's painting, which declares its identity like a Shakespearean actor making a dramatic entrance: "OH I AM ROSE! ROSE! WHITE ROSE."[13] McClure distinguishes his poem from ekphrasis, which James A. W. Heffernan succinctly defines as "the verbal representation of visual representation," by largely bypassing descriptive language. Ekphrasis seeks and invariably fails to overcome the "otherness," as W. J. T. Mitchell has termed it, between verbal and visual media, representation and referent.[14] McClure appears to have attempted to overcome these failures by embodying the painting in the poem—by making a poem in which the painting speaks for itself. That is, by summoning *The Rose* to appear before the reader as a live performer onstage, rather than a described object on the page, the poem sought to conduct the painting's forceful, material presence directly into the reader's sensorium.[15] However, McClure seems to have found the poem's proposed solution to the shortcomings of ekphrasis unsatisfactory: for he crossed out the entire poem, striking through each row of typewritten text. The heavy lines muffle the insistent "shouting" of the poem's capitalized typography, indicating that McClure felt that the poem's attempt to project the painting's "voice," and thus its presence, through the rhetorical tools of repetition, exclamation, and volume had fallen flat.[16]

In August 1965, he tried a different approach, resulting in a second, final poem about the painting. "I'd been in that studio watching her paint," he recalled thirty years later of the process he used to write the second poem. "Then, I did something that I did a lot in those days. When I was asked to make a statement, I would create a deck of cards or the words for a deck of cards and then shuffle them into patterns, and let them repeat back the ideas inherent in the words."[17] His experimentation with word cards was just about to take off when he used them to write about *The Rose*. Later that year, he worked with Dave Haselwood (another old friend from Kansas) at the Auerhahn Press to publish *Dream Table,* a deck of thirty cards bearing two words each. The following year, he and Conner produced LOBE KEY STILLED LIONMAN LACED WINGED APRIL RAPHAEL DANCE WIRY—a deck of square cards rimmed, on one side, with four words provided by McClure and emblazoned, on the other side, with lithographs of mandalic drawings by Conner. Haselwood published a slightly larger version of the deck (under the simplified title CARDS) in 1970, a year after McClure's creation of another set of two-word cards, this time with Pierrepont Press, titled *Lion Fight* (fig. 57).[18]

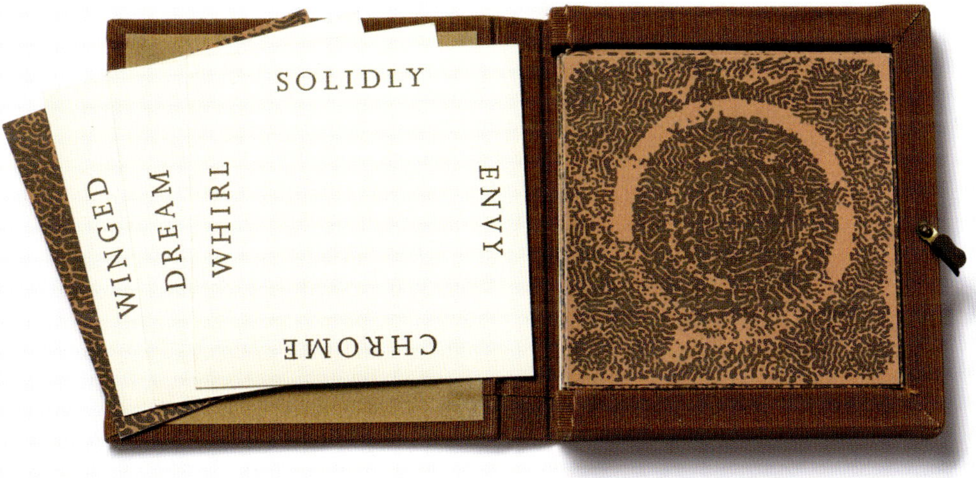

Fig. 57 Bruce Conner and Michael McClure, CARDS, 1970–71. Lithographs on paper and fabric-covered box, edition 19/50, box closed: 5/8 × 4 3/8 × 4 1/8 in. (1.6 × 11.1 × 10.5 cm), each card: 3 7/16 × 3 7/16 in. (8.7 × 8.7 cm). Collection of the Nasher Museum of Art at Duke University, Durham, N.C. Gift of Kristine Stiles [2018.18.1].

The motivations, actions, and outcomes of McClure's stuttering attempt to exceed ekphrasis when writing about *The Rose* are this chapter's primary points of interest. As we will see, understanding that attempt casts new light on the significance of performance to art and writing in postwar San Francisco. McClure's desire to project *The Rose*'s presence directly to the reader suggests that he believed DeFeo was pushing painting in the same direction that he was pushing poetry—toward performance—a conclusion supported by both the content of his poem about *The Rose* and the word-card technique he used to write it. McClure's notebooks from the period indicate that Fillmore artists and writers were inspired to turn to the body by many of the same cultural touchstones—such as Jackson Pollock, Antonin Artaud, and bebop musicians—cited by other early performance artists associated with movements such as Happenings, Gutai, and Fluxus. However, McClure's notebooks also point to a more local motivation—the friction between individual and collective identity and authorship that both McClure and DeFeo felt within the Fillmore community in the late 1950s.

Analysis of McClure's poem and word-card technique, neither of which has previously been the subject of extensive analysis, reveals his belief that performance could alleviate this friction. His description of an intimate association, even identification, between DeFeo and *The Rose* suggests that he viewed her corporeal creative process as transferring energy—a biological, libidinal, and mystical life force—to the painting, a move that, in his view, both consolidated her authority and endowed the work with a living presence. Unlike in standard accounts of action painting, however, McClure thought this liberating energy transfer was dialogical. He believed the creative act instigated "feedback loops" that circulated generative energy or inspiration back and forth between artist, work, and audience—physically connecting them like limbs on a body without channeling specific ideas that might lead to influence or imitation. Through the word-card technique, McClure attempted to translate the corporeal, dialogical dynamic he saw in DeFeo's painting process into his writing process to form a constellation of mutually supporting authors and works that avoided the conformist pressures he observed in postwar American society and experienced within the Fillmore community.

While embodied practice has been emphasized in accounts of San Francisco Renaissance poetry, studies of the city's postwar visual art generally give primacy to assemblage, which is made to represent West Coast artists' anti-formalist embrace of hybridity.[19] Yet McClure's reading of *The Rose* as a version of performance suggests that the body (like the found object) was an important tool for Fillmore artists in their experiments with intermediality. His poem also posits a type of authorship and motivation for performance that is generally left out of narratives of postwar art and literature, both within the Bay Area and beyond. In art history, the transition from action painting to art that takes the body as its medium—an international trend that began in the mid-1950s—is frequently framed as having helped usher in postmodernism by swapping postwar painting's concern with medium specificity, autonomy, and individual expression for an interest in intermedia, heteronomy, and contingent production.[20] In literary studies, by contrast, the emphasis placed on live readings by the Beats and other contemporary poets is often viewed as a return to Romantic lyricism, in which, Michael Davidson explained, "the voice is the outward sign of a unitary, emotive subject."[21] McClure's interpretation of *The Rose,* however, indicates that he saw performance as a means to bridge these possibilities—to merge expressionist autonomy (typically associated with the performative turn in poetry) and postmodernist contingency (typically associated with the performative turn in the visual arts) into a looping relationship between self and world that enabled individual fulfillment through cosmic connection. Reading the poem in relation to McClure's journals also demonstrates that social motivations could complement, as well as complicate, artists' and writers' aesthetic reasons for turning to the body.

DeFeo's response to her friend's interpretation of *The Rose*—which came in the form of a collage she made for McClure some ten years after he wrote the poem—shows that her corporeal experience of producing the work was more multivalent than his poem allows. Through the inherently fractured medium of montage, she adds fragmentation, fatigue, and fragility to McClure's account of the body as labile, libidinal, and liberated. Her amendment to McClure's vision of *The Rose* suggests both the gendered blind spots of his countercultural account of the body and the difficulty of fully realizing the non-oppressive modes of shared authorship and community that he believed the performing body could generate.

A RIVEN COMMUNAL BODY

Beginning in the late 1970s, McClure was frequently called upon to speak and write about the art and literary scenes of postwar San Francisco. The invitations reflected growing historical interest in the city's midcentury cultural underground, as well as the unique position McClure had occupied within it. In these later essays and interviews—many of which were collected in the anthologies *Scratching the Beat Surface* (1982) and *Lighting the Corners* (1993)—he usually characterized the milieu as close-knit and supportive. The scene, he recalled, was composed of small communities of "artists and dissenters who supported and stood up for one another, believed in one another."[22]

Within this intimate context, artists and writers became primary forces shaping one another's work. "We all influenced each other," McClure stated in 1980 of his fellow Bay Area poets. "We felt solid enough in who we were . . . to utilize each other." He elaborated this idea to an interviewer in 1975:

> The wonderful thing that happened to all of us, after we'd got together as a result of the Six Gallery reading was that we got to know

> each other and knock each other's edges off so that we weren't afraid of saying exactly what we thought. And that was at a time when everybody was afraid to acknowledge that anything had influenced them. . . . They weren't chumps like Goethe or Shelley or Shakespeare who were influenced by everything in sight. Like them, the original creators, the discoverers, we took everything, went on every ridge we could go on. We wanted it all.[23]

In McClure's recollections, the collegial atmosphere of San Francisco's literary scene allowed him and his friends to sidestep the "anxiety of influence"—Harold Bloom's term for the friction between continuity and originality felt by modernist poets.[24]

McClure's memories tend to paint a rosier, simpler picture of the community's interpersonal dynamics than do his notebooks from the late 1950s. These understudied archival materials portray San Francisco's midcentury poetic community in a way that is similar to Michael Davidson's portrayal in *The San Francisco Renaissance* (1989), which permits more conflict than do most art-historical accounts of the Fillmore circle.[25] Specifically, the journals indicate that McClure was conflicted about how to develop as a poet: Should he look to the work of others or retreat into himself?

At times, he pursued the former: some entries, for example, describe his plans to write homages and imitations like "'variation on Courbet by Picasso,'" doing "my own way with poems by others."[26] Other times, he rejected all contact, feeling it impeded his individual creativity. He chided himself to "sluff off all influence" and demanded that each "poem must come from myself and not from another poem." In another entry he lamented, "I keep looking for something to inspire myself, but no longer will anything inspire me until I win through and inspire myself."[27] His vacillation between an outward-facing and inward-facing path forward is most strikingly evident in the shifting lists of "heroes"—cultural figures such as Pollock, William Blake, Charles Olson, and Jack Kerouac—that McClure frequently wrote in his notebooks. "You are all incorporate[d] into me / All incorporated into my personality," he announced grandly after one such list. However, only a few entries after so declaring his allegiance to, even indivisibility from, these models, he asserted his independence from them by writing "NOT" followed by the same string of names and, at the end of the list, "BUT MIKE." This expression of Oedipal apprehension is indicative of the struggle of modern writers to assert their independence from tradition, which Bloom identified as the "anxiety of influence."[28]

McClure's equivocations about opening himself creatively went together with doubts about opening himself socially in part, no doubt, because the intimate nature of the city's cultural scene inevitably entangled aesthetic affiliations with social relationships. Under these conditions, artists and writers in postwar San Francisco were more likely to feel the anxiety of influence in relation to their immediate peers than in relation to canonized figures of previous generations, as Bloom emphasized. Some of McClure's notebook entries express a hunger for belonging, if not dependence, that supersedes creative affiliation, reading as a desire for friendship and community. "We become antenna for one another," McClure wrote of his relationship with Duncan's circle. "Robert Jess Helen I etc serve one another as appended organs of senses incomplete in one another."[29] But this feeling of belonging, of wholeness and completeness within the group, could quickly sour. "I learn from RD," McClure noted of Duncan in a later notebook, "but he poisons me. . . . We must preserve individualities. Each of us is separate aloof or we are nothing." The older writer's creative influence is inseparable here from his personal influence; both potentially stifle McClure's individuality. He similarly counseled himself on another occasion: "Don't be dependent upon anyone for anything—approval or amusement or friendship." Clearly, the prospect of friendship could easily become fraught for McClure when cultural allegiances were involved, as is likewise evident in the following entry about his relationship with the Beat poets: "Important realization: There is absolutely no reason to try to please any N. Beach characters. I am disaffiliated from them as well as from anyone else. . . . There is no reason to ever seek or want their friendship."[30]

In the notebooks, McClure's relationships with visual artists generally seem less fraught than his relationships with other writers. DeFeo, for example, appears only occasionally and in entries that are relatively neutral, if not notably favorable. For example, he included "J. & Wally" on an extensive roster of "Friends & acquaintances & enemies in SF," mentioned "J. DeFeo" again in a "TURN-ON LIST" from 1962, and cited her (along with Conner) in a poem about the Rat Bastard Protective Association, which he appears to have written for (but ultimately withdrew from) the 1959 San Francisco Art Association Annual Exhibition catalogue.[31] Perhaps the disparity between McClure's perception of his relationships with artists and with writers indicates that the visual artists of the Fillmore neighborhood experienced less creative and interpersonal conflict than the city's writers, or, alternatively, McClure could simply have been less inclined to feel threatened by acquaintances working outside his field. A journal entry from 1957, however, indicates that McClure also, at times, felt competition playing out across disciplines. "It is our job to tell the painters what to do," he wrote, contradicting the many declarations of admiration for visual artists in his journals. "Painting goes on along behind writing. Painters are dumb."[32]

Either way, McClure's wariness of social belonging echoed popular period apprehensions about the conformity of postwar America. He made this context explicit in the following undated note: "One of the evils of society is that it works upon us continually to prevent us from being affective beings and feeling our interior stalks, and depths and silences, growls, and pleasures. We are constantly turned outward (—or asked to turn ourselves inside outward) for the usage and pleasure of others. The end of this is that at last, in the highest ideal of commercial society, we can no longer claim to be a 'presence' . . . and we are left with so little that is purely our own feeling that we become frightened of our deep emptinesses."[33] In McClure's view, consumerism and social pressure to adopt normative values alienate the individual from intrinsic emotions, intuitions, and desires.

This account of the hollowing out of the self by society resonates with sociologist David Riesman's theory of the rise of "other-directed" individuals in the industrial era, popularized by his book *The Lonely Crowd* (1950). It aligns as well with Herbert Marcuse's theory of "one-dimensional man," proposed in his eponymous book of 1964, which argues that consumer capitalism breeds hegemony, quashing freedom and independent thought by estranging individuals from their authentic needs.[34] As discussed in the introduction to this book, such beliefs were prevalent among the writers and artists of the San Francisco Renaissance, who frequently viewed mainstream society as an oppressive, alienating, and deforming force that prevents individual self-fulfillment.

These views were confirmed by incidents of censorship, including repeated police suppression and high-profile litigation, around McClure's *The Beard* in the mid-1960s. "In the '50s to be an artist was to be an outlaw," McClure recalled. "They were ready to put you in jail."[35] The notion that society was hostile to the individual helped catalyze California's postwar undergrounds and was a driving ideological force behind the later counterculture. McClure's notebooks demonstrate that artists and writers could transfer some version of their suspicions of mainstream society onto their coterie—an intimate community that ideally acted as a buffer between the individual and the postwar public sphere by nurturing, rather than quelling, difference.

In the same period, DeFeo experienced interpersonal and creative tensions that resonate with the sentiments recorded in McClure's notebooks. The incident in question involved the artist Sonia Gechtoff, who with her husband, the painter James Kelly, lived in the same apartment building as DeFeo and Hedrick. Like Hedrick, Gechtoff was affiliated with CSFA, and Gechtoff's mother, Ethel, ran the East and West Gallery several blocks up Fillmore Street. Gechtoff made paintings that, like DeFeo's, featured a virtually monochromatic palette and thick, gestural paint application. DeFeo recalled that the resemblance between their art "started out as a very stimulating thing for me and for her too, I think." The neighbors began to regularly socialize and visit each other's studios—interactions that, according to DeFeo, generated "some mutual influence between us."

Eventually, however, the "continual feedback" between their studios created the impression, intolerable to both artists, that their identities and works had begun to merge. DeFeo remembered: "Oftentimes our ideas would overlap to the point where I would go over and see her, and there would be the painting before my eyes that was still in a germinal state in my head. If you can understand what kind of an impact this had on me psychologically for one thing, it kind of robbed me of my identity, and it also took the joy of discovery away from me, because that's largely the excitement of painting—this groping for the idea." DeFeo felt her individuality slip away as "people in the social scene . . . put us together as two painters who painted alike."[36] The fact that both painters were women and thus more likely to be seen as derivative of male artists, especially by those outside the San Francisco art world, probably amplified the disquiet they felt at being lumped together. Gechtoff responded by accusing DeFeo of plagiarism, even going so far as to solicit an acquaintance to send testimony to that effect to Museum of Modern Art curator Dorothy Miller—actions that left DeFeo feeling "intimidated" and "depressed."[37] In a note to Miller, DeFeo described the stress the situation was causing her: "I haven't any extra energy to expend on those matters which can only upset me far more than it has—to the point where I can't even work."[38] The situation resolved when, upon Ethel's death in 1958, Gechtoff and Kelly moved to New York. While aberrant in its extremity, the evolving relationship between DeFeo and Gechtoff demonstrates that, despite the bonds of their coterie, Fillmore artists were vulnerable to the social tensions and artistic anxieties that plagued their literary counterparts—ills that the intimacy of the underground could, in fact, exacerbate.

In the late 1950s, then, both McClure and DeFeo appear to have felt acutely a particular version of the anxiety of influence: a tension between, on the one hand, the desire for social belonging and creative openness—demonstrated by DeFeo's repeated invitations to McClure to write about her work—and, on the other hand, the desire for individuality and artistic independence that reflected ideals of modernist authorship and period anxieties about conformity. McClure's notebooks and DeFeo's relationship with Gechtoff indicate that the circumscribed nature of San Francisco's avant-garde cultural scene—including the close quarters of the Fillmore neighborhood—fostered opportunities for creative development and friendship; but, contrary to McClure's recollections and later art-historical accounts, it also made hewing one's own creative path and identity as a young artist an anxious affair. They evidence a conflicted process of maturation—of honing one's artistic practice and identity by vacillating between opening oneself to others and chafing against them, between (in McClure's biological lexicon) appending oneself onto the communal body and amputating oneself from it.[39]

In the introduction to *Lighting the Corners,* McClure acknowledged the deeply subjective nature of the essays on the art and literary scenes of his youth collected in the volume. He described the book as "memory itself; it may have error in it or strange shimmers of events just as memory does."[40] The distance of decades as well as the public venues for his later statements, as opposed to the privacy of his notebooks, could account for the relative sanguinity of his later portraits of the community. No matter the explanation, McClure's poem about *The Rose* shows that he attempted to resolve the tension evident in his journals not only retroactively in his memory, but also through his philosophy of performance and word-card technique.

THE ULTIMATE ECSTATIC ART

McClure described his final poem as beginning with a deck of cards on which he wrote words "about the *White Rose*" while or immediately after he watched DeFeo at work on the painting.[41] A typed transcript of the original notebook page on which he composed the poem shows its development over three stages. First, a list of words snakes across the top of the page in two centered lines:

White Rose Muscle Tone Breath Pearl April Venom Musk Cameo Calves
Caress Rage Ankle Musk Snail Breeze Heel

Unconnected by verbs or punctuation, the unbroken string of nouns gives each the concrete, independent feel of a word written on a separate card. Below, another, longer list repeats some of these words and adds others:

> WHITE ROSE is curl, is stretch, is breath, is lips, is gentle, is tongue-tip, is blond, is moving, is powder, is heel, is anger, is brow, is drip, is grace, is plump, is soft, is petal, is pollen, is black, is velvet, is snail, is languor, is smoke, is mount, is cloud, is blue, is pout, is stroke, is strike, is sleep, is envy, is caress, is deep, is thigh, is lisp, is silver, is sweat, is smile, is white, is shine, is ankle, is furnace, is fur, is touch, is cameo, is rage, is pale, is musk, is red, is profile, is toe, is damp, is hook, is high, is hips, is dark, is moist, is pearl, is flowing, is venom.

Here, McClure has made a rudimentary attempt to shape the disparate words into a syntactical whole. His insistent iteration of "is" gives the version the repetitive quality of a mantric chant. In the third and final iteration, which McClure referred to as a "summation," words from the above lists are combined with others to form a coherent poem:

WHITE ROSE is tongue-tip furnace pollen of Jay DeFeo's muscle-
tone. A yogic breath held for five years.—A perfect painting. A
dream of sweat in shape
of petal!
A Veronica!
A pure gesture!
A perfumed thorn
&
spiked blossom
—A damp cameo of hips and rage

—AND SMILES AND VELVET!
I can't separate Jay
from her painting and I think of her Arms.
TOO MUCH![42]

The first sentence of McClure's final poem about *The Rose* signals the ways he changed course after his earlier, inadequate attempt to honor his friend's request. McClure's first, brief poem about *The Rose* had read:

OH I AM ROSE! ROSE! WHITE ROSE
OH I AM ROSE ROSE WHITE ROSE AND READ WITH GOLDEN POLLEN
OF DREAM OH! OH! OH! OH! OH! OH![43]

Almost entirely given over to proclamations of self-existence made emphatic by the repeated use of capitals, exclamation marks, and "ohs," the poem rallies an arsenal of declaration to insistently hammer home the painting's presence to the reader. In the final poem, by contrast, "OH I AM ROSE!" has become "WHITE ROSE is," shifting the point of view from first to third person. Now, DeFeo's painting appears before the reader not as a voice declaring its own identity, but as an object of the author's description, as in traditional ekphrasis. Rather than represent the painting as a self-sufficient entity, however, the first line places it in relation to its maker, as a product "of Jay DeFeo's muscle- / tone." Thus, the final draft still diverges from conventional ekphrasis: its implicit primary focus is DeFeo's painting process, rather than the painting as a finished product. The poem thereby seeks to reproduce the circumstances of its own creation, which involved McClure treating DeFeo's production of *The Rose* as a performance to observe.

In this way, the final poem (like the earlier draft's presentation of DeFeo's painting as an actor) indicates that McClure perceived a kinship between *The Rose* and his intermedial project to push poetry toward performance. In the mid-1950s, McClure began to experiment with ways to make poetry via somatic expression by drawing on diverse contemporary art forms based in embodied and, to varying degrees, improvised action—including bebop jazz, abstract expressionism, Artaud's theater of cruelty, and Olson's projective verse. Looking back on this cultural moment of experimentation, he later recalled how it helped inspire the oracular tendencies of San Francisco's postwar poetry scene, including his own embrace of performance:

> The falsity, the academicism, the love-lack, the inertia of the poetry that was there when we came along . . . said to us, "Go back into yourself and find out what your perceptions tell you, what your sensorium tells you, sight, sounds, smell, touch, taste." Okay, if we look around at who's doing that, we see people like Clyfford Still and Jackson Pollock. . . . There's Miles Davis, Thelonious Monk. . . . You're looking for people who are saying something new with their

bodies. . . . You become more conscious of yourself as an organism, and you find that there's somebody named Charles Olson, and he has an idea that it's by breath and by energy.

Thus inspired, McClure abandoned prescribed forms in order to embrace an embodied writing process that, like Olson's projective verse, involved "the witnessed object, or event, passing through the sensorium of the poet and then being projected onto the page or air in the breath line of the poem."[44]

In the final version of his poem about *The Rose,* the centered text, liberal capitalization and exclamation marks, and seemingly erratic line breaks act as typographic techniques to capture his breathing and vocal modulations. Shape—the visual appearance of the poem printed on the page—was one means by which McClure attempted to make his writing corporeal and gestural. "One of the reasons for the shapes of my poems," McClure explained, "is to give body language to the poem itself."[45] He hoped that translating his physical experience of creating poems in this way would result in texts that escaped the pallid realm of the semiotic and mimetic by conducting not only his ideas but also his presence—the energy generated by the give-and-take between his sensory perception of the world and his bodily action upon it—directly to the listener.

In a later essay, he described first achieving these vivifying effects with his poem "Rant Block" (1961): "I believed that *Rant Block* began to tug and pull and move like an organism—that like a wolf or salmon it could turn its head from side to side to test the elements and seek for breath. I wanted to write a poem that would come to life and be a living organism. . . . The poem . . . was a breakthrough because it went through the crust of the verbal universe for a sea lion swim in the world of physiology."[46] Much as Pollock wanted his drip-painting technique to "express" rather than "illustrate" his feelings, so McClure wanted his corporeal writing process to produce texts with, as literary scholar Stephen Gregory put it, "a greater urgency, vitality, immediacy, and force of expression" that were animate participants in, rather than mere representations of, the world.[47]

McClure believed that, more than any other medium, performance allowed energy to flow directly from the writer's body to the performer's body to the viewer's body, giving words the force of reality and life. In this way he was like many American playwrights and artists of his generation whose concepts of performance were influenced by Grove Press's 1958 publication of the first English edition of Artaud's *The Theater and Its Double.* In this collection of essays, the surrealist Artaud lays out his prescriptions for a "theater of cruelty," which rejects the canon and mimetic, psychological drama in favor of "plastic and physical" drama that utilizes "the vibrations and qualities of voice" to manipulate language not as symbols to communicate meaning, but rather "like a solid object" that can "fascinate and ensnare the organs" of the audience. By calling for theater that communicates "with pure forces" and physically assaults the audience's "entire organism," Artaud offered a solution to some of the difficulty that McClure felt in conveying presence through language.[48] McClure's description of his own plays as "ENERGY DRAMA" and "projective verse turned theater" indicate that he saw them as extensions of his experiments with making poetry that could overcome the limitations of language to "become a breathing creature."[49]

Writing in his notebook in 1958, just as he was beginning to compose plays, McClure suggested that the act of making a visual artwork could be the ideal performance. The entry in question recounts thoughts sparked by a recent conversation with a friend, most likely Wallace Berman:

> Wally has told me of photographs he has just seen in a catalog of Japanese art. A stage performance—a man in a huge box or vat of clay making in front of the audience his work of art. From this I can visualize the ultimate ecstatic art. The making of huge strange Kachinas as a performance with small settings and a small audience watching the birth of the art. The Kachina should be destroyed afterwards. Only photos of the artist and his doll, works, Kachina, left remaining.

The inspiration for McClure's fanciful reimagining likely included Japanese artist Kazuo Shiraga's performance *Challenging Mud* (1955), photographs of which were published in the journal of the Gutai art movement and circulated internationally in the 1950s.[50] Unlike Shiraga's work, however, McClure's vision bears hallmarks of Artaud's emphasis on the ritualized deployment of mise-en-scène, often appropriated from non-Western cultures. By referring to the act of artistic production as a "birth" and the product it yields as "Kachinas" (supernatural beings who some Pueblo peoples believe can be summoned to the world of the living by masked dancers who impersonate them), the passage suggests that McClure saw this ritual as a way to make art that possesses a living presence.[51] Moreover, his prescription to destroy the product of the ritual confirms his intention to make an art of pure presence—of "ecstatic" energy transmission between bodies unmediated by words or objects, and one that could be achieved by intimately witnessing the act of creation, as he did with *The Rose*. McClure, in other words, appears to have read DeFeo's protracted painting process as symptomatic of the interdisciplinary turn to the body that he observed both locally and internationally, and from which he saw his own performances emerging.

McClure's final poem about *The Rose* suggests the type of authorship produced, in his estimation, by DeFeo's transmutation of action painting toward ritual action. His description of *The Rose* as "a pure gesture!" echoes popular period accounts of the abstract expressionist mark as evincing an indexical and existential relationship between artist and work.[52] His use of the terms "sweat," "breath," and "pollen," however, characterize *The Rose* as an index created by emanations (ephemeral and ethereal secretions) from DeFeo's body, rather than by gestures (decisive and discrete actions) made by her body. The relationship his poem conjures between artist and work is thus more intimate and biological than most accounts of action painting. In the penultimate line, this intimate relationship morphs into identification as he confesses: "I can't separate Jay / from her painting." No longer simply an autobiographical trace, the work is now indistinguishable from the artist's body and being. McClure described his own somatic writing process as similarly blurring the boundaries between self and work. As "direct emotional statement[s] from the body (from the organs and from the energy of movements)," his poems were, he claimed, "extensions of myself as much as my hand or arm are extensions of me."[53]

In a later interview, McClure related the corporeal connection he felt to his poems (and that DeFeo, in McClure's view, felt to *The Rose*) to his somewhat idiosyncratic reading of action painting: "A poem can be an overall organism, the direct extension of our biological selves in the sense that Jackson Pollock or Franz Kline imagined Abstract Expressionism to be a spiritual autobiography—an extension of their arm's energy leaving a trail of paint. I picture poems as being the same kind of extension."[54] By generating works that are emanations or extensions of the artist, the turn to performance, in McClure's account, assured the artist's sovereignty—helping, in theory at least, to quell the insecurities about originality that both he and DeFeo had experienced.

Moreover, the mystical and erotic connotations that the poem attributes to DeFeo's relationship to *The Rose* suggest that McClure saw performance as a means not only of consolidating the artist's authority, but of doing so without severing the artist from the communal body. His qualification of "breath" with "yogic" and "sweat" with "dream of" imply that DeFeo's connection to her canvas is simultaneously physical and metaphysical, bodily and visionary. His characterization of the painting as "a Veronica!" continues this pattern. The reference is intriguingly multivalent: it evokes not only the Veil of Veronica but also DeFeo's painting *The Verónica* (1957) and the bullfighting maneuver after which she titled it. By likening *The Rose* to a holy relic—the portrait that Saint Veronica is said to have produced by wiping Jesus's face during his march to Calvary—McClure indicates that the painting too is both a material index and a miraculous image of the artist's body. Additionally, the surreal phrase "tongue-tip furnace pollen" gives the poem's account of corporeality a sensual cast by alluding to heat and animal and plant sexuality. Other lines (for example, "dream of sweat," "damp cameo of hips and rage," and "SMILES AND VELVET") combine references to body parts or functions with haptic descriptors to further portray the relationship between artist and work as distinctly libidinal. Through these mystical and erotic associations, which do not exist in typical accounts of action painting, McClure implicitly attributed aspects of his own somatic writing process—specifically, agnosia and revolt—to DeFeo's making of *The Rose.* In doing so, he asserted that her performative painting process opened abstract expressionism's autonomous act to dialogue and its independent artist to the world, thereby easing tensions between individualism and collectivity.

The spiritual descriptors that McClure peppered throughout his poem about *The Rose* indicate that he saw DeFeo's process as akin to agnosia—a term that was first used by Christian mystics to describe the state of engaged passivity needed to open oneself to divine knowledge. It swaps rational understanding and cultural preconceptions for a more intuitive and experiential state of being that embraces mystery, uncertainty, and multiplicity. McClure—in keeping with the poem's mix of numinous and biological imagery—saw agnosia as a way of inhabiting the world that was not only spiritual but also instinctual and mammalian. By writing in a way that embraced agnosia, which involves a continuous dialogue between self and world, McClure complicated the standard expressionist model of the creative act as a unilateral projection from the inside out. He explained this principle of agnosia in a passage about projective verse: "The creation of projective verse is ideally the flowing or pouring of energy through the system (or *systemless system*). . . . [This] must be loosely, yet complexly looped, and allow for invention and stochastic structuring (and possibly chance) so that it may accommodate . . . agnosia—knowing through not knowing."[55] The concept of agnosia thus helped McClure underscore the contingency of somatic expression, an idea that also surfaces in many of DeFeo's statements about making *The Rose* (as discussed in the previous chapter). Agnosia emphasized that intuitive, corporeal production involves ceding rational control not only to the repressed parts of oneself, but also to one's environment—to, for example, the existing marks on a canvas or a riff laid down by another musician.

In 1989 McClure dedicated a poem about agnosia titled "Dark Contemplation" to DeFeo. The inscription confirmed the earlier poem's hints that he perceived in her production of *The Rose* the intuitiveness, quietude, and dialogical openness that typify agnosia. He reiterated these traits in a later interview, recalling that during his visits to her studio "sometimes she would just sit on this stool, just contemplate, . . . silently and quietly, and not paying attention to anything else. Kind of the way . . . a lion watches a fly."[56] He attributes to DeFeo the tranquil but alert, animal-like receptivity that exemplifies agnosia. The memory indicates that he found the moments of contemplative evaluation in DeFeo's process to be just as important as the moments of physical labor because they evidenced the dialogical nature of her practice. They showed that her manipulation of the paint surface was driven by her open-ended reception of it, creating an "energy loop" between artist and work that propelled the painting's production in a relational, non-teleological manner. For McClure, then, agnosia was a tool that both he and DeFeo used to achieve the creative openness that they had longed for, but been wary of, as young artists.

By including erotic imagery in his poem about *The Rose,* McClure also drew a parallel between DeFeo's production of the painting and revolt, his term for the act of releasing repressed erotic impulses and a crucial component of his somatic writing process. Like many figures associated with the Beat and countercultural movements (including Marcuse), McClure identified society's restriction and regulation of sexuality as a root cause of oppression. He saw the prudishness of mainstream America as a manifestation of Western dualism (the cleaving of soul from body, rationality from instinct, and spirit from substance)—which, he believed, kept individuals both internally fragmented and alienated from one another. Personal, political, and artistic liberation thus required revolt; embracing carnal desire was a path to freedom.[57]

Many of McClure's poems and plays of the later 1950s and 1960s expressed this idea. In *The Beard,* for example, Jean Harlow and Billy the Kid can be seen to represent the false division between mind and body fostered by society's repression of instinctual sexuality. The contentious relationship between the two characters finally gives way to desire as the drama culminates in a simulation of cunnilingus, the union of head and genitals, mind and body—an anti-dualist act par excellence.[58] The belief evident in McClure's work that desublimated desire could help overthrow unjust social strictures undergirded diverse countercultural discourses around sexuality that arose in the 1960s, including in the context of the women's liberation and gay rights movements.[59] The assertion of sexuality in the public sphere is characteristic of both countercultural and identity politics, which frequently use personal experience to counter hegemonic authority and catalyze radical change.

Much like the stereotypical abstract expressionist act, McClure's "revolt" was a rebellious, outward expression of the self against societal strictures that, ideally, dredged up one's muffled inner nature, restoring its unique "presence."[60] Speaking some thirty years later, McClure made explicit the idea, implicit in the poem's sensual account of *The Rose,* that he saw DeFeo's production of the painting as a similar act of boundary breaking. "DeFeo, with *The Rose,* makes an enormous gesture," he declared in 1993, "and frees herself of constriction and follows out the inspiration that she creates as she instructs herself with the painting." Through the unprecedented physical feat of making *The Rose,* DeFeo broke all restraint—limitations imposed by society, aesthetic convention, medium, and even the laws of physics—a liberating act that allowed the painting's production to become a vehicle for self-realization. McClure's notebooks are filled with statements about his use of somatic writing to similarly mold subjectivity—a process that, he noted, blurred existential and physical distinctions between himself and his poems, much as he claimed DeFeo's somatic painting process wedded her to

The Rose. "The act of *writing* is the construction of an inner life," he declared in one such entry, "constructing an inner life as a surface appendage."[61]

While McClure's revolt resembled the action painter's rebellious assertion of existential independence and artistic originality, the intended result was not heroic individualism, but self-fulfillment through cosmic connection. "Revolt is a desire to experience normal physiological processes that give pleasure of fullness and expansion," he explained. "The erotic impulse is the impulse to destroy walls and join units together into larger and larger structures."[62] When libidinal energy overflows its dams, according to McClure, it washes away the false barricades that society erected to separate body and soul, and the natural and cultural sides of the self, uniting them like lovers in an embrace. "Fuck does not mean merely the act of copulation," McClure explained, attempting like many Beat poets to recuperate the expletive, "but all ramifications, doings, and movements that give sexual delight to the spiritbeast who is lonely and cold and in need of touch and warmth in his separateness."[63] Now whole, the liberated being can sense its biological connectedness to the entirety of nature, from the smallest microorganism to the most distant star. McClure often described the experience of this cosmic connection as a sense of proportionlessness, a welcome overwhelming of reason and measurement that sounds a lot like sublime experience. Notably, he also attributed this characteristic of immeasurability to *The Rose,* writing in the 1990s that DeFeo created "a sizeless post-Wagnerian art," a "behemothian," "proportionless" painting that is "epic in intention and form."[64]

Agnosia, as an open exchange between self and environment, similarly supported McClure's idea that the creative act produces a feeling of mystical and material unity—a realization that "the exterior is an extension of the interior. It is myriad, it is one."[65] Thus, in theory, agnosia and revolt remedied society's suppression of individuality while fostering connection instead of atomization—resulting in a utopian balance between self and community that many in the counterculture would attempt to strike through "free love." Read through McClure's understanding of agnosia and revolt, in sum, the poem represents DeFeo's turn to performance as alleviating the authorial and social tensions that both neighbors had experienced within the Fillmore community. As a direct transfer of energy between artist and work, performance, according to McClure, secures the artist's authority while opening the creative process to contingency, dialogue, and connection as energy radiates out from the creative act to encompass environment and audience. Thus, while in most period discourses the postwar subject and the action painter had to break free from social and artistic influence to realize their authentic selves, in McClure's account DeFeo could open her process and studio to dialogue in order to realize, rather than jeopardize, her individual creative sovereignty. The poem not only represented but also, theoretically, demonstrated this power of performance: the text was ostensibly generated by material, metaphysical, and libidinal energy looping from DeFeo's body to the canvas to McClure's body to his word cards—generating an appendage-like relationship between painting and poem, as well as between artist and writer, in which each retained its distinctness while being incorporated within the communal body.

By proposing that performance could solve the anxiety of influence and its concomitant social ills, the poem (like McClure's notebooks) confirms the existence in the Fillmore community of a tension between individualism and collectivity. It also suggests a previously unidentified social, as opposed to exclusively artistic or individually creative, motive for the turn to the body in the art and poetry of postwar San Francisco. Whether or not DeFeo and McClure felt that their intermedial experiments with corporeal processes actually resolved that tension in practice is more difficult to determine. Perhaps McClure's perception that he and his friends did, in fact, alleviate the friction between them—or, at least, that they devised ways to do so in theory—explains why friction is almost entirely excised from his later accounts of the milieu.

SCULPTING *THE ROSE* WITH WORDS

Several of McClure's poems from the late 1950s and early 1960s perform the difficulty of conveying presence through the abstract signs of written language. "Hymns to St. Geryon" (1959), for example, opens with "THE GESTURE" repeated seven times across the page. The hyper-iteration of the words undermines their meaning: read individually, each phrase signals McClure's aspiration to make writing an act of somatic expression akin to action painting; read together, the identical phrases become, as literary critic Geoffrey Thurley observed, a "telltale sign of exasperation, an inability to communicate." The mood of desperation grows until, toward the middle of the poem, McClure explicitly narrates his struggle to create a text that will physically impart his corporeal presence to the reader:

> And I am still not swinging it—there is still confusion
> I PICK IT UP BY THE TAIL AND HIT
> YOU OVER THE HEAD WITH IT.
> WHAP WHAP WHAP WHAP WHAP WHAP WHAP WHAP
> DO YOU BELIEVE ME NOW?[66]

McClure's frustration with language is palpable in this self-consciously misguided performance of using it as a bludgeon to beat understanding or conviction into the reader. The vivid physicality of the passage suggests that the source of McClure's difficulty is his attempt to communicate directly, gesturally through a symbolic medium—written, typeset language—rather than through an immanently material medium such as painting or, better yet, performance, which literally conveys an imprint of the artist's body out into the world.[67] It seems likely that the task that DeFeo set for McClure, of writing about her declaratively material work, made him feel this shortcoming of written language even more acutely.

McClure's turn to the word-card technique when writing about *The Rose* was intended to address the challenge of intermedial translation—of conveying the painting's vital, material presence through written language. Like the cards themselves, the details of precisely how they factored into the poem's composition appear to be lost. However, the three preserved drafts of the poem offer some clues, which we can analyze together with McClure's recollections of writing the poem and his related statements about his word-card technique in general.

Inspiration to use the word cards apparently came from a similar deck made by the daughter of a friend. This origin story contradicts Conner's claim that he suggested the idea to McClure, though both stories could be true, with each instance of inspiration having reinforced the other in McClure's mind.[68] Another touchstone for his word-card method was tarot cards, which are referred to many times in McClure's notebooks from the late 1950s through the 1960s. In an entry from 1956, for example, McClure noted suggestively: "TAROT: A book of poems might be a tarot in that one might refer to it to read himself and his surroundings for the purpose of understanding or admiration." Conner likewise recalled using the deck he made with McClure as one would read tarot cards.[69]

McClure sometimes referred to the word cards he made as "word sculptures."[70] The term emphasizes the cards' materiality, making words into concrete things to be interacted with through the body in three dimensions. It also demonstrates that McClure saw the technique as inherently intermedial—specifically, as a way to endow writing with the physicality generally required to make visual artworks. Shuffling, fanning, and flipping through the cards to dredge up vocabulary made overt the physical dimension of creating a poem, which is usually reserved for the more subdued actions of typing and handwriting. The cards also emphasized the corporeal nature of writing by heightening the involvement of the senses. Composing a poem now involved the whisper and slap of cards being shuffled and dealt, the smoothness of their surfaces, the sharpness of their edges, and the alternating foreignness and familiarity of the shapes of words as they formed novel constellations on juxtaposed cards. By making the act of writing more physical and sensuous, word cards aided McClure's quest to write through the body in a way similar to his "beast language," a form of sound poetry that approximates animal vocalizations, which he used in the collection *Ghost Tantras* (1964).[71] Cards thus helped his writing process become more akin to DeFeo's production of *The Rose* as he described it in the poem: they transformed the act of writing into an act of somatic expression, capable of materially channeling the painting's energy in an unbroken chain through McClure's own senses, body, and breath onto the word cards he generated then into his notebook, only to be reanimated through his or the reader's body when read aloud.

McClure's belief that the cards were a way to "add a sensory quality" to writing indicates that he thought they would help him not only describe DeFeo's painting, but also convey its physical presence. Speaking during a workshop on the technique at the Naropa Institute in 1978, McClure recommended the use of "concrete," "real" words that directly correspond to the author's phenomenological experience of the world. "Stay with things you can see, hear, taste, touch, and smell," he advised.[72] When shuffled into random sequences these vivid words could produce disorienting, synesthetic effects—an "arranged derangement of the senses" that he compared to the "high" of psychedelic drugs.[73] In this way, the expanded corporeal consciousness that the poet experienced when composing using cards was transferred to the reader. In its reliance on nouns and dizzying, vivid imagery, the opening sentence of McClure's poem about *The Rose* ("WHITE ROSE is tongue-tip furnace pollen of Jay DeFeo's muscle- / tone") betrays its origin in his card technique and suggests that he wanted the experience of reading the poem to re-create his powerful sensory experience of viewing *The Rose* in DeFeo's studio.

McClure valued word cards because they made his writing not only more physical but also more spontaneous and intuitive, hallmarks of somatic expression. The author ceded control while composing the poem as the word order was generally determined by drawing cards at random. Instead of obeying calcified rules of grammar, syntax, and literary convention, he allowed chance or, more specifically, stochastics (which McClure defined as "controlled chance," "drawing randomly from a *limited* number of possibilities") to suggest how to combine the words into a poem. The stochastic manipulation of the cards also suppressed the poet's rational control, decreasing the likelihood of interference with the phenomenological, intuitive process of transferring presence across bodies and media. The cards also opened the writing process to accident by courting interaction. McClure noted, "There are lots of things you can do with the cards: play games with them, make conversations with them, tell jokes with them, make sound poems with them." The cards could be played physically, manipulated by multiple people like game tiles or tarot cards, or they could be played vocally. Footage produced in 1966 for the documentary television series *USA: Poetry* shows McClure and Conner engaged in the latter activity (fig. 58). They sit facing each other on the floor of McClure's apartment. Each holds a deck of cards that they shuffle through simultaneously but out of synch, reading words aloud as they go. Through this spontaneous, interactive reading, the series' narrator declares, "a poem is improvised."[74] By heightening both the corporeality and spontaneity of the writing process, McClure's word cards furthered his goal of making poetry an intuitive, gestural process—closer, that is, to action painting.

By courting chance, the cards also helped McClure make his writing process dialogical and thus more in line with the concept of agnosia that he associated with DeFeo's production of *The Rose*. Even if McClure generated

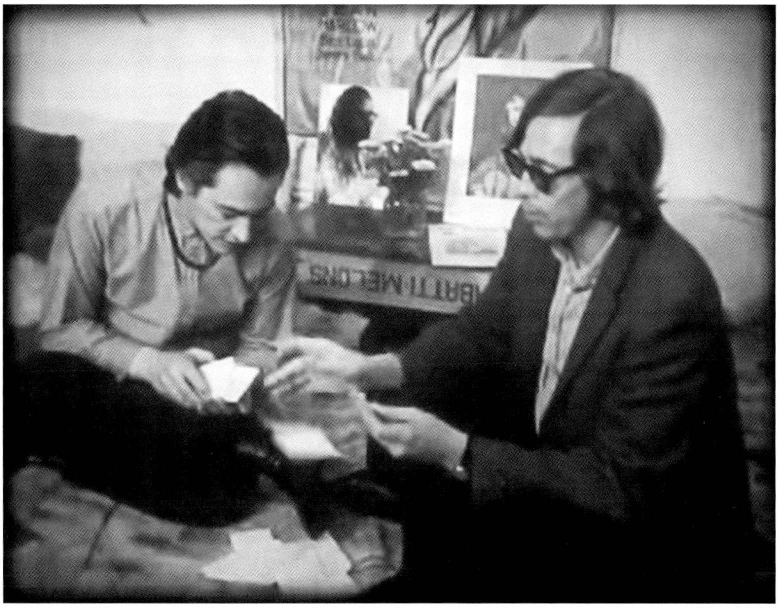

Fig. 58 Still of Michael McClure and Bruce Conner from *USA: Poetry,* "Brother Antoninus and Michael McClure," directed by Richard O. Moore, 1966. WNET, New York.

words for a deck, as he generally did, through free association—an introspective, intuitive process that involved, according to the poet, finding "a rapport with yourself"—the act of externalizing his "interior personal universe" onto note cards and mediating his perception of them through chance made the creative act interactive, an exchange between subject and object. Rather than words flowing in a unidirectional stream from the poet's embodied consciousness, that is, the cards fostered an exchange between poet and world. In this way, the card technique also complemented what McClure called the "systemless system" of projective verse, and the agnosia it breeds, by augmenting its "looped," "stochastic structuring."[75]

When composing poems about external objects, such as *The Rose,* the word cards exaggerated the already relational nature of the act of writing. Indeed, McClure highlighted the inherently dialogical nature of the card process in his description of writing about *The Rose.* "I would create a deck of cards or the words for a deck of cards," he recalled, "and then shuffle them into patterns, and let them repeat back the ideas inherent in the words." By converting internal intuitions into external objects, the cards echoed McClure's thoughts and feelings back to him—a process of defamiliarization that generated new emotions, ideas, and experiences. As with the agnosia that he identified in DeFeo's production of *The Rose,* there was, for McClure, something mysterious about the generative nature of this process. He likened the effect of the cards' interactions, the ways their words unexpectedly reacted with and against each other to catalyze new meanings and associations, to "alchemical" transformation.[76]

The content and form of the poem suggest that the dialogue between DeFeo's creation of the painting and McClure's creation of the poem, which the word cards helped facilitate, was fueled by desire. The interplay between repetition and difference in the poem's structure—the way each sentence proposes a different possibility for completing the opening phrase ("WHITE ROSE is")—mimics the interplay in psychoanalytic accounts of erotic desire between mastery and deferral, between the drive to possess the other and the recognition of the other's elusiveness.[77] McClure's iteration of this formula, increasing use of exclamation marks, and the hourglass shape that the lines make on the page create a sense of swelling momentum, making the poet's attempt to vivify the painting feel increasingly insistent. This crescendo culminates in the final three lines, which erupt into the first person:

I can't separate Jay
from her painting and I think of her Arms.
TOO MUCH!

A driving force behind McClure's frenzied description of *The Rose* is revealed to be not only his enthusiasm for the painting, but also his desire for its author. DeFeo's arms are no longer simply emblems of her gestural technique or signs of the painting's appendage-like relationship to her body; they are also a fetish for McClure, the fixated locus of his desire. "I believe now," McClure confessed in 2015, "I was more in love with Jay than I ever knew. She's heart-shakingly beautiful. . . . I used to love just watching her arms."[78] McClure's encounter with DeFeo's creation of *The Rose,* the experience he wants to transfer to the reader, is shown to be sensual in the fullest meaning of the term—both perceptually stimulating and erotically charged. The poem thus draws a parallel between McClure's writing of it and DeFeo's painting of *The Rose:* both poet and artist channeled the full range of their corporeal experience into the production of their works, achieving McClure's ideal of experiencing artistic creation as a liberating gesture of sexual expression.

As we have seen, McClure's countercultural view of sexuality defined desire as "the impulse to destroy walls and join units together." Desire's ambiguous, seemingly pervasive location in the poem—belonging to *The Rose,* DeFeo, McClure, and, implicitly, the spaces between them—emphasizes its ability to connect. The poem suggests that as libidinal energy drives the creation of DeFeo's painting and McClure's poem about it, it binds them together, merging DeFeo with her painting ("I can't separate Jay / from her painting") and McClure's thoughts with her body ("I think of her Arms. / TOO MUCH!"). The poem thus suggests that desire, as a catalyst of creativity and connection, plays an important role in the production of texts that strive to overcome the material paucity of language—texts that, like *The Rose,* have the ability to physically and spiritually connect creator and receiver. Specifically, the poem implies that sparking desire helps poetry overcome the intangibility of words and the abstraction of ideas by transmitting their energy from the body of the writer to that of the reader.

In a later statement, McClure described viewers of *The Rose* similarly fusing with the work. "We are led so intensely to believe what we see," he claimed, "that we bond or merge with the painting and imagine the stages, steps, dances, layerings, scrapings, and sweat drops that led to that surface." As in typical accounts of viewing abstract expressionist paintings, McClure's viewers decode *The Rose*'s facture to imaginatively reconstitute the artist's actions from the indexical traces of them on the painting's surface. However, in McClure's account, those viewers also "bond or merge with the painting," suggesting that their experience of the work, including signs of its making, are not only seen but felt. McClure later clarified, in 1995, that viewers identify with DeFeo's painting and with her embodied production of it through both the work's hulking physical presence and "the spirit of the painting."[79] To view *The Rose,* McClure contends, is to experience a sense of physical and mystical union with its material heft and, thereby, to empathize with the body that produced it.

One of McClure's goals, then, was for the process he used to write about *The Rose* to help address the challenge (endemic to ekphrasis and evident in the earlier, rejected version of the poem) of intermedial translation—of conveying the painting's presence through the written word. The card technique made his writing process more physical, spontaneous, dialogical, and sensuous. These were qualities that McClure observed in DeFeo's production of *The Rose* and, to varying degrees, in the creative practices (such as action painting and projective verse) that influenced his conception of performance. McClure believed these modes of making allowed artists and writers to overcome, in effect, the mediation of the work to project their corporeal presence directly to the viewer or reader. By mimicking these processes, the word-card technique was intended to aid McClure's quest to channel *The Rose*'s presence—specifically, the energy generated by the material interaction between DeFeo's body and the canvas—directly to the reader. Cards, in short, were an instrument that McClure used to try to endow words with, as he and Kevin Power articulated in conversation, "gestural identities" with "an immense energy charge" that allowed them to "directly work on people." They were a way, as Power articulated elsewhere, "to get this energy of the brushstroke into the verbal stroke."[80]

Word cards, for McClure, provided a potential means not only to exceed ekphrasis, but also to overcome the oppressive nature of influence by generating novel relationships between works and between their makers. He described this power in an untitled lecture, likely written around 1970, about his application of word cards to Percy Bysshe Shelley's "Lift Not the Painted Veil" (1819). The process involved dispersing the key words of Shelley's poem onto cards, using free association to generate more words for each card, shuffling the deck, and finally, using the random cards he drew as the springboard for a long, spontaneous poem. By facilitating an exchange between Shelley and himself, the cards created a poem that McClure felt perched between an "analysis" of Shelley's poem—the truth “beneath the veil”—and an original composition. According to McClure, the word-card method generated relationships that eluded precise definition between not only works, but also authors. “In writing the Shelley game,” he explained, “it was my hope to make some new constellation of experience for myself or a constellation using myself as Shelley and using myself and Shelley.”[81]

This is to say that, by making his writing process dialogical and stochastic, word cards enabled McClure to use other works (by other artists and, potentially, in other mediums) as catalysts for his poems while resisting any conflation with or mimicry of the artists or their works. They made space for difficult-to-categorize relationships between artists and between their works that could, in theory at least, alleviate the anxiety of influence. In this way, the technique potentially eased some of the tension between individualism and collectivity that McClure and DeFeo felt within the Fillmore circle by helping him strike a balance between imitation and originality, influence and independence. He believed, that is, that the word-card process could help open a middle ground between appropriation, an authorial mode often associated with postmodernism and the postwar turn to performance in the visual arts, and autonomous expression, an authorial mode often associated with high modernism and the postwar turn to performance in poetry. Cards thus provided a method for courting the fluidity between self and other and the resulting mysterious creativity that characterize McClure’s accounts of projective verse and agnosia. It stands to reason, however, that McClure’s anxiety of influence was easier to quell when the author he engaged was, like Shelley, dead—his body and words fixed and distant, in sharp contrast to DeFeo’s dynamic, proximate presence.

Expressions of tension concerning authorship are rare in McClure’s retrospective accounts of the Fillmore community, suggesting that he believed his word-card technique provided a means to work around them. Starting in the 1970s, McClure began to use the terms “inspiration” and “feedback loops” to describe the relational creative activity that he believed the word-card technique could facilitate. The concepts demonstrate McClure’s belief that dialogical production across works, artists, and media—like his poem about *The Rose*—generated non-oppressive forms of collectivity that countered the conformity of postwar America. “Inspiration” and “feedback loops” thus offer frameworks for understanding the constellations between individual and collective authorship that McClure’s poem articulates through its content and, ideally, performed through its making—not unlike the concepts of esoteric hermeneutics and domestic utopia that figured, respectively, in Berman’s and Hedrick’s exchanges with DeFeo around *The Rose*, as discussed in chapters 1 and 2.

In a 2015 interview, McClure identified “inspiration” as the connective, generative tissue that bound his creative practice to DeFeo’s:

> Now, back to being around Jay's painting and around Jay's art and person. I embraced her work. I love her work. I believe that by seeing the inspiration of others we are led to believe in our own inspiration. In other words, we need to see what inspiration is in an active artist to believe in our own inspiration and then that fills us up. Then we think: "Yes, my God, me too, I'm there! We. It's WE. We are artists."[82]

He states that it was not DeFeo's work per se, but rather the inspiration evident in her art, person, and process, that ignited his inspiration, catalyzing his creativity. As he describes it, inspiration is a somewhat mysterious process akin to the simultaneously mystical and physical transmission of energy from object to writer to poem to reader in projective verse. McClure's concept of inspiration differs from aesthetic influence and intellectual exchange in that only the spark of creativity—shorn of ideas, formal characteristics, and other specifics—transfers from one artist to the next. Thus, it eludes rational explanation. "I would sit, when I had time, in her studio," McClure recalled of his visits to DeFeo. "And I would watch her paint. . . . We didn't talk, I just watched. . . . See we didn't talk much. We were alive."[83] Inspiration, according to McClure, is physically contagious: it passes from one warm body to the next without the aid of linguistic communication, spreading in all who catch it the will to create but not to imitate.

McClure's poem could thus, in theory, be both about and of *The Rose*—that is, both an interpretation of DeFeo's painting and a physical extension of it, its literary appendage—without threatening the originality of either work or author. His version of inspiration fosters solidarity while avoiding conformity; it circumvents the power dynamics and homogenizing effects of influence, yet cultivates belonging or, as he put it, the realization that: "Yes, my God, me too, I'm there! We. It's WE. We are artists." In retrospect, McClure saw inspiration as a significant, even structural, dynamic of San Francisco's postwar artistic and literary avant-garde. "It was a community," he stated almost sixty years after writing his poem for *The Rose,* "of people inspiring and counter-inspiring each other."[84] According to McClure, inspiration flowed in his community—as it did in his own practice—in a dialogical circuit that cultivated interaction while suppressing the dominance of any one voice.

McClure also used the term "feedback loop" to describe this dynamic. For example, he employed the concept to characterize the relationship between authors and between works enacted in "Shelley Game," engaging his friend the psychiatrist and ecologist Sterling Bunnell's definition of feedback to do so: "A cell creates catalytic agents that cause, in another part of the body, hormones to be made that in turn affects the cells that created the original catalyst."[85] As the biological metaphor suggests, McClure drew his understanding of "feedback" largely from non-art discourses—including ecology, systems theory, and cybernetics—that he investigated further after reading biologist Ramon Margalef's *Perspectives in Ecological Theory*

(1968). McClure was far from the only cultural practitioner looking to these fields and their formulation of "feedback" circa 1970.[86] This interdisciplinary engagement is evident in works by early video artists and experimental composers, such as Nam June Paik and John Cage, that incorporate visual and audio feedback from electronic equipment; and in installation and conceptual works by visual artists, such as Hans Haacke and Les Levine, that involve environmental and social feedback—projects that the critic Jack Burnham classified under the label "system aesthetics."

Cybernetics, systems theory, and ecology were useful to avant-gardes of the late 1960s and 1970s because they emphasized relationality over discrete objects and identities. They investigated the mutually affecting nature of components within systems: the dynamic relationships that form, for example, between organism and environment, or between user and technology. Feedback—in the form of static on a screen, reverb from a speaker, or changes viewers make to an installation—was evidence of this interaction. As such, feedback provided a valuable framework and tool for attempts to shatter formalism's autonomy of the artwork and humanism's autonomy of the subject. Most artists, writers, and musicians focused on fostering feedback loops between author and work and/or between work and environment. Haacke's *Condensation Cube,* which was realized the same year that McClure wrote his poem for *The Rose,* is an elegant example of the latter (fig. 59). Water inside a sealed Plexiglas cube condenses and evaporates as the temperature of the air around the cube falls and rises, at times due to the addition of more viewers. McClure's understanding of the energy loop generated between author, work, and audience through performance is another prime example of conceiving the work as a dynamic connector, rather than a self-contained entity.[87]

Unlike most of his peers, however, McClure also saw the creative relationships he formed with other artists and writers as operating in a feedback loop, as his application of the term to "Shelley Game" demonstrates. He reiterated this connection in an essay from the 1980s by borrowing the term "veil" from Shelley to summarize his understanding of ecology: "The organism is, in itself, a tissue or veil between itself and the environment—it is also simultaneously the environment itself." Jonathan Skinner aptly interpreted the passage to mean: "It is the very closure ('the veil') of the organism that enables it to multiply points of contact with its environment and to alter its own structural states. In other words, it is only through our disconnection that we are connected to the environment."[88] Like the Plexiglas skin of Haacke's *Condensation Cube,* the veil both seals off the organism and enables its interaction with the surrounding environment. This dynamic parallels McClure's understanding of his creative exchanges, in which the independence of an author and his or her work allows the author to inspire new creations by equally independent authors whose works are then taken up, continuing the circuit of inspiration while avoiding imitation. For McClure, as inspiration boomeranged around the "body" of the community—aided

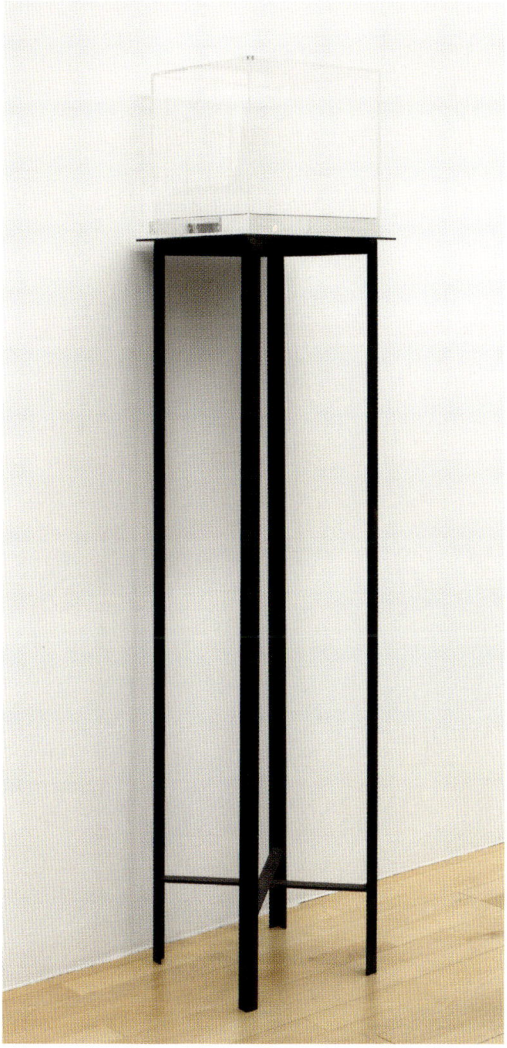

Fig. 59 Hans Haacke, *Condensation Cube,* 1963–65. Perspex, steel, and water, 120 × 120 × 120 in. (305 × 305 × 305 cm). Tate, London.

by dialogical, stochastic techniques such as the word cards—it supposedly entangled authorship in ways that defied the logic of a hard line between individual and collective, organism and environment, cell and corpus, thus shattering the protectionist conception of identity that caused McClure so much grief as a young poet. Feedback thus modeled a balanced, mutually constitutive relationship between separation and connection, closed and open, autonomy and dependence, that resonates with the relationships enacted through the interindividual collaborations around *The Rose.*

By using a biological metaphor to describe the dialogical dynamic of creativity in his community, McClure also suggested that it cultivated the sense of corporeal connectivity that he believed was also produced by unrestricted erotic expression. Hence, inspiration paralleled sexual liberation as a method for producing non-oppressive forms of collectivity that countered both the conformity and the alienation of postwar America. McClure's poem about *The Rose* furthermore suggests that he experienced the circuits

Fig. 60 Photograph by Larry Keenan on the cover of Michael McClure's *September Blackberries* (New York: New Directions, 1974). © Larry Keenan.

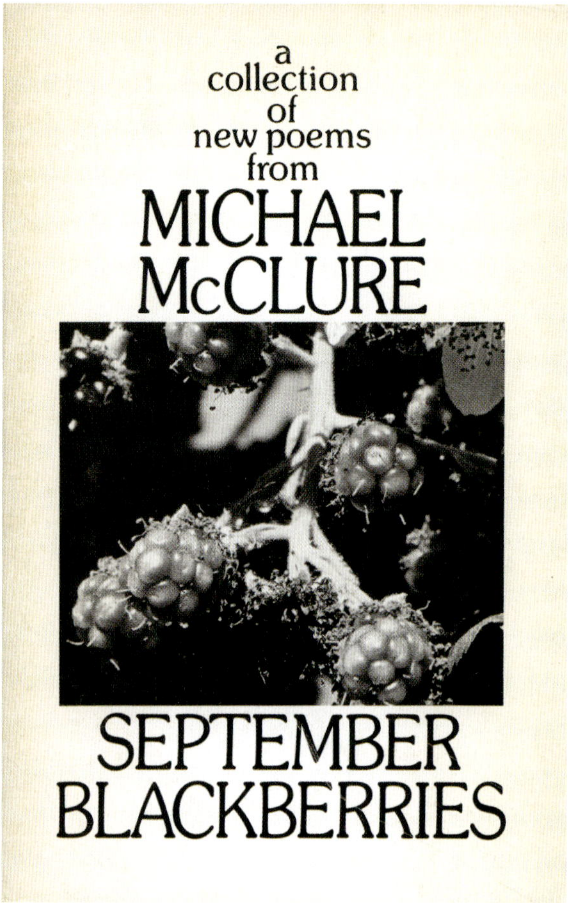

of inspiration and desire that pulsed through his community, liberating his friends as it bound them together, to be not only parallel but also entwined. The poem's characterization of a libidinal relationship between McClure and DeFeo indicates that he believed desire helped propel "feedback loops" of inspiration, like the one between his poem and her painting—that the unifying power of the "erotic impulse," the fluidity it cultivates between internal and external, catalyzed an opening of the self and a tending toward the other that enabled artists in their circle to recycle one another's works while mitigating the anxiety of influence. Another member of the Fillmore coterie, Carlos Villa, similarly suggested that romantic feelings for DeFeo contributed to her male friends' attachments to and creation of works about *The Rose.* "I could see," he recalled, "Fred Martin and Bruce Conner having these kinds of, 'Oh, I can't really say how I feel,' . . . unrequited love for this personage [DeFeo]."[89] The 1965 poem adds McClure to Villa's list.

However, McClure's statement of desire for DeFeo at the end of the poem is notably conflicted. The poem's final line ("TOO MUCH!") has two possible meanings: it could express either the poet's feeling of being overwhelmed by the enormity of his desire or the poet chastising himself for that desire. Either way, as a call for restraint, the exclamation is at odds with

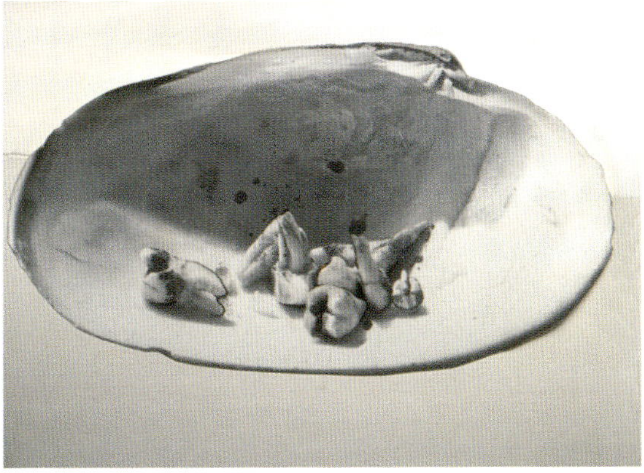

Fig. 61 Jay DeFeo, *September Blackberries,* 1973. Gelatin silver print with ink and paint on paper, 8 × 11 in. (20.3 × 27.9 cm). Private collection.

his typical celebration of uninhibited sexuality. His friendship with DeFeo, and the fact that they were both married to other people, may have made it uncomfortable for him to admit (and for her to accept) his attraction to her, an uneasiness likely exacerbated by the potentially reductive nature of his account of sexuality, particularly female sexuality. The final line, in short, reads as an admission by McClure that the "feedback loops" of desire and inspiration between bodies, works, and media that helped generate his community and its art were entangled in webs of interpersonal relationship (friendships, marriages, and so on) and identity (gender, sexuality, and so on) that often made their generative, dialogical paths more complex and strained in practice than they were in theory.

COMPLETING THE CIRCUIT

Nearly a decade after McClure wrote his poem about *The Rose*—long after he, DeFeo, and the painting had vacated the Fillmore Street apartment building—he sent her a copy of his poetry collection *September Blackberries* (1974, fig. 60). DeFeo responded by sending him a collage of the same title (fig. 61). "Yeah, I gave Jay *September Blackberries,* my book," McClure recalled in 2015 of the exchange. "And, so, as a return gift, she gave me that little collage hanging on my wall there." The work is one of several photographs, photo collages, and paintings that DeFeo created in the early 1970s that feature her teeth and dental bridge that had to be extracted in 1967 due to periodontal disease.[90] Three of these works bear the same title as McClure's anthology: the mixed-media work she sent him, a photomontage, and an acrylic painting modeled on the photomontage (figs. 62, 63). All three were created between 1972 and 1973, roughly contemporaneous with McClure's writing of *September Blackberries,* suggesting that the works and poems were created in dialogue with one another. The photomontage in particular seems to confirm this connection (see fig. 62). It overlays a photograph of her pulled teeth atop a photographic detail of *The Rose* that was possibly taken in the context of recent efforts to conserve the painting (which the next chapter will elaborate). The montage not only references the friends' earlier interactions around *The Rose* but also the changes that they and their works had undergone in the intervening years, thereby bringing the creative circuit between them into the present.

By visually merging her iconic work with a part of her body, DeFeo's collage literalizes McClure's notion that *The Rose,* due to the somatic process that generated it, is continuous with its maker—an idea he reiterated in the introduction to *September Blackberries* by describing "poetry and theatre" as "organisms and biological extensions of the artist."[91] DeFeo's translation of the painting and her teeth into the gray scale of black-and-white photography homogenizes them tonally. Her compositional choices also visually meld the materially distinct components: by affixing the teeth to a dark patch of the painting's surface, she creates the illusion that they are nestled in one of *The Rose*'s many crevices. The bulbous crowns of molars and jutting roots of incisors help carve out space even as they blend with the irregular paint surface, making the amalgamation of the work of art and the artist's body appear both organic and mystifying. The cluster of teeth seems both to burrow into the painting's substantial mass and to rest (as the photograph does) on its surface. The painting thus appears to serve as both a foundational cradle for the emissaries of DeFeo's body and a precarious surface support to which they miraculously cling, thereby evoking *The*

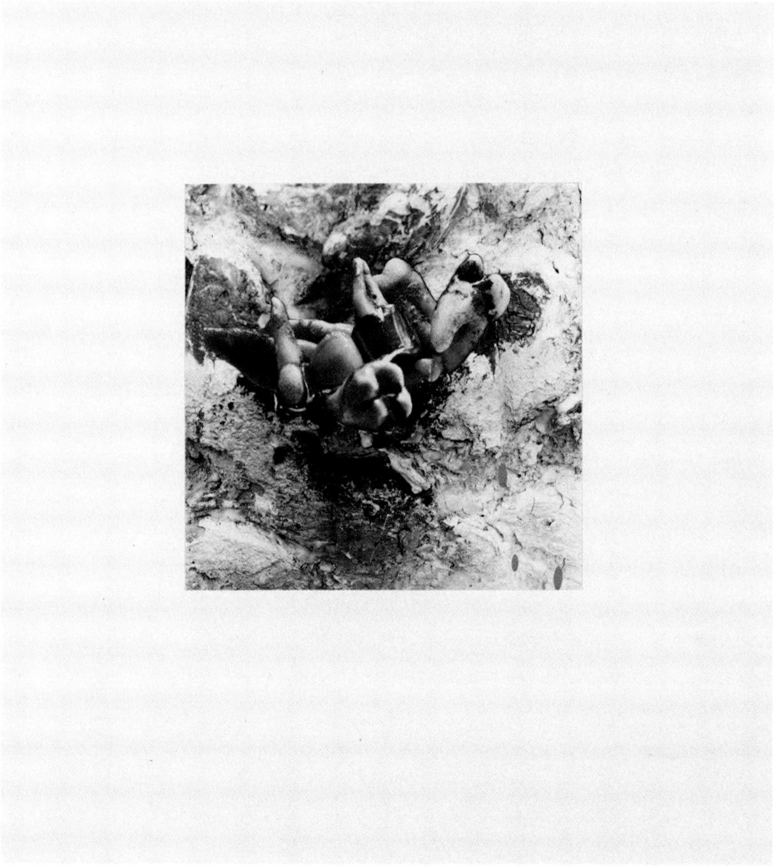

Fig. 62 Jay DeFeo, *Study for September Blackberries,* c. 1972–73. Gelatin silver prints and paint mounted on paperboard, image: 7⅝ × 7⅝ in. (19.4 × 19.4 cm). Whitney Museum of American Art, New York. Purchase, with funds from the Photography Committee [Inv.: 2004.18].

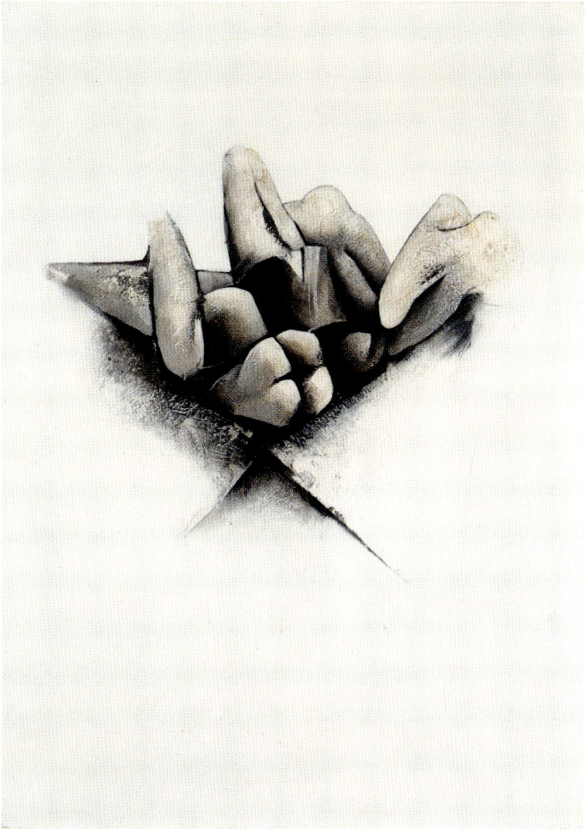

Fig. 63 Jay DeFeo, *September Blackberries,* 1973. Acrylic and mixed media on Masonite, 48⅝ × 35⅝ in. (123.5 × 90.5 cm). Private collection.

Rose's hybridity between sculpture and painting. The way DeFeo juxtaposed distinct images within the collage, in sum, makes it difficult to separate and identify her body (as represented by her teeth) from her painting—thereby representing through montage the simultaneously physical and metaphysical blending of artist and work that McClure's poem about *The Rose* evoked ten years prior.

DeFeo's collage speaks further to McClure's account of embodied creativity insofar as it disorients the viewer with regard to scale. The extreme close-up view emphasizes the painting's uneven, scabrous texture. Without an image to orient to, the fragmentary view of *The Rose* resembles an aerial view of arid earth, and the jutting teeth assume the architectonic grandeur of rock formations—an illusion that DeFeo magnified in the subsequent painting. Once the teeth have been identified as such, however, the viewer's sense of scale shrinks from monumental to miniscule. This equivocation of scale recalls McClure's fascination with proportion or, more precisely, with instances in which he found proportion missing. Proportionlessness, for McClure, was symptomatic of the liberating realization that the self is both physically and spiritually united with all of nature. He reiterated this feeling in the foreword to *September Blackberries,* declaring: "I see all beings as a finger or tentacle of a universe that is a surge of living matter." For McClure, the relationship between artist and work that results from embodied processes was symptomatic of this corporeal connection. "When I make a poem I create an extension of myself," he wrote in the collection's foreword. "A poem is like an ear or shoulder."[92] With the photo collage, DeFeo asked: Can it also be a tooth?

But a tooth, as the collage makes clear, is not the same as an ear or a shoulder. For all the ways in which DeFeo's work translates into visual form McClure's ideal of the work as an extension of the artist's body (a model epitomized for the poet by *The Rose*), the collage also diverges from his ideas in decisive ways. For McClure, the connection between artist and work was indicative of the cosmic totality created by, among other things, the somatic creative act. The liberating activity of performance, like that of sex, brought about the realization that each being is inseparable from the totality of nature. DeFeo's photo collage, by contrast, vehemently denies wholeness. Both the artist's work and her body are fragmented. The close-up view of *The Rose* refuses, adamantly, to convey any sense of the painting's gestalt that, along with its colossal mass and stature, is the source of its compelling presence. The artist's body too has been reduced to shards. Unlike an ear or shoulder (or any of the parts such as arms and hips that McClure named in his poem about *The Rose*), pulled teeth do not evoke a laboring, sensing, or whole body that is the seat of heroic action and cosmic connection. Instead, they evoke a body in pieces—a body of immanently detachable, brittle parts rather than interconnected, resilient, and motile ones. While in McClure's thinking the integrity of the self is realized through merger with the nonself, in the collage connection between work and body requires each to sacrifice wholeness.

DeFeo replaces her friend's celebration of a perfect, immortal, desired, and desiring body with an anxious and macabre depiction of the vulnerable body, shattered and subject to decay. The zoomed-in view reveals imperfections in both teeth and painting, likening the craggy, spotted roots below the pearly enamel and glistening crowns to the flaking, pitted paint surface. Both seem to evidence trauma and entropy. By using a "model . . . out of my own head!," as DeFeo put it, she literalized McClure's expressionist understanding of the creative act as a way of extending and externalizing "our inner life."[93] Instead of leading to self-actualization and completeness, however, this externalization in DeFeo's deliberately flat-footed interpretation leads to a shattering of the self and a sense of loss.

With these features of the collage, DeFeo highlighted aspects of her relationship with *The Rose* that McClure's somewhat romanticized account left out. Her montage alludes to the bodily toll of the physical labor of making *The Rose* and the psychic toll of identifying so thoroughly with her painting—both potential downsides of McClure's model of corporeal authorship that his writings omit. DeFeo believed that the high lead content in the white paint she used for *The Rose* was largely responsible for her poor dental health.[94] In pairing her teeth with her painting, the collage thus brought together not only artist and work but also, from DeFeo's perspective, victim and culprit. The work's representation of the fragmented body also poignantly conveys the anxiety that DeFeo felt about having her teeth pulled—fear about not only the physical pain of the procedure, but also the physic pain of losing a part of herself. In correspondence, DeFeo often expressed the difficulty of reestablishing her identity during this difficult period, such as when she wrote to David Simpson in 1967: "This year has been such a unique chapter in my life I sometimes have difficulty remembering my own name."[95]

Her physical alienation from *The Rose* is staged in the collage precisely by reversing the relationship between maker and made that McClure described: in the collage, the painting unmakes the body of its author. Instead of the painting stemming from DeFeo's body (being the "pollen" of her "muscle-tone"), in the collage, the painting serves as the ground for her deteriorated body, as her teeth sprout from its craggy surface like alien mushrooms or crystals growing, improbably, from a cliff face. The collage thus gestures to the way in which the conflation of work and artist, as in McClure's account of performance, can easily lead to the work subsuming the artist. This reversal generally detracts from, rather than testifies to, the artist's authorial strength, especially, as Greil Marcus has noted, if the artist is a woman. "The myth is now part of *The Rose,*" Marcus explained of this trope, "where the artist is replaced by, subsumed by, the work. The work becomes the artist, and the myth becomes the tomb that holds both the painting and the woman who made it."[96]

DeFeo's divergent account of embodied creativity also raises new questions about McClure's countercultural view of the body. While radical for its time, McClure's account of the body as, to summarize Norman Bryson's definition of the depoliticized body, "a pre-social and biological given" and "a source of mystical value" failed to acknowledge an increasingly common claim among contemporary participants in feminist, queer, and postcolonial movements—namely, that culture mediates corporeal experience by inscribing bodies with socially determined categories of difference and power.[97] Poet Jason Camlot articulated such a critique of McClure's view in 2003, arguing that what is "ultimately absent" in McClure's "poetics is a sociological awareness of the particularities of reception, an acknowledgement that one person's mammalian plasm (so to speak) may not be the same as another's due to cultural or even personal circumstances," a characteristic "most evident in the maleness of the sexuality expressed in his poems."[98] Like so many attempts by Beat authors to valorize marginalized aspects of American culture, McClure's celebration of female sexuality, evident in his poem about DeFeo, risked reinforcing the stereotypes it sought to revalue. His many writings that represent Jean Harlow as an emblem of liberated sexuality, for example, recapitulate primitivizing accounts of the femme fatale that have historically been mobilized to justify the regulation and subordination of women. In contrast, the notable lack of plenitude that DeFeo attributed, through the collage, to her experience of inhabiting and creating art through her body—a body marked by gender and other forms of difference—reveals the limitations of McClure's supposedly universal model of corporeal creativity.

In addition to pushing back against McClure's characterization of *The Rose* from a decade before, DeFeo's photomontage acknowledges the changes that the painting and artists had undergone in the intervening years—the subject to which we will turn in Chapter 4. The "sense of loss" conveyed by the photomontage acknowledges, as Corey Keller observed, "the closure of the chapter sealed by the completion of *The Rose* and its physical removal from her studio," an event that coincided with the dispersal of the Fillmore community.[99] At the time of their exchange, both McClure and DeFeo had been living outside of the neighborhood for a number of years: he in San Francisco's Haight-Ashbury district and she across the Golden Gate Bridge in Marin County. *The Rose,* meanwhile, was installed in a conference room at the San Francisco Art Institute, a limbo from which DeFeo was actively working to free it.

DeFeo's collage signals this new reality by depicting the joint presence of the painting and the artist's body, which McClure fetishized in his portrayal of *The Rose,* as shot through with absence. Their relationship is now founded on the mutual vulnerability of bodies and paintings, rather than on gesture and desire, and is therefore subject to the passage of time. Her montage asserts that change—a force that, for McClure, was indicative of life—also includes decay.[100] By acknowledging the effects of time, *The Rose*'s completion, and the scattering of the circle of artists that formed around it, the collage proposes a relationship between DeFeo and *The Rose* that decisively diverges from the one McClure presented in his 1965 poem. In gifting a work from her *September Blackberries* series to McClure, however, DeFeo expressed her desire to continue their simultaneously personal and creative conversation. It showed that she wanted to share the transformation of her art, body, identity, and relationships during this transitional period with her old friend and former neighbor, despite the distance that had opened between them. The gesture suggests that though she may have experienced the "feedback loop" between them as difficult and problematic at times, she also saw it, like McClure, as generative.

By invoking late-season fruit, the title of McClure's poetry collection also speaks to the passage of time. Comparing DeFeo's photo collage to the cover of McClure's *September Blackberries*—a close-up photograph by Larry Keenan of ripe berries on the vine—shows that the collage emphasizes both the melancholy and the hopefulness of the collection's lyrical title in ways that echo her vision of *The Rose* and her relationship with McClure. By sharing a title with McClure's book, DeFeo's collage prompts the viewer to perceive her pulled teeth as blackberries—a surreal substitution aided by the similarity in scale, detail, and structure between DeFeo's montaged incisors and molars and Keenan's photographed fruit. The association subverts the allure of the plump, dusky berries, which appear just within reach.

DeFeo's reimagining of the book cover further emphasizes waning vitality by clustering the teeth on the close-up of *The Rose* like berries in a bowl—berries, that is, that have been plucked from the vine as they were from DeFeo's head, hastening their inevitable decomposition.

Yet DeFeo's invocation of late-harvest fruit also conjures pleasant associations with time's passage by reminding the viewer that the sweetest fruits are those that have had the most time to ripen—their savor made more poignant by the impending chill of autumn. The collage's likening of DeFeo's teeth to September blackberries, bearers of nourishment and seeds, also frames them as agents of future growth and continued vitality. It asserts the miraculousness of life's persistence in the face of change, even trauma. In this way, the botanical theme shared by book and collage, like the entirety of the exchange that happened through them, confirmed the continued generative potential of DeFeo and McClure's friendship as their lives entered a new season.

McClure's poems, in sum, appear to have impelled DeFeo to express the ways in which his conception of the kind of authorship generated by performance, which he had refined a decade earlier through his poem on *The Rose* and reiterated in *September Blackberries,* converged with and diverged from her experience. This interaction fits McClure's description of a "feedback loop" of artists "inspiring and counter-inspiring" each other in that DeFeo's openness to McClure's poetry, which reflected his reception of her art, motivated her to create new work. However, it also suggests that those circuits of inspiration were often propelled as much by friction as by harmony—that artists in the Fillmore community found one another's works generative because they not only opened toward them, but also pushed against them.[101] Even though it took place across the divide between the written and visual arts, then, McClure and DeFeo's exchange around *The Rose* displayed a similarly fraught dynamic to the other interindividual collaborations charted in this book. The way DeFeo's collage decisively overturns the eroticism of McClure's characterization of her relationship with *The Rose,* moreover, hints that the dialogue between their works provided a means for her to articulate and refine not only her creative project but also her identity as she responded to, in ways that alternately confirmed and contradicted, her friend's perceptions of her art and person. In these ways, DeFeo and McClure's *September Blackberries* exchange suggests that the interweaving of art and community in the Fillmore neighborhood was more complex and conflicted than McClure's theories of performance and inspiration, as well as subsequent scholarship, have suggested. Though less idyllic than McClure's "feedback loops," the concrete examples of DeFeo and McClure taking up each other's works (like many of the exchanges around *The Rose* discussed in this book) also exhibit a dialectic between connection and separation, identity and difference, influence and independence, that the poet believed was necessary to create art within a community and to create community through art.

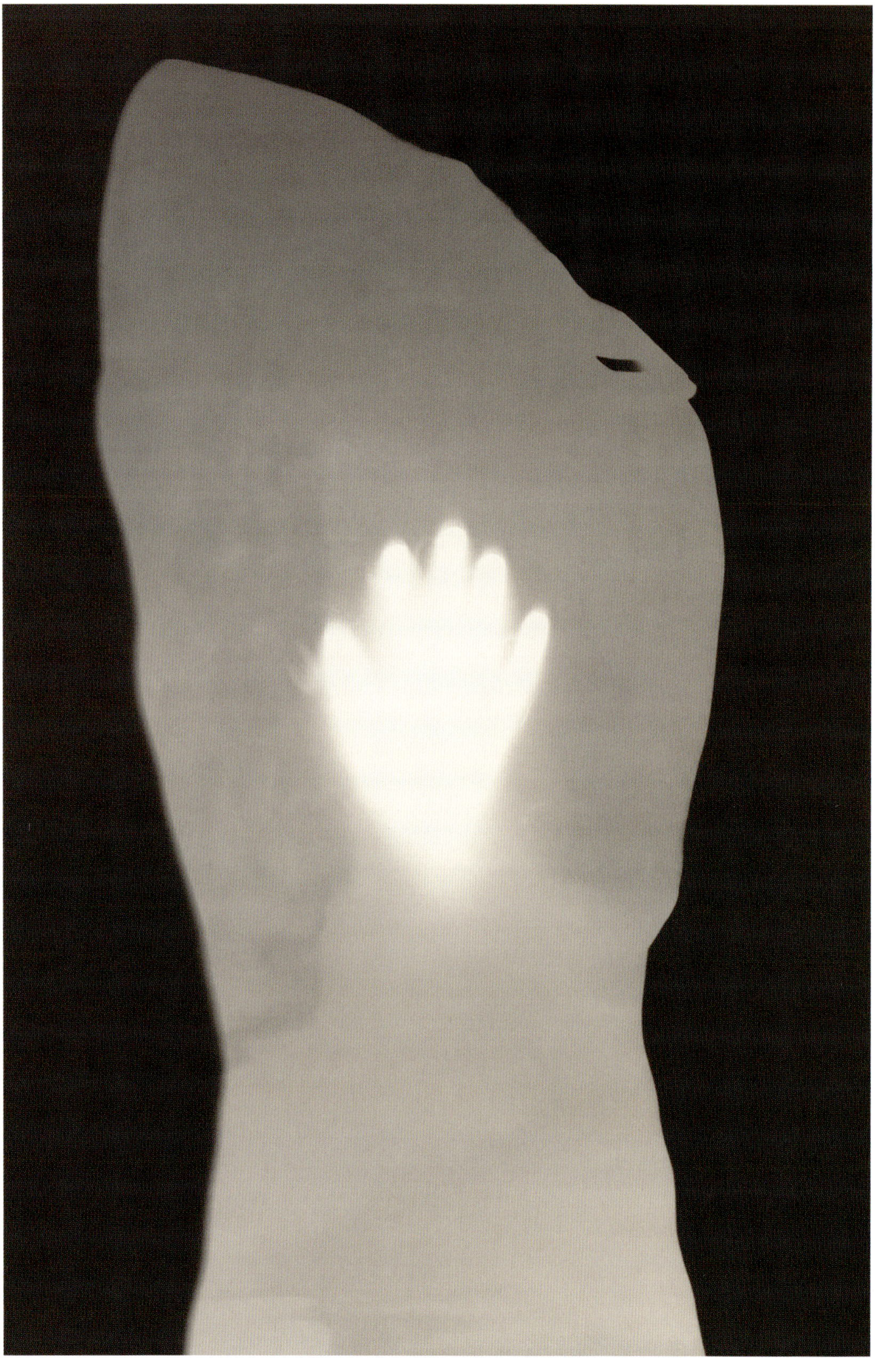

CHAPTER 4

Afterlives

A WAKE FOR *THE ROSE*

On May 21, 1973, Jay DeFeo and the artist Bruce Conner held a wake for *The Rose.* The service took place at the San Francisco Art Institute (SFAI) in the conference room that had housed the massive painting for the past four years.[1] The school was the last stop on the painting's brief and belated debut exhibition tour in 1969, four years after it left DeFeo's studio. By that time, interest that curators and collectors had shown in the painting a decade earlier had faded, and the SFAI conference room that was supposed to be a passing stop for *The Rose* had become a more permanent resting place. In 1971 DeFeo began to solicit museums and private collectors to purchase *The Rose.* After a particularly frustrating round of failed negotiations with the Oakland Museum of California (OMCA), she enlisted Conner in her efforts.[2] The wake was one manifestation of their partnership. Attending mourners—mostly friends and local art-world luminaries—watched Conner's film THE WHITE ROSE (1967), which dramatized *The Rose*'s removal from DeFeo's studio.[3] After the viewing, gathered grievers listened to Conner eulogize the painting and solicit their contributions to fund its conservation.

DeFeo first met Conner in 1957, after he and his wife, the artist Jean Conner, moved to San Francisco. The Conners were following in the steps of Bruce's childhood friend from Kansas, Michael McClure. They settled on Jackson Street, two blocks away from the apartment building on Fillmore Street where McClure lived one floor above DeFeo. Conner quickly became active in the Fillmore art scene, showing in area galleries and attending parties at DeFeo's apartment with Jean in tow. Jean recalled:

> When we first lived in San Francisco in the fall of 1957 she [DeFeo] had a Christmas party . . . and Bruce and I were invited. And, for some reason, Bruce decided to dress me for that occasion. . . . Bruce had seen her [DeFeo] more, because he was always going over there with that crowd of people. He bought a beaded dress from probably the 1920s. So, I wore the beaded dress, and he had some black and

Detail, fig. 80

white feathers that I fixed in my hair. . . . I went to the party with Bruce, and, oh, there were lots of people there and we were milling around and everything, and Jay DeFeo came up to me and said, "Who ARE you?" She was just amazed![4]

The Conners' willingness to create and perform for private audiences of friends shows their easy compatibility with the circle of other artists that was forming in the Fillmore District.

Not long after his arrival, Conner organized artists from the neighborhood, including DeFeo, into an informal collective called the Rat Bastard Protective Association (RBPA). The collective's name (a wry mash-up of the Scavengers Protective Association, a local trash collectors' guild, and the Pre-Raphaelite Brotherhood, an erudite Victorian art movement) signaled Conner's identification with the margins of American society and his wary stance toward mainstream art institutions—values that drove him to embrace San Francisco as his home. Unlike in New York, art in 1950s San Francisco "wasn't a product," according to Conner, who liked that there was "little concern for the art establishment and society's requisites for diplomas, what is art and what is not art, etc."[5]

Those first years in the Fillmore District also saw Conner's art transform in ways that reflected his new surroundings, at times literally. He began creating works from castoff objects purchased from local thrift shops and debris scavenged from the demolition of old Victorian houses in the area. After Conner titled the first of these works RATBASTARD in 1958, the insult became an unofficial moniker for his early assemblages, signaling both their grubby materiality and lowly themes. The assemblages acted like Freudian slips of American culture, revealing aspects of it that were repressed in and by mainstream media, such as sexual fetishism and state-sanctioned violence. The works expressed the distrust that Conner, like so many artists and writers who chose to live in San Francisco, felt toward postwar society. "I think one of the themes of the work," he explained to an interviewer in 1974, is that "the society which we have is alienating to the animal. It expresses power and violence and death and that's its main structure. . . . That people have to deal with that crucifixion of the spirit all the time, and how well they shine through that is the triumph of those individuals."[6] In the Fillmore community, Conner found a group of artists who largely shared his disaffection—a situation that encouraged him to address alienation and repression through his art.

The declarative hybridity, tenuous materiality, and, at times, provocative content of Conner's RATBASTARD works have led many scholars to see them as indicative of the experimental, anti-formalist tendencies bred by the bohemian commitments and non-commercial nature of California's postwar artistic undergrounds.[7] Although he succeeded professionally more than many of his Fillmore peers (for example, he was represented by the Charles Alan Gallery in New York from 1956 to 1965 and was included in William Seitz's *The Art of Assemblage* show at the Museum of Modern Art in 1961), Conner did so while, nonetheless, embracing the marginal status of his chosen home.[8] He believed the integrity of his art depended on his personal and creative freedom, which he cultivated by evading and, often, actively foiling established art-world conventions. For example, he consciously avoided a signature style and medium, working instead across assemblage, collage, drawing, film, photography, installation, and performance.

Conner and DeFeo quickly developed a mutual admiration for each other's art. Even before Conner's arrival in the Bay Area, DeFeo "marveled at the skill" evident in drawings he had sent McClure, and she later referred to the artist as one of her "muses."[9] Conner likewise drew inspiration from DeFeo, recalling that her inventive Christmas decorations prompted him to experiment with hanging his assemblages.[10] Perhaps to acknowledge the source of his inspiration, Conner titled one of them HOMAGE TO JAY DEFEO (1958, fig. 64). The strap from which it hangs indicates that portability is an essential element of the work and recalls how Conner would carry this and other RATBASTARDS to neighbors' homes for intimate, informal viewings.

Conner witnessed the full span of *The Rose*'s development, helping install the work in DeFeo's studio during its remounting and filming its exit some six years later.[11] *The Rose*'s departure marked the unraveling—or, at least, slackening—of the social bonds that had formed around the painting during its seven-year development in DeFeo's studio. By 1965 nearly all the artists and writers who had made the Fillmore District their home in the 1950s had dispersed—including Conner, who relocated to the Haight-Ashbury neighborhood, and DeFeo, who moved fifteen miles north to the town of Ross.[12]

By the time the friends organized the wake, their priorities had shifted from finding a suitable home for *The Rose* to arresting its deterioration. DeFeo's experimental, sculptural use of oil paint was raising pressing concerns about the work's structural integrity. Its location in a busy classroom exacerbated worries about its physical peril—apparently, for good reason. A friend told her that he saw the painting "standing there with two or three brooms and mops leaning against it!" In 1974 she used funds raised by the wake and a personal grant from the National Endowment for the Arts to hire conservator Tony Rockwell to clean the painting and encase it in a plaster cast, in the hopes of stabilizing it enough to safely transport to the San Francisco Museum of Art's (SFMA) conservation lab.[13] Conner described the process as "an even stranger transmutation" than the stylistic cycles the painting went through in DeFeo's studio; *The Rose* was becoming "a mummy wrapping, plaster wall, chrysalis." DeFeo similarly framed the conservation efforts in anthropomorphizing terms, confessing to Conner: "I feel like we are foolishly struggling to sustain the life of a terminal patient, . . . who would just as soon not be fucked with."[14] DeFeo's reservations proved prescient. When Rockwell and his team finished coating *The Rose* in plaster, it

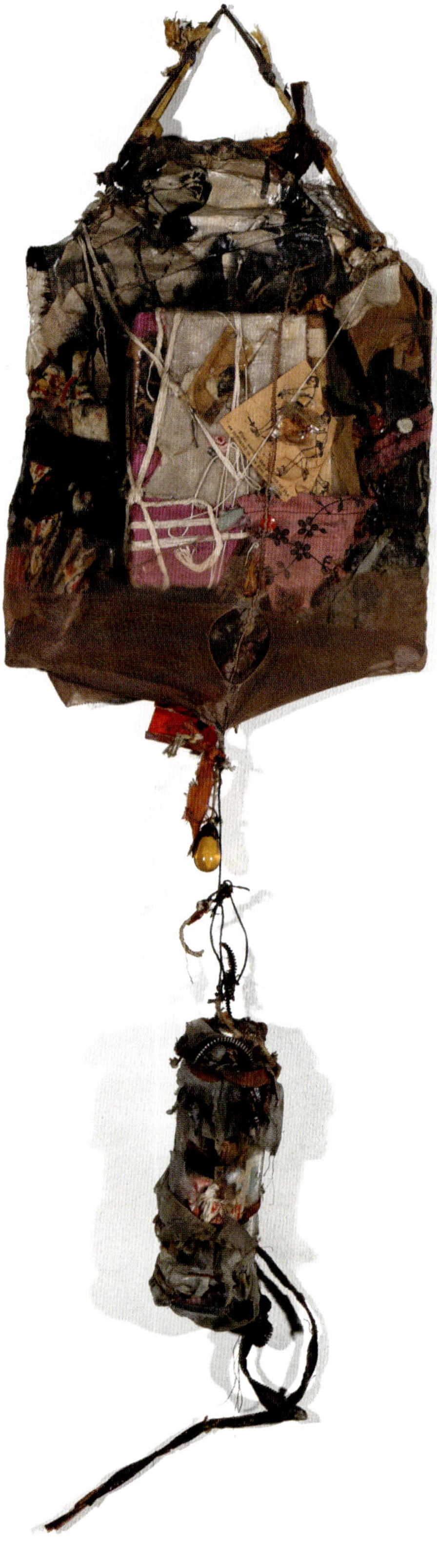

Fig. 64 Bruce Conner, HOMAGE TO JAY DEFEO, 1958. Cardboard, nylon, costume jewelry, book wrapped in fabric and twine, beads, paper, plastic, glass, postage stamps, rubber bands, burned fabric, staples, and zipper, 32 × 10 × 4 in. (81.3 × 25.4 × 10.2 cm). mumok—Museum moderner Kunst Stiftung Ludwig Wien, former Hahn Collection, Cologne.

was not transferred to SFMA, probably due to the prohibitively high cost of doing so. In 1979 drywall was placed in front of the now-occluded painting, and it remained immured until 1995, six years after DeFeo's death.

DeFeo and Conner's wake for *The Rose* posited an unusual ontological status for the work. Hosting a vigil to raise funds for a painting's preservation is as paradoxical as throwing a funeral to raise funds for a patient's continued medical treatment. The event simultaneously declared that the work was dead—that it had irrevocably passed into an afterlife—and that there was still hope of recovery or, at least, resuscitation. It suggested, that is, that either *The Rose* was perched on the boundary between life and death, like a patient on life support, or *The Rose* was somehow occupying both states at once, like a corpse at a wake—still physically present but spiritually departed. Only the possibility of resurrection could smooth over the illogic at the event's heart. By characterizing *The Rose* as suspended, zombie-like, between life and death, the wake implied that the painting possessed an uncanny vitality during its production that was now in question: Was the completed work a matured organism or a corpse? Did *The Rose* leave DeFeo's studio like a butterfly emerging from its chrysalis or like a lifeless body heading off to the morgue for mummification?

DeFeo and Conner conversed about this question for a decade or so after *The Rose*'s dramatic departure from 2322 Fillmore Street. This chapter reassembles that conversation to investigate the afterlives, or post-studio identities, that the two artists fashioned for *The Rose.* By taking Conner's interpretation of *The Rose* seriously, this approach diverges from recent scholarship on DeFeo that downplays the many myths—romanticized tales of obsession and martyrdom, for example—that arose to discursively fill voids in the public's perception of the painting during its quarantine at SFAI.[15] The purpose of the following account is to advance art-historical understanding of how a work of art's role in artists' personal and creative lives can change over time—specifically, in this case, how the meaning and function of *The Rose* shifted in the ten-year period after both the painting and the artists around it left the Fillmore neighborhood.

Much like the wake, Conner's THE WHITE ROSE represents *The Rose*'s removal from DeFeo's studio as a death. The film presents itself as a melancholic memory that underscores the loss of *The Rose,* DeFeo, and the artists' community. DeFeo responded to the film by taking up the framework of memory in the early 1970s during her first attempts to return to art-making after *The Rose.* Instead of emphasizing loss, however, she viewed the painting's simultaneous physical absence and psychic presence as performing the generative functions—the incessant agglomerations and transmutations—of memory. By seeing *The Rose* as a bridge between her past and present oeuvres, DeFeo resuscitated the work as a catalyst for her renewed art practice. She and Conner reincarnated *The Rose* yet again during their efforts to place the work in the mid-1970s—this time, bringing the painting back as a delightful playmate, rather than a plaintive memory. Through collaged correspondence, the friends both constructed a fantasy world for *The Rose* that magically resolved its current predicament and ignited DeFeo's return to recycling her friends' artworks.

Studying Conner's film with DeFeo's response to it in mind highlights a little-discussed dimension of the art practices that arose from the ideological, social, and material conditions of the Fillmore neighborhood. Specifically, it illuminates the vitality that artists attributed to their works due to their mutable materiality and embeddedness in place and community—a quality of liveness emblematized for Conner by *The Rose.*

Looking at Conner's film and DeFeo's collages from the 1970s together against the backdrop of their efforts to conserve and place *The Rose* also reveals that the painting continued to serve as a vital, though now virtual, locus for artistic and interpersonal exchange post-Fillmore. As the gathering of old friends for the wake suggested, *The Rose* lived on as a nexus for community even after its "death." Indeed, many of DeFeo and Conner's interindividual collaborations from the 1970s display an authorial and interpersonal push and pull like those that occurred around the painting during its production. However, the conceptual frameworks of memory and play that DeFeo and Conner applied to *The Rose* in the 1970s indicate that their perception of the work's generative nature shifted to reflect its current purgatorial circumstances. *The Rose* was now seen to catalyze creativity and interpersonal relationships by enacting, like reminiscence and make-believe, a transformative interplay between presence and absence. By hinting at the distances that had recently opened between the artists, this new dynamic freshened the urgency and redefined the poignancy of their exchanges.

IN MEMORY OF *THE ROSE*

According to Conner, he first conceived of documenting *The Rose*'s removal from DeFeo's studio at its remounting party in 1959–60. "Once we glued it [*The Rose*] on [its new canvas]," he recalled, "you couldn't get it out the door. . . . So since that moment, I started thinking about when it had to go out I wanted to film it." When that time finally arrived, some six years later, Conner shot footage for THE WHITE ROSE over two days, documenting *The Rose* in situ during its last day in DeFeo's studio and returning the following morning to record the crew of movers gingerly crating the monumental painting, extracting it through a hole that they sawed in the sill of the studio's bay window, lowering it to the street via hydraulic lift, and trucking it away.[16] Over the next two years, Conner edited the six-hour proceedings down to a seven-minute film titled THE WHITE ROSE: JAY DEFEO'S PAINTING REMOVED BY ANGELIC HOSTS, which he later abbreviated by dropping the subtitle.[17]

Dana Miller has observed that screenings of the film at *The Rose*'s debut exhibition helped shape the press's reception of the painting as "an incongruous relic . . . and the artist as a lost figure" and, moreover, that screenings after the work's immurement "helped perpetuate" its "mythic status."[18] One therefore needs to proceed with caution when using one work of art to tell a story about another, as there is great potential for distortion and disempowerment, especially when discussing the work of a male artist in reference to that of a female artist. That said, examining the film's interpretation of *The Rose* and DeFeo's response to the film can help elucidate both artists' conceptions of *The Rose*'s post-studio identity and how those conceptions developed, in part, from the specific conditions for artistic practice within the Fillmore neighborhood. So, let us proceed, caution in hand.

THE WHITE ROSE diverges in several respects from the found-footage films that brought Conner acclaim among experimental filmmakers in the 1960s. It uses original instead of archival footage and is structurally distinct from his most commonly cited films—A MOVIE (1958), COSMIC RAY (1961), and REPORT (1967)—which splice stretches of blank frames between developed ones.[19] Like his frequent use of disjunctive cuts, the interruptive hiccups in the moving picture (the longer of which register as interminable suspensions) remind viewers of the constructed nature of the projected world and thus refuse to transport them into it. THE WHITE ROSE largely inverts these deconstructionist strategies and, instead, uses cuts in the service of story. It takes the unexposed frames that intrusively erupt seemingly at random in Conner's other films and codifies them into punctuation marks that deliberately divide the narrative action into seven movements. Even the film's somewhat dizzying use of a wide variety of shots helps engross viewers in the plot, as the changes in pacing generally correspond to cadence shifts in the film's wistful soundtrack, an excerpt from Miles Davis's version of Joaquín Rodrigo's "Concierto de Aranjuez" from the album *Sketches of Spain* (1960).[20] While the film offers a legible narrative, some of its cuts still create disjunctive ruptures that seem to perform, as Kevin Hatch observed, "the deficiencies and deceptions that memory entails."[21] The film's structure thus mimes its subject—*The Rose*'s transition from presence (the plenitude it garnered from DeFeo's studio and person) to absence, from present tense to past tense, from life to afterlife. It is little wonder, then, that DeFeo and Conner chose to screen the film at the painting's wake.

The film underscores loss not only by miming the structure of memory but also by representing *The Rose*'s removal from DeFeo's studio as a death. Its first two acts are establishing sequences that introduce the two settings and casts of characters that the narrative brings together. THE WHITE ROSE opens on the site where *The Rose* is destined to end up—the street below DeFeo's apartment (fig. 65). This is the light and lively domain of the angelic hosts of the erstwhile subtitle, who file out of their van wearing white jumpsuits and mill about with ladders, waiting to ascend. The second scene introduces their destination—DeFeo's second-floor studio. Rather

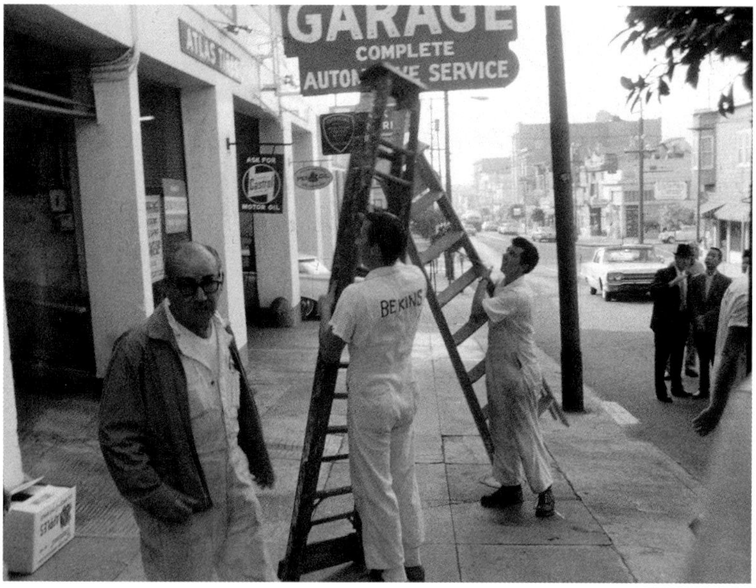

Fig. 65 Bruce Conner, THE WHITE ROSE, 1967. 16mm, black/white, sound, 7 min. Conner Family Trust.

than a feeling of airy movement, Conner's rapid cuts and twirling pans give the studio an unsettling air of insanity and enclosure, as if the camera were entering a madwoman's lair or the unconscious mind—a representation that resonates with gallerist Walter Hopps's description of DeFeo's studio as a "primordial cave."[22] Conner first focuses on the dilapidated quality of the room, tracing exposed wires and lingering on the gagged mouth of a caved-in fireplace. He then turns to its decrepit population—a copse of defoliated Christmas trees (souvenirs from DeFeo's annual holiday parties) and a workbench petrified under layers of paint.

Suddenly, the camera shifts from the room's shadowy periphery to the luminous painting, using jerky zoom sequences and soaring, vertiginous close-ups to augment its splendor and scale (fig. 66). He focuses in on the paint-splattered stool in front of *The Rose,* which begs DeFeo's presence and which she would later gift Conner. The whirling camerawork and brisk splicing endow the painting with an uncanny aliveness: *The Rose* appears as the magnificent, living heart of an enchanted but dying dominion. This effect creates the impression of a symbiotic, probably parasitical, relationship between the work and its environment that is sundered by the movers' invasive maneuvers. Greil Marcus has catalogued the many narratives of violent demise ("the hero and the dragon," the film-noir "murder investigation," and so on) conjured by Conner's multivalent depiction of the painting's reorientation from upright to recumbent in the film's later acts.[23] By drawing on these tropes, Conner's account of *The Rose*'s removal from 2322 Fillmore Street has the capacity to move viewers emotionally despite being self-consciously melodramatic.[24]

Conner marshaled similar metaphors of mortality when discussing *The Rose*'s relationship to DeFeo's studio. "The room itself was the work," he declared. "The stool, the floor was covered with the chunks of almost flesh-like paint that would be scraped off the canvas. . . . It was almost alive." In 2004 he articulated the consequences of destroying the site-specific dimension of the work in ways that speak to the film's portrayal of it as a death (as well as to the significance the painting's domestic setting assumed for DeFeo and her circle, as discussed in Chapter 2): "It is important to understand that not only was the environment, place and time integral to the meaning of *The Rose,* so was the specific geography and plan of the 2322 Fillmore Street flat—*the* specific site. The particularity of the proportion and character of the space where *The Rose* thrived for seven years created the impression of a living and breathing physical being." Plucked from its nurturing surrounds and placed in a museum, *The Rose* became a "remnant and artifact of its magnificent and majestic living form," a corpse that the friends would publicly mourn a decade later.[25]

The film also emphasizes loss by depicting DeFeo's reaction to the painting's deportation as a series of mysterious, possibly mad, mourning rituals. She appears halfway through the film sitting on the fire escape of her apartment, a liminal space between the movers' domain of the street and the artist's domain of the studio. After a shot of a worker sawing through the windowsill, Conner cuts to DeFeo; her legs swing back and forth in a graphic match to the action of the saw, thereby contrasting the mover's purposeful labor with DeFeo's whimsical play. The next scene shows her sitting in the new opening, as if the sawing enabled her entrance.

But even after entering the studio proper, DeFeo remains unengaged with the hubbub of disassembly, hovering nearby instead, like a spirit haunting the proceedings. Her interactions with *The Rose,* while deliberate, decidedly lack the rationality and teamwork of the movers' carefully coordinated efforts. Her gestures are mysterious, reflective, and symbolic;

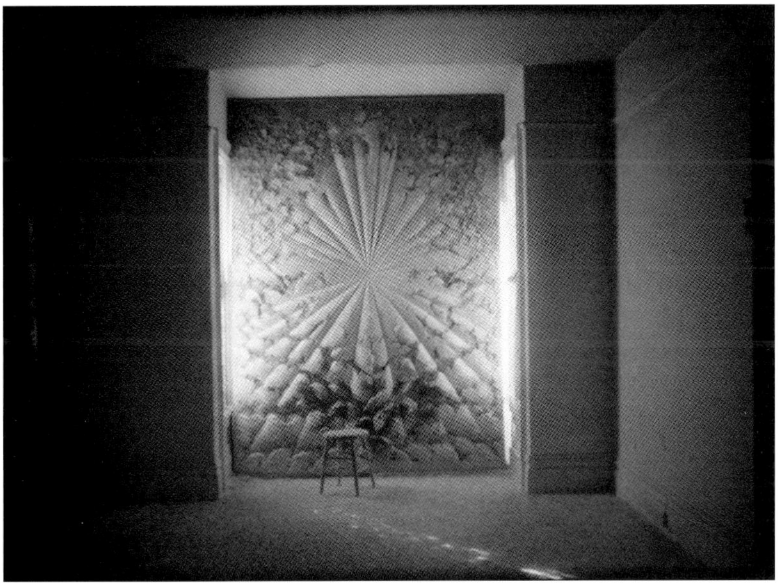

Fig. 66 Bruce Conner, THE WHITE ROSE, 1967. 16mm, black/white, sound, 7 min. Conner Family Trust.

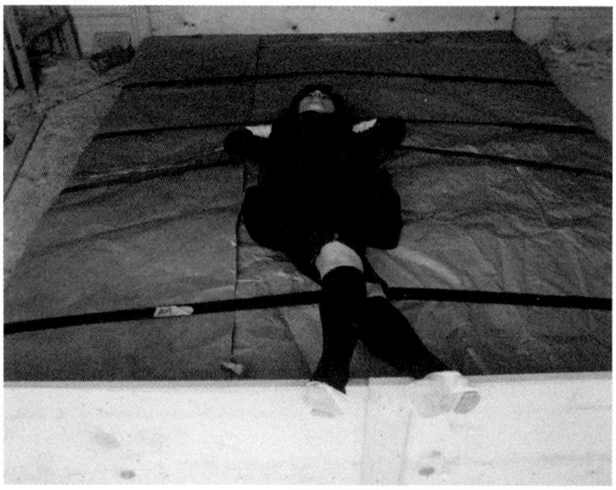

Fig. 67 Bruce Conner, THE WHITE ROSE, 1967. 16mm, black/white, sound, 7 min. Conner Family Trust.

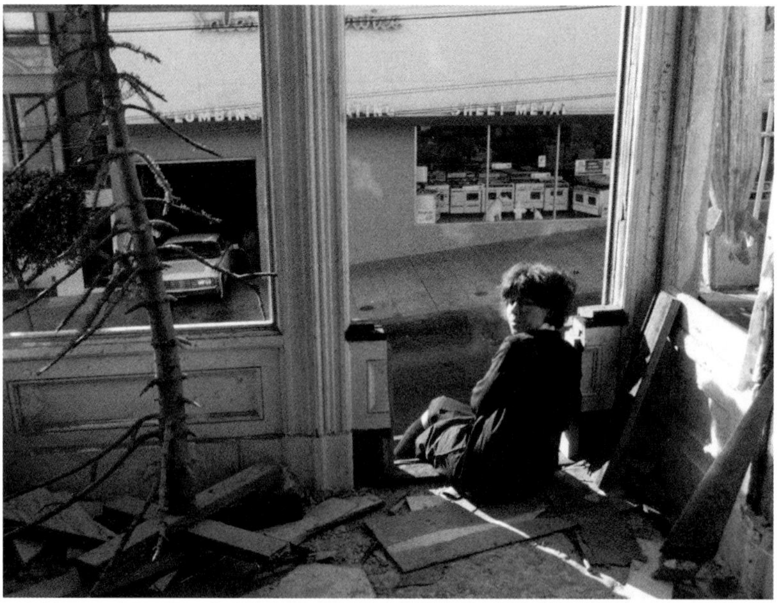

Fig. 68 Bruce Conner, THE WHITE ROSE, 1967. 16mm, black/white, sound, 7 min. Conner Family Trust.

they read as personal rituals performed in response to the workers' intrusive manipulation of her painting and its environment. She not only sits in the fresh wound made by the workman's saw in the studio windowsill, but also, in a brief yet haunting sequence, stretches across the surface of the shrouded and bound canvas as it reclines on the floor of her studio, fidgeting, in Conner's words, "as though she were trying to sleep fitfully on a large bed" (fig. 67). Conner also read DeFeo's cryptic performance as evidence of her identification with the work; speaking of the crate that the movers constructed around *The Rose,* he remarked, "So it seemed symbolically as if she were packaged into it herself and set out onto the forklift."[26]

After the painting has been lowered to the street and is about to be swallowed by the van, DeFeo brings an atrophied Christmas tree to the window where *The Rose* once stood (fig. 68). As souvenirs of an annual event, the denuded and desiccated trees DeFeo kept in her studio were markers of the procession of time. While the painting marked time's passage largely through growth, the accumulation of layers of paint, the trees marked it through enumeration and decomposition—a difference that makes the insufficiency of the substitution, like that of memory, profound. The scrawny specter that DeFeo brings to the window reads as both her co-witness to the painting's departure and a futile attempt to fill the physical void created by that event. As the movers drive away and the film closes, DeFeo appears to perform the same compensatory action with her body by lounging, precariously, in the hole through which the work exited.

By characterizing DeFeo's first attempts to cope with the painting's absence as pitiful and slightly unhinged, the film knowingly likens her to the stereotype of the Romantic genius who is tragically damaged (driven insane, maimed, and/or killed) by his obsessive devotion to art. As previous chapters have shown, this myth was a common lens through which DeFeo's male friends viewed her in relation to *The Rose,* in part because it made the work a symbol for their self-marginalization within the art world and society. Narratives of martyrdom were indeed present in Conner's mind when he made the film, as he cited Carl Theodor Dreyer's *The Passion of Joan of Arc* (1928) as a precedent for THE WHITE ROSE.[27]

Conner reinforced this trope in later statements, claiming, for example, that toward the end of DeFeo's production of *The Rose,* the painting "was the only identity she had with any kind of exterior reality." He borrowed this familiar narrative yet again in 1995: "The painting is a masterpiece of spirit and transformation that almost destroyed her through lead poisoning and its dominance over her relationship to the conscious world. When Jay and *The Rose* were evicted by their landlord, the thread was lost and Jay's life unraveled."[28] According to Conner, production of *The Rose* consumed DeFeo so utterly that its loss shattered her both physically and psychically. The film, then, frames her as both a mourner for and a victim of her painting. By representing an intense identification between (even conflation of) artist and work, the film presents the loss of one as the loss of the other. "It was the end of *The Rose,*" Conner declared of the removal, "and it was the end of Jay. . . . And all that day, I wondered if Jay was going to go out the window herself."[29]

DeFeo's response to Conner's portrayal of *The Rose* was mixed. She characterized the film as "pretty melodramatic" and more indicative of Conner's work than her own, suggesting that she felt its romanticized equation of the painting's removal to death exaggerated and thus misrepresented her experience, as Miller argued. However, DeFeo also expressed her gratitude for the film in a letter written to Conner while they were working to conserve *The Rose:* "But back to the cost of restoration . . . I have had to rationalize . . . not just cost, but more important motive . . . in all this trouble and expense . . . and all I come up with that is philosophically reasonable in my own thinking . . . is that I feel I must do whatever I can to perpetuate the *myth of the Rose* . . . and the poor painting is the physical symbol of that myth . . . in its decline, but I must care for it as long as it may serve to remind others of loftier ideas. I appreciate your film so much for that reason . . . it says a lot the Rose can't say for itself."[30] Her description of the painting post-Fillmore as a "physical symbol" of "the myth of the Rose" resembles Conner's description of it as a "remnant and artifact of its magnificent and majestic living form." Both accounts characterize *The Rose* after it left the studio as a ruin that (not unlike a corpse or a memory) no longer provides direct experience but instead points to its past, to the "loftier ideas" represented by its epic making. In this way, DeFeo agreed with Conner that *The Rose*'s prolonged production complicated its reception by creating significant aspects of the work's identity that the finished canvas could not fully represent.

DeFeo further acknowledged that resurrecting *The Rose*—providing the fullest possible experience of it for public audiences—required narratives that vivified its past production and attachment to her studio, supplements created by the few who witnessed its life on Fillmore Street. Her statement that she appreciated Conner's film because "it says a lot the Rose can't say for itself" suggests that she saw THE WHITE ROSE in these terms. Here, the film literally speaks for the painting, telling the inspirational story that the canvas—muted by its abstract materiality and imprisonment in the SFAI conference room—is unable to communicate. Her comments also underscore that Conner's film, like many of the works discussed in this book, undercuts the solitude of the studio, even as it celebrates it; for its existence testifies to the presence of intimate witnesses who interpreted *The Rose* during its creation and, in doing so, snagged the recalcitrant masterpiece and autonomous artist in a net of intertextual works and interpersonal relationships. While DeFeo expresses her gratitude for the film's assistance, her wistful tone suggests regret that the "poor" painting's unfortunate circumstances have magnified its limitations, increasing its reliance on more articulate and agile ambassadors, such as THE WHITE ROSE.

For Conner, the quickened quality he observed in *The Rose* was also a key element of his own art. "The greatest attraction in creating any work is to see that it never dies," he declared in 1985. "It is still alive . . . as long as it keeps changing."[31] His assemblages both figure and perform this change: agglomerations tenuously banded together by webs of torn nylon stockings, they simultaneously conjure pupal metamorphosis and rotting flesh. As Hopps and others have observed, Conner used "fragile," "fugitive," and "vulnerable" materials, such as "fabrics, cardboard, [and] melted wax," to ensure that his assemblages not only expressed the concept of transformation but forever enacted it.[32] Many of these materials, such as fur and feathers, are also haptically appealing—inviting viewers to touch the works and thus hasten the works' disintegration. Conner asserted this dimension of his art in 1963 when SFMA placed a "Do Not Touch" sign next to his multimedia painting DARK BROWN (1959). He responded by printing cards reading: "THE BEARER OF THIS CARD is authorized / to alter any collage or assemblage made by Bruce / Conner which is displayed for public

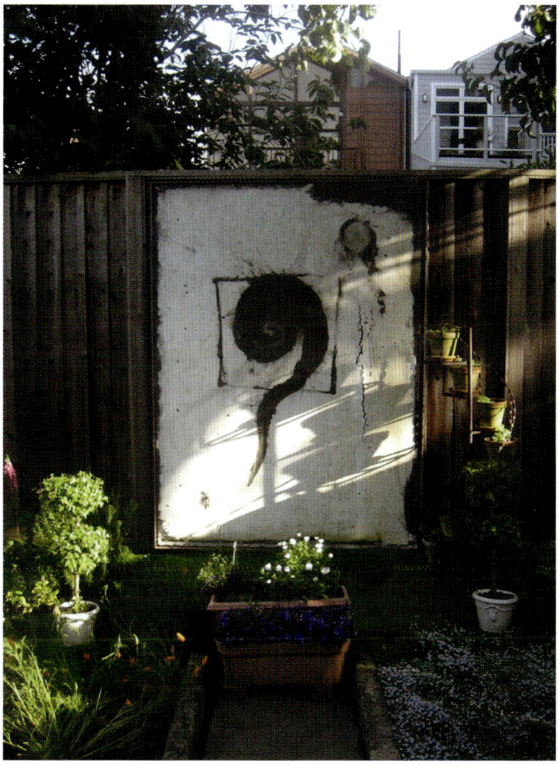

Fig. 69 Anonymous, HOMAGE TO JAY DEFEO, 1991. Photographed by Brian Lucas in 2011. On loan to Steven Fama, San Francisco.

consumption."[33] The card maintained the radical openness of his work to change and interaction, going against the museum's customary perception of the work of art, once it has left the studio, as a static, finished product to be preserved.

Conner's account of the vitality granted to his works by their mutability parallels DeFeo's characterization of *The Rose*'s production as a life cycle—a dialectic between creation and destruction that endowed the work with the presence of a living organism. "The work developed through metamorphosis," DeFeo explained of *The Rose* in 1973. "The feeling was organic—'it grew like a living plant.'" In DeFeo's prolonged painting process, Conner perceived the potential for the endlessly transforming work of art to which he aspired. "It had to take an uncontrolled event to make it stop," he stated of *The Rose*. "She kept changing it."[34] Conner's second HOMAGE TO JAY DEFEO (1991), which he created under the pseudonym "Anonymous" two years after her death, further evinces his association of her work with perpetual change (fig. 69). He lent the large painting to a friend in 2007 with the stipulation that it be displayed outdoors, where it would be subject to "the sun, heat, cold, rain, and the other elements of the San Francisco weather along with the expected and various incursions of natural plants and animals."[35] Thus, he specified that the work dedicated to DeFeo participate in the natural forces at play in his friend's garden, so that it could enact the entropic mutations that he envisioned both *The Rose* and his own art performing.

These links to Conner's practice suggest that *The Rose* was not the only work of art created in the Fillmore community that the group perceived as possessing the qualities of a living thing. (Indeed, this book's third chapter charted McClure's projection of presence and agency onto both DeFeo's painting and his poetry.) As Fillmore artists turned to one another as their primary audience—due to both the weak local art market and the suspicions that many, including Conner, harbored toward the art world and broader society—the idea of what a work of art could be expanded and transformed. *The Rose* and Conner's assemblages each manifest this shift, though in divergent ways. Once reception became a private activity—an intimate exchange between friends at a RBPA meeting, local co-op opening, or party—process could become indefinite; works could become ephemeral, portable, or architectural; and viewing could become interactive and entwined with production.

The mutation of art practices under the peculiar conditions of San Francisco's postwar art world has been noted before, of course. Anastasia Aukeman has rightly observed that many of these transformations paralleled contemporary developments toward environmental, process, and performance art that occurred in New York and elsewhere circa 1960.[36] Conner's film and DeFeo's comments about it help complicate this narrative by underscoring an aspect of this turn specific to San Francisco: they reveal that artists in the Fillmore District often ascribed agency to the physical and social site of a work's production. By integrating a work with its context, that is, the artists seemed to endow it with a life force and a capacity for infinite change. This perception of art as alive—an uncommon trope in American art discourses of the period—spoke to the private nature of artistic practice in their community and the intersubjective and existential agency it thus acquired. Given, as this book has shown, that Fillmore artists used the making and viewing of art to produce and shape their relationships and daily existence, it is little wonder they began to perceive their works as possessive of the willful, agential presence of living organisms. As Conner's film demonstrates, the flip side of the magical animus the work acquired within the private, protected sphere of the coterie and studio was the "death" it suffered beyond them—the work's inability to communicate its full range of meanings and experiences to public audiences in institutional settings.

The card that Conner created to accompany DARK BROWN indicates his acute awareness of this conundrum. By asserting his authorial power over institutional control and catalyzing interactive viewing, it gave the museum audience the combination of creative independence and dialogue cultivated within the Fillmore neighborhood. Conner originally made the painting for McClure and added its fur border as an invitation to the poet's touch, knowing from experience that his friend was likely to accept. However, there were limits to Conner's embrace of Cagean contingency. Specifically, he wanted the public to activate the vitality of his works by manipulating them, but he also wanted to retain his position as the works' author.[37] Rather than being continuously collaborative, in other words, they were works by an individual artist that others were expected to perpetuate. This mode of reception echoes the balance between individual authority and collective production that, this book argues, artists attempted to strike through their interindividual collaborations around *The Rose*—exchanges that emblematize the fluidity between production and reception cultivated by the informal, intimate viewing conditions of the Fillmore neighborhood. Ultimately, Conner stopped making assemblages because gallerygoers failed to respond to their invitation to interaction.[38] This failure confirms that the balance to which Conner aspired between static object and living thing, production and reception, individual and collective-making, was difficult to strike beyond the circumscribed borders of the coterie.

The incident involving DARK BROWN also highlights ways in which Conner's embrace of change was distinct from DeFeo's—a difference that likely followed from the fact that she harbored much less anti-institutional sentiment than Conner. DeFeo never fully resigned herself to the notion that *The Rose*'s development was complete, but neither did she ask that the painting continue to transform during its public reception. On the contrary, her efforts to conserve the painting demonstrated a desire to stave off the deterioration that Conner courted. At least, for the most part. Niccolo Caldararo, who led the team that eventually conserved *The Rose* in the 1990s, recalled advice DeFeo gave him about a work he was conserving: "Don't make it look too new. It should feel like it's been someplace. I have."[39] Works of art, she appears to have thought, should bear the marks of experience: they should physically evidence the vicissitudes of life as all bodies do.

THE WHITE ROSE, in sum, expressed Conner's belief that *The Rose*'s continually transmuting surface, physical integration with DeFeo's studio, and function as a creative nexus made it exemplify the living presence that works of art could achieve within the Fillmore community. Comments that Conner made about his 1964 exhibition at the Batman Gallery, located a block away from DeFeo's apartment, reveal he saw the painting as not only an example of vitality, but also as a source of it. Conner's unconventional display choices—which included occupying the gallery for the show's three-day run and painting the walls matte black—attempted to re-create the intimate, interactive, and domestic conditions under which his friends and neighbors customarily viewed his works. By thus preserving some of the connections between his art and life in the gallery's public setting, Conner may have hoped the exhibition design would act as life support, sustaining the vivacity of his works as they moved out into the world, as he had attempted to do for DARK BROWN the year before. The *San Francisco Chronicle*'s description of the exhibition as a "magic grotto, full of things that have been put under enchantment and left for years to the bats and spiders, but are still alive and waiting to be revivified" suggests that Conner's installation bore out this existential dimension in ways that strikingly predicted his representation of the life-giving/-draining symbiosis of studio and work in THE WHITE ROSE.[40]

Conner perceived a further connection between his exhibition and *The Rose,* claiming that the show "was partially conceived and structured in relation to 2322 Fillmore." This statement implies that DeFeo's studio served as both a model for Conner's ambitions to create environmental art, evident in the exhibition's unconventional design, and a site toward which he physically oriented his installation. "[It] was not only a centering emblem to Jay," Conner explained of *The Rose* in 2004. "It became a basic reference point for myself and many others. A reference point from which it was possible to gauge everything else."[41] His Batman exhibition suggests that this statement be taken literally as well as metaphorically—that Conner believed *The Rose* radiated life force along its painted rays beyond the walls of 2322 Fillmore Street to nourish the creative practices of those who oriented toward it, as worshippers might toward Mecca, the Vatican, or Stonehenge. Sundering the painting from its site would thus decimate not only work and artist, but also the nurturing, generative place their union created.

THE ROSE AS MEMORY

Another loss that *The Rose* would come to represent for Conner was the cessation of DeFeo's creative activity following its production. Between 1966 and 1970, when DeFeo was living in Ross and then in the neighboring town of Larkspur, she made no new works. She later referred to this time as her "happening period." She mused, "Everyone else was staging happenings during that period. I was living one."[42] In the early 1970s, she had transitioned back to art-making not with the large-scale paintings she created during her Fillmore days, but with small, multimedia works largely based in drawing and photomontage (such as the *September Blackberries* collage discussed in the previous chapter) that better suited her new circumstances, especially her more confined studio space.

In statements, such as the following one from 1994, Conner extended the Romantic narrative he crafted in THE WHITE ROSE to encompass both DeFeo's multiyear break from art-making and her return to creative practice: "Jay worked on *The Rose* for seven years to the virtual exclusion of any other artwork. It took her another seven years, the amount of time it takes to replace every cell in the human body, before she could begin to reassemble the parts into a whole image. The fragments of value around her in a small house among the redwoods north of San Francisco were photographed and collaged and rephotographed as the most solid images her mind could bring close and secure. She chose the objects that she saved and used from the past as if they were holy artifacts."[43] He characterizes her collage work as a therapeutic activity, as part of her slow recovery from the physical, mental, and spiritual trauma incurred by *The Rose.* For Conner, montage represented more than the medium DeFeo chose after her

Rose-induced hiatus from art-making: it was a metaphor for her recuperation. He likens her montage activity to the body's ceaseless regeneration of cells and the assembly of reliquaries—to pursuits that are restorative and redemptive. THE WHITE ROSE's representation of DeFeo's strange ritual with the Christmas tree prefigures Conner's reading of her collage practice as rearranging the remnants of her life from Fillmore Street to fill the gaping hole left in both her life and her psyche by *The Rose.*

In the early and mid-1970s, DeFeo also framed her current creative activity in relation to *The Rose,* though she envisioned this association quite differently from Conner. Instead of seeing the painting as pointing mournfully to its irretrievable past, she repeatedly described it as a conduit between her past works and present production. "I view all my ideas with an ever changing retrospective eye," she wrote to Thomas Albright in 1971. "It is like a kaleidoscope. I see the Rose as something like that [. . .] absorbing all that preceded it [. . .] as if it were the core of my creative universe [. . .] but unlike the idiot who wondered about my 'encore' I see it emitting my ~~private collection of images~~ vocabulary of visual symbols into ever changing patterns of images."[44] Four years later, she described *The Rose* in similar terms: "With some perspective, I see the Rose as a kind of culmination of all the painting experience that preceded it. Now it is providing (graciously) a kind of feed-back . . . so much [is] growing out of it in terms of future ideas." DeFeo repeated this idea yet again in 1978: "But when I once again had a place to work and the energy was restored, I began to see the Rose as a storehouse for all the symbol shapes and imagery that went into it, releasing all the ideas that have come since."[45]

Whether likening *The Rose* to a "kaleidoscope," a "culmination," or a "storehouse," DeFeo portrays the painting as "absorbing" all aspects of her past creative activity (from the distinctive forms, symbols, and ideas that characterize her works to the skill and experience that produced them) and "releasing" them into the present. Around 1972–73 DeFeo drew a diagram that visualizes this dynamic (fig. 70). A schematic sketch of *The Rose* sits in the middle of the page as a spiraling line unfurls from its center, ending in arrows that point to lists of her pre- and post-*Rose* works on either side of the page. These works are further grouped into pairs and trios, demonstrating her long-standing penchant for thinking of her works in relation to one another (discussed in the introduction). She represents *The Rose* as the epicenter of her oeuvre, as a vortex that cuts across—mixes up and mediates between—her past and present production.

The drawing suggests that DeFeo viewed *The Rose* in the early 1970s as performing the tasks of memory. The images she evoked to describe the painting's curious but crucial function in her practice are common metaphors for memory. Her depiction of the work as a "storehouse" fits the conceit that memory is a containing structure for past experience, while the figure of the "kaleidoscope" conveys the familiar notion that the mind's largely subconscious stores color our experience of the present, like glass

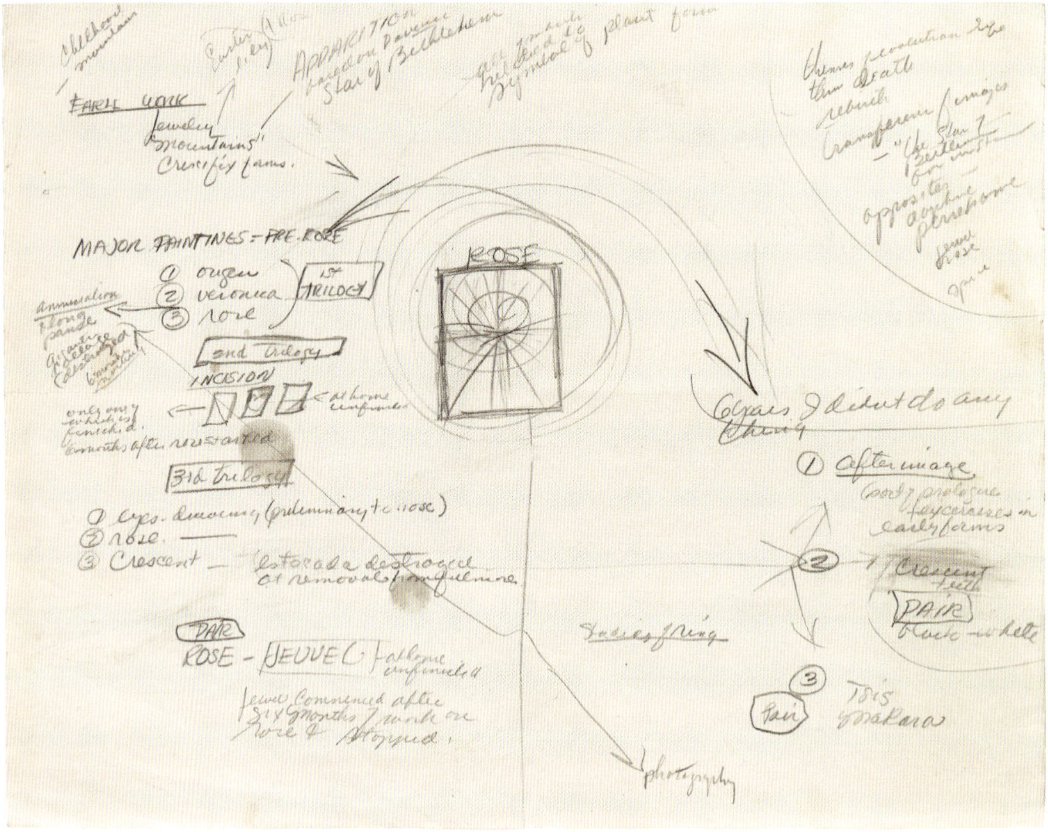

Fig. 70 Jay DeFeo, Diagram of relationships among her works, c. 1972–73. Graphite on paper. The Jay DeFeo Foundation, Berkeley, Calif. [JDF no. Doc0001].

beads refracting the view of what lies directly in front of us.[46] In the first quoted passage, DeFeo applies the kaleidoscope metaphor to both her "ever changing retrospective eye" and *The Rose*—a slippage that effectively conflates her memory with her painting. Doing so reveals how she adapted the processes and ideas that she developed through making *The Rose,* including her exchanges with other artists, to life after its production.

By taking up *The Rose* under the sign of memory and montage, DeFeo's mixed-media practice of the 1970s established an implicit dialogue with Conner's film that is echoed in the statements quoted above. While DeFeo's kaleidoscope simile and Conner's allegory of healing both evoke fragmentation and, thus, her chosen medium of collage, they assign *The Rose* disparate roles in her montage practice. For Conner, the figurative shattering of *The Rose* (and, by extension, DeFeo's life and self) is symbolic of the trauma and loss incurred by her draining experience creating the work—an account that resonates with the melancholic portrayal of artist and painting in his film. In his narrative, she uses collage to recover from the painting. By contrast, DeFeo's kaleidoscope metaphor depicts *The Rose*'s shattering as inherently generative. The fragmented painting engenders "future ideas" by constantly recombining shards of her past and present creative activity into novel constellations, as a kaleidoscope's spinning prism churns the contents of its barrel and the view beyond into a whirling amalgam. Her kaleidoscope metaphor animates the moribund "fragments" and "artifacts" from Fillmore Street that Conner evokes, transforming them from scraps representing a lost whole into enlivened building blocks for future works. Her account thus endows *The Rose* with agency and generosity, qualities that contrast sharply with Conner's characterization of it as a depleting drain on her creative powers. In this way, her interpretation of *The Rose* in the 1970s allowed the painting to retain some of the vitality that both she and Conner perceived during its production, while still acknowledging that the work's plenitude, as with all memories, had depleted.

As *The Rose* transformed, in DeFeo's estimation, from a work in progress into an avatar for her memory, its temporal structure also shifted. According to DeFeo, the painting conveyed a chronological conception of time when it was under production. Her equation of the painting's development to the stylistic evolution of Western art (detailed in Chapter 2) expressed this idea. The finished work manifests sequential organization in a geological way: its layers of paint resemble sediment accumulated on Earth's crust. The kaleidoscope metaphor explodes these fossilized strata into swirling smithereens, creating a temporal complexity that differs from cinema's reanimation of the past. While the painting-as-object calcifies time into a static sequence, the painting-as-memory draws disparate moments together to generate a future. It represents time as a dynamic pattern rather than a petrified, unilinear progression. This distinction is reminiscent of one that Walter Benjamin drew between his account of history as a dialectical image—in which liberated splinters of "the Then and the Now come together into a constellation"—and historicism's view of time as an additive succession of homologous moments.[47] Like Benjamin, DeFeo judged this montage-like temporality to be both melancholic and potentially redemptive.

The mnemonic character that DeFeo attributed to her creative practice manifested in the procedures and formal languages that she developed upon returning to art-making in the early 1970s. Echoing Conner's cinematic portrayal of *The Rose,* DeFeo turned to a film-based and, hence, temporally complex medium to manifest the mnemonic character of her art. In 1971 she began to regularly photograph her work space and to compile proof sheets of the resulting images in binders (fig. 71). "I've got a 'visual diary' of the progress of my work since 1971," she explained in 1977. "I've made books out of literally hundreds of contact prints that say far more at a glance about my work patterns and thought processes over the years than any words can hope to convey."[48] Some photographs appear to be candid snapshots of her work space, while others seem to depict staged arrangements of the works and objects in her studio. Like the photographs that DeFeo and others took of *The Rose* in her Fillmore Street studio, the proof sheets chart the evolution of individual works over time, but they also map spatial relationships between works—specifically, between the unfinished drawings, paintings, and collages that cluttered her work space. In

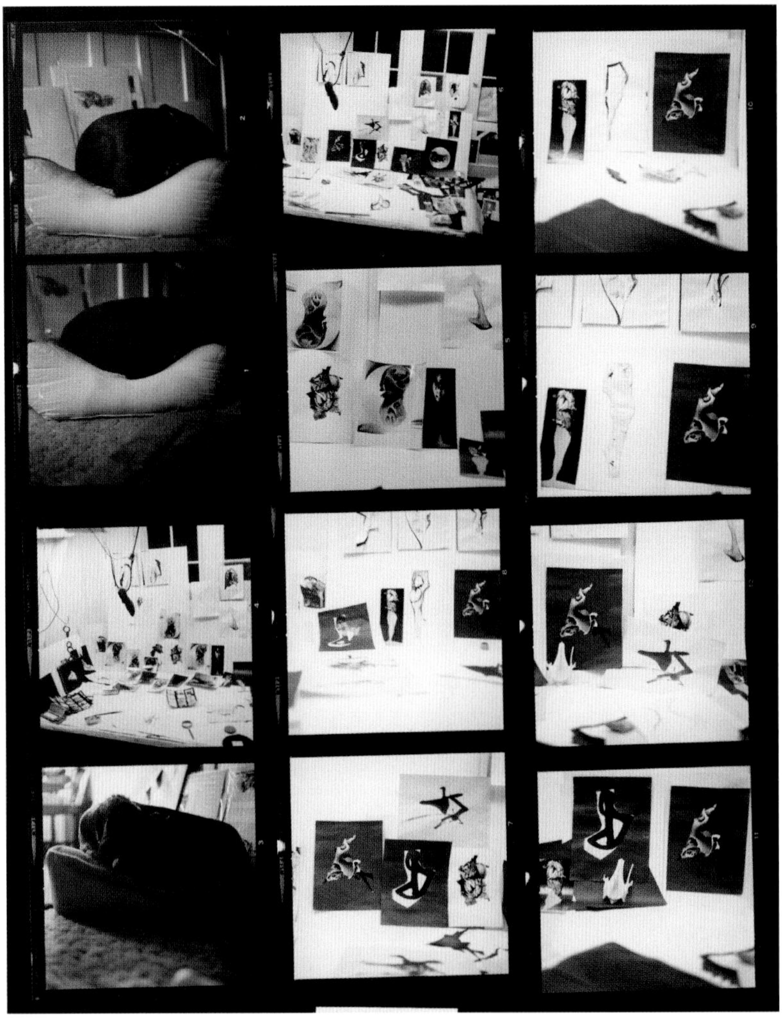

Fig. 71 Jay DeFeo, Untitled, 1976. Gelatin silver contact print, 10 × 8 in. (25.4 × 20.3 cm). The Jay DeFeo Foundation, Berkeley, Calif. [JDF no. C0009].

this way, the catalogues associate the changes that discrete works undergo from frame to frame with the constellations into which they are arranged within each frame. They suggest, in other words, that juxtaposition propelled DeFeo's creative process—that the direction in which she took a work emerged, in part at least, from its relation to the works around it. Some photographs show that she interspersed previous studio shots and works into her arrangements, implying that she drew inspiration from connecting works across not only space but also time. Incorporated back into the studio space, the old images acted like *The Rose:* they provided feedback between her past and future works. The artistic process depicted in her "visual diary" therefore accords with the kaleidoscope metaphor she used to describe it: both identify the juxtaposition of past and present as a catalyst for transformation.

After Image (1970), the first work DeFeo made after *The Rose,* demonstrates one kind of temporal complexity that her montage-like studio arrangements yielded (fig. 72). The modestly scaled work on paper is a

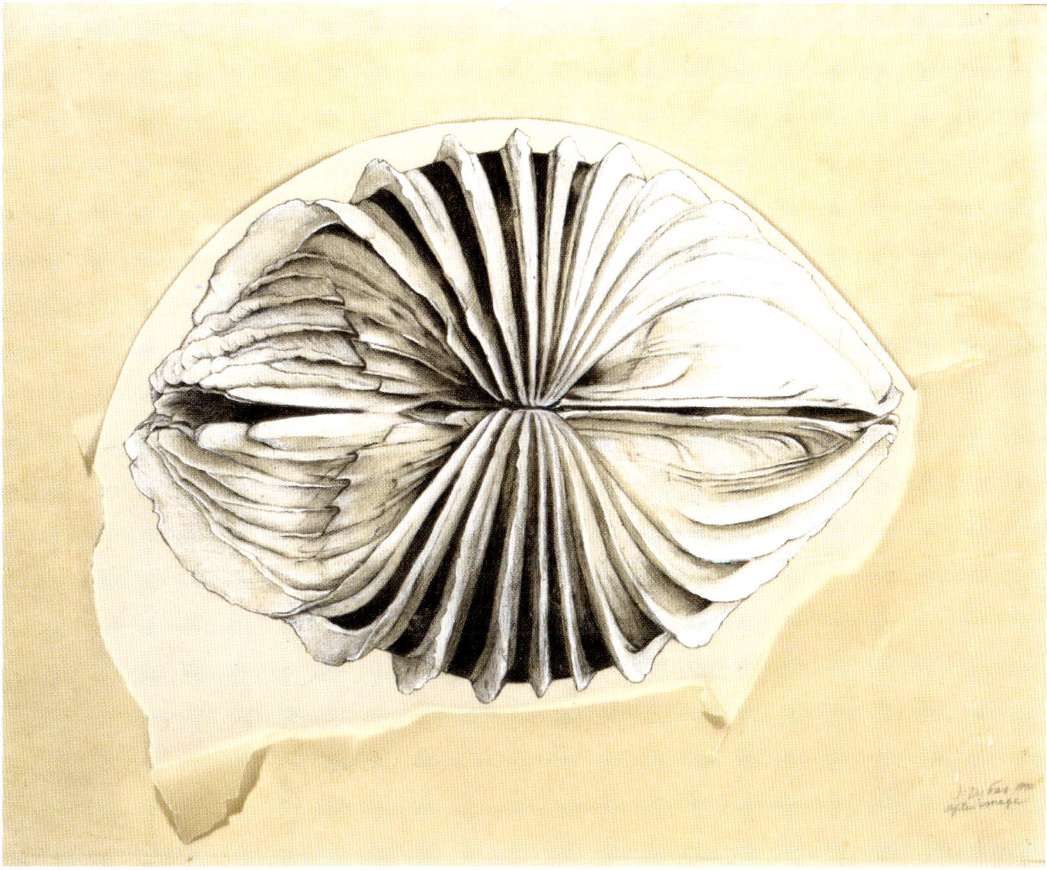

luscious medley of materials and textures. A fine graphite drawing shellacked with a dazzling coat of transparent acrylic paint rests inside a torn frame of tracing paper. The jagged hole in the gauzy top layer usually (depending on the light source) casts a thin shadow that imperfectly traces the centered drawing. The tissue's delicateness rhymes with the brittleness of DeFeo's line, but its matte fragility sharply contrasts with the glossy lushness of the drawing's sealed surface. The drawn form—an involuted ovoid composed of thin, undulating corrugations—evokes organic connotations, but the references that it conjures are many and mixed. As Brigid Doherty observed, the image's "ridges and crevices . . . alternately resemble brittle, razor-edged stone and pliant, supple petals." I would add to this list crisply layered plumage and the elegant whorls of a seashell. While the figure is visually and materially evocative, it is also frustratingly unplaceable, like a word on the tip of one's tongue. Writing to DeFeo in 1971, Thomas Albright, DeFeo's friend and art critic for the *San Francisco Chronicle,* remarked on *After Image*'s mix of precarity and persistence, and the temporal effect it conveys: "It's a curious thing about those creases and torn edges and faded colorations; . . . I thought they were immensely effective, projecting a kind of feel of age and decay through which the images, for all their fleeting, elusive qualities, manage to preserve, like some magical symbol discovered

Fig. 72 Jay DeFeo, *After Image*, 1970. Graphite, gouache, and transparent acrylic on paper with cut and torn tracing paper, overlay: 10⅞ × 13¾ in. (27.6 × 34.9 cm), primary support: 14 × 19½ in. (35.6 × 49.5 cm). Menil Collection, Houston. Gift of Glenn Fukushima in honor of the artist [1900–04].

on an ancient papyrus manuscript."[49] Elusive yet effective, decayed yet discoverable, *After Image* conveys the feeling of the past emerging, with simultaneous power and intangibility, into the present. The form's presence is similarly commanding and tenuous: the glimmering shape appears to have burst triumphantly through the thin veil of translucent paper, even as the shadow that paper casts threatens to obscure the drawing.[50]

DeFeo based the image on a photograph of a seashell that she encountered in a book, but she added that the form also "connected me with *The Rose* as well as my large *Eyes* drawing" (see fig. 47).[51] *After Image* thus resulted from the cross-pollination of images and works that populated DeFeo's studio, a hybridization recorded in the proof sheets. In *After Image,* past works haunt present images through formal allusion. Doherty noted that the "orificial image recalls the shape of *The Eyes,* and the shell's regular folds emerge from its center, recalling the radial convergence of *The Rose.*"[52] DeFeo's statement that *After Image* "connected" her with the Fillmore period works suggests that the references embedded in the drawing were unintended—that the act of depicting the seashell dredged up recollections of her past pieces that, in turn, molded her perception and representation of the object before her.

The work's title and many of its formal aspects similarly evoke involuntary memory. An afterimage is the negative trace of something beheld (a bright light, for example) that temporarily lingers in the visual field after the object vanishes or the viewer looks away.[53] As a reflexive intrusion of the past into the present, the perceptual phenomenon crystallizes DeFeo's description of *After Image*'s production. The drawing's simultaneous insistence and precariousness also corresponds with the automatic yet ephemeral nature of afterimages and involuntary memories in general—with the way they intrude unexpectedly into view only to disappear in an instant. Like her kaleidoscope metaphor, the work's title implies that memory drives creativity by mediating vision, causing images to interpenetrate. *After Image*'s veil of tracing paper likewise suggests superimposition, as does the specific way the drawing combines its three referents; instead of appending individual features of each work side by side to create a declarative hybrid, it layers *The Rose*'s cruciform composition onto *The Eyes*' ovoid shape and onto the shell's brittle texture to form a haunting whole. The resulting amalgam mimes the way involuntary memory coats perceived objects with a cascade of unconscious associations, enacting a mutual permeation of present and absent, external and internal, matter and mind, that makes sight transformative.

After Image speaks to DeFeo's understanding of the ways that mnemonic processes mold our view of not only the present but also the past. It translates *The Rose*'s sculptural ridges and valleys into illusionistic ripples and shrinks the monumental painting and drawing down to handheld scale. In addition to flattening and miniaturizing, *After Image* turns the older works' expansive compositions in on themselves: it wraps *The Rose*'s reaching rays and *The Eyes*' rocketing perspectival lines around the shell, containing their infinity within the object's delimited circumference. By making the earlier, epic, and outward-turning images intimate and self-contained, *After Image* suggests that memory distills unwieldy experience into manageable, possessable figments. The drawing's resemblance to a shell likens this psychic process to the slow, accretive, and depletive action of ocean currents. Adrift in DeFeo's memory, the colossal works have been coalesced and whittled down to wash up on the shore of her consciousness as an enigmatic souvenir.

The product of this sea change retains some of the mystery of the deep. Its horizontal seam unfurls just enough to reveal a dark interior without disclosing the contents of that recess, implying that its most valuable feature is hidden, like a pearl, behind mute lips. Although *After Image* underscores the generative power of memory, this detail hints at the loss incurred by mnemonic transfiguration—the aspect of memory most salient in Conner's film. The shell's latent cargo suggests the aspects of previous experience that are withheld from consciousness in the morphed form that the past assumes in reminiscence. Loss may also have been an aspect of DeFeo's drawing process. A conservation report written for the Menil Collection, which currently houses *After Image,* notes that the drawing's contour is heavy and gouged, suggesting that it was made by tracing. The torn top layer of copying paper testifies to this otherwise hidden procedure, like an erased note (repressed memory) preserved on the wax slab (unconscious) of Sigmund Freud's "mystic writing pad."[54] If the report is accurate, then the drawing is a literal afterimage, an index of a vanished original, and making it involved the same interplay of dependence and separation, presence and absence, that the work conveys through its form and media.

After Image suggests that the guise of memory allowed *The Rose* to continue to serve as a nexus for intertextual exchange, as it had during its production in DeFeo's studio. Memory reiterated the relational dynamic that her practice acquired while she was living at 2322 Fillmore Street, when she developed her art in dialogue with works by both herself and her friends, but it added temporal complexity. She envisioned her multimedia works of the 1970s evolving from the push and pull not only between different works, forms, and media but also between different moments—between then and now, absent and present. The strategy proved productive for DeFeo: in the early 1970s she made other mixed-media works by recycling art from her Fillmore days through formal allusion, photographic representation, and material appropriation. Notable examples include *Tuxedo Junction* (1965/74)—which consists of mounted fragments of *The Estocada* (1965), a massive mixed-media work on paper that DeFeo produced while completing *The Rose*—and *White Spica* (1958/73), a collection of four pieces of an untitled drawing that she started when beginning *The Rose* in 1958. She photographed the individual fragments of *White Spica* multiple times in the 1970s.[55]

The adjustments that DeFeo made to her working methods in the 1970s reflected *The Rose*'s changed circumstances. The temporal complexity of her process paralleled her contemporary efforts to conserve the painting, which similarly scrambled chronology by imaginatively projecting an old work into the future. Her concern over *The Rose* likewise increased the painting's appearance in her thoughts while, at the same, underscoring its physical distance from her—a paradoxical effect similar to memory's poignant interplay of presence and absence. Like THE WHITE ROSE, then, *After Image* represents memory as entailing loss. Unlike Conner's film, however, DeFeo's work also characterizes memory as transformative and thus innervating—as a source of renewal, even reincarnation. To DeFeo, memory was a useful sign under which to rebuild her creative life, not only because it provided a familiar foundation (namely, *The Rose* and the relational modes of making it spawned); memory was also productive because it showed that continuity could be a catalyst of change, the past a progenitor of the future, and death an impetus for reincarnation. She acknowledged the importance of this idea to her art practice by writing "evolution of life / thru death / rebirth" at the top of the list of "themes" on the diagram that she drew of her oeuvre—reasserting the idea, which both she and Conner had cultivated during their Fillmore days, that art is a living, ever-changing presence (see fig. 70). Against Conner's tale of dispossession and decrepitude, DeFeo asserted the vigor and continued evolution of *The Rose* and its maker. Her artistic dialogue with Conner around the theme of memory thus displayed the interplay between harmony and discord that characterized many of the intertextual conversations she engaged in around *The Rose* during its production. This parallel suggests that interindividual collaboration was one dimension of the creative life nurtured by *The Rose* that DeFeo resuscitated following its departure from her studio.

PLAYING WITH ROSE

Montage continued to play a prominent role in DeFeo's practice long after her tentative return to art-making. In 1971 she began to experiment with exposing and developing photographs. She frequently used prints of objects in her studio and of the flowers and vistas around her home as raw materials for her collages. DeFeo's friendship with Conner is often identified as the biographical backdrop for these photo collages because he suggested that she look to her domestic environs for artistic content.[56] The old friends became even closer around 1972, when Conner started to assist her efforts to conserve and place *The Rose*. They regularly conversed for hours over the phone (so much so that DeFeo began to refer to Conner as "telephone"), exchanged numerous letters, and even sent the occasional telegram between her home in Larkspur and his home in San Francisco. Their discussions revolved around *The Rose*'s future and the creative doldrums both artists were currently experiencing. Both personal and professional, the

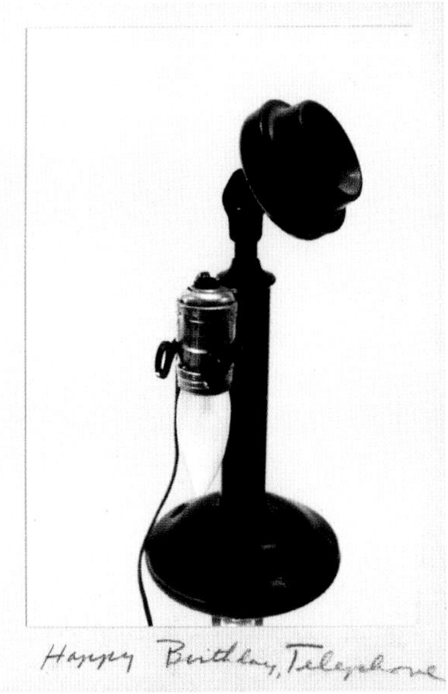

Fig. 73 Jay DeFeo, Correspondence for Bruce Conner, 1973. Inscribed copy print of photographic collage. Bruce Conner photograph collection, BANC PIC 1997.069, Bancroft Library, University of California, Berkeley

relationship they cultivated in the 1970s is difficult to categorize. Conner made this point in a letter to DeFeo when describing how he introduced himself to her new gallerist in 1973: "I called myself manager because it has a better effect and sounds better than other phrases like psychic advisor, jester, minister, old pal, etc."[57]

From 1973 on, DeFeo frequently incorporated overt references to her exchanges with Conner into her photo collages. Many of the montages conjure the pair's main medium of communication by picturing parts of an antiquated candlestick telephone that DeFeo kept in her studio. She unequivocally linked such works to Conner by labeling them Untitled (*for B.C.*). Some of the visual references to their relationship that appear in her photo collages reentered their correspondence, as when DeFeo converted a photograph of the telephone into Conner's birthday card (fig. 73). The card's scrawled message, "Happy Birthday, Telephone!," converts the image into a Picabia-like portrait of the recipient. The photograph reveals the surrealist alterations she made to the actual telephone—mounting it on a tripod and replacing its hanging receiver with a flame-shaped light bulb, a punning play on the phone's "candlestick" form. The ersatz flame emerges from the cord like a flash of insight above the head of a cartoon character. Her modifications thus imagine the telephone as both an instrument for art-making (a camera) and a source of inspiration. They suggest, in short, that she found conversing with Conner to be creatively invigorating. She would confirm this association later in the decade, writing, "Bruce has played [a part] in feeding my imagination, most particularly in the photography-collage area."[58]

Reexamining the oft-cited yet under-theorized connection between DeFeo's *for B.C.* photo collages and her relationship with Conner reveals that this association extended beyond the biographical fact that Conner provided his friend with moral support and direction in this period. Indeed, DeFeo's production of photo collages developed out of her and Conner's creative correspondence around *The Rose,* an activity that they construed as play. Like so many of the interindividual collaborations prompted by *The Rose,* these telegrams, notes, and collaged cards have largely been overlooked because they blur the boundary between interpersonal and artistic exchange, archive and museum. Through these occasional (in Paul Goodman's sense of the term) works, the friends reincarnated *The Rose* yet again, not as memory, but as a site for, creation of, and participant in their make-believe play.[59]

Play, according to Johan Huizinga, is a "well-defined quality of action which is different from 'ordinary' life."[60] Such technical definitions of play from modern psychologists helped shape popular conceptions of it in the twentieth century. According to these discourses, which Susanna Millar summarized in her 1968 text *The Psychology of Play,* ludic activity offers a respite from our accustomed modes of dealing with the world by permitting a "certain degree of choice, lack of constraint from conventional ways of handling objects, materials and ideas." This freedom is especially apparent in make-believe play when, as the pediatric psychoanalyst D. W. Winnicott explained, the pretending "child manipulates external phenomena" to conform to "inner or personal reality."[61] Sigmund Freud influentially interpreted imaginative play as a vehicle for wish fulfillment: "Unacknowledged, not yet achieved, or impossible wishes continue to find expression in play" as the child "uses objects and situations from the real world" but orders and alters them "in the way that pleases him best." According to this account, play serves the same purpose for children as daydreaming does for adults: it allows individuals to experience the feeling of mastering or resolving unpleasant or threatening events.[62] As Huizinga concluded, play "creates order, *is* order. Into an imperfect world and into the confusion of life it brings a temporary, a limited perfection."[63]

These defining qualities of play also characterize a portion of DeFeo's correspondence with Conner in the early 1970s. In addition to long, dry letters detailing their frustrating dealings on behalf of *The Rose,* the friends exchanged notes, postcards, and telegrams that plucked the painting from its dreary reality and inserted it into fantastical scenarios. In 1973, for example, Conner amended the following intentionally puerile fairy tale to a letter for DeFeo that chronicled the most recent travails of *The Rose*'s restoration: "This is the story: THE WHITE ROSE has moved to Happy Valley where the giant Pandas live and everyone eats as much ice cream and cake as they want. Rose is happy there and sends you best and fondest wishes and says not to worry. Rose eats well and gets plenty of rest." DeFeo then sent Conner a postcard to corroborate the fanciful travel narrative: "Dear Bruce and Jay, / Having a wonderful time. Wish you were here. / love from Pandaland, / Rose."[64] On the front of the card, she collaged a black-and-white photograph of a rose into the embrace of a diminutive, Technicolor gorilla

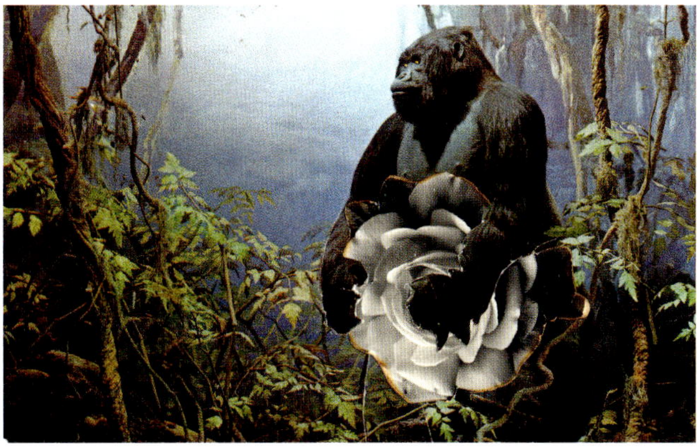

Fig. 74 Jay DeFeo, Collaged postcard for Bruce Conner, c. 1973. Gelatin silver print mounted on a postcard. Bruce Conner correspondence concerning Jay DeFeo's *The Rose*, BANC MSS 98/32 c, Bancroft Library, University of California, Berkeley.

(fig. 74). By translating the story's protagonist as a flower and the pandas as gorillas, the collage continues the process of metamorphosis enacted by the card's message. Recalling the absurdist collages of Berlin dada, the montage's humorous hodgepodge of incongruous objects, palettes, and scales makes it an appropriate pictorial analogue to the preposterous message scribbled on its reverse.

Like children contriving imaginary worlds through make-believe, the friends constructed their fables by mining their serious discussions about the painting and using the harvested contents to absurd ends. DeFeo's anthropomorphization of *The Rose* into Rose, for example, transformed the disabused painting into a happily-ever-after princess with the efficiency of a fairy godmother's wand. Both their work to conserve *The Rose* and their myths about it imagined a safe future for the endangered painting, but the latter magically resolved the anxieties, frustrations, and disappointments that burdened their real-life preservation efforts. The narratives, in other words, whimsically manifested the friends' deepest desires for the painting and thus performed the therapeutic function that Freud attributed to play. DeFeo spoke to this function in her story by including the line, "Rose says not to worry." A telegram that DeFeo sent Conner in 1974 further demonstrates how their mirthful exchanges with and about Rose held a fun house mirror up to their business dealings around *The Rose*. It reads: "DEAR TELEPHONE TELL ROSE A SILLY STORY LOVE."[65] Like most of their exchanges at the time, the telegram takes the painting as its subject; however, the task that DeFeo charges Conner to perform converts his usual tedious and trying managerial duties into the frivolous and pleasurable activity of recounting "A SILLY STORY." Hence, Huizinga's definition of play as a liberating suspension of reality describes both the telegram and the action that it orders.

Another postcard that DeFeo sent Conner around 1973 further indicates that she employed collage to exorcise her frustrations and disappointments about the painting (fig. 75). She created the card in response to her long, unfruitful negotiations with OMCA over *The Rose*, which prompted her to recruit Conner. On the back, she composed a note expressing her indignation at the museum's mistreatment of her. She then pasted scraps of

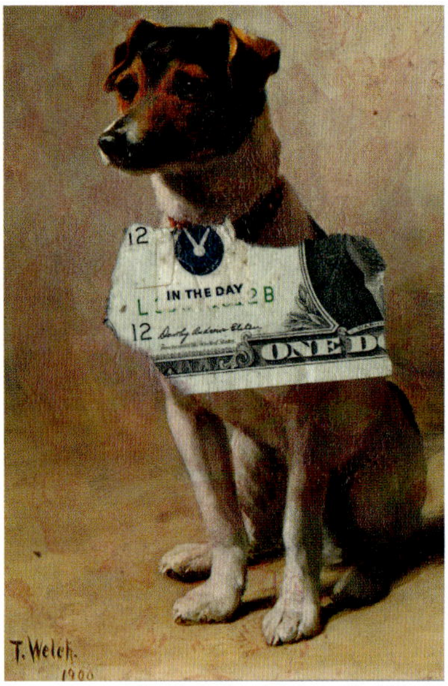

Fig. 75 Jay DeFeo, Collaged postcard for Bruce Conner, c. 1973. Torn paper currency mounted on a postcard. Bruce Conner correspondence concerning Jay DeFeo's *The Rose*, BANC MSS 98/32 c, Bancroft Library, University of California, Berkeley.

both a dollar bill and a drawing by Conner across the card's back and front. The torn strips obscure swaths of her writing like black bars on a censored document, and they maul the quaint portrait of a terrier on the front of the card with intimations of avarice. Before sending the postcard to Conner, she enclosed it in an envelope addressed to the museum's director in script that mocks his wildly illegible signature. In a note on the envelope's verso, she explained her motivations for the creation: "Bruce—This was never sent of course—little expressionistic games of this nature kept me relatively sane during all this."[66] By referring to her collage correspondence as "little expressionistic games," DeFeo suggests that the activity provided a means of enacting desires that she could not act on in real life. As she points out, the card "was never sent of course." Her confession that such "games" kept her "relatively sane" during her difficult dealings with the museum once again assigns the purpose that Freud ascribed to play—emotional recalibration—to her collage practice. When Conner began to help her find a home for *The Rose,* DeFeo's solitary games gained a second player.

The salutation that DeFeo used on the telegram discussed above indicates that she and Conner were also subject to the transformative powers of their make-believe play. By addressing Conner as "TELEPHONE," the missive confuses her interlocutor with the typical means by which they conversed. Such slippages abound in the artists' lighthearted epistles. DeFeo almost always refers to herself and Conner with nicknames derived from the media and motifs of their recent discussions. He is "Telephone" and, occasionally, "Music-page."[67] The latter appellation alludes to a drawing on staff paper that Conner gave DeFeo on the occasion of *The Rose*'s debut exhibition and that she, in turn, incorporated into a collage via photography (fig. 76). She goes by more varied pseudonyms, including "Telegram" (a nod to her proclivity for sending them), "Elephant" (a reference to her realization that

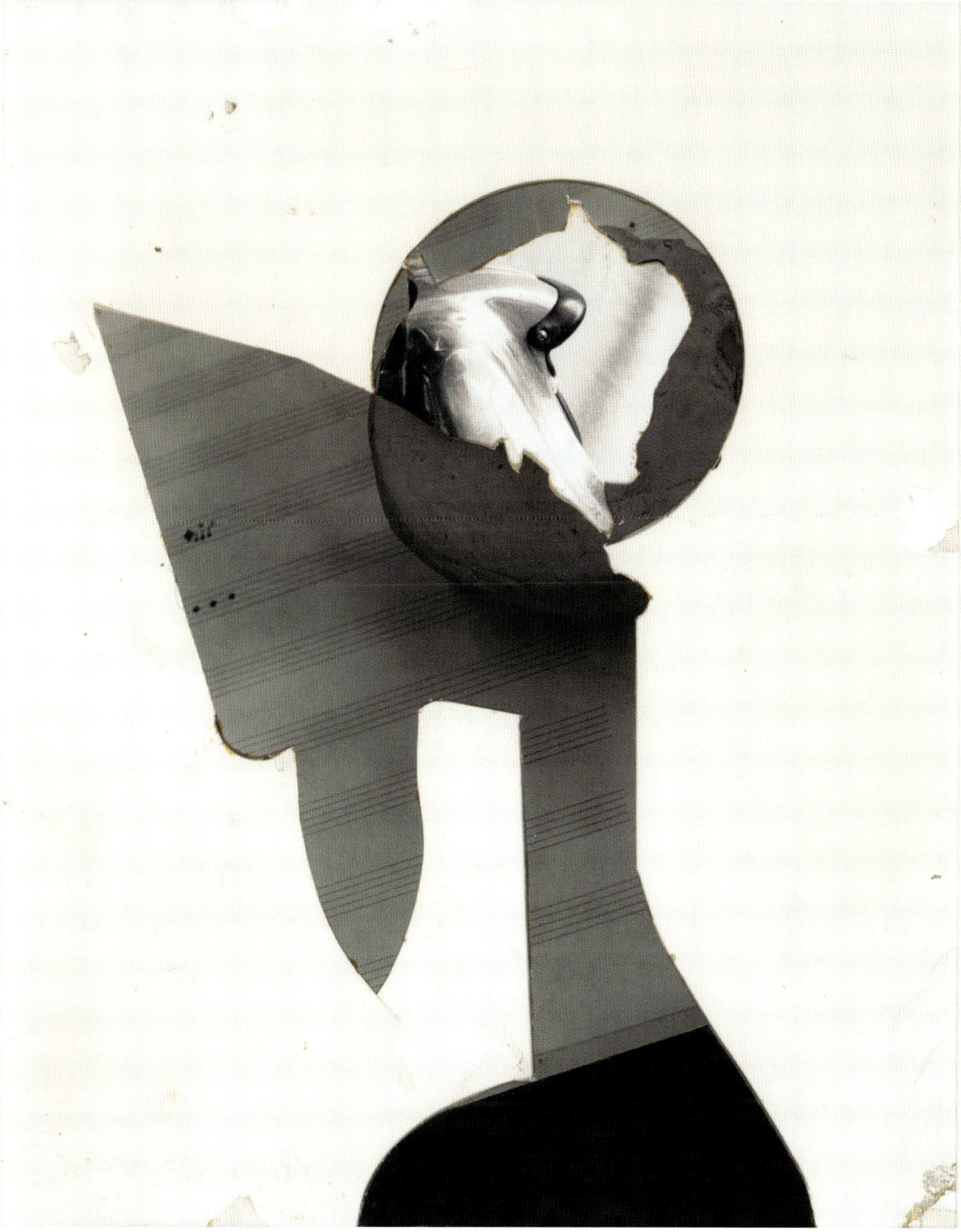

Fig. 76 Jay DeFeo, Untitled, 1973. Collage of gelatin silver prints on board, 9³⁄₁₆ × 7³⁄₁₆ in. (23.3 × 18.3 cm). San Francisco Museum of Modern Art. Purchase through a gift of Demetrios Scourtis, Phyllis Kempner Stein and David Stein, Helen Johnston Collection Bequest Fund, Accessions Committee Fund and anonymous donors.

"the Rose has become something of a white elephant to us all"), and "Drawing Board" (a declaration of her beginner's mind following *The Rose*).[68] Some of her notes are little more than nonsensical strings of pet names, codes composed of inside jokes. For example, one of her Western Union dispatches reads: "Rose Sends Greetings to Telephone Love Telegram."[69] By adopting nonsensical identities like these, DeFeo and Conner entered the imaginary world that they constructed around *The Rose*. It is tempting to liken their use of nicknames to a game of dress-up, in which, according to Huizinga, "the masked individual 'plays' another part, another being. He *is* another being."[70] Similar to the rotating contents of a costume chest, the aliases assumed by DeFeo, Conner, and *The Rose* circulated unstably between them. Sometimes, for example, "Rose" referred to the painting and sometimes it referred to DeFeo—a transfer that mirrors the name's uncanny blurring of object and subject, as well as the conflation between DeFeo and her painting by Fillmore figures, such as McClure.

The friends' seemingly endless stream of nicknames also echoed Conner's play with identity in his public life as an artist. From the mid-1960s on, the interrogation of artistic identity became increasingly central to Conner's art practice. He refused to sign his works, staged his death twice, created works under a succession of pseudonyms, and attributed an entire exhibition of his collages to the actor, artist, and filmmaker Dennis Hopper. By thus performing his own transmutation, Conner sought to avoid the feelings of self-alienation caused by the institutionalization of his art and, by extension, identity. "I have a feeling of death from the 'recognition' I have been receiving," Conner wrote to McClure in 1965. "Ford grant, shows, reviews, interviews, prizes . . . I feel like I am being cataloged and filed away and I have a refusal to produce something by which I will be 'recognized.'"[71] Conner responded to this stultification by changing. Like his constantly transforming assemblages, his artistic identity was never static.[72]

Conner's deep suspicion of the institutions of art and constant challenging of them made him both an odd and savvy candidate to help DeFeo place *The Rose*. Like her, he felt marginalized by the mainstream art world. Unlike her, however, he deliberately courted marginality in ways that gave him insight into the art world and made him a fierce advocate for artists' rights. "One of the purposes of my work," he reflected in 1996, "has been to try to change the way in which people relate to artists, how museums deal with the art work; to alter the process."[73] Just as Conner used a string of pseudonyms to evade the reifying power of art-world expectations and to keep his artistic identity vital, so the friends' endless stream of anthropomorphizing nicknames for *The Rose*—which they generated through the dialogic dynamic of play—revived some of the vitality and agency that the painting possessed in DeFeo's studio, when both her painting process and the creations it sparked subjected the work to constant change.

The artists' excessive use of nicknames suggests that their antic exchanges also performed the social function of play. According to

Huizinga, play fosters a sense of belonging because the "feeling of being 'apart together' in an exceptional situation, of sharing something important, of mutually withdrawing from the rest of the world and rejecting the usual norms, retains its magic beyond the duration of the individual game." The "us versus them" mentality cultivated by play finds expression in children's secret clubs, coded languages, inside jokes, and nicknames.[74] By mimicking these exclusionary juvenile behaviors, DeFeo and Conner signaled their solidarity around the Herculean task of ensuring *The Rose*'s future. While seemingly frivolous, their mythmaking around *The Rose* was arguably integral to their real-life efforts, as it helped cultivate the emotional resources and solidarity required for their difficult task. Furthermore, their zany missives mirrored, and thus may have been cathartic expressions of, the absurdity of their situation—the ridiculousness of petitioning institutions about which they felt, to some degree, ambivalent. At the very least, the friends' imaginative exchanges interjected some much-needed levity into their angst-ridden crusade to save *The Rose*. The fact that DeFeo occasionally incorporated photographs of herself and Conner as children into her dispatches indicates that she consciously framed their interactions as play. The jaunty invitation that she appended to a snapshot-cum-postcard of herself as a young girl makes this association overt: "I am feeling better as you can see!! Can you come and play next Friday? Your friend, J.D." (fig. 77).[75]

As a technique that involves decontextualizing, fragmenting, and rearranging images, collage lends itself to representing the playing child's cannibalization of reality. Indeed, theorists often use terminology that evokes montage to describe make-believe play. Winnicott, for example, observed that children construct their imaginary worlds out of "fragments from external reality." Freud added the act of rearranging to the process of world-building through play: "Might we not say that every child at play behaves like a creative writer, in that he creates a world of his own, or, rather, rearranges the things of his world in a new way which pleases him?"[76] Although Freud compared the pretending child to the creative writer, his characterization of play as an inventive recombination of bits scavenged from everyday life vividly conjures the activities of the photomonteur.

DeFeo drew a similar connection by attributing the same sense of fun and frivolity to making the *for B.C.* collages that she ascribed to her blithe exchanges with Conner. As Constance Lewallen noted, DeFeo did not "take seriously her photocollages of the early seventies; she once called them 'after hours fun things.'"[77] To make the *for B.C.* collages, DeFeo mined her correspondence with Conner, culling its telltale tropes (such as the telephone) and mimicking its inventive appropriation of reality, which is indicative of make-believe. One of the simplest works in the *for B.C.* suite crystallizes this dynamic (fig. 78). It combines black-and-white photographs of a leather golf bag and the modified telephone's bulb-receiver on a sheet of black paper. The outsized receiver-hook sprouts from the upright

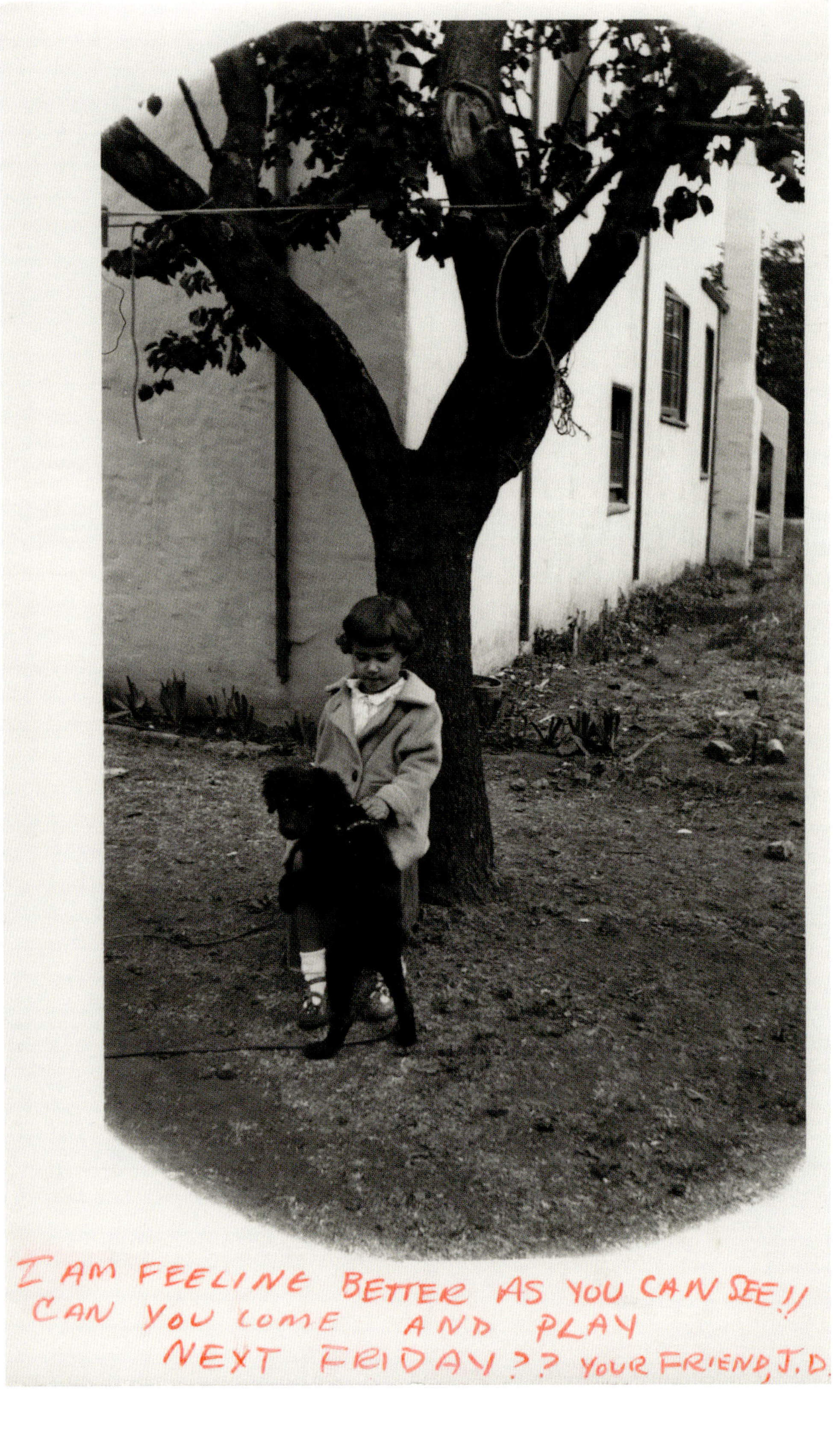
I AM FEELING BETTER AS YOU CAN SEE!!
CAN YOU COME AND PLAY
NEXT FRIDAY?? YOUR FRIEND, J.D.

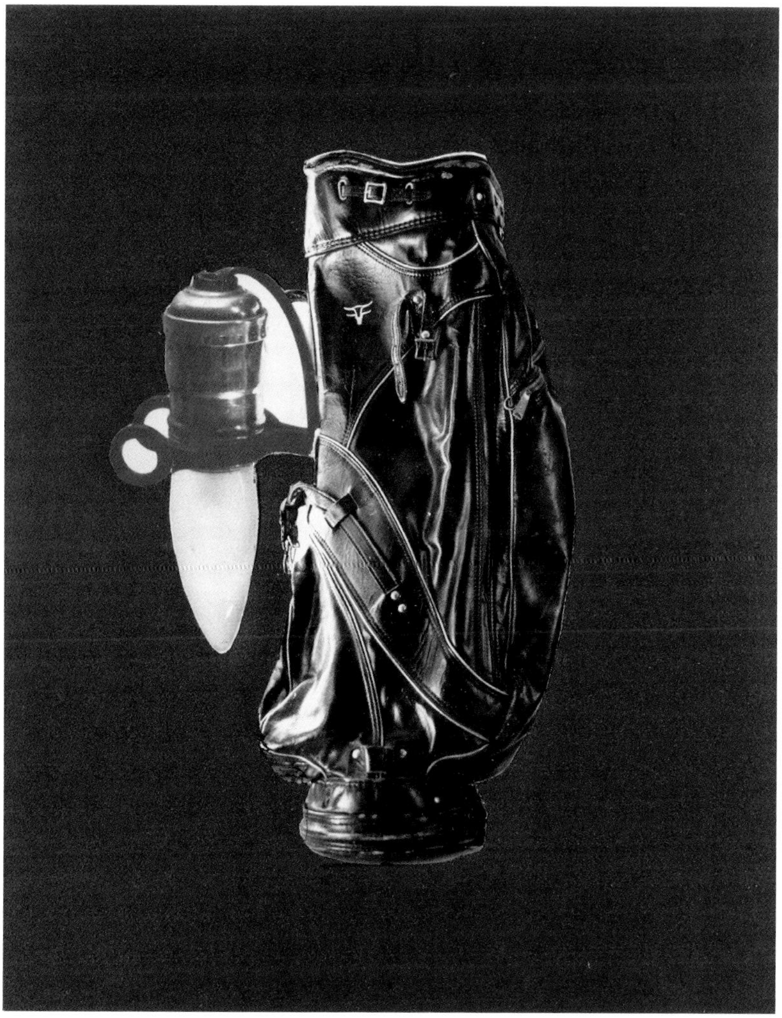

Fig. 77 Jay DeFeo, Correspondence for Bruce Conner, c. 1970s. Bruce Conner photograph collection, BANC PIC 1997.069, Bancroft Library, University of California, Berkeley.

Fig. 78 Jay DeFeo, Untitled (*for B.C.*), 1973. Photo collage on black matboard, 9¾ × 7¾ in. (24.7 × 19.7 cm). Michael Rosenfeld Gallery LLC, New York.

bag's right side, approximately where it would on a telephone. The collage is a blatant visual pun: it elides objects (bulb and receiver, golf bag and telephone stem) based on their formal resemblance, with utter disregard for function. DeFeo's play with visual resemblances between otherwise unrelated things resonates with prominent avant-garde practices from earlier in the twentieth century.[78] In this case, the unexpected associations between incongruous elements have a humorous, comical effect, giving the montage a light, amusing tenor.

By dislodging objects from their customary contexts and narratives of use and combining them according to alternative criteria, the collage demonstrates an indicative aspect of play, which Millar describes as "the lack of constraint from conventional ways of handling objects, materials and ideas." The fact that the same objects (telephone, fan, table, light bulb, and so on) reappear in different combinations throughout the series further likens her artistic process to a child's inexhaustible invention of new significations for the worn contents of her toy chest. "A telephone," Conner

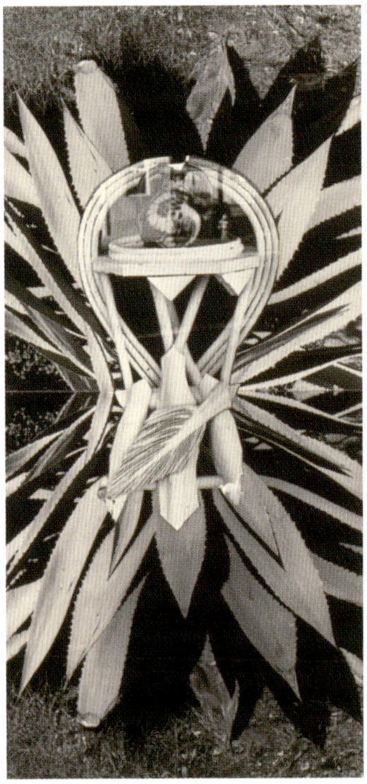

Fig. 79 Jay DeFeo, Untitled (*for B.C.*), 1973. Photo collage, 14½ × 7 in. (36.8 × 17.8 cm). Collection of the Honolulu Museum of Art. Gift of the Contemporary Museum, Honolulu, 2011, and purchased with funds given by the Judith Rothschild Foundation [TCM.1998.5.2].

wrote of DeFeo's collages in 1994, "could transform itself into a golf bag or a human figure or a flower, like a scene in a Betty Boop cartoon."[79] By comparing the transformative nature of her collages to cartoon antics, he suggests that the works possess the qualities of imagination, fantasy, and humor shared by animation and pretend play.

The bag's new appendage forces the viewer to perceive it as a telephone stem, yet the image never fully relinquishes its former identity: it flickers unstably between tote and telephone, just as its prosthesis shuttles between bulb and receiver. The perceptual tug-of-war that the collage induces imitates the liminal vision generated by make-believe, which Winnicott described as "the interplay in the child's mind of that which is subjective (near-hallucination) and that which is objectively perceived (actual, or shared reality)."[80] As a distinct appended form, the receiver has the look of an accessory that the bag has donned to pretend to be a telephone, like an apron that a child has wrapped around his or her neck to "become" a superhero. As in a game of dress-up, only one out-of-the-ordinary item is needed to signal that the player (the bag) has transformed into another. The dramatic metamorphosis that DeFeo and Conner enacted simply by dropping the definite article from "*The Rose*" also demonstrates the creative efficiency of imaginative play. While other entries in the *for B.C.* series are more elaborate than the golf-bag collage, they also read as masquerading objects. In one work, a photograph of a drawing by Conner assumes the identity of a telephone/flower (see fig. 76). In another, a table poses as a light bulb, while a succulent impersonates DeFeo's painting *The Jewel* (1959) in the background (fig. 79).[81] These examples indicate that DeFeo often created multivalent images by combining montage juxtaposition with other mischievous, surrealist-tested methods of photographic manipulation, such as doubling and silhouette.[82]

The conception of play as a kind of waking dream accounts for the collages' resemblance to surrealist objects, which generally bring together two or more familiar yet unassociated things, such as the fur pelt and tea setting coupled in Meret Oppenheim's notoriously disquieting *Object* (1936). Such unexpected combinations were meant to mimic the psyche's illogical manipulation of waking experience. The objects were supposed to shock viewers by forcing their conscious minds to grapple with the kinds of disconcerting distortions usually reserved for dreams. By simulating the liminal vision of the playing child, DeFeo's montage works of 1973 similarly use juxtaposition to confuse internal and external experience. Her lamp-telephone assemblage is a surrealist object par excellence because it mixes incongruous objects to simultaneously humorous, ominous, and erotic effect (see fig. 73). On the surface, her exchange of receiver for light bulb is merely amusing—a visual pun that confuses sound and sight. Like every good surrealist object, however, the amalgam is also unsettling: one cringes when imagining what would happen if the glass spike were brought into contact with an ear. Swapping the concave receiver for the elongated bulb also scrambles the telephone's gender to erotic ends as the phallic flame now rests suggestively in its cradle. Her collages of the modified telephone, as well as those featuring other objects in her home, continue these themes in two dimensions.

Viewing the *for B.C.* series in the context of DeFeo and Conner's fanciful correspondence, in sum, suggests that the photo collages model artistic practice on make-believe play. Although the frolicsome montages bear little formal resemblance to her earlier works from the 1970s that recycle Fillmore-era pieces, they offer a similar account of creativity. Each suite likens the process of aesthetic invention to modes of experience (make-believe and memory, respectively) in which consciousness permeates sensory perception, enacting a transformative, but fleeting, interpenetration of mind and matter, internal and external, absent and present. Winnicott articulated these dynamics: "The thing about playing is always the precariousness of the interplay of personal psychic reality and the experience of control of actual objects. This is the precariousness of magic itself." While their informality conjures ephemerality, the works that DeFeo produced under the sign of play shed the vestiges of trauma, loss, and death—as well as the temporal complexity—evident in the mnemonic works in favor of ludic fantasy and pure glee. DeFeo and Conner's tales of Rose's travels (to Happy Valley and Pandaland, among other majestic spots) were more overt acts of wish fulfillment than her metaphor of *The Rose* as memory. The unabashedly fantastical myths blatantly inverted the meaning of the painting's separation from them, transforming it from a sign of impotence and danger into evidence of the work's well-being. Their exchanges also acknowledged that, unlike the solitary chamber of memory, the "magic circle" that play creates—where, in Huizinga's definition, an "influx of mind" infuses "the matter of the world"—is often an intersubjective space.[83] The friends' construction of a shared imaginary world that revived *The Rose* as the happy-go-lucky Rose thus also revived, across the distance that now separated them, the possibility for the kinds of dialogical making that they had practiced around the painting when living in the Fillmore District.

THE ANGELIC HOSTS RETURN

Two years after making the *for B.C.* works, DeFeo enhanced the connection between her current practice and the interindividual collaborations she engaged in during *The Rose*'s production by making a series of collages that directly appropriated Conner's art. The collages brought together her photographs with reproductions of works from Conner's ANGELS series, which consists of twenty-nine photograms produced between 1972 and 1975. The images cast Conner in the divine, titular role that his film assigned to the Bekins movers. He made each life-size photogram by posing naked in front of a large sheet of photo-sensitive paper that the photographer Edmund Shea, Conner's collaborator on the project, then subjected to a burst of bright light from a slide projector. Once developed, the areas of paper that were exposed to light turned black, while those that were blocked by Conner's body turned varying shades of gray to white, depending on the proximity of his skin to the surface.[84]

To make her collages, DeFeo borrowed images of two works from the series, SOUND OF ONE HAND ANGEL (1974) and SOUND OF TWO HAND ANGEL (1974), taking them from the announcement Conner sent her for his recent show at the Braunstein/Quay Gallery in San Francisco (figs. 80, 81). According to Conner, DeFeo offered the angel collages to him "as a gift," but he asked her to keep them instead.[85] She seems, then, to have intended to use the angel collages in a way that harkened back to the Fillmore circle's practice of privately circulating artworks instead of selling them on the market.

Conner's experiments with photograms started the same year DeFeo began her *for B.C.* works, and he turned to camera-less photography for one of the same reasons she turned to collage: to shake off artist's block. "The ANGELS occurred," he recalled in 1997, "at a time when I didn't feel comfortable with what I was doing in drawing, films, or whatever else I was doing at the time. I was feeling very nebulous about my own identity, and uncertain how to cope with that." The series was indicative of the personal, creative, and career struggles Conner had experienced since 1967, not unlike the unmooring DeFeo felt after leaving Fillmore Street. He originally planned to use the silhouettes as templates for black velvet cutouts that he could carry around and unfurl like portable shadows, to remind him of his creative impasse. Conner was so pleased with the results, however,

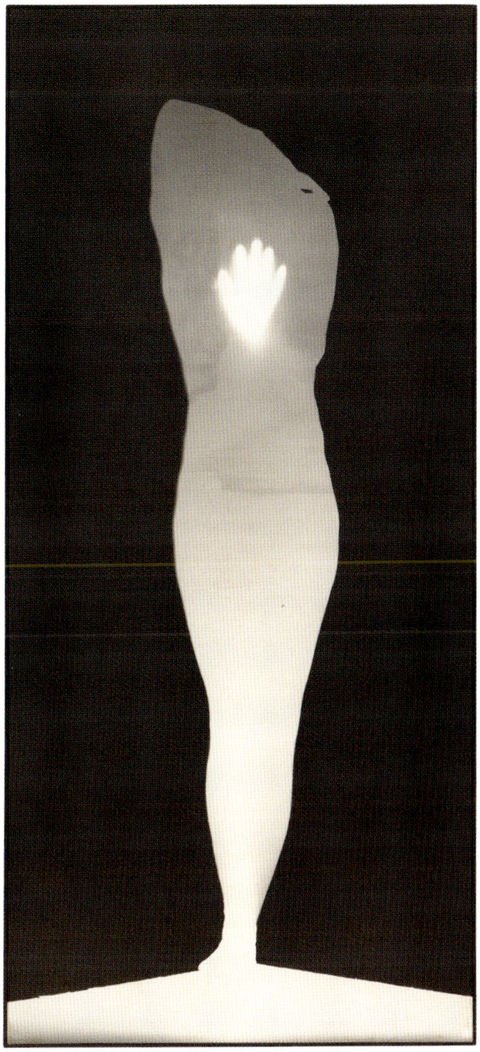

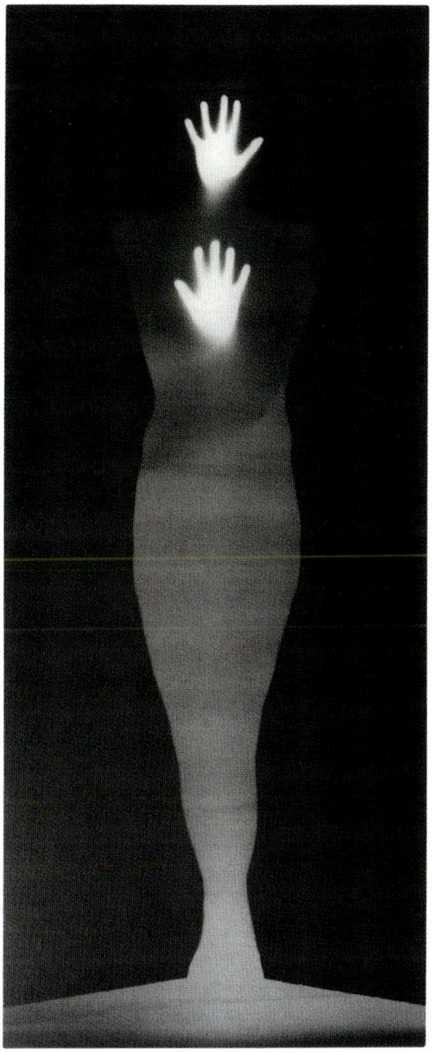

that he decided to preserve the photograms as artworks in their own right, foregoing the translation from light to dark and paper to fabric.[86] Instead of haunting emblems of stagnation and failure, they became angels—signs of transcendence and redemption. He signaled the series' connection to creative renewal by associating the photograms with transformation, a quality that—as we have seen—he felt endowed both his works and *The Rose* with vitality. "The photograms obviously have a sequential nature in how they related to one another," he explained in 1986. "Some of them in sequence appear to have that kind of transformational process of growth or alternation that we might find in motion picture film. Part of it is my interests in the process of change, of decay, of birth, rebirth, growth."[87]

As this statement suggests, the figure of the angel resonates with the ways in which Conner and DeFeo thought about their art following the breakup of the Fillmore community.[88] Angels mediate. They exist between and serve to connect discrete states (death and life) and worlds (heaven

Fig. 80 Bruce Conner and Edmund Shea, SOUND OF ONE HAND ANGEL, 1974. Gelatin silver print, 87¾ × 41¼ in. (222.9 × 104.8 cm). San Francisco Museum of Modern Art. Purchase.

Fig. 81 Bruce Conner and Edmund Shea, SOUND OF TWO HAND ANGEL, 1974. Gelatin silver print, 88 × 37 in. (223.5 × 94 cm). Collection of Tim Savinar and Patricia Unterman.

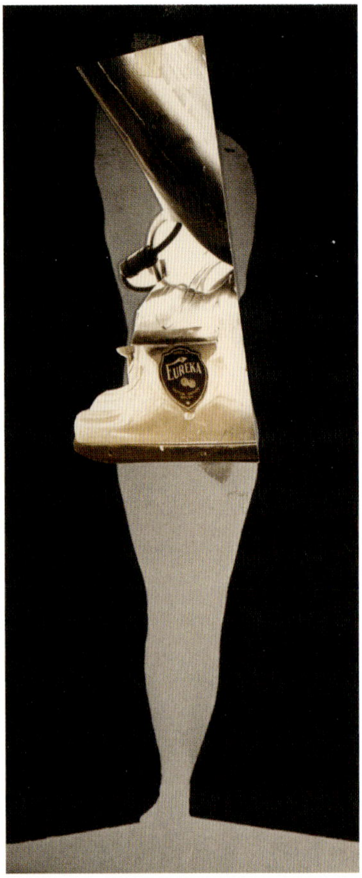

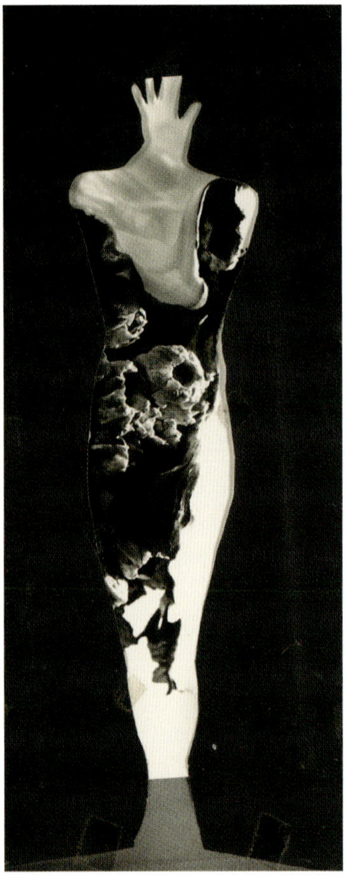

Fig. 82 Jay DeFeo, Untitled, c. 1975–76. Collage of photomechanical reproduction, gelatin silver print, and transparent pressure-sensitive tape, $9\frac{1}{2} \times 3\frac{15}{16}$ in. (24.2 × 10 cm). The Jay DeFeo Foundation, Berkeley, Calif. [JDF no. E2925].

Fig. 83 Jay DeFeo, Untitled, c. 1975–76. Collage of photomechanical reproduction, gelatin silver print, and transparent pressure-sensitive tape, $9\frac{3}{8} \times 3\frac{3}{4}$ in. (23.8 × 9.5 cm). The Jay DeFeo Foundation, Berkeley, Calif. [JDF no. E2922].

and earth). But they occupy this ambiguous ontological territory in a more agreeable way than a corpse at a wake. Angels are animate souls, rather than lifeless bodies: physically dubious, but spiritually full. Instead of causing impotence, their suspension between realms endows them with miraculous powers.[89] They demonstrate that agency and being can continue once life has departed, even without reincarnation or resurrection. Angels were thus an ideal vehicle for DeFeo and Conner's dialogue—which this chapter has traced—around the status of their artworks, especially *The Rose,* once they left the Fillmore District and dismantled the attachments to site, process, and community that seemed to give their art life. The figure of the angel resonates particularly strongly with DeFeo's perception of *The Rose* in the 1970s, when she saw its suspension between life and death, presence and absence, as the source of its continued power and vitality—a way for the painting to fuel her renewed creativity by bridging disparate moments in time (her past and present oeuvres) and space (the distance between herself and Conner).

DeFeo's recycling of Conner's photograms into collages fit with the ANGELS' significance to Conner—his view of them as symbols of transformation and creative renewal. Almost all eighteen collages that DeFeo based on the series combine one of the two photograms reproduced on the

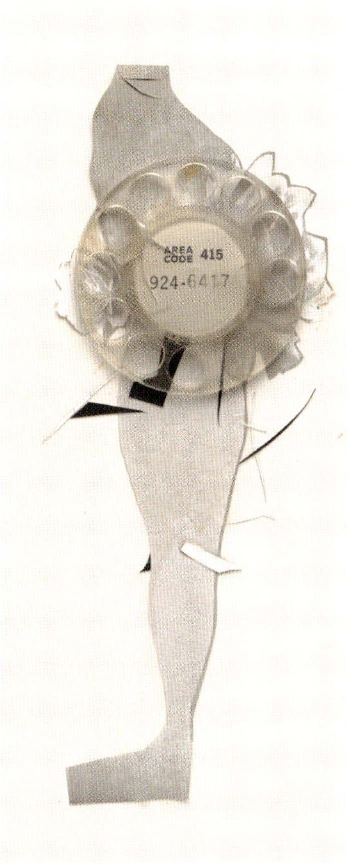

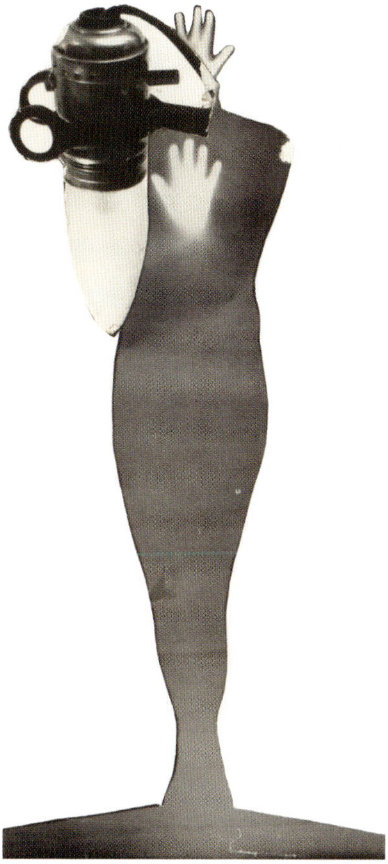

Fig. 84 Jay DeFeo, *Collage for Bruce Conner,* 1975. Collage of photocopy and gelatin silver prints with telephone dial on matboard, 10¾ × 4⅛ in. (27.3 × 10.5 cm). Private collection.

Fig. 85 Jay DeFeo, Untitled, c. 1975–76. Collage of photomechanical reproduction, gelatin silver print, and transparent pressure-sensitive tape, 8$^{13}/_{16}$ × 4 in. (22.4 × 10.2 cm). The Jay DeFeo Foundation, Berkeley, Calif. [JDF no. E2943].

announcement with cutouts from one or more of her photographs. Using cellophane tape, she affixed image fragments on top of Conner's ghostly figure (fig. 82) and sometimes cut around the contour of his form to slip her photographs partially or completely behind the photogram's black background (fig. 83). Through these methods, she used the reproduced photograms as supports and apertures for a variety of her photographs, ranging from botanical and landscape images to depictions of the motley collection of objects (candlestick telephone, fragmented teacup, vacuum cleaner, and suchlike) that populated her studio. She also cannibalized her studio shots for the collages, extracting fragments of the space and details of works in progress to combine with Conner's form. By thus modifying Conner's photograms, by continuing their production into their reception, DeFeo kept them alive, much as the pair's playful correspondence reanimated *The Rose.*

DeFeo's angel collages further signal the generative energy of artistic rebirth by exhibiting many of the playful elements found in her *for B.C.* series. They often act as visual puns and as analogues for her practice of nicknaming Conner. Two collages, for instance, imagine him as a telephone by appending both real and represented telephone parts to the slender, upright trace of his body (figs. 84, 85). She also reversed this pretend play

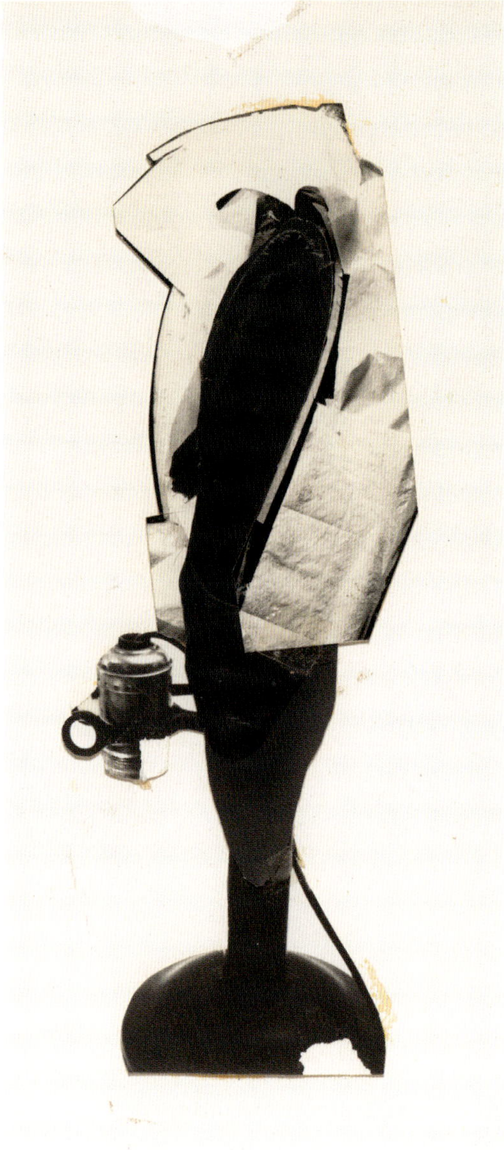

Fig. 86 Jay DeFeo, Untitled, 1975–76. Photo collage with transparent pressure-sensitive tape, 10 × 4½ in. (25.4 × 11.4 cm). The Jay DeFeo Foundation, Berkeley, Calif. [JDF no. E2921].

to dress the phone up as Conner by wrapping a detail from one of her in-progress *Loop* paintings around the phone like a stole to approximate the tapered form of his ANGELS (fig. 86). DeFeo's studio logs demonstrate that she produced the series with the same exuberant experimentation that characterized her previous collage production (fig. 87). The eighth frame of the contact sheet shows approximately a dozen modified photograms mounted on various backings and strung up in sloppy rows with other drawings and paintings. These examples suggest a serial process of permutation through recombination: through the interplay of repetition and difference, the collages fed off each other as they materially cannibalized her photographs. Mounted on her studio wall, the reproduced photograms resemble a troop of paper dolls sporting two-dimensional costumes. As with the earlier

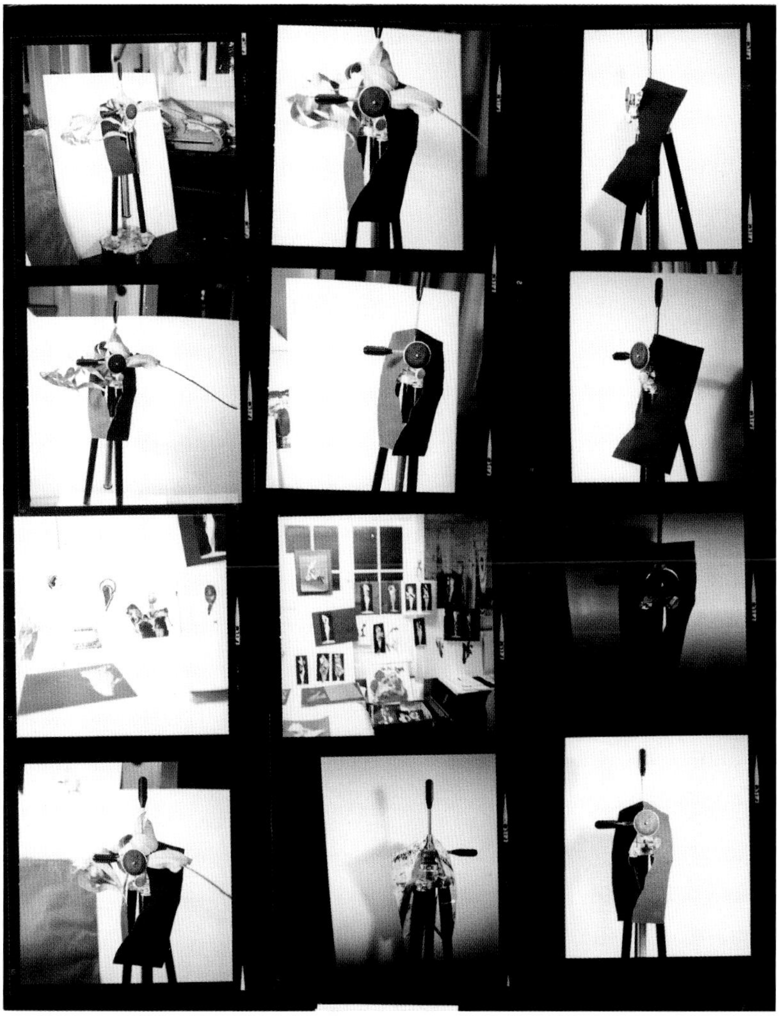

Fig. 87 Jay DeFeo, Untitled, January 1976. Gelatin silver contact print, 10 × 8 in. (25.4 × 10.3 cm). The Jay DeFeo Foundation, Berkeley, Calif. [JDF no. C0003A].

montages, which invert the contents of DeFeo and Conner's serious dealings with *The Rose,* the angel collages appropriate a material artifact from Conner's public life as a professional artist (the exhibition announcement) and turn it into something private—an inside joke shared between friends.

However, DeFeo's angel collages combine the playful techniques and aesthetics of her recent photo collages with the intertextual dynamics of the exchanges she engaged in while living on Fillmore Street more overtly than her *for B.C.* series by directly recycling Conner's art. Like her past interindividual collaborations around *The Rose,* her modifications both amplify and interrupt the formal language of Conner's photograms. Many of her manipulations magnify the photograms' mystery by heightening the ambiguity inherent in silhouettes. They also exaggerate the way his ghostly figures confuse absence and presence by alternately treating the indexes as solid supports for her photographs and as windows through which to view them. However, her collages also multiply and miniaturize his unique, life-size works. Moreover, many of the guises she used to "dress" the ANGELS are incongruous with their original, awe-inspiring manifestations: they pollute Conner's pure, radiant beings with the stuff of her everyday world. In one collage, for example, DeFeo appended the bottom of a vacuum cleaner to Conner's upper body (see fig. 82). The addition both echoes the shape of his torso and appears to be responsible for sucking out his hollowed form, mischievously converting the otherworldly ethereality of his image into mundane vacancy.

A note that DeFeo sent Conner regarding the series further indicates how she adapted the dialogical style of making that developed in the Fillmore community to her life after it (fig. 88). She wrote the note on a photocopy of a modified announcement for Conner's ANGELS show. Cut-out photographs of roses dapple the pair of reproduced photograms that flank information about the exhibition; blossoms wedge into the crook of one gracefully tapered figure's waist and between the outstretched hands of the other. In addition to these amendments, DeFeo scribbled a request, in looping cursive script, between the regimented lines of blocky type: "Send more vases! / love, Rose."[90] By signing the note with the name of her imaginary alter ego, DeFeo confirmed that she viewed her request for more announcements and, by extension, the angel collages that she would produce from them as part of the friends' long-standing game around *The Rose.*

Read together, the note and collaged images identify the reproduced photograms as the sought-after "vases," indicating that DeFeo viewed the ANGELS as containers for arranging not cut flowers but cut photographs. This metaphor suggests that the photograms were useful to her because their liminal status—the fact that the indexes hover perceptually and materially between presence and absence—meant that they provided both a

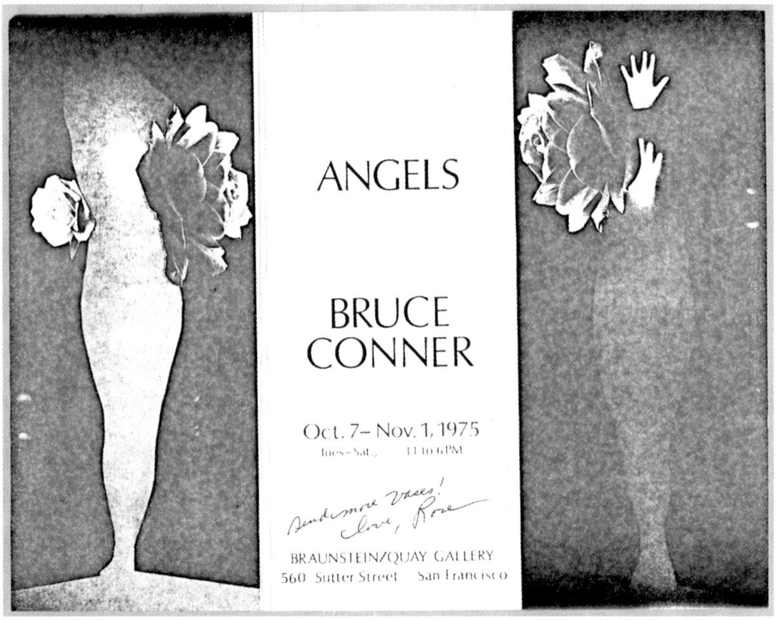

Fig. 88 Jay DeFeo, Note to Bruce Conner on a photocopy of an untitled collage made from an announcement for Conner's exhibition ANGELS, 1975. Photocopy, 8¾ × 11½ in. (22.2 × 29.2 cm). Bruce Conner correspondence concerning Jay DeFeo's *The Rose*, circa 1930–96, BANC MSS 98/32c, Bancroft Library, University of California, Berkeley.

foundational structure for her collage compositions and an empty space in which they could reside.[91] It is tempting to see DeFeo's note about Conner's photograms as indicative of how Fillmore artists perceived one another's art more generally—that they viewed their friends' works as creative catalysts because they provided both structuring foundations and open spaces to fill with their own making. The works their interindividual collaborations yielded often remained assemblages of distinct objects, media, and authors even as they amalgamated into something new, much as a vase and the flowers it contains remain distinguishable entities even as they fuse to form an arrangement. DeFeo's angel collages perform this dance with Conner's photograms: her interpenetrating images invert the perfect totality and autonomy of his silhouette, transforming his solitary image into a site of dialogue.

DeFeo's perception of Conner's photograms also echoes her view of *The Rose* in the early 1970s, which this chapter has endeavored to illuminate. By framing the painting as both her memory and her imaginary friend, DeFeo endowed it with the same mixture of absence and presence that she assigned Conner's ANGELS when referring to them as "vases." Like a vessel, and like angels, both modes of experience are liminal: they are characterized by the interplay of absence and presence. Whether conjured by remembrance or imagination, the mind's illusory images mold our perception of the tangible objects in front of us as the vase's negative space shapes the flowers it holds. And, like the coming together of vase and flowers (or the scraps that make up a montage), the intermediate experiences of memory and make-believe produce precarious hybrids—transformative amalgamations of mind and matter that are unstable and fleeting.

The liminality that DeFeo attributed to *The Rose* reflected the paradoxical relationship that she seems to have developed with the work as it languished in SFAI. During this time, the painting's physical distance from her made it loom large in her thoughts, inspiring her and Conner's many thwarted plans to bring it back to life. The fact that the painting remained the "core" of her "creative universe" despite being "in its decline" supports the idea that DeFeo viewed the work as simultaneously present and absent, vital and decrepit.[92] The note's indication that she found the liminality of Conner's photograms to be creatively invigorating suggests that she likewise saw *The Rose* as an effective creative catalyst because of, rather than in spite of, her paradoxical impression of it. Like a vase, *The Rose* provided the ideal marriage of structure (formal and conceptual foundation) and space to spur artistic invention. It played a vital role in rebooting DeFeo's practice by acting as a generative vacancy—a container for her and Conner to fill with fertile myths. In this way, *The Rose* continued to serve as a hub for intertextual exchanges through which the artists negotiated ideas, authorship, and intersubjectivity. As a vase of water can prolong the life of a cut flower, so DeFeo and Conner's exchanges around *The Rose* during its period of seclusion prolonged its vitality as a source of creativity.

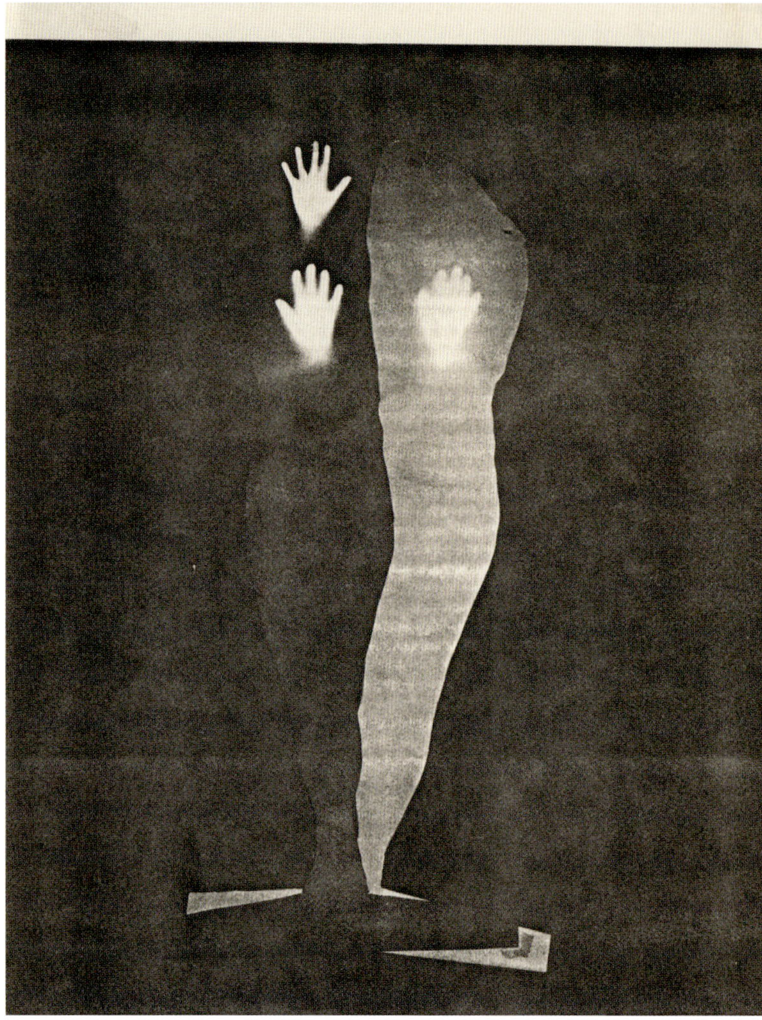

Fig. 89 Jay DeFeo, Untitled, c. 1975–76. Photocopy, 11 × 8½ in. (28 × 21.6 cm). The Jay DeFeo Foundation, Berkeley, Calif. [JDF no. E2955A].

Another angel collage, a photocopy of which DeFeo sent Conner, reasserts the social dynamic of the creative exchanges that she took part in during her years on Fillmore Street (fig. 89). During that time, this book has argued, *The Rose* became a nexus for intertextual collaborations that figured alternative modes of authorship and community. These experiments were both predicated on and helped shape the intimate social bonds of the Fillmore coterie. Specifically, they were a means to negotiate non-oppressive relationships between self and other that, ideally, struck a balance between individual freedom and collective belonging—a balance that many members of San Francisco's postwar artistic underground, including Conner, felt was sorely lacking in the broader art world and society of postwar America. The collage suggests that, even after the community's dispersal, DeFeo saw her appropriative montages performing the interpenetration not only of images and artistic practices, but also of subjectivities.

The montage uncharacteristically bypasses DeFeo's photographs to combine the two photograms reproduced on the ANGELS exhibition announcement, liberating the spectral figures from their cells on either side of the flyer and joining them at the hip, imbricating their limbless and headless bodies. This union grants the ANGELS the contact for which their pale hands seem to reach.[93] In this way, the collage foregrounds the dialectic between isolation and contact that makes each ANGEL's solitary confinement—as well as the collaborations of the Fillmore community, especially after its dispersal—so poignant. While the silhouettes merge to form one body, their respective shades distinguish them as separate entities. The ANGELS thus merge to form a one that is two, and a two that are one. Like all of DeFeo's angel collages, their rendezvous performs the vagaries of intersubjective space—the destabilizing transformations of identity and being that occur when two people come together.

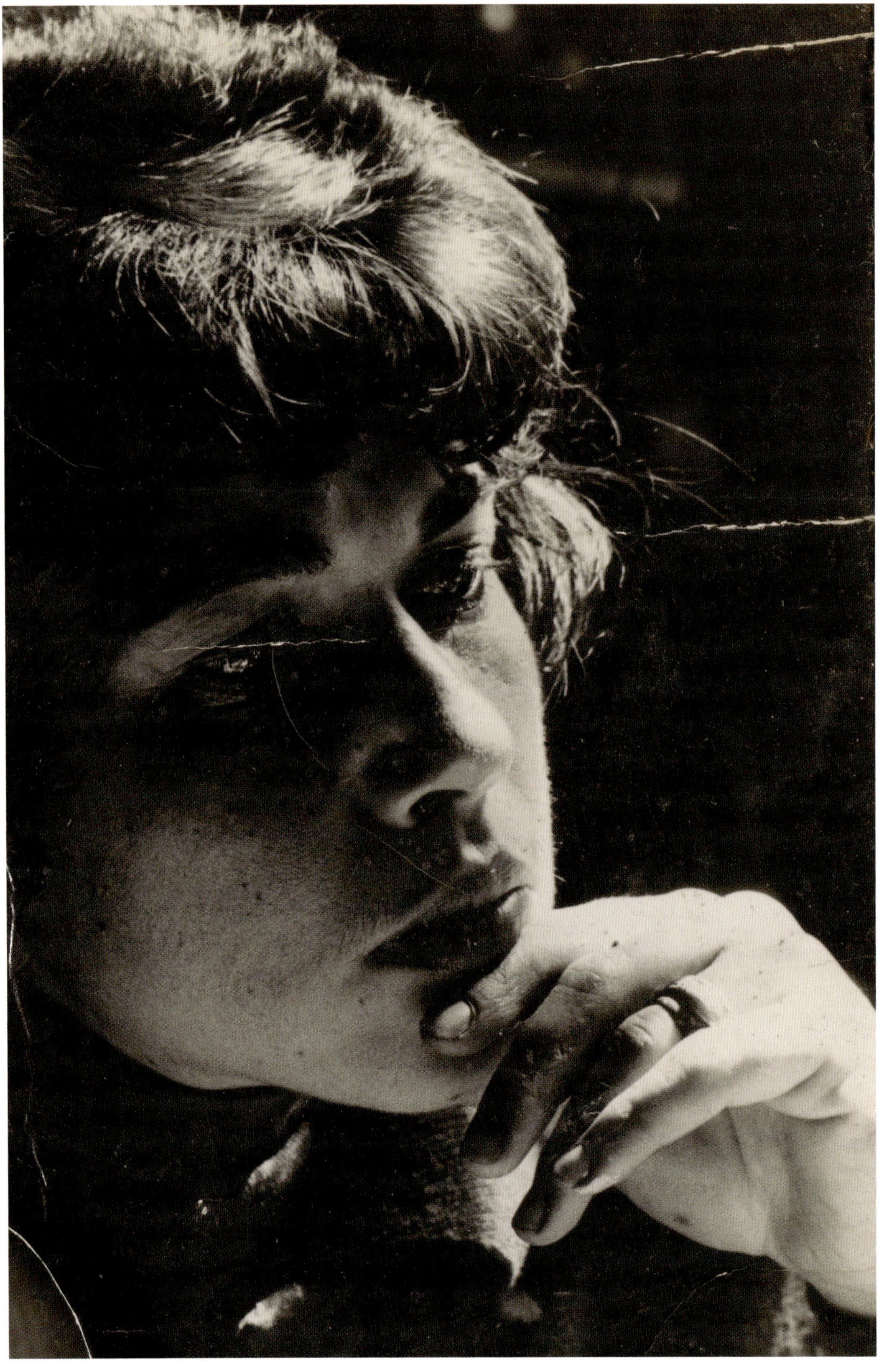

Coda

The Rose served as a site for the construction of not only community and authorship, but also gender identity, which was integral to the subjectivities and relationships that DeFeo and her fellow artists formed through their exchanges around the painting. In each case, a male artist's portrayals of DeFeo and her painting proposed a certain script for her gender identity that she, in turn, modified or outright contradicted in creative response. The interindividual collaborations that took place around *The Rose* thus became vehicles for gender play that sometimes subverted but other times confirmed the rigid gender binaries and hierarchies that structured the patriarchy of postwar America.

Such has been, for the most part, implicit in the findings presented in the preceding chapters. Let us address the gender dynamics of the exchanges around *The Rose* explicitly now, with the luxury of having all four chapters in mind, to see what they reveal about how gender affected the lives and practices of artists in the Fillmore circle. In each case, the gender identities of the artists were negotiated primarily through private, reciprocal exchanges. The collaborations also placed a woman artist (DeFeo) at the center of a circle of male artists. In both respects, the gender dynamics of the exchanges differed from typical accounts of gender and art at midcentury—a fact that has led several scholars to claim that artists in the Fillmore neighborhood experienced a high degree of gender equality in comparison to contemporary artists elsewhere in the United States. We will find, however, that the Fillmore community's gender politics in fact fell somewhere between the utopian egalitarianism that some have attributed to it and the crippling misogyny to which such a vision is opposed.

THE EXCEPTIONALISM OF SAN FRANCISCO

Like most women artists of her generation, DeFeo was reluctant to make gender an overt framework for her art practice.[1] The formalist education she received at Berkeley instilled the idea that art is universal and thus transcends all aspects of difference, including gender. As was standard for women artists in the 1940s and 1950s, DeFeo adopted the masculine models that modernism provided for artistic identity and creativity as best she could, assuming a gender-neutral nickname and deploying a formal vocabulary that—in its scale, gestural quality, materiality, and palette—was often coded male despite its ostensibly universal abstractness. These beliefs and practices meant that DeFeo, like so many of her contemporaries, as

Detail, fig. 90

Anne M. Wagner has written, "hesitated over how to understand an artist's status as a woman (and vice versa) and worried about the relationship of feminism to art and aesthetics."[2]

Even though DeFeo has been retroactively embraced by feminist art history, she was reluctant to view her work in relation to women's liberation, as evidenced by her rejection in the 1970s of readings of *The Rose* as yonic (quoted in Chapter 1).[3] For women artists such as DeFeo, who spent their careers ignoring or masking their gender, making their identity as women suddenly matter to their artistic practice and identity usually seemed absurd and/or dangerous. "If the awakening of feminism meant that one had to identify with other women," Helen Molesworth explained, "it also meant that one had to identify oneself as not equal to men—a position some embraced with the proper anger and others avoided with an equally reasonable ambivalence."[4] DeFeo, like most American women artists born before the late 1930s, adopted the latter stance of ambivalent avoidance.

While scholars generally note that DeFeo's attitudes toward gender are typical for her generation, the reason most give for her perspective on gender diverges significantly from the usual explanation of how women artists her age acquired their similar views. The latter narrative goes something like this: for artists working in New York in the decades following World War II, masking one's female identification was crucial to surviving an art world structured by overt sexism. Abstract expressionism's focus on individual expression meant that artistic identity gained increasing importance in the popular imagination. As the movement became entangled in Cold War discourses, so its stereotypical artist came to embody, in Ann Gibson's words, the "ideal postwar American male subject"—a heroic individual who was "a bastion of autonomy in an age of encroaching collectivity and conformity." While straight, white, male abstract expressionists appropriated characteristics (such as the unconscious) stereotypically associated with women and people of color, artists who occupied such "marked categories" risked threatening their already-tenuous claims to artistic authority if they similarly claimed characteristics linked to the "primitive" subjectivities they supposedly possessed. As Wagner has argued, adopting an approach to art-making founded on self-expression was an inherently conflicted proposition for women abstract expressionists, given that a vital part of their identity, their gender, was seen to disqualify them from authorship.[5]

Commentators and historians have established that the art world of postwar Los Angeles and the literary scenes fostered by Beat writers in Greenwich Village, North Beach, and Venice, California, were similarly macho and sexist. The Ferus Gallery, Los Angeles's premier venue for avant-garde art in the 1950s and 1960s, rivaled New York's Cedar Tavern as, in Molesworth's words, a "boys' club par excellence."[6] DeFeo was one of few women admitted into the "all kings stable," the artist Kenneth Price's descriptor for Ferus. As in New York, gender discrimination was a matter of course in Southern California. "The art world was very macho then," Henry

Hopkins, who was highly involved in the Los Angeles art scene in the 1950s and 1960s, recalled. "You'd hear dealers saying things like 'I can't represent a woman. She's gonna get married and have children and she won't keep producing.' That was the standard line."[7]

Reactionary gender politics similarly pervaded the Beat movement, undercutting its claims to social radicalism. The author Joyce Johnson ironically labeled women Beat writers like herself "minor characters," to signal how their male counterparts relegated them to passive, conventionally feminine roles such as witness and supporter—viewing them as merely "silent 'girls' in black," to borrow scholar Ronna Johnson's potent phrase. Given the pervasive male chauvinism of the New York and Los Angeles art worlds, as well as various Beat undergrounds, it is little wonder that downplaying one's femininity was, as Maggie Nelson put it, "something of a prerequisite for women to get in and stay in the conversation—the way to get ahead, get seen, get heard."[8]

Scholars of postwar San Francisco have given essentially the opposite explanation for DeFeo's downplaying of gender. Instead of reading her hesitancy over the label "woman artist" as an ingrained defense mechanism against gender discrimination, they see it as evidence of the "relative gender equality," to quote Lucy Lippard, of the Bay Area art world in the 1950s.[9] According to these accounts, San Francisco's weak art market largely inoculated it against the sexism that plagued the art scenes of other major American cities. With commercial competition eliminated, male artists were much less likely to marginalize their female colleagues because they had no practical reason to view them as threats. The vacuum left by commercial art institutions also helped shift the locus of art practice to the traditionally female-coded domestic sphere (as discussed in Chapter 2), which arguably helped women occupy more central positions within the aesthetic philosophies and practices of postwar San Francisco.

The argument goes that these factors fostered an environment of "unparalleled opportunity, in which women were not just participants, but became leaders of artistic activity," as Susan Landauer asserted. DeFeo confirmed this narrative of exceptionalism in a 1988 interview: "I really felt that I had the respect of all my male friends who were artists. It [being a woman] wasn't an issue maybe because there wasn't any competition for wall space, even any competition for jobs." This statement led Landauer to speculate that "perhaps" so few women abstract expressionists in San Francisco "concerned themselves with gender-specific imagery or attributes" because they "faced relatively little resistance" to being a woman.[10] This account inverts the standard explanation of why women artists tended to downplay gender prior to 1970: while women artists in New York and Los Angeles were forced to actively suppress their gender in the face of systematic sexism, DeFeo and her Bay Area peers had the luxury of ignoring gender because the virtual absence of sexism in the local art scene prevented gender difference from meaningfully registering in their lives as artists.

DIFFERENCE AND DESIRE

It is rare in the history of Western art for a woman artist to form the center of a group of male artists.[11] That this demographic dynamic crystallized around *The Rose* thus seems to confirm the relative gender parity of the Fillmore community. It is almost impossible to imagine that a woman artist could have achieved a similarly central and elevated position within a contemporaneous coterie elsewhere in the United States, given the emphatically masculine conception of the postwar American artist and the structural sexism of most art institutions at the time. However, the fact that all of the artists who created works about *The Rose* were men also complicates our notion of gender in the Fillmore circle; for it means that none of the many female artists and writers who were involved in the scene (including Joan Brown, Sonia Gechtoff, Jean Conner, Joanna McClure, Bernice Bing, Patricia Jordan, Nell Sinton, and Deborah Remington) chose to respond to DeFeo's painting. While the reasons for this gender disparity remain somewhat obscure, this book's analysis of the exchanges between DeFeo and her male neighbors provides some clues.

Her collaborations with Wallace Berman, Michael McClure, Bruce Conner, and, to a lesser extent, Wally Hedrick display a mix of separation and contact that, I have argued, qualify them as "interindividual." DeFeo and her friends put their works, processes, and identities in dialogue with one another while still maintaining some distinction between them. In doing so, they attempted to foster an intersubjective space that still allowed for their independence as individual subjects and authors. There is evidence that this mix of dependence and autonomy was key to sustaining relationships that the artists found creatively productive. When characterizing Berman and Conner as her "muses" (quoted in Chapter 1), for example, DeFeo described her creatively stimulating relationships with the men as a dance between closeness and solitude, identification and distance. Likewise, McClure's notebooks and DeFeo's falling-out with Gechtoff (both described in Chapter 3) indicate that, even without a strong art market fueling competition, relationships within the Fillmore community could sour when intimacy slipped into identification, threatening one's individuality and originality.

The mix of gender difference and heterosexual desire between DeFeo (who identified as a straight woman) and Berman, Hedrick, Conner, and McClure (who identified as straight men) complemented the interplay between separation and contact that defines interindividual collaboration. Gender difference guaranteed a degree of alterity between artists who otherwise shared similar racial and socioeconomic backgrounds. In doing so, it helped ensure that the artists' identities remained discrete from each other—individuation that DeFeo notably struggled to sustain in her relationship with Gechtoff, another woman artist. At the same time, some degree of sexual desire between the artists, especially the men's attraction to DeFeo, helped propel their coming together. McClure's poem makes explicit the undercurrent of desire that helped stoke DeFeo's male friends' admiration for her and, in turn, fuel their homages to *The Rose.*

Perhaps DeFeo and other women artists of the Fillmore circle never exchanged works around *The Rose* because their relationships lacked the combination of alterity and attraction needed to motivate and sustain interindividual collaboration. Speaking in the 1970s, DeFeo described her relationships with Gechtoff and Brown, who consecutively occupied the flat next to 2322 Fillmore Street, in terms that differ decidedly from the combination of intimacy and isolation she used to characterize her association with Berman and Conner. "On a very personal level," she recalled, "between Joan and I for instance, or between Sonia and I . . . , there was a lot of exchange because we were painting next door to each other and we'd see each other at the end of a good day or bad day as the case may be. So in that case, there may be an exchange, not just social talk, but talk about our work."[12] Her daily contact with the female painters suggests an intimate bond that lacked the countervailing distance she attributed to her relationships with male artists of her circle. The fact that DeFeo, Gechtoff, and Brown all identified as female likely helped foster the easy familiarity among them. It also likely helped edge that familiarity into the unhealthy identification DeFeo experienced with Gechtoff. A photomontage DeFeo made that amalgamates her portrait with Brown's and, in doing so, highlights the similarity between their features to uncanny effect suggests that a similar blurring of boundaries may have occurred between the neighbors—though, it would seem, without the same dire interpersonal and professional consequences (fig. 90).

DeFeo also states that her routine contact with Gechtoff and, later, Brown, prompted them to talk about their work—a topic that was generally off-limits when Fillmore artists socialized. (Recall, for instance, McClure's statement that when he visited DeFeo's studio, "we didn't talk much. We were alive.")[13] DeFeo and her female neighbors thus exchanged aesthetic advice and emotional support rather than homages. They stimulated one another's creativity through daily conversations rather than dialogues carried out across works.

The distinction between DeFeo's relationships with the men and women of her coterie highlights the double-edged nature of the gender dynamics that developed around *The Rose*—a duality that manifested in each of this book's case studies. On the one hand, the fact that male artists enthusiastically engaged the work of a female artist suggests that they respected her as an equal. On the other hand, this arrangement risked replicating the conventional gender hierarchy of Western art and society, which was particularly marked in postwar America, by potentially positioning DeFeo as an object that is spoken for, rather than a subject who is spoken with. Simone de Beauvoir articulated the difference between these two possibilities for male-female relations in *The Second Sex* (1949): "Thus it is

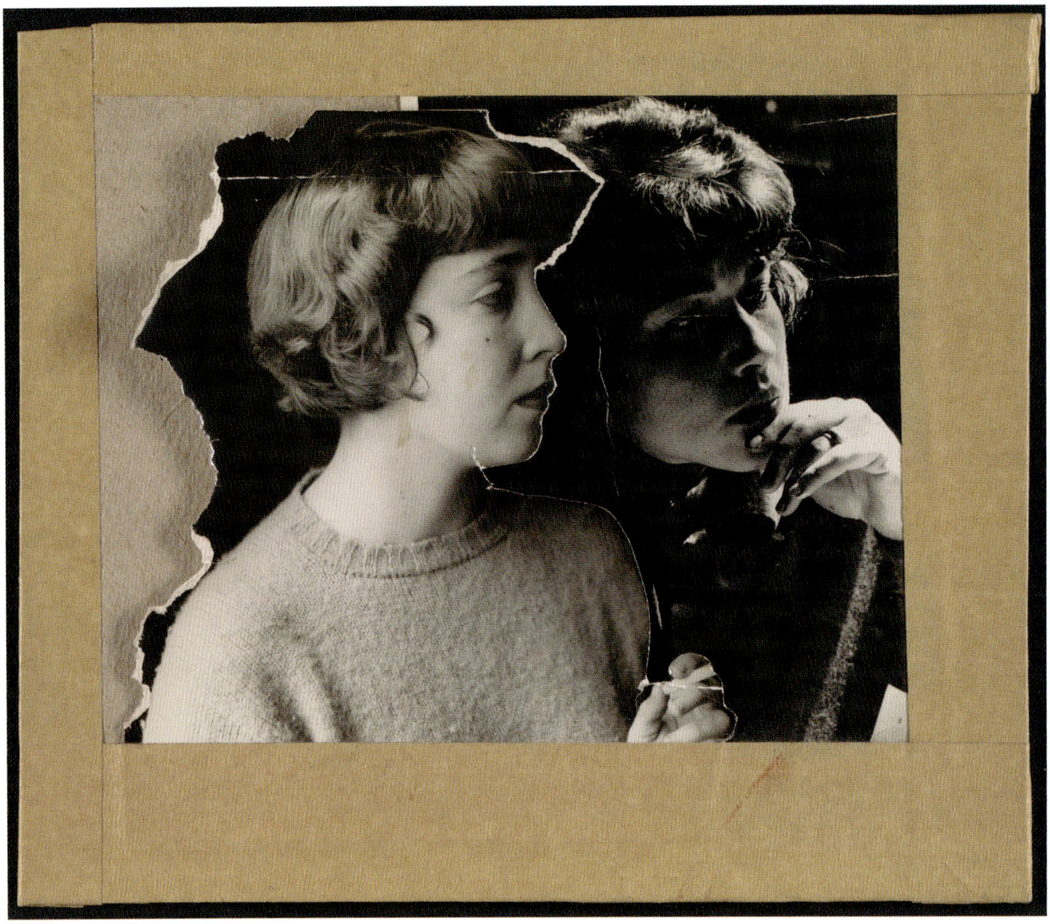

Fig. 90 Jay DeFeo, Collage of Joan Brown and Jay DeFeo, c. 1958. Photographic prints, card stock, and tape, 8⅕ × 9⅘ in. (21 × 25 cm). Jay DeFeo papers, Archives of American Art, Smithsonian Institution, Washington, D.C.

quite true that woman is other than man, and this alterity is directly felt in desire, the embrace, love; but the real relation is one of reciprocity; as such it gives rise to authentic drama. Through eroticism, love, friendship, and their alternatives, deception, hate, rivalry, the relation is a struggle between conscious beings each of whom wishes to be essential, it is the mutual recognition of free beings who confirm one another's freedom, it is the vague transition from aversion to participation. To pose Woman is to pose the absolute Other, without reciprocity, denying against all experience that she is a subject, a fellow human being."[14] The preceding chapters show that the relationships that DeFeo and her male friends negotiated around *The Rose* often uncomfortably skirted the line between these contrasting possibilities: while gender difference facilitated the artists' attempts to strike a balance between individual and collective authorship, it also complicated—to the point of jeopardizing—this project by creating a power imbalance between DeFeo and her male collaborators.

AUTHENTIC DRAMA

The private nature of the exchanges that occurred around *The Rose* helped foster the kind of reciprocal, participatory gender relations that Beauvoir championed. As Wagner has demonstrated, gender identity is constructed relationally through a process of "disjunction and recognition" as "the self apprehends and claims its difference from and similitude with other selves."[15] In this case, Wagner was referring primarily to instances in which women artists working in the United States during the twentieth century were forced to renegotiate how gender figured into their artistic identity in response to public (mis)representations of them that, more often than not, framed them within feminine stereotypes that were both alienating and marginalizing.

The collaborations around *The Rose* show how this process of subjective negotiation could shift when it played out mainly within the private, interpersonal space of the coterie, rather than the public, professional space of criticism. As the "*Artforum* incident" discussed in Chapter 1 showed, one important way in which encountering oneself in photographs hung in a friend's home or in an unpublished poem written by a neighbor was different from encountering similar portrayals in magazines or exhibition reviews was that the former allowed for, even encouraged, a response. Within the coterie, the representations that DeFeo's male friends crafted of *The Rose* operated as opening salvos, rather than definitive statements, as she replied to them in ways that both built upon and pushed against the gendered artistic identities they proposed for her. This book's chapters show, for example, that she tempered Berman's binary depiction of artist and model by posing as a tomboyish sandlot slugger; answered McClure's vision of her generative sensuality with a stark, desexualized image of the corporeal damage wrought by her artistic labor; and inverted Conner's portrait of her as broken by framing *The Rose*'s loss as a source for her continued creative powers.

Judith Butler has observed that "silence is the performative effect of a certain kind of speech, where the speech is an address that has as its object the deauthorization of the speech of the one to whom the speech act is addressed."[16] The fact that DeFeo responded to her male friends' interpretations of *The Rose* by continuing the conversation, rather than with silence, suggests that she saw them as a source of agency more than as a source of alienation—that is, that she perceived the men in her circle to be speaking *with* her more than *for* her. Like most of her female contemporaries, DeFeo often had misgivings about the ways men portrayed her. This book records reservations she expressed over Berman's photographs, Conner's film, and McClure's and Fred Martin's written statements about her art. Yet, unlike most female artists prior to women's liberation, she felt empowered to speak back to these misrepresentations largely because, I believe, they were proposed in the context of interpersonal relationships conditioned on trust and mutual respect, rather than in the context of public, institutional forums (such as the art press, art schools, and commercial galleries) structured by judgment and exclusion.

Indeed, the tension that characterizes the dialogues that played out around *The Rose* resonates with the "authentic drama" that, according to Beauvoir, arises within equitable relationships between men and women when gender alterity is negotiated reciprocally. The friction between DeFeo's works and those of her male friends could be seen to express the "struggle" that Beauvoir describes "between conscious beings each of whom wishes to be essential." Meanwhile, the consonance between their works (the way they build off of and amplify one another) could be seen to manifest the countervailing aspect of that relationship—"the mutual recognition of free beings who confirm one another's freedom."[17]

The intimate, dialogical nature of gender construction around *The Rose* guarded against "mythical thought." According to Beauvoir, this essentialist way of conceptualizing identity proposes the "Eternal Feminine, unique and changeless," "against the dispersed, contingent, and multiple existences of actual women." The gendered identities that DeFeo's male friends proposed for her were unlikely to calcify into an image of her as "the absolute Other" for two reasons. First, the fact that their depictions of her arose from their personal relationships with her—that they were based on firsthand knowledge of her and her painting—meant that they were less likely to utterly abstract her individual gender expression into stereotypical notions of "the feminine." As Beauvoir noted, "The more relationships are concretely lived, the less they are idealized."[18] Second, their depictions of DeFeo were formulated in dialogue with her and, thus, as discussed above, were always open to revision. This process of proposal and counterproposal posited her gender identity as performative, evolving, situational, constructed, and individual, rather than expressed, static, innate, and universal. The interindividual collaborations around *The Rose* thus manifested Beauvoir's assertion that gender is, as Diane Richardson summarized, "something that is acquired through the social process of *becoming gendered,*" an idea that Butler influentially elaborated some forty years later in her theory of gender as "performative."[19]

Many of the exchanges examined in this book also nod to the fluid, constructed nature of identity by playing with conventional gender signifiers in ways that defy postwar stereotypes. The works DeFeo's friends made about *The Rose,* and her responses to them, frequently scrambled the strict binaries that structured mainstream America's perception of gender in the decades following World War II. For example, DeFeo's collaborators often pictured her as possessing some version of Romantic, expressionist subjectivity—an ideal from which women artists were almost categorically barred in the period. By representing DeFeo as a god-like creator ex nihilo, an intrepid mountaineer, a liberated action painter, and a tragic visionary, her male friends challenged not only the adamantly masculine gendering of the postwar artist, but also, in Nelson's words, the "misogyny which for centuries has posited women as the antithesis to abstraction or transcendence."[20] By thus mobilizing period tropes of artistic identity in ways that altered their standard gendering, DeFeo and her circle exercised some of the limited freedom they had to redefine gender categories and determine their own gender identifications. In this way, they used *The Rose* as a vehicle for gender play—as a means, according to Sharon Marcus's definition of "play," to exploit "the *elasticity* of systems, their ability to be stretched without permanent alteration." This finding accords with research by Richard Cándida Smith and Michael Davidson, who have each argued that California's midcentury cultural undergrounds served as incubators for alternative masculinities.[21]

POSING WOMAN

The gender play that occurred around *The Rose* thus, in some ways, supports the narrative that gender relations inside the Fillmore circle were more equitable and reciprocal than they were prior to the women's liberation movement in most of the United States, not least in the art world. However, evidence presented here also tempers that somewhat celebratory account, showing that exchanges around *The Rose* often subverted but also sometimes replicated the essentialist thinking and stereotypes that pervaded "common sense" understandings of gender in the period. The intimacy and reciprocity of the Fillmore coterie is therefore revealed to have created a space that mitigated but did not fully escape the patriarchy of postwar society.

Exchanges within DeFeo's circle occurred between individuals who occupied distinct positions within the period's dominant binary and hierarchical gender imaginary. The power imbalance between these positions—that is, between DeFeo and her male collaborators—meant that the act of representing her risked portraying her in ways that confirmed broader society's conception of her as "Other," rather than in ways that invited dialogue and challenged existing stereotypes. This possibility was mitigated, to some degree, by the fact that DeFeo's male friends developed their depictions of her in the context of their established personal relationships, and through dialogue, with her. Ultimately, however, their representations of her at times still edged into essentialization. The predominant culture was not so easily eschewed.

For example, the idealization evident, to varying degrees, in Berman's, Hedrick's, McClure's, and Conner's portrayals of DeFeo evidences their respect for her, but it also exaggerates her alterity in ways that threaten to other her. Idealization both elevates an individual ("places them on a pedestal") and abstracts them (to represent an "ideal"). While the distance this act creates between self and other is typically experienced as admiration, the process courts objectification as the other is no longer approached as "another" (as a unique subject equal to the self) but as an "Other" (as a distant, abstract archetype). The preceding chapters show that many works about *The Rose* fall somewhere between being individualized portraits that confirm DeFeo's subjectivity and universalizing symbols that objectify, even as they elevate, her.

DeFeo's collaborators heightened this risk of objectification when they represented her using identities already freighted with essentialist connotations. Sometimes they mobilized "mythical" identities in ways that inverted expectations, as when they denaturalized the masculinity of the "expressionist genius" by casting DeFeo in that role. Other times, however, their depictions of DeFeo rehearsed worn gender stereotypes. By representing her as, for example, a sexualized model, a domestic burden, an embodiment of primitive sexuality, and a piteous martyr, her male friends repeated all-too-familiar tropes of "the Eternal Feminine" that have been used to support the idea that women are inherently "Other" and subservient to men. The fact that works by DeFeo's male friends frequently romanticize, idealize, and sexualize her in ways that are absent from both her responses to them and her relationships with women artists speaks to a lack of complete parity between men and women in the Fillmore community.

This observation points to other possible reasons for the unusual gender composition of the ring that formed around *The Rose.* DeFeo's male neighbors may have been more willing than her female neighbors to enter into the nontraditional constellations of authorship generated by interindividual collaboration because their creative authority was more secure. As previously discussed, the ability of women to be artists, especially "great" ones, was always in doubt in postwar America. Even if this sexism was muffled within the Fillmore coterie, it may have dissuaded women artists from engaging in practices that potentially compromised their artistic originality and independence, traits they were often forced to defend. The fact that DeFeo was willing to take such a risk is notable.

Furthermore, the subaltern position that DeFeo occupied because of her identity as a woman—even when tempered by friendship and the coterie—may have made her an appealing creative partner for male artists; for it meant that she posed less of a threat to their authorial agency than other male artists. In other words, men may have felt freer to take up DeFeo and her painting as the basis for their own works in part because women have traditionally been viewed as an object/material/site for men to transform through art-making. As I see it, the interindividual collaborations around *The Rose* evidence some persistence of these gender hierarchies and essentializing modes of representation, even if the artists attempted to enact the opposite—reciprocal, mutually empowering dialogues between male and female artists.

SOMEWHERE ON A SLOW CURVE

"The White Rose," DeFeo wrote on the collaged poster she sent Berman (discussed at the end of Chapter 1), "is a Fact painted somewhere on a slow curve between destinations."[22] Her description poetically articulates *The Rose*'s dual identity as an art object (a colossal one, at that) and a process piece. It encapsulates the way the painting embodied the prototypical modernist "work" even as it performed the work's (postmodernist) dispersal—a combination that throws a "curveball" into standard narratives of postwar American art.[23] This book has argued that *The Rose*'s monumental materiality and seemingly interminable production also encouraged DeFeo's neighbors to respond to it, generating interindividual collaborations that likewise blurred boundaries that have historically been drawn between modernism and postmodernism by merging expression and appropriation, individual and collective authorship.

DeFeo's statement can also be read in relation to the understanding of gender enacted through these exchanges, which this coda has elaborated. Through their creative dialogues, DeFeo and her male friends treated gender identity as a "slow curve between destinations"—as an ongoing process of becoming, of endless negotiation between ideals of masculine and feminine. At times, however, gender identity manifested in their exchanges as a "Fact"—as an immutable, innate part of the self that is expressed rather than constructed.

The simultaneous existence of these opposing conceptions of gender identity (one post-structuralist, the other positivist) within the interindividual collaborations that developed around *The Rose* supports my argument that these exchanges fostered gender play, again in Marcus's sense of the term. Their dialogues tested "the elasticity" of postwar America's "system" of patriarchy by fostering alternatives to the strict gender binaries and hierarchies that kept women artists on the margins. Yet, as with all forms of play, according to Marcus, the change they enacted was relatively circumscribed.[24] Their exchanges sometimes reiterated mainstream gender stereotypes and were largely contained within the private space of the coterie. They thus "stretched" hegemonic notions of gender identity without causing any "permanent alteration" to society's system of structural gender inequality.

In *Bodies That Matter* (1993), Butler asserts that practices that do not radically denaturalize or subvert gender norms risk reconsolidating their "hegemonic status."[25] Her warning, we have seen, applies to the works that Berman, Hedrick, McClure, and Conner created about *The Rose*. When these works were made public, their complex (at times conflicted) representation of gender became flattened in ways that often affirmed DeFeo's subaltern status as a woman artist. Decontextualized from the artists' dialogues, the tension the works convey between representing gender as a fluid construct and a given fact, speaking with and speaking for DeFeo, became inaudible as the latter, hegemonic side of the conversation was amplified. In other words, the identities that DeFeo's male friends proposed for her often became reified into "mythical thought" once they were removed from the reciprocal relations of the Fillmore community. No longer up for discussion, their provisional proposals became immutable truths that supplanted DeFeo and her painting in the public imagination.

This book, I realize, risks perpetuating that mythologization. A study that largely focuses on men's interpretations of the work of a woman artist potentially exacerbates the disenfranchisement that DeFeo suffered when their works came to substitute for hers. This project would not have been responsible, in my opinion, were it not for pioneering work, spearheaded by The Jay DeFeo Foundation and the Whitney Museum of American Art, that over the past thirty years has pushed back against the "myths" around *The Rose* to present DeFeo's work on its own terms (as discussed in the introduction). I am happy to report that these efforts are gaining momentum, as evidenced by many recent and upcoming solo exhibitions and monographs on diverse aspects of DeFeo's oeuvre.

I knowingly took a divergent approach here to complement the growing body of monographic research on DeFeo. Swapping one established line of feminist art-historical inquiry (reclaiming the muffled "voice" of overlooked women artists) for another, this book has followed Wagner's influential proposal that feminist art history investigate the processes—aesthetic, professional, and personal—through which artists form gendered subjectivities.[26] These processes are difficult, if not impossible, to see when an artist is viewed in isolation. Focusing on moments when DeFeo's art practice intersected with the art practices of male members of her coterie was thus a way to throw into relief how gender formation played out within the Fillmore circle, especially around *The Rose.* While it can be uncomfortable to treat women artists as anything other than fully realized and autonomous Authors, as this role has long been denied them, looking at how DeFeo forged her authorial subjectivity in relation to others was, from my perspective, worth the discomfort. For scrutinizing this process—especially the agency DeFeo gained and the risks she faced from it—expands both our understanding of her significance as an artist and our knowledge of the ways female artists navigated gender identity prior to women's liberation.

Notes

INTRODUCTION

1. Clement Greenberg, "Modernist Painting," in *Modern Art and Modernism: A Critical Anthology*, ed. Francis Francina and Charles Harrison (New York: Harper and Row, 1982), 5–10.

2. Carlos Villa, untitled notes, Wally Hedrick, Archival Artist's File, San Francisco Art Institute Archives.

3. I am using "work" and "text" as defined by Roland Barthes in "The Death of the Author," in *Image Music Text*, trans. Stephen Heath (London: Fontana, 1977), 142–48.

4. Facts for this biographical sketch of DeFeo derive from Judith Dunham, "Chronology," in *Jay DeFeo and "The Rose,"* ed. Jane Green and Leah Levy (Berkeley: University of California Press; New York: Whitney Museum of American Art, 2003), 155–68; and Diana Kamin and Meredith George Van Dyke, "Chronology," in *Jay DeFeo: A Retrospective*, ed. Dana Miller, exh. cat. (New York: Whitney Museum of American Art; New Haven: Yale University Press, 2012), 281–83. Details of DeFeo's travels are from Dana Miller, "Jay DeFeo: A Slow Curve," in Miller, *Jay DeFeo: A Retrospective*, 16–17.

5. "Jay DeFeo: Interview with Leela Elliott," in *Connecting Conversations: Interviews with 28 Bay Area Women Artists*, ed. Moira Roth (Oakland: Eucalyptus, Mills College, 1988), 46; oral history interview with Jay DeFeo, June 3, 1975–January 23, 1976, Archives of American Art (AAA), Smithsonian Institution, Washington, D.C.; Jay DeFeo, letter to Dorothy C. Miller, August 18, 1959, Museum of Modern Art (MoMA) Archives, New York: Dorothy C. Miller Papers, I.15.k.

6. DeFeo, letter to Miller, August 18, 1959, MoMA Archives.

7. The final quote is from Jay DeFeo, letter to Henry Hopkins, June 21, 1978, republished as "My Visual Vocabulary," in *Jay DeFeo: The Ripple Effect*, ed. Seungduk Kim and Franck Gautherot, exh. cat. (Dijon: Les presses du réel, 2018), 141; all other quotes in this paragraph are from DeFeo interview, AAA.

8. Quoted in John Baur, Dorothy Sekler, and Dorothy Miller, "New Talent U.S.A.: Painting," *Art in America* 49, no. 1 (1961): 30.

9. For more on the work's material and structural composition, see Niccolo Caldararo, "Conserving *The Rose*," in Green and Levy, *Jay DeFeo and "The Rose,"* 111–25.

10. Jay DeFeo, letter to Bruce Conner, October 27, 1972, Jay DeFeo papers, circa 1940s–1970s, AAA; Jay DeFeo, "Biography of J. DeFeo," 1975, Jay DeFeo's artist file, archives of the Oakland Museum of California.

11. Rebecca Solnit, *Secret Exhibition: Six California Artists of the Cold War Era* (San Francisco: City Lights, 1990), 79; Miller, "Slow Curve," 30. Facts about *The Rose*'s journey after it left DeFeo's studio derive from Dunham, "Chronology," 159–68; and Kamin and Van Dyke, "Chronology," 287–94.

12. Dunham, "Chronology," 159–68; Kamin and Van Dyke, "Chronology," 287–94.

13. Dunham, "Chronology," 157.

14. Baur, Sekler, and Miller, "New Talent U.S.A."; Kenneth Tynan, "San Francisco: The Rebels," *Holiday* 29, no. 4 (April 1961): 92–97, 188, 191, 194–97; John F. Kennedy, "The Arts in America," *Look*, December 18, 1962, 104–23; *Creative America* (New York: Ridge, 1962).

15. Caldararo, "Conserving *The Rose*," 112; Jerome Tarshis, "The Art Doctors," *San Francisco*, November 1973, 35. I would like to thank Leah Levy for bringing the latter article to my attention.

16. *The Rose* was included in the following exhibitions at the Whitney: *Beat Culture and the New America: 1950–1965* (1995), curated by Lisa Phillips; *Beside* The Rose*: Selected Works by Jay DeFeo* (2003), curated by Dana Miller; and various installations of its permanent collection, including *America Is Hard to See* (2015). Miller also curated *Jay DeFeo: A Retrospective*.

17. See, especially, Jane Green and Leah Levy, "Introduction," in Green and Levy, *Jay DeFeo and "The Rose,"* 4; and Miller, "Slow Curve," 15.

18. Solnit, *Secret Exhibition;* Richard Cándida Smith, *Utopia and Dissent: Art, Poetry, and Politics in California* (Berkeley: University of California Press, 1995); Anastasia Aukeman, *Welcome to Painterland: Bruce Conner and the Rat Bastard Protective Association* (Berkeley: University of California Press, 2016). Other significant projects on art in Northern California in the 1950s and 1960s include, in chronological order: *Art as a Muscular Principle: 10 Artists and San Francisco, 1950–1965—Roots and New Directions*, an exhibition curated by Merril Greene for the Warbeke Gallery, Mount Holyoke College, in 1975; Thomas Albright, *Art in the San Francisco Bay Area, 1945–1980: An Illustrated History* (Berkeley: University of California Press, 1985); Rebecca Schoenthal, "North Beach to Haight-Ashbury: Underground Artists and Community in 1950s San Francisco" (Ph.D. diss., University of Virginia, 2005); *Semina Culture: Wallace Berman and His Circle*, a traveling exhibition curated by Michael Duncan and Kristine McKenna for the Santa Monica Museum of Art in 2006; *Looking for Mushrooms: Beat Poets, Hippies, Funk, Minimal Art—San Francisco, 1955–68*, an exhibition held at the Museum Ludwig in Cologne, Germany, in 2008; Richard Cándida Smith, *The Modern Moves West: California Artists and Democratic Culture in the Twentieth Century* (Philadelphia: University of Pennsylvania Press, 2009); *An Opening of the Field: Jess, Robert Duncan, and Their Circle*, a traveling exhibition curated by Michael Duncan and Christopher Wagstaff for the Crocker Art Museum in Sacramento in 2013; Kevin Hatch, *Looking for Bruce Conner* (Cambridge, Mass.: MIT Press, 2016); *Bruce Conner: It's All True*, an exhibition curated by MoMA and the San Francisco Museum of Modern Art

in 2016; Tara McDowell, *Householders: Robert Duncan and Jess* (Cambridge, Mass.: MIT Press, 2019); and Kevin Hatch, "'Thinking of You: Bruce Conner's Epistolary Practice," *American Art* 33, no. 1 (Spring 2019): 52–73.

19. Given the ambiguity surrounding the area's name, I refer to it as the "Fillmore District" or the "Fillmore neighborhood," as is customary in literature on DeFeo and her coterie. For a more detailed history of the neighborhood, see Schoenthal, "North Beach to Haight-Ashbury," 145–58; and Aukeman, *Welcome to Painterland*, 38–40. For more on the long-standing connections between art and gentrification in the United States, which has negatively impacted neighborhoods inhabited by the working class and people of color, see Rosalyn Deutsche, *Evictions: Art and Spatial Politics* (Cambridge, Mass.: MIT Press, 1998); Aaron Shukda, *The Lofts of SoHo: Gentrification, Art, and Industry in New York, 1950–1980* (Chicago: University of Chicago Press, 2016); Kim Charnley and Gregory Sholette, eds., *Delirium and Resistance: Activist Art and the Crisis of Capitalism* (London: Pluto, 2017); and Kellie Jones, *South of Pico: African American Artists in Los Angeles in the 1960s and 1970s* (Durham, N.C.: Duke University Press, 2017).

20. DeFeo interview, AAA; Aukeman, *Welcome to Painterland*, 238n7.

21. Quoted in Jack Foley, "O Her Blackness Sparkles," in *The Beat Generation Galleries and Beyond*, ed. John Natsoulas, exh. cat. (Davis, Calif.: John Natsoulas Gallery, 1996), 170; quoted in Bruce Nixon, "The 6 Gallery," in *Beat Generation Galleries*, 85.

22. For a definition of "community," see Louis Kaplan, *American Exposures: Photography and Community in the Twentieth Century* (Minneapolis: University of Minnesota Press, 2005); for "circle," see Michael P. Farrell, *Collaborative Circles: Friendship Dynamics and Creative Work* (Chicago: University of Chicago Press, 2001); for "coterie," see Lytle Shaw, *Frank O'Hara and the Poetics of Coterie* (Iowa City: University of Iowa Press, 2006); for "group," see Bridget Alsdorf, *Fellow Men: Fantin-Latour and the Problem of the Group in Nineteenth-Century French Painting* (Princeton, N.J.: Princeton University Press, 2012).

23. See, for example, Solnit, *Secret Exhibition*, viii–ix, 43; and Aukeman, *Welcome to Painterland*, 3.

24. Other notable incidents of legal and critical censure include Berman's conviction for public obscenity over his exhibition at the Ferus Gallery in Los Angeles in 1957 (Rebecca Solnit, "Ferus: The End of the Beginning," in *Secret Exhibition*, 18–23), which spurred his move to San Francisco, and the controversy over Conner's assemblage CHILD (1959–60) when it was shown at the de Young Museum; see Roger Griffith and Megan Randall, "The Life, Death, and Resurrection of Bruce Conner's *CHILD*," in *Bruce Conner: It's All True*, ed. Rudolf Frieling and Gary Garrels, exh. cat. (San Francisco: San Francisco Museum of Modern Art; Berkeley: University of California Press, 2016), 293–97. Articles that vexed Fillmore writers and artists by portraying them as beatniks included George B. Leonard, "The Bored, the Bearded, and the Beat," *Look*, August 1958, 64–68; Miriam Dungan Cross, "Shocking 'Beat' Art Displayed," *Oakland Tribune*, November 29, 1959; and Paul O'Neil, "The Only Rebellion Around," *Life*, November 30, 1959, 114–30.

25. This overview of the CSFA's significance draws from Caroline A. Jones, *Bay Area Figurative Art, 1950–1965*, exh. cat. (San Francisco: San Francisco Museum of Modern Art; Berkeley: University of California Press, 1989); Susan Landauer, *The San Francisco School of Abstract Expressionism*, exh. cat. (Laguna Beach, Calif.: Laguna Art Museum; Berkeley: University of California Press, 1996); and Richard Cándida Smith, "Revolution at the California School of Fine Arts: Abstract Expressionism in San Francisco," in *Utopia and Dissent*, 90–137.

26. Quoted in Solnit, *Secret Exhibition*, 7. For more on the galleries of the Fillmore District, see *Beat Generation Galleries and Beyond;* and Anastasia Aukeman, "Artist-Run Galleries of the Fillmore," in *Welcome to Painterland*, 107–27.

27. The introductions to Solnit's *Secret Exhibition*, Cándida Smith's *Utopia and Dissent*, and Aukeman's *Welcome to Painterland* contain crystallized expressions of this narrative.

28. Cándida Smith, *Utopia and Dissent*, xix.

29. This idea and related reading of *The Rose* are both articulated in Solnit, *Secret Exhibition*, 49–50, 77–78; Cándida Smith, *Utopia and Dissent*, 197; and Aukeman, *Welcome to Painterland*, 182–83.

30. Cándida Smith, *Utopia and Dissent*, 197, 199. Dana Miller has convincingly argued against the characterization of DeFeo as wary of mainstream institutions and the market; Miller, "Slow Curve," 27.

31. Literary scholars, such as Michael Davidson, have arguably been more successful at teasing out the ways in which the "new poetics" of San Francisco's Beat generation writers "implied not only formal innovation but also discovery of alternative social forms"; Michael Davidson, *The San Francisco Renaissance: Poetics and Community at Mid-Century* (Cambridge: Cambridge University Press, 1991), xi. See also Michael Davidson, *Guys Like Us: Citing Masculinity in Cold War Poetics* (Chicago: University of Chicago Press, 2003).

32. These studies include Branden Joseph, *Beyond the Dream Syndicate: Tony Conrad and the Arts after Cage* (Cambridge, Mass.: MIT Press, 2008); Alsdorf, *Fellow Men;* Bibiana Obler, *Intimate Collaborations: Kandinsky and Münter, Arp and Taeuber* (New Haven: Yale University Press, 2014); and Tirza True Latimer, *Eccentric Modernisms: Making Differences in the History of American Art* (Berkeley: University of California Press, 2016).

33. Paul Goodman, "Advance-Guard Writing, 1900–1950," *Kenyon Review* 13, no. 3 (Summer 1951): 357–80. Literary scholars generally refer to this coterie as the New York School; I have chosen not to use that label because it is also an alternative term for abstract expressionism. Studies that were particularly influential to this book's approach include Michael Magee, "Tribes of New York: Frank O'Hara, Amiri Baraka, and the Poetics of the Five Spot," *Contemporary Literature* 42, no. 4 (Winter 2001): 694–726; Gavin Butt, "How New York Queered the Idea of Modern Art," in *Varieties of Modernism*, ed. Paul Wood (New Haven: Yale University Press, 2004), 315–38; Gavin Butt, *Between You and Me: Queer Disclosures in the New York Art World, 1945–1963* (Durham, N.C.: Duke University Press, 2005); Andrew Epstein, *Beautiful Enemies: Friendship and Postwar American Poetry* (Oxford: Oxford University Press, 2006); Shaw, *Poetics of*

Coterie; Jonathan Katz, "'Committing the Perfect Crime': Sexuality, Assemblage, and the Postmodern Turn in American Art," *Art Journal* 67, no. 1 (2008): 38–53; and Ryan Dohoney, "Spontaneity, Intimacy, and Friendship in Morton Feldman's Music of the 1950s," *Modernism/modernity* 2, no. 3 (September 2017), https://doi.org/10.26597/mod.0030.

34. Joseph, *Beyond the Dream Syndicate,* 57. In addition to Joseph's treatment of the multimedia artist Tony Conrad as a "minor" figure, the structure of my study resonates with MoMA's 2017 "open monograph" of Robert Rauschenberg, *Robert Rauschenberg: Among Friends.*

35. Latimer, *Eccentric Modernisms,* 119; Joseph, *Beyond the Dream Syndicate,* 57. Other studies that informed this aspect of my approach include Hatch, *Looking for Bruce Conner,* 5–7; and Butt, *Between You and Me,* 18–19.

36. Epstein, *Beautiful Enemies,* 5.

37. See, for example, Cándida Smith, *Utopia and Dissent;* Schoenthal, "North Beach to Haight-Ashbury"; and Aukeman, *Welcome to Painterland.*

38. Another work that has inspired historians to ask similar questions to those posed in this book is Marcel Duchamp's *The Bride Stripped Bare by Her Bachelors, Even* (*The Large Glass*) (1915–23), which like *The Rose* was produced during a long, somewhat hermetic process and became a locus of creative response for avant-garde artists. See, for example, Dalia Judovitz, *Drawing on Art: Duchamp and Company* (Minneapolis: University of Minnesota Press, 2010); and Susan Rosenbaum, "Brides Stripped Bare: Surrealism, the Large Glass, and U.S. Women's Imaginary Museums," *Dada/Surrealism* 21 (2017), https://ir.uiowa.edu/dadasur/.

39. Critiques of the binary opposition between modernism and postmodernism are myriad. The approach taken in this book resonates most closely with feminist and postcolonial arguments that traditional periodizations, such as the progression from modernism to postmodernism, perpetuate the invisibility of historical actors from marginalized groups by reinforcing categories created in reference solely to those with privileged social identities, such as white male authors. See, for example, Joyce W. Warren and Margaret Dickie, eds., *Challenging Boundaries: Gender and Periodization* (Athens: University of Georgia Press, 2000); Susan Stanford Friedman, "Periodizing Modernism: Postcolonial Modernities and the Space/Time Borders of Modernist Studies," *Modernism/modernity* 13, no. 3 (September 2006): 425–43; and Alexandra Shepard and Garthine Walker, eds., *Gender and Change: Agency, Chronology, and Periodisation* (Hoboken, N.J.: Wiley-Blackwell, 2010). Many art historians have also challenged inherited narratives of the transition from modernism to postmodernism by carefully reexamining postwar art and its contexts, as this study attempts to do. See, for example, Alex Potts, "Autonomy in Post-War Art, Quasi-Heroic and Casual," *Oxford Art Journal* 27, no. 1 (2004): 45–59; Valerie Hellstein, "The Cage-iness of Abstract Expressionism," *American Art* 28, no. 1 (Spring 2014): 56–77; and Elise Archias, *The Concrete Body: Yvonne Rainer, Carolee Schneemann, Vito Acconci* (New Haven: Yale University Press, 2016).

40. Harold Rosenberg, "The American Action Painters," *Art News* 51, no. 8 (December 1952): 22–23, 48–50; Allan Kaprow, "The Artist as a Man of the World," in *Essays on Blurring Art and Life,* ed. Jeff Kelley (Berkeley: University of California Press, 1993), 46–58.

41. For an extended example of this narrative, see Moira Roth, "The Aesthetics of Indifference," in *Difference/Indifference: Musings on Postmodernism, Marcel Duchamp, and John Cage* (Amsterdam: Gordon and Breach, 1998), 33–48.

42. Alternatively, an openness to collectivity is sometimes presented as a connecting thread between modernism—as it manifested in the interwar avant-gardes, rather than in postwar formalism—and postmodernism; see, for example, Hal Foster, "Postmodernism: A Preface," in *The Anti-Aesthetic: Essays on Postmodern Culture,* ed. Hal Foster (Port Townsend, Wash.: Bay, 1983). For further discussion of artistic collectivity at midcentury, see Blake Stimson and Gregory Sholette, *Collectivism after Modernism: The Art of Social Imagination after 1945* (Minneapolis: University of Minnesota Press, 2007); and Meredith A. Brown and Michelle Millar Fisher, eds., *Collaboration and Its (Dis)Contents: Art, Architecture, and Photography since 1950* (London: Courtauld, 2017), https://courtauld.ac.uk/research/courtauld-books-online/collaboration-and-its-discontents.

43. This paragraph's sketch of well-known midcentury social discourses is indebted to Michael Davidson, "Introduction: Enabling Fictions," in *San Francisco Renaissance,* 1–32; Andrew Epstein, "Situating the Avant-Garde in Postwar America: Community, Individualism, and Cold War Culture," in *Beautiful Enemies,* 26–52; Lytle Shaw, "In Memory of My Feelings: The Limits of Kinship," in *Poetics of Coterie,* 81–114; and Blake Stimson and Gregory Sholette, "Introduction: Periodizing Collectivism," in *Collectivism after Modernism,* 1–15.

44. David Riesman, Nathan Glazer, and Reuel Denney, *The Lonely Crowd: A Study of the Changing American Character* (New Haven: Yale University Press, 1950); Sloan Wilson, *The Man in the Gray Flannel Suit* (New York: Simon and Schuster, 1955); *The Man in the Gray Flannel Suit,* dir. Nunnally Johnson (Los Angeles: 20th Century Fox, 1956); William H. Whyte, *The Organization Man* (New York: Simon and Schuster, 1956).

45. See, for example, Schoenthal, "North Beach to Haight-Ashbury," 230; Aukeman, *Welcome to Painterland,* 197–98; and Susan Landauer, "The Advantages of Obscurity: Women Abstract Expressionists in San Francisco," in *Women of Abstract Expressionism,* ed. Joan Marter, exh. cat. (New Haven: Yale University Press, 2016), 42.

46. Jay DeFeo, letter to Dorothy C. Miller, December 18, 1960, MoMA Archives: Dorothy C. Miller Papers, I.15.k.

CHAPTER 1
MODEL ARTIST

1. Jay DeFeo, letter to Dorothy C. Miller, October 19, 1959, Museum of Modern Art (MoMA) Archives, New York: Dorothy C. Miller Papers, I.15.k.

2. In this chapter, I define the series as the nine photographs currently owned by the Whitney Museum of American Art because they were likely printed by Berman and shown in the original exhibition. The full series is reproduced in Dana Miller, ed., *Jay DeFeo: A Retrospective,* exh. cat. (New York: Whitney Museum of American Art; New Haven: Yale University Press, 2012), 136–39.

Several other negatives that were clearly exposed during the shoot have been printed posthumously by the Estate of Wallace Berman. Some of these have been reproduced in Michael Duncan and Kristine McKenna, *Semina Culture: Wallace Berman and His Circle* (New York: D.A.P.; Santa Monica: Santa Monica Museum of Art, 2005), 116; Kristine McKenna and Lorraine Wild, eds., *Wallace Berman: Photographs*, exh. cat. (Santa Monica: Rose Gallery, 2007), 37–40; Kristine McKenna, ed., *SHE: Images of Women by Wallace Berman and Richard Prince* (Los Angeles: Kohn Gallery, 2009), 19; and Claudia Bohn-Spector and Sam Mellon, eds., *Wallace Berman: American Aleph*, exh. cat. (Los Angeles: Kohn Gallery, 2016), 68. In a late interview, DeFeo claimed that Hedrick "was present" during her photo shoot with Berman: Jay DeFeo, interview with Rebecca Solnit, March 12, 1984, Oakland, Calif., interviews for the book *Secret Exhibition*, Phonotape 4000 C: 1–19, Bancroft Library, University of California, Berkeley; quoted here with the permission of Rebecca Solnit.

3. Jay DeFeo, letter to Dorothy C. Miller, November 18, 1959, MoMA Archives: Dorothy C. Miller Papers, I.15.k.

4. Kristine McKenna details Berman's darkroom procedures in "Wallace Berman and Photography," in Duncan and McKenna, *Semina Culture*, 308.

5. DeFeo, interview with Solnit, Bancroft Library. Berman briefly exhibited the photographs in his home again after moving back to Los Angeles in 1961; see McKenna, "Wallace Berman and Photography," 305.

6. Dorothy C. Miller, letter to Jay DeFeo, October 22, 1959, MoMA Archives: Dorothy C. Miller Papers, I.15.k. Photographs from the series were first shown publicly in the exhibition *A Kind of Beatness: North Beach in the 1950s*, which was curated by Mark Green at the Focus Gallery in 1975. In a letter from 1978, DeFeo claims that she personally selected two images to hang in the show; Jay DeFeo, letter to Mark Himelstein, June 14, 1978, Archive of The Jay DeFeo Foundation, Berkeley, Calif. For more on the photographs' early public appearances, see Jason Goldman, "Concealed Exposures: Jay DeFeo, *The Rose*, and the Photographic Image," in "Open Secrets: Publicity, Privacy, and U.S. Artistic Practice in the Sixties" (Ph.D. diss., University of Southern California, 2011), 93–104.

7. This background information on Berman draws from Ken D. Allan, "City of Degenerate Angels: Wallace Berman, Jazz and *Semina* in Postwar Los Angeles," *Art Journal* 70, no. 1 (Spring 2011): 70–91; Rebecca Solnit, "Wallace Berman and Los Angeles, 1947–1957," in *Secret Exhibition: Six California Artists of the Cold War Era* (San Francisco: City Lights, 1990), 1–23; Michael Duncan, "Wallace Berman and His Circle," in Duncan and McKenna, *Semina Culture*, 8–15; Richard Cándida Smith, "Utopia and the Private Realm: Wallace Berman on Career, Family, and Community," in *Utopia and Dissent: Art, Poetry, and Politics in California* (Berkeley: University of California Press, 1995), 212–68; and Sandra Leonard Starr, *Lost and Found in California: Four Decades of Assemblage Art*, exh. cat. (Los Angeles: James Corcoran Gallery, 1988).

8. Many accounts exist of Berman's arrest and trial; see especially Rebecca Solnit, "Ferus: The End of the Beginning," in *Secret Exhibition*, 18–23.

9. Quoted in Solnit, *Secret Exhibition*, 6.

10. This detail is recounted in Dana Miller, "A Slow Curve," in Miller, *Jay DeFeo: A Retrospective*, 25. For further information on the series' production, see note 54 of Miller's essay.

11. For more on DeFeo's thoughts about her career during this period, see Miller, "Slow Curve," 28.

12. For this narrative of postwar art on the West Coast, see Solnit, *Secret Exhibition;* Richard Cándida Smith, *Utopia and Dissent* and *The Modern Moves West: California Artists and Democratic Culture in the Twentieth Century* (Philadelphia: University of Pennsylvania Press, 2009); and Anastasia Aukeman, *Welcome to Painterland: Bruce Conner and the Rat Bastard Protective Association* (Berkeley: University of California Press, 2016). See Mary Anne Staniszewski, *The Power of Display: A History of Exhibition Installations at the Museum of Modern Art* (Cambridge, Mass.: MIT Press, 1998), for a discussion of the ways MoMA's exhibition strategies foreground artistic individualism.

13. Jay DeFeo, letter to Dorothy C. Miller, October 21, 1959, MoMA Archives: Dorothy C. Miller Papers, I.15.k.

14. Solnit, *Secret Exhibition*, 83; Rebecca Schoenthal, "North Beach to Haight-Ashbury: Underground Artists and Community in 1950s San Francisco" (Ph.D. diss., University of Virginia, 2005), 234. Also, see Solnit, *Secret Exhibition*, 75–76; Cándida Smith, *Utopia and Dissent*, 118–19; Carter Ratcliff, "Romance of *The Rose*," *Modern Painters* 16, no. 1 (Spring 2003): 92; and Schoenthal, "North Beach to Haight-Ashbury," 233–36. For extended meditations on DeFeo's participation in the exhibition, see Bill Berkson, "Without *The Rose:* DeFeo in *Sixteen Americans*," in *Jay DeFeo and "The Rose*," ed. Jane Green and Leah Levy (Berkeley: University of California Press; New York: Whitney Museum of American Art, 2003), 43–54; and Cándida Smith, *Modern Moves West*, 110–20. For Miller's counterargument, see Miller, "Slow Curve," 51n71.

15. *The SBL Handbook of Style* (Atlanta: Society of Biblical Literature, 2014) specifies this English spelling of the Hebrew character (56). For a discussion of the symbolism associated with tsade, see Robert Berg, "Jay DeFeo: The Transcendental Rose," *American Art* 12, no. 3 (Autumn 1998): 68–78.

16. Carter Ratcliff, "Jay DeFeo: Selfhood Self-Defined," in *Jay DeFeo: Ingredients of Alchemy*, exh. cat. (New York: Michael Rosenfeld Gallery, 2002), 12–13.

17. Kristen van Diggelen Sloan, a recent resident of DeFeo's Fillmore Street apartment complex, owns a painting of DeFeo modeling that appears to have been created at CSFA in 1957; Kristen van Diggelen Sloan, email message to the author, January 16, 2014.

18. Jay DeFeo, letter to *Artforum*, undated (c. 1978), Archive of The Jay DeFeo Foundation; Michael Duncan, "Biography of Jay DeFeo," in Duncan and McKenna, *Semina Culture*, 118; John Bowles, "Shocking 'Beat' Art Displayed: California Artists and the Beat Image," in *Reading California: Art, Image, and Identity, 1900–2000*, ed. Stephanie Barron, Sheri Bernstein, and Ilene Susan Fort, exh. cat. (Berkeley: University of California Press; Los Angeles: Los Angeles County Museum of Art), 235.

19. Jay DeFeo, letter to Mark Himelstein, April 20, 1978, Archive of The Jay DeFeo Foundation; Miller, "Slow Curve," 26. Both The Jay DeFeo Foundation and the Estate of Wallace Berman, which

is administered by the Kohn Gallery, likewise attribute the series to Berman alone. As Miller rightly notes, DeFeo was likely motivated to craft divergent representations of the photo shoot in the two letters quoted here because they were intended for very different audiences, as will be discussed toward the end of this chapter; Miller, "Slow Curve," 50n59.

20. Goldman, "Open Secrets," 102. Lorraine Wild has noted that the authorship of many of Berman's photographs occupy a similar gray zone between photographer and model; Lorraine Wild, "Afterword," in McKenna and Wild, *Wallace Berman: Photographs,* 144–45.

21. Until the mid-1970s, Berman always exhibited the photographs together. DeFeo likewise referred to them as a unit, calling them on different occasions a "series portrait" and a "composite portrait"; DeFeo, letter to Himelstein, April 20, 1978, Archive of The Jay DeFeo Foundation; DeFeo, interview with Solnit, Bancroft Library. She repeated this sentiment more vehemently in her interview with Solnit, noting that she "took great exception" when a "single portrait" was used because she thought that "out of the context of the whole it misrepresented me."

22. See the introduction of this book for a list of publications that circulated images of *The Rose* during its production. For further discussion of *The Rose*'s relationship to these images, see Goldman, "Open Secrets"; and Martha Prather, "Beside *The Rose:* DeFeo's Work at the Whitney Museum," in Green and Levy, *Jay DeFeo and "The Rose,"* xvi–xvii.

23. *Creative America* (New York: Ridge, 1962), 3.

24. Harold Rosenberg, "The American Action Painters," *Art News* 51, no. 8 (December 1952): 22. Goldman drew similar conclusions about Glinn's photograph in Goldman, "Open Secrets," 67–68.

25. See, for example, Berg, "Transcendental Rose," 72; Miller, "Slow Curve," 26; Prather, "Beside *The Rose,*" xvi; and Schoenthal, "North Beach to Haight-Ashbury," 293–95.

26. "Women Artists in Ascendance," *Life,* May 13, 1957, 74–77. Several of these remarks draw on Anne M. Wagner's observations about the article in "Pollock's Nature, Frankenthaler's Culture," in *Jackson Pollock: New Approaches,* ed. Kirk Varnedoe and Pepe Karmel (New York: Museum of Modern Art, 1999), 185.

27. Cándida Smith, *Modern Moves West,* 120.

28. McKenna, "Wallace Berman and Photography," 305.

29. McKenna, *SHE,* 11–12; Natalie Haddad, "SHE: Images of Women by Wallace Berman and Richard Prince," *Brooklyn Rail,* March 6, 2009, http://www.brooklynrail.org/2009/03/artseen.

30. David Meltzer, "The Secret Text Lost in the Processor," in *Wallace Berman: Support the Revolution,* exh. cat. (Amsterdam: Institute of Contemporary Art, 1992), 57; Jack Keroauc, "Aftermath: The Philosophy of the Beat Generation," *Esquire,* March 1958, 24–26. For more on the role of sex and eroticism in Berman's art, see Cándida Smith, *Utopia and Dissent,* 212–98; and Stephen Fredman, *Contextual Practice: Assemblage and the Erotic in Postwar Poetry and Art* (Stanford: Stanford University Press, 2010), 99–117.

31. Goldman, "Open Secrets," 86–87. While the largest images in both collages are of naked women, *Blossom* also includes images of men at its center, and *Applaud* prominently features a horse and ambiguously gendered hands. I would like to thank Leah Levy for bringing these details of *Blossom* to my attention.

32. Several scholars have asserted this connection, including Miller, "Slow Curve," 25; Lucy R. Lippard, "Transplanting *The Rose,*" in Green and Levy, *Jay DeFeo and "The Rose,"* 55–64; and Goldman, "Open Secrets," 77–78.

33. Kelly Dennis, *Art/Porn: A History of Seeing and Touching* (Oxford: Berg, 2009), 66.

34. Goldman, "Open Secrets," 79; Lippard, "Transplanting *The Rose,*" 56.

35. Jay DeFeo, letter to Henry Hopkins, June 21, 1978, republished as "My Visual Vocabulary," in *Jay DeFeo: The Ripple Effect,* ed. Seungduk Kim and Franck Gautherot, exh. cat. (Dijon: Les presses du réel, 2018), 140.

36. DeFeo, letter to Himelstein, April 20, 1978, Archive of The Jay DeFeo Foundation.

37. Bruce Conner recalled seeing a photograph matching its description displayed at the exhibition in Berman's Scott Street apartment; see Schoenthal, "North Beach to Haight-Ashbury," 290–91.

38. Carol Duncan, "Virility and Domination in Twentieth-Century Vanguard Painting," in *The Aesthetics of Power: Essays in the Critical History of Art* (Cambridge: Cambridge University Press, 1993), 81–109.

39. Goldman, "Open Secrets," 70–71; Dennis, *Art/Porn,* 1.

40. For the distinction between naked and nude, see Lynda Nead, "Part I: Theorizing the Female Nude," in *The Female Nude: Art, Obscenity, and Sexuality* (London: Routledge, 1992), 8–32.

41. The link between the postcard and the series is circumstantial but likely given the card's date and message; Miller supports this connection in "Slow Curve," 25. Kristine McKenna claims that the self-portrait on the postcard was taken in DeFeo's apartment in 1959; McKenna and Wild, *Wallace Berman: Photographs,* 149. This attribution suggests that the series was shot over the course of two sessions instead of one, an idea that McKenna explicitly states in "Chronology," in Duncan and McKenna, *Semina Culture,* 338. I have not ascertained evidence that supports this timeline of the series' production.

42. E. A. Wallis Budge, *Amulets and Superstitions* (London: Oxford University Press, 1930); Kurt Seligmann, *The Magic Mirror: A History of Magic in the Western World* (New York: Pantheon, 1948). Lamantia's connection with Seligmann (which Fredman notes in *Contextual Practice,* 113) makes the latter's book a likely source for Berman's collage. However, *Amulets and Superstitions* was reissued by Dover in 1978, suggesting that there was continued demand for the volume and, thus, increasing the likelihood that Berman knew it.

43. Fredman, *Contextual Practice,* 104–5.

44. For more on Artaud's significance to Berman, see Lucy Bradnock, "'Mantras of Gibberish': Wallace Berman's Visions of Artaud," *Art History* 35, no. 3 (June 2012): 622–43. Other evidence of the poet's currency within DeFeo and Berman's circle includes frequent references to him in Michael McClure's journals from the period (Michael McClure Papers: Additions, BANC MSS 2003/222 c, Bancroft Library, University of California, Berkeley); the *Artaud Anthology*

edited by Hirschman and published by San Francisco's City Lights Bookstore in 1965; and Lamantia's inclusion of a translation of Artaud's diatribe "I Demand Extinction of Laws Prohibiting Narcotic Drugs!" in his anthology *Narcotica* (1959), which Berman illustrated. For analysis of Artaud's impact on American postwar avant-gardes, especially San Francisco's literary and theater circles, see Joanna Pawlik, "Artaud in Performance: Dissident Surrealism and the Postwar American Literary Avant-Garde," *Papers of Surrealism* 8 (2010): 1–21, http://www.surrealismcentre.ac.uk.

45. Schoenthal, "North Beach to Haight-Ashbury," 292–93. For more on Berman's reception of surrealism, see Tosh Berman, "Wallace and His Film," in *Support the Revolution*, 73–77; and Claudia Bohn-Spector, "Wallace Berman: Forms of Things Unknown," in *Wallace Berman: American Aleph*, 36. For surrealism's influence on the artistic undergrounds of postwar California, see Stephen Fredman, "Surrealism and Kabbalah in Semina Culture," in *Contextual Practice*, 99–124; and Christine A. Meilicke, "Abulafianism among the Counterculture Kabbalists," *Jewish Studies Quarterly* 9, no. 1 (2002): 71–101.

46. Wallace Berman, note to Jay DeFeo, undated, Jay DeFeo papers, circa 1940s–1970s, Archives of American Art (AAA), Smithsonian Institution, Washington, D.C. For more on the intersection of drugs and esotericism in Berman's art, see Louis Kaplan, "*Aleph* Beat: Wallace Berman between Photography and Film," in *Still Moving: Between Cinema and Photography*, ed. Karen Beckman and Jean Ma (Durham, N.C.: Duke University Press, 2008), 196–225.

47. Rosalind Krauss and Jane Livingston, eds., *L'Amour Fou: Photography and Surrealism* (New York: Abbeville, 1985).

48. See, especially, Chelsea Behle Fralick, "'Musical and Magical Counterpoint': Language, Sound, and the Image in Wallace Berman's *Aleph*, 1956–66," in *The Global Sixties in Sound and Vision*, ed. Timothy Scott Brown and Andrew Lison (New York: Palgrave Macmillan, 2014), 103–5; Fredman, "Surrealism and Kabbalah," 99–124; Walter Hopps, "An Interview with Walter Hopps," in *Wallace Berman Retrospective*, exh. cat. (Los Angeles: Otis Art Institute, 1978), 13–15; and Cándida Smith, *Utopia and Dissent*, 289–94. Berman's papers at the Archives of American Art contain the following publications on Kabbalah: Knut Stenring, *The Book of Formation or Sepher Yetzirah* (London: William Rider, 1923); Rabbi Levi L. Krakovsky, *Kabbalah* (New York: Kabbalah Foundation, 1950); Dagobert D. Runes and S. L. MacGregor Mathers, eds., *The Wisdom of the Kabbalah, as Represented by Chapters Taken from the Book Zohar* (New York: Philosophical Library, 1957); Simon Kasdin, *The Esoteric Tarot: The Key to the Cabala* (New Jersey: Emerson Society, 1965); Rabbi Moses C. Luzzatto, *General Principles of the Kabbalah* (New York: Press of the Research Centre of Kabbalah, 1970); and Charles Ponce, *Kabbalah* (San Francisco: Straight Arrow, 1973).

49. Moshe Halbertal, *Concealment and Revelation: Esotericism in Jewish Thought and Its Philosophical Implications* (Princeton, N.J.: Princeton University Press, 2007), 151, 161.

50. Meltzer, "Secret Text," 55, 54, and 59.

51. Ken D. Allan, "Radio-Mastery of the Ether," in *American Aleph*, 84.

52. Attribution from Allan, "Radio-Mastery of the Ether," 74; Allan explains the Verifax process on page 80 of his essay.

53. Allan, "Radio-Mastery of the Ether," 73. Also see Meilicke, "Abulafianism among the Counterculture Kabbalists," 72; Fralick, "'Musical and Magical Counterpoint,'" 104; Kaplan, "*Aleph* Beat," 209–10; and Meltzer, "Secret Text," 59.

54. Betty Rojtman, *Black Fire on White Fire: An Essay on Jewish Hermeneutics from Midrash to Kabbalah*, trans. Steven Randall (Berkeley: University of California Press, 1998), 1–2.

55. Moshe Idel, *Old Worlds, New Mirrors: On Jewish Mysticism and Twentieth-Century Thought* (Philadelphia: University of Pennsylvania Press, 2010), 182.

56. Harold Bloom, *Kabbalah and Criticism* (New York: Seabury, 1975), 30.

57. Elliot R. Wolfson, *Language, Eros, Being: Kabbalistic Hermeneutics and Poetic Imagination* (New York: Fordham University Press, 2005), 30.

58. Halbertal, *Concealment and Revelation*, 146.

59. Runes and MacGregor Mathers, *Wisdom of the Kabbalah*, 22.

60. I do not think, however, that esotericism was the only cultural frame Berman borrowed to conceptualize communal modes of making; Allan, for example, has convincingly argued that Berman modeled *Semina* on bebop jazz; Allan, "City of Degenerate Angels."

61. Guy Debord, *The Society of the Spectacle*, trans. Donald Nicholson-Smith (New York: Zone, 1994); Michel de Certeau, *The Practice of Everyday Life*, trans. Steven Rendall (Berkeley: University of California Press, 2011).

62. Michael McClure, "On *Semina*," in *Support the Revolution*, 61. Issues one, four, five, seven, and eight of the nine editions of *Semina* are loose-leaf; see Duncan and McKenna, *Semina Culture*, 49.

63. See, for example, Michael Duncan, "*Semina* as Art," in Duncan and McKenna, *Semina Culture*, 22; Fredman, *Contextual Practice*, 104; McClure, "On *Semina*," 60–61; and Cándida Smith, *Utopia and Dissent*, 239.

64. Prather, "Beside *The Rose*," xvi.

65. Halbertal, *Concealment and Revelation*, 3.

66. McClure, "On Semina," 60.

67. Michael Warner, *Publics and Counterpublics* (New York: Zone, 2002).

68. DeFeo, interview with Solnit, Bancroft Library.

69. Fred Martin, "For the Death Rose," in *The Rose: J. DeFeo*, exh. brochure (Pasadena, Calif.: Pasadena Art Museum, 1969), unpaginated.

70. Fred Martin, interview with the author, May 6, 2009, Piedmont, Calif.

71. Halbertal, *Concealment and Revelation*, 149.

72. Jay DeFeo, letter to Bruce Conner, July 25, 1973, Jay DeFeo papers, AAA. DeFeo's protracted production of *The Rose* has led several commentators to liken her to Balzac's fictional genius, including Lennard J. Davis, "'Play It Again, Sam, and Again': Obsession in Art," *Journal of Visual Culture* 5, no. 2 (August 2006): 242–66; and John Perreault, "Jay DeFeo's *The Rose*: Into the Light," *Artopia: John Perreault's Art Diary* (blog), January 11, 2004, http://www.artsjournal.com/artopia/2004/01.

73. Halbertal, *Concealment and Revelation*, 159.

74. Solnit, *Secret Exhibition,* xi.

75. The display includes photographs of John Wieners, Jan Balas, Joe Dunne, Howard Shulman, and Richard Constantino. The far-left image is an altered still of Susan Hayward depicting Barbara Graham in the film *I Want to Live* (1958), which Berman used for the cover of *Semina 7* (1961); see Duncan and McKenna, *Semina Culture,* 63.

76. Jean-Luc Nancy, "The Inoperative Community," in *The Inoperative Community,* ed. Peter Conner, trans. Peter Connor, Lisa Garbus, Michael Holland, and Simona Sawhney (Minneapolis: University of Minnesota Press, 1991), 1–42.

77. Nancy paraphrased by Louis Kaplan in *American Exposures: Photography and Community in the Twentieth Century* (Minneapolis: University of Minnesota Press, 2005), 82.

78. Jay DeFeo, letter to Mark Himelstein, August 31, 1978, Archive of The Jay DeFeo Foundation; Mark Himelstein, letter to Jay DeFeo, February 6, 1979, Archive of The Jay DeFeo Foundation. The article in question is Merril Greene, "Portrait of the Artist as an Underground Man," *Artforum* 16, no. 6 (February 1978): 53–81.

79. Mark Himelstein, letter to *Artforum,* March 30, 1978, Archive of The Jay DeFeo Foundation.

80. Jay DeFeo, letter to *Artforum,* undated, Archive of The Jay DeFeo Foundation. She elaborated this sentiment in her interview with Solnit, Bancroft Library.

81. Halbertal, *Concealment and Revelation,* 146.

82. DeFeo, letter to Himelstein, April 20, 1978, Archive of The Jay DeFeo Foundation.

83. Notable examples include a drawing DeFeo made in 1972 of a ring that she had previously gifted to Shirley Berman; this is discussed in Miller, "Slow Curve," 34. DeFeo also sent Berman a card featuring two photographs, each of an object lying on the ground. One shows her recently extracted dental bridge, and the other depicts a rock or shell with Hebrew letters on it; see Jay DeFeo, letter to Wallace Berman, May 9, 1972, Wallace Berman papers, 1907–1979, bulk 1955–1979, AAA. It is likely that Berman gave her the latter object. The Whitney owns several possibly related works—abstracted oil portraits that DeFeo painted of a long-haired Berman in 1974, possibly based on a photograph he sent her of himself in front of *Topanga Seed* (1969–70), one of his Kabbalah rock works; see Wallace Berman, letter to Jay DeFeo, November 4, 1970, Jay DeFeo papers, AAA.

84. Jay DeFeo, letter to Wallace Berman, April 30, 1965, Wallace Berman papers, AAA. This quote combines several snippets of the fragmentary letter.

CHAPTER 2
MAKING HOME

1. Oral history interview with Wally Hedrick, June 10–24, 1974, Archives of American Art (AAA), Smithsonian Institution, Washington, D.C. Michael Duncan identified the image in *Life Game* as a roulette wheel; Michael Duncan, "Chancing the Ridiculous," in *Jay DeFeo: A Retrospective,* ed. Dana Miller, exh. cat. (New York: Whitney Museum of American Art; New Haven: Yale University Press, 2012), 65. Fred Martin identified it as an alchemist's star; Fred Martin, "Wally Hedrick," in *Wally Hedrick/Sam Tchakalian,* exh. cat. (Balboa, Calif.: Balboa Pavilion Gallery, 1967), unpaginated. Hedrick may have coated the surface of *Life Game* with black paint in protest against the Vietnam War, as he did with many of his paintings from the 1950s. For more on this practice, see Hedrick, AAA interview; and Rebecca Solnit, *Secret Exhibition: Six California Artists of the Cold War Era* (San Francisco: City Lights, 1990), 80–82.

2. Hedrick identified the original source of this imagery ("Russian . . . jewelry or something") and the process by which he abstracted it ("I stopped depending on the imagery but kept the modeling") in his AAA interview.

3. Quoted in William S. Rubin, "Wally Hedrick (The Secret Life of Harry Fallick)," in *Wally Hedrick: Selected Works,* exh. cat. (San Francisco: San Francisco Art Institute, 1985), 9. Mark Van Proyen reiterated this interpretation in "Atypical Prototypes: The Art of Wally Hedrick," *Artweek* 16 (April 27, 1985): 1.

4. Jay DeFeo, "J. De Feo," in *Sixteen Americans,* ed. Dorothy Miller, exh. cat. (New York: Museum of Modern Art, 1959), 8; Wally Hedrick, "Wally Hedrick," in Miller, *Sixteen Americans,* 13; Wally Hedrick, *Wally Hedrick,* exh. cat. (San Francisco: California School of Fine Arts, 1956), unpaginated.

5. Quoted in Harold Rosenberg, "Young Masters, New Critics: Frank Stella," in *The De-Definition of Art* (Chicago: University of Chicago Press, 1972), 125.

6. Duncan, "Chancing the Ridiculous," 64–65; Solnit, *Secret Exhibition,* 44. Mark Van Proyen reiterated this idea in "Sight/Vision: The Inward Gaze," *Artweek* 14 (October 29, 1983). Scholars have also noted formal resonances between DeFeo's *Origin* (1956) and Hedrick's *Spirit* paintings of the 1950s, and between DeFeo's *Doctor Jazz* (1958) and Hedrick's *Anger* (1959).

7. Martin, "Wally Hedrick," unpaginated; Rebecca Schoenthal, "North Beach to Haight-Ashbury: Underground Artists and Community in 1950s San Francisco" (Ph.D. diss., University of Virginia, 2005), 240. Carlos Villa included a similar assessment in his memorial address for Hedrick; Carlos Villa, untitled notes, Wally Hedrick, Archival Artist's File, San Francisco Art Institute Archives.

8. Hannah Arendt, "The Public and the Private Realm," in *The Human Condition* (Chicago: University of Chicago Press, 1958), 28; Richard Cándida Smith, "Utopia and the Private Realm," in *Utopia and Dissent: Art, Poetry, and Politics in California* (Berkeley: University of California Press, 1995), 212–68. Also see Anastasia Aukeman, *Welcome to Painterland: Bruce Conner and the Rat Bastard Protective Association* (Berkeley: University of California Press, 2016), 199; and Tara McDowell, *Householders: Robert Duncan and Jess* (Cambridge, Mass.: MIT Press, 2019).

9. Aukeman, *Welcome to Painterland,* especially "The Art of Assemblage, New York–San Francisco," 49–67. Allan Kaprow, "The Legacy of Jackson Pollock," in *Essays on the Blurring of Art and Life,* ed. Jeff Kelley (Berkeley: University of California Press, 1993), 7; Robert Rauschenberg, "Robert Rauschenberg," in Miller, *Sixteen Americans,* 58.

10. Rita Felski, "The Invention of Everyday Life," in *Doing Time: Feminist Theory and Postmodern Culture* (New York: New York University Press, 2000), 78. I use Felski's summary of twentieth-century philosophical perspectives of everyday life as a touchstone for this chapter because I have found no one model—

including those presented in important period texts, such as Henri Lefebvre's *The Critique of Everyday Life* (1947) and Erving Goffman's *The Presentation of the Self in Everyday Life* (1956)—capable of illuminating the artists' understandings of and approaches to the everyday.

11. Aukeman, "Rat Bastards in Painterland," in *Welcome to Painterland*, 69–101.

12. "Wally Hedrick Biography," Wally Hedrick, http://www.wallyhedrick.org.

13. This account of the couple's early life together, including any unattributed quotes, derives from oral history interview with Jay DeFeo, June 3, 1975–January 23, 1976, AAA.

14. Richard Cándida Smith, *The Modern Moves West: California Artists and Democratic Culture in the Twentieth Century* (Philadelphia: University of Pennsylvania Press, 2009), 70.

15. Cándida Smith, "Utopia and the Private Realm," 257.

16. Photographs of Jay DeFeo's studio, Jay DeFeo papers, circa 1940s–1970s, AAA.

17. Fred Martin, interview with the author, May 6, 2009, Piedmont, Calif.

18. Martin wrote statements at DeFeo's request for the *Sixteen Americans* catalogue and for the brochure that accompanied *The Rose*'s debut exhibition at the Pasadena Art Museum, as detailed in Chapter 1. Aukeman discusses Martin's exhibition at the Six Gallery in *Welcome to Painterland*, 105.

19. Fred Martin, press release for *The Individual and His World*, Museum of Modern Art (MoMA) Archives, New York: Dorothy C. Miller Papers, I.15.k. Martin references Keats's sonnet "On First Looking into Chapman's Homer" (1816). My discussion of the exhibition follows Martin's use of masculine pronouns to refer to the artist.

20. The concept of "domesticized high modernism" that I identify in Martin's exhibition is a version of Cándida Smith's "domestic utopia." Both terms signify the belief that the home protects and nurtures self-expression. I have found my own term preferable to use at times throughout this chapter because it situates this ideology within larger postwar art discourses, thus clarifying its implications for authorship.

21. Caroline A. Jones, "The Romance of the Studio and the Abstract Expressionist Sublime," in *Machine in the Studio: Constructing the Postwar American Artist* (Chicago: University of Chicago Press, 1996), 1–59.

22. Felski, "Invention of Everyday Life," 82–84.

23. David Riesman coined the term "other-directed" in his classic sociological text *The Lonely Crowd: A Study of the Changing American Character* (New Haven: Yale University Press, 1950) to designate individuals who lack autonomy. John Keats, *The Crack in the Picture Window* (Boston: Houghton Mifflin, 1957), 124.

24. Ugo Mulas and Alan Solomon, *New York: The New Art Scene* (New York: Holt, Rinehart and Winston, 1967), exemplifies this shift.

25. Charles Rice, *The Emergence of the Interior: Architecture, Modernity, Domesticity* (New York: Routledge, 2006).

26. Quoted in Solnit, *Secret Exhibition*, 56. Contrary to Martin, the mainstream press often represented 1950s bohemia as a bastion of conformity; see, for example, Paul O'Neil, "The Only Rebellion Around," *Life* 47, no. 22 (November 30, 1959): 114–30.

27. In chapter three of *Welcome to Painterland*, Aukeman discusses photographs that Burchard took for the exhibition, but she does not discuss the photo panels themselves.

28. Miriam Dungan Cross, "Shocking 'Beat' Art Displayed," *Oakland Tribune*, November 29, 1959. For more on the article, see John Bowles, "Shocking 'Beat' Art Displayed: California Artists and the Beat Image," in *Reading California: Art, Image, and Identity, 1900–2000*, ed. Stephanie Barron, Sheri Bernstein, and Ilene Susan Fort, exh. cat. (Berkeley: University of California Press; Los Angeles: Los Angeles County Museum of Art , 2000); and Aukeman, *Welcome to Painterland*, 71–79.

29. Bill Brown, *A Sense of Things: The Object Matter of American Literature* (Chicago: University of Chicago Press, 2003).

30. Fred Martin, "The Birth of the Thing, or, Some Recent Developments in the San Francisco Bay Area," undated, Fred Martin papers, 1949–1975, AAA. All quotes in this paragraph are from Martin's essay, pages 7–8.

31. Alex Potts, "Tactility: The Interrogation of Medium in Art of the 1960s," *Art History* 27, no. 2 (April 2004): 301.

32. DeFeo, AAA interview. Hedrick's works that thematize mountain climbing include *Tenzing Zindabad* (1956), *American Everest* (1956–57), and *Wind in the South Col* (date unknown). Constance Lewellan details the couple's fascination with mountaineering in "Mountain Climbing," in *Jay DeFeo: Selected Works, 1952–1989*, ed. Constance Lewellan, exh. cat. (Philadelphia: Goldie Paley Gallery, Moore College of Art and Design, 1996), 6–25. I would like to thank Leah Levy and Dawn Troy of The Jay DeFeo Foundation for their assistance in researching DeFeo and Hedrick's interest in mountain climbing.

33. Wally Hedrick, interview with Meredith Tromble, "A Conversation with Wally Hedrick," *Artweek* 27, no. 10 (October 1996): 14–15.

34. Jay DeFeo, lecture at the University of California, Santa Cruz, May 10, 1989, video recording, Archive of The Jay DeFeo Foundation, Berkeley, Calif.; DeFeo, AAA interview; Jay DeFeo, lecture at the Oakland Museum of California, May 21, 1979, audio recording, Archive of The Jay DeFeo Foundation.

35. Jay DeFeo, interview with Moira Roth, "Talking with Jay DeFeo," *Artweek* 21 (February 8, 1990): 19.

36. Quoted in Greil Marcus, "Ritual in Transfigured Time," *Film Comment* 41, no. 1 (2005): 63.

37. Jay DeFeo, "Jay DeFeo: Interview with Leela Elliott," in *Connecting Conversations: Interviews with 28 Bay Area Women Artists*, ed. Moira Roth (Oakland: Eucalyptus, 1988), 48–49; Felski, "Invention of Everyday Life," 79.

38. Such metaphors can be found in Joseph R. Wolin, "Jay DeFeo: A Retrospective," *Time Out: New York*, March 18, 2013, http://www.timeout.com/newyork/art/jay-defeo-a-retrospective; David Littlejohn, "Art: Cosmology on Canvas," *Wall Street Journal*, November 20, 2012; Walead Beshty, "The Ritual of Everyday Life: On the Migrating Objects of Jay DeFeo," in *Jay DeFeo*, exh. cat. (New York: Mitchell-Innes and Nash, 2014), 13; and Kenneth Baker, "Jay DeFeo Review: Fearless Art," *SF Gate*, November 2, 2012, http://www.sfgate.com/art/article/Jay-DeFeo-review-Fearless-art-4003945.php. Laura Meyer insightfully discusses the gradual nature

of DeFeo's painting process in "Constructing a New Paradigm: European American Women Artists in California, 1950–2000," in *Art/Women/California: Parallels and Intersections, 1950–2000,* ed. Diana Burgess and Daniela Salvioni (Berkeley: University of California Press, 2002), 99–100.

39. Hannah Arendt, "Labor," in *Human Condition,* 79–135.

40. Jay DeFeo, letter to Henry Hopkins, June 21, 1978, republished as "My Visual Vocabulary," in *Jay DeFeo: The Ripple Effect,* ed. Seungduk Kim and Franck Gautherot, exh. cat. (Dijon: Les presses du réel, 2018), 141.

41. Marshall Brown, "The Classic Is the Baroque," *Critical Inquiry* 9, no. 2 (December 1982): 379–404. The terms "archaic," "classic," and "baroque" appear frequently in English translations of Heinrich Wölfflin's most canonical text, *Principles in Art History: The Problem of the Development of Style,* trans. M. D. Hottinger (New York: Dover, 1932). Many German émigrés were on the art and art history faculty at the University of California, Berkeley, when DeFeo was a student there, including Walter Horn, Otto J. Mäenchen-Helfen, and Eugene Neuhaus. DeFeo took courses in medieval, Renaissance, and Asian art with Horn and Mäenchen-Helfen; see Kirsten Chen, "DeFeo at Berkeley: Developing the Art Department from 1946–1951," *Caliber* (March 23, 2018), https://www.calibermag.net/blog/2018/3/23/defeo-at-berkeley-developing-the-art-department-from-1946-1951. Even if DeFeo never read Wölfflin's texts, her accounts of *The Rose* indicate that the art historian's vocabulary and methods permeated her education and helped shape her understanding of her art practice.

42. Hannah Arendt, "Work," in *Human Condition,* 136–74; Julia Kristeva, "Women's Time," *Signs: Journal of Women in Culture and Society* 7, no. 1 (Autumn 1981): 17.

43. Felski, "Invention of Everyday Life," 84.

44. Bruce Conner, undated letter to the Berkeley Art Museum, Bruce Conner correspondence concerning Jay DeFeo's *The Rose,* circa 1930–1996, BANC MSS 98/32 c, Bancroft Library, University of California, Berkeley. By portraying the studio as a space elevated above everyday life, the photograph hems closer to the conventions for depicting the abstract expressionist studio that most of Burchard's other photographs rejected. Given this disconnect, it is little wonder Burchard and Martin left this studio shot off of DeFeo's panel for *The Individual and His World.* Catherine Spencer also describes DeFeo's studio as "liminal" space in "Coral and Lichen, Brains and Bowels: Jay DeFeo's Hybrid Abstraction," *Tate Papers* 23 (Spring 2015), http://www.tate.org.uk/research/publications/tate-papers/23.

45. DeFeo emphasized that the Fillmore Street apartment was large enough for her and Wally to have separate studios; Jay DeFeo, interview with Sidra Stich, August 19, 1988, audio recording, Archive of The Jay DeFeo Foundation.

46. In a 1959 letter, DeFeo acknowledged that restretching *The Rose* and *The Jewel* meant "tearing the front of the house out to get them out"; Jay DeFeo, letter to Dorothy C. Miller, August 18, 1959, MoMA Archives: Dorothy C. Miller Papers, I.15.k.

47. Jay DeFeo, letter to Terry St. John, April 30, 1971; Jay DeFeo, letter to Thomas Albright, May 30, 1971, Bruce Conner correspondence concerning *The Rose,* Bancroft Library.

48. Oral history interview with Carlos Villa, June 20–July 10, 1995, AAA. Sandra S. Phillips makes a similar point in "Photographing *The Rose,*" in *Jay DeFeo and "The Rose,"* ed. Jane Green and Leah Levy (Berkeley: University of California Press, 2003), 66–67.

49. Dana Miller, "Slow Curve," in Miller, *Jay DeFeo: A Retrospective,* 24.

50. Quoted in Solnit, *Secret Exhibition,* 78.

51. Hedrick, AAA interview. Aukeman likewise points to Schwitters as a significant precedent for the assemblage practices of the Fillmore circle; Aukeman, *Welcome to Painterland,* 66–67. Other evidence of Schwitters's importance to DeFeo includes a handmade, undated "Merz Award" given to her by an unknown friend (Jay DeFeo papers, AAA) and a clay hamburger that she took a bite out of and titled *Merzberger* (discussed in DeFeo, "My Visual Vocabulary," 144). She also mentions Schwitters in correspondence about the precariousness of *The Rose*'s situation at the San Francisco Art Institute: "They suddenly discovered Dada at the school God forbid! And are having a Merz show in the conference room where the Rose is. . . . I hate to say it but I once joked about having a dada demolition party on the last day of school. What a final irony it would be if my dream came true now that I've lost the courage of my convictions!" DeFeo, letter to Albright, May 30, 1971, Bancroft Library.

52. Elizabeth Burns Gamard, *Kurt Schwitter's Merzbau: The Cathedral of Erotic Misery* (Princeton, N.J.: Princeton Architectural Press, 2000).

53. Quoted in *Wally Hedrick/Seymour Locks: A Selected Survey,* exh. cat. (Davis, Calif.: Natsoulas Novelozo Gallery, 1990), 33.

54. Schoenthal observed that Hedrick "rides the line between seriousness and irony so closely that the work can always be considered both and neither"; Schoenthal, "North Beach to Haight-Ashbury," 209. I believe this ambiguity applies to most of Hedrick's statements, as well as his works.

55. I have adapted the term "junk artist" from Lawrence Alloway's idea of "junk art," proposed in "Junk Art," *Architectural Design* 31 (March 1961): 123–33. Rauschenberg articulated the concept of "random order" in "Random Order," *Location* 1, no. 1 (Spring 1963): 28.

56. Allan Kaprow, "Untitled Guidelines for Happenings" (1965), in *Theories and Documents of Contemporary Art: A Sourcebook of Artists' Writings,* ed. Kristine Stiles and Peter Selz (Berkeley: University of California Press, 2012), 835. Kaprow articulates this goal most clearly in his writings of the 1970s and 1980s, such as "Participation Performance" (1977), "Performing Life" (1979), and "Art Which Can't Be Art" (1986), reprinted in *Essays on Blurring Art and Life,* ed. Jeff Kelley (Berkeley: University of California Press, 1993), 181–94, 195–200, 219–22. For more on Kaprow's Happenings, especially their challenge to consumer capitalism, see Judith Rodenbeck, *Radical Prototypes: Allan Kaprow and the Invention of Happenings* (Cambridge, Mass.: MIT Press, 2011).

57. Walter Benjamin, "The Work of Art in the Age of Mechanical Reproduction," in *Illuminations,* trans. Harry Zohn (New York: Schocken, 2007), 217–52; Peter Bürger, "Avant-Gardiste Work of Art,"

in *The Theory of the Avant-Garde,* trans. Michael Shaw (Minneapolis: University of Minnesota Press, 1984), 55–82.

58. See, for example, Solnit, *Secret Exhibition,* 83; Lippard, "Transplanting *The Rose,*" in Green and Levy, *Jay DeFeo and "The Rose,"* 55–64; Schoenthal, "North Beach to Haight-Ashbury," 234; and Lennard J. Davis, "'Play It Again, Sam, and Again': Obsession in Art," *Journal of Visual Culture* 5, no. 2 (August 2006): 242–66.

59. Wally Hedrick, interview with Leslie Goldberg, "di Rosa Artist Interview Series," 2009, http://www.wallyhedrick.org/pdfs/di_rosa_artist_interview_series.pdf; Wally Hedrick, interview with Mark Van Proyen, "An Interview with Wally Hedrick," *Expo-See* (Summer 1985), unpaginated, http://www.wallyhedrick.org/pdfs/exposee_1985.pdf.

60. DeFeo, AAA interview; Betty Friedan, *The Feminine Mystique* (New York: W. W. Norton, 1963).

61. Jay DeFeo, letter to Dorothy C. Miller, February 9, 1960, MoMA Archives: Dorothy C. Miller Papers, I.15.k. In the mid-1970s, DeFeo glued fig. 50 over the image of fig. 13 reproduced on the announcement for the exhibition *Art as a Muscular Principle* and sent copies of the collage, which humorously underscores the complex relationship between her domestic and artistic personae, to friends.

62. Cándida Smith, "Utopia and the Private Realm."

63. Helen Molesworth, "House Work and Art Work," *October* 92 (Spring 2000): 71–97; also see Mierle Laderman Ukeles, "Maintenance Art Manifesto" (1969), in Stiles and Selz, *Theories and Documents of Contemporary Art,* 733–35.

64. Lippard, "Transplanting *The Rose,*" 56. I adopt the term "prefeminist generation" from Norma Broude and Mary D. Garrard to describe women who began their careers prior to the women's liberation movement of the late 1960s; Norma Broude and Mary D. Garrard, "Introduction: Feminism and Art in the Twentieth Century," in *The Power of Feminist Art: The American Movement of the 1970s, History and Impact,* ed. Norma Broude and Mary D. Garrard (New York: Harry N. Abrams, 1994), 17. For discussion of other prefeminist artists who similarly adopted masculine-connoted means of self-presentation, see Linda Grasso, *Equal under the Sky: Georgia O'Keeffe and Twentieth-Century Feminism* (Albuquerque: University of New Mexico Press, 2017), 9; and Anne M. Wagner, "Lee Krasner as L. K.," *Representations* 25 (Winter 1989): 42–57.

65. Jay DeFeo, undated note, Jay DeFeo papers, AAA.

66. Facts about DeFeo and Hedrick's separation are from Diana Kamin and Meredith George Van Dyke, "Chronology," in Miller, *Jay DeFeo: A Retrospective,* 287–88. Precisely how the couple's displacement from 2322 Fillmore Street affected DeFeo's completion of *The Rose* is unclear. While DeFeo sometimes claimed that the move forced her to finish the painting prematurely, Miller has demonstrated that DeFeo felt it was nearing completion before she and Hedrick received notification of the rent increase; Miller, "Slow Curve," 30.

67. Jay DeFeo, interview with Sidra Stich, September 16, 1988, Archive of The Jay DeFeo Foundation.

68. All quotes by DeFeo in this paragraph are from DeFeo, AAA interview. Duncan interprets *Life Game* in relation to this interpretation of *The Rose;* Duncan, "Chancing the Ridiculous," 65.

69. Hedrick, interview with Goldberg. Bill Berkson includes a similar account from Hedrick in "In the Heat of the Rose," *Art in America* 84 (March 1996): 69–73, 110–11.

70. Whitney Chadwick and Isabelle de Courtivron, "Introduction," in *Significant Others: Creativity and Intimate Partnership,* ed. Whitney Chadwick and Isabelle de Courtivron (London: Thames and Hudson, 1996), 1.

71. Hedrick, AAA interview.

72. Quoted in *Jay DeFeo, An Intimate View: Small Paintings, 1986–1989* (Santa Cruz: Art Museum of Santa Cruz County; Oakland, Calif.: Mills College, 1990), 2.

73. Jackson Pollock voiceover in *Jackson Pollock '51,* dir. Hans Namuth (1951).

74. Jackson Pollock, "Interview with William Wright" (1950), in Stiles and Selz, *Theories and Documents of Contemporary Art,* 26.

75. Chadwick and Courtivron, *Significant Others,* 1–2; Anne M. Wagner, *Three Artists (Three Women)* (Berkeley: University of California Press, 1996); Bibiana Obler, *Intimate Collaborations: Kandinsky and Münter, Arp and Taeuber* (New Haven: Yale University Press, 2014).

76. Hedrick, *Wally Hedrick,* unpaginated. The following year, Hedrick created a related sculpture titled *J. Me et Bat* that incorporates one of DeFeo's jewelry pieces and bears some resemblance to the sculpture depicted in the painting. He employed the tower figure yet again in *Love Feeling* (1957), a painting that also features a heart inscribed with "W.H. + J.D."

77. Hedrick, *Wally Hedrick,* unpaginated.

CHAPTER 3
BODY LANGUAGE

1. The assumption that McClure wrote the poem at DeFeo's request and that she intended to use it for *The Rose*'s debut exhibition is based on a letter DeFeo wrote in 1965 explaining that she, Fred Martin, and McClure were writing "brief statements" for the exhibition brochure; DeFeo, letter to Walter Hopps, May 10, 1965, archives of the Norton Simon Museum, Pasadena, Calif. Likely due to the exhibition's three-year delay, McClure's poem was never used. It was made public thirty years later when he read it at "A Day with *The Rose,*" a symposium held at the San Francisco Art Institute on August 12, 1995, to celebrate the painting's successful return to public view. The following year, a version of his remarks was published in Michael McClure, "Thoughts on Jay DeFeo's *The Rose,* from a notebook, August 1965," in *Jay DeFeo: Selected Works, 1952–1989,* ed. Constance Lewellan, exh. cat. (Philadelphia: Goldie Paley Gallery, Moore College of Art and Design, 1996), 31.

2. Michael McClure, interview with the author, July 26, 2015, Oakland, Calif.

3. Oral history interview with Jay DeFeo, June 3, 1975–January 23, 1976, Archives of American Art (AAA), Smithsonian Institution, Washington, D.C.; quoted in Anastasia Aukeman, *Welcome to Painterland: Bruce Conner and the Rat Bastard Protective Association* (Berkeley: University of California Press, 2016), 84; McClure, interview with author; Michael McClure, note to Jay DeFeo, March–April 1961 notebook, Michael McClure Papers: Additions, 1874–2003, bulk 1949–2002, BANC MSS 2003/222 c, Bancroft Library, Berkeley, Calif.

4. Quotes from Michael McClure, "Poetry of the 6," in *The Beat Generation Galleries and Beyond*, ed. John Natsoulas, exh. cat. (Davis, Calif.: John Natsoulas Gallery, 1996), 67; and McClure, interview with author. Also see Michael McClure, interview with David Meltzer, "Interview with Michael McClure," in *San Francisco Beat: Talking with the Poets*, ed. David Meltzer (San Francisco: City Lights, 2001), 150.

5. Steven Watson, "Michael McClure," in *The Birth of the Beat Generation: Visionaries, Rebels, and Hipsters, 1944–1960* (New York: Pantheon, 1995), 209.

6. "Michael McClure at the Spatsa Gallery," in Natsoulas, *Beat Generation Galleries and Beyond*, 156.

7. See, for example, Aukeman, *Welcome to Painterland*, 105.

8. Quotes from Michael McClure, interview with Kevin Power, "Interview with Michael McClure," in *Where You're At: Poetics and Visual Art* (Berkeley: Poltroon, 2011), 48; and Michael McClure, "Poetry of the 6," in *Beat Down Your Soul: What Was the Beat Generation?*, ed. Ann Charters (New York: Penguin, 2001), 373. Also see Michael McClure, "The Beat Surface," in *Scratching the Beat Surface* (San Francisco: North Point, 1982), 13. For a detailed account of McClure's role in the reading, see Aukeman, *Welcome to Painterland*, 104–5, 262.

9. For more on the oracular emphasis of poetry in postwar San Francisco, see Michael Davidson, *The San Francisco Renaissance: Poetics and Community at Mid-Century* (Cambridge: Cambridge University Press, 1991), 20–23.

10. Robert Duncan, *Faust Foutu: A Comic Masque* (Barrytown, N.Y.: Station Hill, 1985); McClure, interview with author; Michael McClure, "An Empire of Signs: Jack Spicer," in *Lighting the Corners: On Nature, Art, and the Visionary* (Albuquerque: University of New Mexico Press, 1993), 114.

11. McClure, interview with Power, 54.

12. *The Maze: Haight/Ashbury* (1967), Bay Area Television Archive, https://diva.sfsu.edu/collections/sfbatv/bundles/189371. For more on McClure's involvement in the Fillmore art scene and the later counterculture, see Anastasia Aukeman, "The Centrality of Michael McClure," in *Welcome to Painterland*, 85–88.

13. Michael McClure, untitled poem, undated, Michael McClure Papers: Additions, Bancroft Library. Although undated, the poem's reference to "White Rose" (which was the title of DeFeo's painting at the time) and its use of terms (such as "pollen" and "dream") that appear in the final draft of the poem suggest that it was McClure's initial response to DeFeo's request.

14. James A. W. Heffernan, *Museum of Words: The Poetics of Ekphrasis from Homer to Ashbery* (Chicago: University of Chicago Press, 1993), 4; W. J. T. Mitchell, "Ekphrasis and the Other," in *Picture Theory: Essays on Verbal and Visual Representation* (Chicago: University of Chicago Press, 1995), 151–81.

15. With this strategy, McClure followed (probably unknowingly) Gotthold Ephraim Lessing's argument that dramatic speech ameliorates the abstraction of language and the absence that undergirds mimesis by deploying words within theater's "lifelike" embodied action, creating illusions superior to those produced in other media; see Murray Krieger, *Ekphrasis: Illusion of the Natural Sign* (Baltimore: Johns Hopkins University Press, 1992), 51.

16. For McClure's explanations of his use of capitalization, see Michael McClure, "After Thoughts," in *Huge Dreams: San Francisco and the Beat Poems* (New York: Penguin Poets, 1999), 169; and Michael McClure, untitled statement, January–June 1961 notebook, Michael McClure Papers: Additions, Bancroft Library.

17. Michael McClure, remarks at the symposium "A Day with *The Rose*," San Francisco Art Institute, August 12, 1995, audio recording, Archive of The Jay DeFeo Foundation, Berkeley, Calif.

18. Imagery from the second deck was also used for *Mandala*, a book that Conner and McClure jointly produced in 1966. Details of the card projects are from Taylor Zakarin, "The Oracle in the CARDS: Robert Rauschenberg, Bruce Conner, and Michael McClure," Robert Rauschenberg Foundation, http://shuffle.rauschenbergfoundation.org/exhibitions/nasher/essays; Kevin Hatch, "'Thinking of You': Bruce Conner's Epistolary Practice," *American Art* 33, no. 1 (Spring 2019): 65; and Christopher Luna, ed., "The Flame Is Ours: The Letters of Stan Brakhage and Michael McClure, 1961–1978," *Big Bridge* 15 (Spring 2011), https://bigbridge.org/BB15/toc.html. For more on Conner's *Mandala* series, see Kevin Hatch, "Really Looking," in *Looking for Bruce Conner* (Cambridge, Mass.: MIT Press, 2016), 193–249.

19. Kevin Hatch notably brings these discourses together by reading Conner's assemblage practice through the lens of performance; Kevin Hatch, "'It Has to Do with the Theater,'" in *Looking for Bruce Conner*, 31–110.

20. See, for example, Paul Schimmel, ed., *Out of Actions: Between Performance and the Object, 1949–1979* (Los Angeles: Museum of Contemporary Art; London: Thames and Hudson, 1998).

21. Davidson, *San Francisco Renaissance*, 154. Davidson complicates this narrative in his reading of Jack Spicer, which shares several features with my reading of McClure; Michael Davidson, "'The City Redefined': Community and Dialogue in Jack Spicer," in *San Francisco Renaissance*, 150–71.

22. Michael McClure, "The First Reading of the Environmental Movement: The Six Gallery Reading," in *Beats at Naropa: An Anthology*, ed. Anne Waldman and Laura Wright (Minneapolis: Coffee House, 2009), 15.

23. Quoted in Robert Basil, "Michael McClure: Charming and Articulate," *Prodigal Sun/The Spectrum* (March 28, 1980): 11; McClure, interview with Power, 55–56.

24. Harold Bloom, *The Anxiety of Influence: A Theory of Poetry* (New York: Oxford University Press, 1973). Occasionally, McClure's retrospective accounts acknowledge that criticism and competition also played a role in the city's cultural underground; see, for example, McClure, "After Thoughts," 166.

25. Aukeman, for example, describes the Fillmore community as possessing a "tender utopianism"; Aukeman, *Welcome to Painterland*, 199.

26. Michael McClure, untitled entry, December 29–March 2, 1957 notebook, Michael McClure: Additions, Bancroft Library; Michael McClure, untitled entry, March–July 1960 notebook, Michael McClure: Additions, Bancroft Library.

27. Michael McClure, untitled entry, October–November 1957 notebook, Michael McClure: Additions, Bancroft Library; Michael McClure, untitled entry, November 1959 notebook, Michael McClure: Additions, Bancroft Library.

28. Michael McClure, "Shout ODE for John Webster," November 1958 notebook, Michael McClure: Additions, Bancroft Library; Michael McClure, untitled entry, December 1958–May 1959 notebook, Michael McClure: Additions, Bancroft Library.

29. Michael McClure, untitled entry, December 1956 notebook, Michael McClure: Additions, Bancroft Library. "Jess" refers to Duncan's partner, the artist Jess (Collins), and "Helen" is Helen Adam, a poet and close friend of the couple.

30. Michael McClure, untitled entry, March–September 1957 notebook, Michael McClure: Additions, Bancroft Library; Michael McClure, untitled entry, December–September 1960 notebook, Michael McClure: Additions, Bancroft Library; Michael McClure, untitled entry, March–June 1957 notebook, Michael McClure: Additions, Bancroft Library.

31. Michael McClure, "Friends & acquaintances & enemies in SF," undated notebook, Michael McClure: Additions, Bancroft Library; Michael McClure, "TURN-ON LIST," March 29–May 12, 1962 notebook, Michael McClure: Additions, Bancroft Library; Michael McClure, "RATBASTARDS/BRUCE CONNER," June 1958 notebook, McClure: Additions, Bancroft Library (reprinted in Aukeman, *Welcome to Painterland,* 98–99).

32. Michael McClure, "Supplementary Notes to the Critique on Sonia," March–September 1957 notebook, Michael McClure: Additions, Bancroft Library.

33. Michael McClure, untitled statement, Michael McClure: Additions, Bancroft Library.

34. David Riesman, Nathan Glazer, and Reuel Denney, *The Lonely Crowd: A Study of the Changing American Character* (New Haven: Yale University Press, 1950); Herbert Marcuse, *One-Dimensional Man: Studies in the Ideology of Advanced Industrial Society* (Boston: Beacon, 1964). For more on Marcuse's significance to McClure, see Jack Foley, "Livingness: A Review of *REBEL LIONS,*" *Poetry Flash* 227 (February 1992), reprinted on Michael McClure Home Page, http://www.thing.net/~grist/l&d/mcclure/mc-fol1.htm; and Anis Shivani, "Exclusive: Beat Poet Michael McClure on Jim Morrison, The Doors, Allen Ginsberg, Jack Kerouac," Huffington Post, March 3, 2011, http://www.huffingtonpost.com/entry/exclusive-beat-poet-mcclure_b_823425.

35. Quoted in Aukeman, *Welcome to Painterland,* 91. For more on incidents of censorship, including those involving *The Beard,* see Maurice Berger, "Libraries Full of Tears: The Beats and the Law," in *Beat Culture and the New America, 1950–1965,* ed. Lisa Phillips, exh. cat. (New York: Whitney Museum of American Art, 1995), 122–37; and Dawn B. Soba, "The Beard," in *Banned Plays: Censorship Histories of 125 Stage Dramas* (New York: Facts on File, 2004), 12–14.

36. DeFeo, AAA interview.

37. Miller's papers in the Museum of Modern Art (MoMA) Archives contain letters from Edith Posel, writing in support of Gechtoff, and David Simpson, writing in defense of DeFeo. Miller dismissed Gechtoff's accusations.

38. Jay DeFeo, letter to Dorothy C. Miller, December 31, 1959, MoMA Archives, New York: Dorothy C. Miller Papers, I.15.k.

39. Richard Cándida Smith discusses the maturation of California artists and writers at midcentury in "Part II: Mythopoesis and Self-Narration," in *Utopia and Dissent: Art, Poetry, and Politics in California* (Berkeley: University of California Press, 1995), 143–298.

40. McClure, *Lighting the Corners,* ix.

41. McClure, interview with author.

42. Poem transcribed from McClure, "Thoughts on Jay DeFeo's *The Rose,* from a notebook, August 1965." McClure described the final version of the poem as a "summation" at "A Day with *The Rose,*" Archive of The Jay DeFeo Foundation.

43. McClure, untitled poem, undated, Michael McClure Papers: Additions, Bancroft Library.

44. Quoted in Don Shewey, "Michael McClure Is an Animal," *Soho News,* archived in Michael McClure: Additions, Bancroft Library; Michael McClure, "Poet Playwright Director Magic," in *Lighting the Corners,* 266.

45. Michael McClure, interview with Harald Mesch, "Writing One's Body," in *Lighting the Corners,* 18. For further discussion of McClure's use of shape and typography, see Davidson, *San Francisco Renaissance,* 86.

46. Michael McClure, "The Shape of Energy," in *Scratching the Beat Surface,* 89, 96.

47. Jackson Pollock voiceover in *Jackson Pollock '51,* dir. Hans Namuth (1951); Stephen Gregory, *The Daybreak Boys: Essays on the Literature of the Beat Generation* (Carbondale: Southern Illinois University Press, 1990), 109.

48. Antonin Artaud, *The Theater and Its Double* (New York: Grove, 1958), 71, 72, 90–91.

49. Michael McClure, *The Mammals* (San Francisco: Cranium, 1972), 7, 5–6. For more on McClure's reception of Artaud, see Michael McClure, "Artaud: Peace Chief," in *Meat Science Essays* (San Francisco: City Light, 1963), 77–78.

50. Michael McClure, untitled entry, June 1958 notebook, Michael McClure Papers: Additions, Bancroft Library. I would like to thank Namiko Kunimoto for linking the passage to Shiraga's performance.

51. Dennis Tedlock, "Stories of Kachinas and the Dance of Life and Death," in *Kachinas in the Pueblo World,* ed. Polly Shaafsma (Salt Lake City: University of Utah Press, 2000), 171.

52. See, for example, Harold Rosenberg, "The American Action Painters," *Art News* 51, no. 8 (December 1952): 22–23, 48–50.

53. Michael McClure, *The New Book/A Book of Torture* (New York: Grove, 1961), back cover; McClure, "Shape of Energy," 89.

54. Michael McClure, interview with Mick McAllister, "The Beat Journey: An Interview," in *Lighting the Corners,* 132.

55. McClure, "Shape of Energy," 57. For McClure's thoughts on agnosia, see McClure, "Writing One's Body," 22–23; and Foley, "Livingness." McClure has used "negative capability," a term coined by the English Romantic poet John Keats, virtually interchangeably with agnosia; see Li Ou, *Keats and Negative Capability* (New York: Continuum International, 2009).

56. Michael McClure, "Dark Contemplation," in *Jay DeFeo: Works on Paper,* ed. Sidra Stich (Berkeley: University Art Museum, University of California, Berkeley, 1989), 29; McClure, interview with author.

57. Herbert Marcuse, *Eros and Civilization: A Philosophical Inquiry into Freud* (Boston: Beacon, 1955); Michael McClure, "Revolt," in *Meat Science Essays,* 81.

58. Rod Phillips, *Michael McClure* (Boise,

Idaho: Boise State University Press, 2003), 23–28; and Stephenson, *Daybreak Boys,* 115–18.

59. Lauren Berlant, *Desire/Love* (Goleta, Calif.: Punctum, 2012), 46.

60. McClure, "Revolt," 75. Also see Jason Camlot, "Mammals and Machines: Michael McClure's Embodying Poetics," *Atenea* 23, no. 1 (June 2003), http://ece.uprm.edu/artssciences/atenea/Atenea-XXIII-1.pdf.

61. Michael McClure, "Seventeen Things about Jay DeFeo," in Lewellan, *Jay DeFeo: Selected Works,* 32; Michael McClure, untitled statement, November 1959 notebook, Michael McClure Papers: Additions, Bancroft Library.

62. McClure, "Revolt," 76–77.

63. Michael McClure, "Phi Upsilon Kappa," in *Meat Science Essays,* 20. Also see Franca Bellarsi, "Sex and the Body in Michael McClure's Quest 'For the Mammal Self,'" in *The Body and the Book: Writings on Poetry and Sexuality,* ed. Glennis Byron and Andrew J. Sneddon (Amsterdam: Rodopi, 2008), 173–91.

64. McClure, "Seventeen Things," 32. For McClure's thoughts on proportionlessness, see "Phi Upsilon Kappa," 15.

65. McClure, interview with Meltzer, 164.

66. Michael McClure, "Hymns to St. Geryon," in *Hymns to St. Geryon and Other Poems* (London: Cape Goliard, 1969), unpaginated; Geoffrey Thurley, *American Moment: American Poetry in the Mid-Century* (London: Edward Arnold, 1977), 197. Davidson makes a similar point; Davidson, *San Francisco Renaissance,* 89.

67. Camlot, "Mammals and Machines," 56; and K. C. Power, "WOLF RIMBAUD SNOW-LEOPARD HARLOW BLOSSOM FRICK STAR POLLOCK ANGEL ODUM MEAT MICHAEL MCCLURE," *Margins* 18, no. 3 (1975): 50.

68. Michael McClure, "Cinnamon Turquoise Leather," in *Lighting the Corners,* 311; oral history interview with Bruce Conner, April 16, 1973, AAA.

69. Michael McClure, untitled entry, 1956 notebook, Michael McClure Papers: Bancroft Library; Conner, AAA interview. Other precedents include *Semina*—Berman's underground literary journal, which due to its card-like format has also been compared to tarot—and the word-card deck *Game for Angels* that Paul Beattie and Herms, two members of California's artistic underground with ties to the Fillmore District, published with MC Press in 1963; see Cándida Smith, *Utopia and Dissent,* 231; and Michael Duncan and Kristine McKenna, *Semina Culture: Wallace Berman and His Circle* (New York: D.A.P.; Santa Monica: Santa Monica Museum of Art, 2005), 27–28.

70. McClure, "Cinnamon Turquoise Leather," 311.

71. McClure explicitly connected the two techniques at "A Day with *The Rose*" by calling the list of words at the top of the 1965 notebook page "beast language." Conner also connects McClure's *Ghost Tantras* to their word cards in his AAA interview.

72. McClure, interview with author; McClure, "Cinnamon Turquoise Leather," 301–12.

73. McClure similarly used a string of words unburdened by punctuation and syntax to describe his experience of the world while on peyote in Richard O. Moore's 1966 televised documentary series *USA: Poetry.* Conner's drawings for the 1970 deck also suggest a connection to drugs in their resemblance to psychedelic art.

74. McClure, "Cinnamon Turquoise Leather," 301–12; *USA: Poetry,* "Brother Antonius and Michael McClure," National Educational Television, dir. Richard O. Moore (March 27, 1966).

75. McClure, "Shape of Energy," 57.

76. McClure, "Day with *The Rose.*"

77. Berlant, *Desire/Love,* 26.

78. McClure, interview with author.

79. McClure, "Seventeen Things," 32; McClure, "Day with *The Rose.*"

80. McClure, interview with Power, 61; Power, "WOLF RIMBAUD," 50.

81. Michael McClure, "The Shelley Game," October 23, undated notebook, Michael McClure Papers: Additions, Bancroft Library.

82. McClure, interview with author.

83. McClure, interview with author.

84. McClure, interview with author.

85. McClure, "Shelley Game." This summary of McClure's engagement with scientific discourses draws from Rod Phillips, "'Let Us Throw Out the Word Man': Michael McClure's Mammalian Poetics," in *"Forest Beatniks" and "Urban Thoreaus": Gary Snyder, Jack Kerouac, Lew Welch, and Michael McClure* (New York: Peter Lang, 2000), 103–24; and Jonathan Skinner, "Visceral Ecopoetics in Charles Olson and Michael McClure: Proprioception, Biology, and the Writing Body," in *Ecopoetics: Essays in the Field,* ed. Angela Hume and Gillian Osborne (Iowa City: University of Iowa Press, 2018), 65–83.

86. This discussion of feedback is informed by Luke Skrebowski, "All Systems Go: Recovering Jack Burnham's 'Systems Aesthetics,'" *Tate Papers,* no. 5 (Spring 2006), https://www.tate.org.uk/research/publications/tate-papers/05; Dario Sanfilippo and Andrea Valle, "Feedback Systems: An Analytical Framework," *Computer Music Journal* 37, no. 2 (Summer 2013): 12–27; and William Kaizen, "Video Ecologies," in *Against Immediacy: Video Art and Media Populism* (Hanover, N.H.: Dartmouth College Press, 2016).

87. Both Phillips, "'Let Us Throw Out the Word Man,'" and Skinner, "Visceral Poetics," discuss this idea in relation to McClure's understanding of projective verse.

88. Michael McClure, "Shape of Energy," 44; Skinner, "Visceral Poetics," 79.

89. Oral history interview with Carlos Villa, June 20–July 10, 1995, AAA.

90. McClure, interview with author. Information on DeFeo's creative use of her teeth derives from Corey Keller, "My Favorite Things," in *Jay DeFeo: A Retrospective,* ed. Dana Miller, exh. cat. (New York: Whitney Museum of American Art; New Haven: Yale University Press, 2012), 76; and Stephen F. F. Jost, *"Out of my own head": Photographs by Jay DeFeo,* exh. cat. (Oakland: Mills College Art Museum, 2004). For a sampling of these works, see plates 71–77 of Miller, *Jay DeFeo: A Retrospective,* 150–57.

91. Michael McClure, *September Blackberries* (New York: New Directions, 1974), back cover. Keller cites the same quote; Keller, "My Favorite Things," 76.

92. McClure, *September Blackberries,* foreword.

93. Quoted in Jost, *"Out of my own head"*; McClure, *September Blackberries,* foreword.

94. Jay DeFeo, lecture at the San Francisco Art Institute, February 11, 1980, audio recording, Archive of The Jay DeFeo Foundation. Conservator Niccolo Caldararo lays out conflicting evidence regarding *The Rose*'s lead content in

"Conserving *The Rose*," in *Jay DeFeo and "The Rose,"* ed. Jane Green and Leah Levy (Berkeley: University of California Press; New York: Whitney Museum of American Art, 2003), 123.

95. Jay DeFeo, letter to David Simpson, undated, Jay DeFeo papers, circa 1940s–1970s, AAA.

96. Greil Marcus, "Valentine's Day," in Green and Levy, *Jay DeFeo and "The Rose,"* 108. Marcus specifically cites McClure's invocation of the saying "It is not Goethe who creates Faust but Faust who creates Goethe" at "A Day with *The Rose*" as indicative of this myth; Marcus, "Valentine's Day," 105.

97. Norman Bryson, "Intertextuality and Visual Poetics," *Style* 22, no. 2 (Summer 1988): 189.

98. Camlot, "Mammals and Machines," 64. Similar critiques can be found in Skinner, "Visceral Ecopoetics," 78; and Ruby Cohn, *New American Dramatists, 1960–1980* (New York: Grove, 1982), 146.

99. Keller, "My Favorite Things," 76.

100. For McClure's views on change, see Michael McClure, "Towards Perception: An Interview with Francesco Clemente," in *Lighting the Corners*, 210–11.

101. DeFeo's correspondence with the curator of *Sixteen Americans*, Dorothy Miller, reveals that this generative interplay between consonance and friction was an established pattern for artist and poet. DeFeo's letters show that her reservations about McClure's characterization of her art prompted her to write her own statement to accompany his and Martin's in the catalogue; see Jay DeFeo, letter to Dorothy C. Miller, October 21, 1959, MoMA Archives: Dorothy C. Miller Papers, I.15.k.

CHAPTER 4
AFTERLIVES

1. Registry for "A Wake for *The Rose*," Jay DeFeo, Archival Artist's File, San Francisco Art Institute (SFAI) Archives. According to Judith Dunham, DeFeo helped organize the wake but did not attend it; Judith Dunham, "Chronology," in *Jay DeFeo and "The Rose,"* ed. Jane Green and Leah Levy (Berkeley: University of California Press, 2003), 162.

2. Bruce Conner, letter to Jay DeFeo, December 15, 1973, Bruce Conner photograph collection, BANC PIC 1997.069, Bancroft Library, University of California, Berkeley. See the introduction to this book for a more extensive description of *The Rose*'s post-studio journey.

3. This chapter follows Conner's preference for formatting the titles of his works and series in all capitals instead of the customary italics; see Rudolf Frieling and Gary Garrels, eds., *Bruce Conner: It's All True*, exh. cat. (San Francisco: San Francisco Museum of Modern Art; Berkeley: University of California Press, 2016), 13.

4. Jean Conner, interview with the author, July 22, 2015, San Francisco.

5. Quoted in Laura Hoptman, "Beyond Compare: Bruce Conner's Assemblage Movement, 1958–64," in Frieling and Garrels, *It's All True*, 273. For more on the RBPA, see Anastasia Aukeman, *Welcome to Painterland: Bruce Conner and the Rat Bastard Protective Association* (Berkeley: University of California Press, 2016).

6. Oral history interview with Bruce Conner, August 12, 1974, Archives of American Art (AAA), Smithsonian Institution, Washington, D.C.

7. See, for example, Rebecca Solnit, *Secret Exhibition: Six California Artists of the Cold War Era* (San Francisco: City Lights, 1990), 68; Kevin Hatch, *Looking for Bruce Conner* (Cambridge, Mass.: MIT Press, 2016), 35; and Anastasia Aukeman, "The Art of Assemblage, New York–San Francisco," in *Welcome to Painterland*, 49–67.

8. Facts from Kevin Hatch, "'It Has to Do with the Theater': Bruce Conner's Ratbastards," *October* 127 (2009): 114, 121. For further discussion of Conner's uneasy relationship with the art world, see Gerald Matt, "I'm Bruce Conner, I'm Not Bruce Conner: On a Man with Qualities," in *Bruce Conner: The 70s: Painting, Drawing, Film*, ed. Gerald Matt and Barbara Steffen, exh. cat. (Vienna: Verlag für moderne Kunst Nürnberg, 2010), 132–43; and Kevin Hatch, "Introduction: A Tomfool in the Emerald City," in *Looking for Bruce Conner*, 1–30.

9. Oral history interview with Jay DeFeo, June 3, 1975–January 23, 1976, AAA; Jay DeFeo, interview with Rebecca Solnit, June 20, 1988, Oakland, Calif., interviews for the book *Secret Exhibition*, Phonotape 4000 C: 1–19, Bancroft Library; quoted here with the permission of Rebecca Solnit. See Chapter 1 for a full transcription of the latter statement.

10. Conner, AAA interview. Many scholars have cited this anecdote, including Aukeman, *Welcome to Painterland*, 137; Michael Duncan, "Chancing the Ridiculous," in *Jay DeFeo: A Retrospective*, ed. Dana Miller, exh. cat. (New York: Whitney Museum of American Art; New Haven: Yale University Press, 2012), 66; and Rachel Federman, "Bruce Conner: Fifty Years in Show Business: A Narrative Chronology," in Frieling and Garrels, *It's All True*, 29; and Hatch, *Looking for Bruce Conner*, 15.

11. Conner lived outside San Francisco, in Mexico and Massachusetts, for part of 1962 and 1963 and, therefore, was not present for some months of *The Rose*'s production. There is also some question as to whether Conner was present for *The Rose*'s remounting, as he claimed: Jean Conner recalled attending the event in her husband's place (Conner, interview with author).

12. Scholars who frame *The Rose*'s removal as marking the end of the Fillmore District's artistic community include Hatch, *Looking for Bruce Conner*, 166, 169; and Dana Miller, "A Slow Curve," in Miller, *Jay DeFeo: A Retrospective*, 31.

13. Thomas Albright, letter to Jay DeFeo, April 6, 1971, Bruce Conner correspondence concerning Jay DeFeo's *The Rose*, circa 1930–1996, BANC MSS 98/32 c, Bancroft Library. This account of the conservation effort derives from Bruce Conner, letter to Tony Rockwell, May 23, 1973, Jay DeFeo, Archival Artist's File, SFAI Archives; and Jerome Tarshis, "The Art Doctors," *San Francisco*, November 1973, 35. I would like to thank Leah Levy for bringing the latter article to my attention.

14. Bruce Conner, letter to Elizabeth Wendt, undated, Bruce Conner correspondence concerning *The Rose*, Bancroft Library; Jay DeFeo, letter to Bruce Conner, October 27, 1972, Jay DeFeo papers, circa 1940s–1970s, AAA.

15. For more on this trend in the literature on DeFeo, see the introduction to this book.

16. Quoted in Miller, "Slow Curve," 29. These facts about the film's production are from page 31 of Miller's essay.

17. Aukeman, *Welcome to Painterland*, 269n33.

18. Miller, "Slow Curve," 33, 38.

19. In its use of shot (as opposed to found) footage, focus on a female acquaintance, and prominent soundtrack, THE WHITE ROSE most closely resembles Conner's films VIVIAN (1964) and BREAKAWAY (1966), which respectively feature Vivian Kurz and Toni Basil. COSMIC RAY (1961) also incorporates shots of Conner's friends and fellow artists Joan Brown and Beth Pewther. For more on these films, see Dara Birnbaum, "Three Women, Three Films: Bruce Conner in the 1960s," in Frieling and Garrels, *It's All True,* 50–52; and Johanna Gosse, "Pop, Collaboration, Utopia: Bruce Conner's BREAKAWAY in 1960s Los Angeles," *Camera Obscura: Feminism, Culture, and Media Studies* 30, no. 2 (2015): 1–27.

20. Stan Brakhage, who was active in San Francisco's fledgling experimental film scene in the late 1950s, stated that, unlike with his other films, Conner "deliberately worked with 'A' and 'B' roll printing" when editing THE WHITE ROSE "to conceal the splices"; Stan Brakhage, "Bruce Conner," in *Film at Wit's End: Eight Avant-Garde Filmmakers* (New Paltz, N.Y.: Documentext, 1989), 135. Much has been made of Conner's distinctive and influential use of music in his films; see, for example, James Peterson, "Bruce Conner and the Compilation Narrative," *Wide Angle* 8, nos. 3–4 (1986): 53–62; and Thomas Miessgang, "Me, Myself, and Eye," in Matt and Steffen, *Bruce Conner: The 70s,* 81–82.

21. Hatch, *Looking for Bruce Conner,* 116.

22. Quoted in Aukeman, *Welcome to Painterland,* 146. For an alternative analysis of DeFeo's studio in the film, see Rebecca Schoenthal, "North Beach to Haight-Ashbury: Underground Artists and Community in 1950s San Francisco" (Ph.D. diss., University of Virginia, 2005), 142–45.

23. Marcus, "Ritual in Transfigured Time," *Film Comment* 41, no. 1 (2005): 64–65.

24. Conner aptly described THE WHITE ROSE as having "the character of a documentary with overtones of humor and drama"; "*The Rose:* A eulogy as well as a proposal that *The Rose* be seen in a different light," Bruce Conner correspondence concerning *The Rose,* Bancroft Library. For more on the tonal multivalence of Conner's films, see Hatch, *Looking for Bruce Conner,* 9; David Mosen, "Report," *Film Quarterly* 19, no. 3 (Spring 1966): 56; Dave Sterritt, "Wrenching Departures: Mortality and Absurdity in Avant-Garde Film," in *The Last Laugh: Strange Humors of Cinema,* ed. Murray Pomerance (Detroit: Wayne State University Press, 2013), 98; and V. Vale, *Bruce Conner: The Afternoon Interviews* (San Francisco: Re/Search, 2016), 8–10.

25. Quoted in "Jay DeFeo's *The Rose:* The Enormous Painting That Was 'Almost Alive,'" San Francisco Museum of Modern Art, https://www.sfmoma.org/watch/jay-defeos-the-rose-the-enormous-painting-that-was-almost-alive/; Conner, "*The Rose:* A eulogy," Bruce Conner correspondence concerning *The Rose,* Bancroft Library.

26. Quoted in "Enormous Painting That Was 'Almost Alive.'"

27. Miller, "Slow Curve," 31.

28. Bruce Conner, "A Conversation," *Grand Street* 52 (1995): 233.

29. Hatch, *Looking for Bruce Conner,* 168; "Enormous Painting That Was 'Almost Alive.'"

30. DeFeo, letter to Bruce Conner, October 27, 1972, AAA. Emphasis in original.

31. Quoted in Peter Boswell, "Bruce Conner: Theater of Light and Shadow," in *2000 BC: The Bruce Conner Story Part II,* ed. Joan Rothfuss, exh. cat. (Minneapolis: Walker Art Center, 1999), 32.

32. Walter Hopps, "Bruce Conner," *Bomb* 80 (Summer 2002): 10. Also see Matt, "I'm Bruce Conner, I'm Not Bruce Conner," 325–27; and Gary Garrels, "Soul Stirrer," in Frieling and Garrels, *It's All True,* 339.

33. The card is reproduced in Rachel Federman, "Twenty-Four-Hour Art: Bruce Conner's Environments," in Frieling and Garrels, *It's All True,* 305.

34. Jay DeFeo quoted in Kristin M. Wennesland, "*The Wise and Foolish Virgins* of Jay DeFeo: The Work's History and Symbolic Significance" (master's thesis, University of Oslo, 2009), 61; Bruce Conner quoted in "Enormous Painting That Was 'Almost Alive.'"

35. Quoted in Rudolf Frieling, "Ch-Ch-Ch-Changes," in Frieling and Garrels, *It's All True,* 326.

36. This idea is foundational to both Solnit's *Secret Exhibition* and Aukeman's *Welcome to Painterland,* especially the latter's "Rat Bastard Protective Association and the Making of Assemblage," 128–67.

37. Frieling, "Ch-Ch-Ch-Changes," 324. Information about DARK BROWN is from Garrels, "Soul Stirrer," 339. The mixed-media work is in dialogue with McClure's poem "Dark Brown" (1961).

38. Greil Marcus, "Bruce Conner's BLACK DAHLIA," in Frieling and Garrels, *It's All True,* 79.

39. Quoted in Niccolo Caldararo, "Conserving *The Rose,*" in Green and Levy, *Jay DeFeo and "The Rose,"* 111.

40. Quoted in James Boaden, "San Francisco, Ruin of the Nineteenth Century: The Assemblage Work of Bruce Conner, 1957–1962," *Papers of Surrealism* 2 (Summer 2004): 8, https://www.research.manchester.ac.uk/portal/files/63517386/surrealism_issue_2.pdf. This paragraph's characterization of Conner's Batman exhibition relies on Federman, "Twenty-Four-Hour Art," 305.

41. Quoted in Federman, "Fifty Years of Show Business," 90n85.

42. DeFeo, AAA interview. For details of DeFeo's life during this period, see Miller, "Slow Curve," 31–34; and Kamin and Van Dyke, "Chronology," in Miller, *Jay DeFeo: A Retrospective,* 288–89.

43. Conner, "Conversation," 233.

44. Jay DeFeo, letter to Thomas Albright, May 13, 1971, Bruce Conner correspondence concerning *The Rose,* Bancroft Library. The "idiot" who "wondered about" DeFeo's "encore" was Gerald Adams in "Lady in Search of an Encore," *San Francisco Sunday Examiner and Chronicle,* September 21, 1969.

45. Jay DeFeo, "Biography of J. DeFeo," 1975, Jay DeFeo's artist file, archives of the Oakland Museum of California; Jay DeFeo, letter to Henry Hopkins, June 21, 1978, republished as "My Visual Vocabulary," in *Jay DeFeo: The Ripple Effect,* ed. Seungduk Kim and Franck Gautherot, exh. cat. (Dijon: Les presses du réel, 2018), 140.

46. My argument draws on Myrian Sepúlveda Santos's summary of humanistic thinking on memory in the twentieth century in "Memory and Narrative in Social Theory," *Time and Society* 10, nos. 2–3 (September 2001): 163–89.

47. Quoted in Santos, "Memory and Narrative in Social Theory," 181. It should be noted that DeFeo's conception of the montage-like temporality of her art

practice lacks the Marxist politics and geopolitical implications of Benjamin's theory of history.

48. Quoted in Elizabeth Sussman, "Behold! The Tripod!," in *Jay DeFeo: Her Tripod and Its Dress*, exh. cat. (New York: Michael Rosenfeld Gallery, 2003), 10. My analysis of DeFeo's studio records draws on Sussman, "Behold! The Tripod!," 10–11; Miller, "Slow Curve," 35; and Corey Keller, "My Favorite Things," in Miller, *Jay DeFeo: A Retrospective*, 78. Keller similarly argues that photography helped DeFeo explore time in her art.

49. Brigid Doherty, "Imaging Seeing," in *Jay DeFeo: Works on Paper*, ed. Sidra Stich (Berkeley: University Art Museum, University of California, Berkeley, 1989), 37; quoted in Constance Lewallen, "Mountain Climbing," in *Jay DeFeo: Selected Works, 1952–1989*, ed. Constance Lewellan, exh. cat. (Philadelphia: Goldie Paley Gallery, Moore College of Art and Design, 1996), 17–18.

50. Lewallen, "Mountain Climbing," 17.

51. Miller, "Slow Curve," 34; quoted in Marla Prather, "Beside *The Rose*," in Green and Levy, *Jay DeFeo and "The Rose,"* xvii.

52. Doherty, "Imaging Seeing," 37.

53. Doherty similarly notes that the work's title foregrounds both contingency and irretrievability; Doherty, "Imaging Seeing," 37.

54. Conservation Report on *After Image*, Menil Collection, Houston; Sigmund Freud, "A Note Upon the Mystic Writing Pad" (1925), in *General Psychological Theory: Papers on Metapsychology*, ed. Philip Rieff (New York: Simon and Schuster, 2008), 211–16. Since *After Image* is larger than its reference image, any tracing would have occurred from now-lost intermediary drawings that DeFeo did based on the seashell photograph.

55. For a discussion of these works and their relation to memory, see Claire Elliott, "Fragments and Photographs: Reflections on an Unfinished Work by Jay DeFeo," Menil Collection, https://www.menil.org/read/articles/21; Keller, "My Favorite Things," 77; and Miller, "Slow Curve," 35–36.

56. See, for example, Sussman, "Behold! The Tripod!," 6; Lewallen, "Mountain Climbing," 18; and Miller, "Slow Curve," 37.

57. Conner, letter to Jay DeFeo, December 15, 1973, Bruce Conner photograph collection, Bancroft Library. My account of DeFeo and Conner's relationship in this period derives from their correspondence and Conner's statement for DeFeo's 1994 show at the Kohn Turner Gallery (later published in *Grand Street* as "A Conversation"). Other facts are drawn from Dunham, "Chronology," 161.

58. DeFeo, "My Visual Vocabulary," 145. Keller similarly notes that these collages conjure the surrealists' "magical circumstantial"; Keller, "My Favorite Things," 75.

59. Paul Goodman, "Advance-Guard Writing, 1900–1950," *Kenyon Review* 13, no. 3 (Summer 1951): 357–80. Kevin Hatch touched upon Conner and DeFeo's correspondence around *The Rose* in "'Thinking of You': Bruce Conner's Epistolary Practice," *American Art* 33, no. 1 (Spring 2019): 52–73. His analysis of the role that epistolary exchange played in Conner's art practice raises many issues also explored in this chapter.

60. Johan Huizinga, *Homo Ludens: A Study of the Play-Element in Culture*, trans. R. F. C. Hull (London: Routledge and Kegan Paul, 1949), 4.

61. Susanna Millar, *The Psychology of Play* (New York: J. Aronson, 1974), 13–14; D.W. Winnicott, *Playing and Reality* (London: Tavistock, 1971), 51.

62. Sigmund Freud paraphrased in Millar, *Psychology of Play*, 148, 25; Sigmund Freud, "Creative Writers and Day-Dreaming" (1907), in *Criticism: The Major Statements*, ed. Charles Kaplan (New York: St. Martin's, 1991), 419–28.

63. Huizinga, *Homo Ludens*, 10.

64. Bruce Conner, letter to Jay DeFeo, February 28, 1973, Jay DeFeo papers, AAA; Jay DeFeo, postcard to Bruce Conner, undated (early 1970s), Bruce Conner correspondence concerning *The Rose*, Bancroft Library.

65. Jay DeFeo, telegram to Bruce Conner, August 27, 1974, Bruce Conner correspondence concerning *The Rose*, Bancroft Library.

66. Jay DeFeo, letter to Bruce Conner, undated, Bruce Conner correspondence concerning *The Rose*, Bancroft Library.

67. DeFeo addresses Conner as "Telephone" in the following correspondence: Jay DeFeo, telegram to Bruce Conner, 1974, Bruce Conner correspondence concerning *The Rose*, Bancroft Library; and Jay DeFeo, letter to Bruce Conner, undated, Bruce Conner photograph collection, Bancroft Library. She refers to him as "Music-page" in Jay DeFeo, letter to Bruce Conner, 1976, Bruce Conner correspondence concerning *The Rose*, Bancroft Library.

68. DeFeo named herself "Telegram" in DeFeo, telegram to Conner, 1974, Bruce Conner correspondence concerning *The Rose*, Bancroft Library. She called herself "Elephant" in Jay DeFeo, letter to Bruce Conner, undated, Bruce Conner photograph collection, Bancroft Library. She likewise referred to *The Rose* as her "white elephant" in Jay DeFeo, letter to Irving Blum, 1966, Jay DeFeo papers, AAA; and in Jay DeFeo, letter to Thomas Albright, April 4, 1971, Bruce Conner correspondence concerning *The Rose*, Bancroft Library. Finally, she christened herself "Drawing Board" in Jay DeFeo, letter to Bruce Conner, undated, Bruce Conner correspondence concerning *The Rose*, Bancroft Library.

69. DeFeo, telegram to Bruce Conner, 1974, Bruce Conner correspondence concerning *The Rose*, Bancroft Library.

70. Huizinga, *Homo Ludens*, 14.

71. Quoted in Hatch, *Looking for Bruce Conner*, 152. For more on Conner's play with artistic identity, see Matt, "I'm Bruce Conner, I'm Not Bruce Conner," 135–38; and Joan Rothfuss, "Escape Artist," in Rothfuss, *2000 BC*, 163, 179.

72. Federman, "Fifty Years in Show Business," 18.

73. Quoted in Federman, "Fifty Years in Show Business," 18–19.

74. Huizinga, *Homo Ludens*, 13; Millar, *Psychology of Play*, 187.

75. Jay DeFeo, letter to Bruce Conner, undated, Bruce Conner photograph collection, Bancroft Library. This collection contains two other examples of baby photos that DeFeo converted into postcards for Conner.

76. Winnicott, *Playing and Reality*, 51; Freud, "Creative Writers and Day-Dreaming," 421.

77. Lewallen, "Mountain Climbing," 18–19.

78. Lewallen, "Mountain Climbing," 19.

79. Millar, *Psychology of Play*, 13–14; Conner, "Conversation," 233.

80. Winnicott, *Playing and Reality*, 52.

81. Miller identifies these referents in "Slow Curve," 37.

82. Rosalind Krauss, "Photography in the Service of Surrealism," in *L'Amour Fou: Photography and Surrealism*, ed. Rosalind Krauss and Jane Livingston (New York: Abbeville, 1985), 14–42. Sussman similarly links DeFeo's photo collages to avant-garde precedents; Sussman, "Behold! The Tripod!," 8.

83. Winnicott, *Playing and Reality*, 47; Huizinga, *Homo Ludens*, 11 and 4.

84. This description of the process that produced the ANGELS series draws on Boswell, "Theater of Light and Shadow," 72–75; and Rothfuss, "Escape Artist," 165.

85. Conner, "Conversation," 234.

86. Quoted in Federman, "Fifty Years in Show Business," 186. This account of the photograms' production relies on Judith Cizek, "Angels: Bruce Conner, 1973–1975," exh. brochure (San Francisco: San Francisco Museum of Modern Art, 1992); Rothfuss, "Escape Artist," 165, 167; and Hatch, *Looking for Bruce Conner*, 269–70.

87. Bruce Conner, interview with Peter Boswell, "Bruce Conner in Conversation with Peter Boswell," in Matt and Steffen, *Bruce Conner: The 1970s*, 184.

88. Several scholars have noted that the photograms crystallize the "thematic struggle of light overcoming darkness that was, increasingly surfacing in his [Conner's] work at the time"; see Hatch, *Looking for Bruce Conner*, 264. Also see Boswell, "Theater of Light and Shadow."

89. Kristine Stiles, "Bruce Conner's Eyes," in Frieling and Garrels, *It's All True*, 317.

90. Jay DeFeo, note to Bruce Conner, undated (c. 1975), Bruce Conner correspondence concerning *The Rose*, Bancroft Library.

91. Boswell and Cizek both echo DeFeo's assessment of Conner's ANGELS, referring to them as "vessel[s] of light" and "vessel[s] of radiance"; see Boswell, "Theater of Light and Shadow," 74; Cizek, "Angels: Bruce Conner," unpaginated.

92. DeFeo, letter to Thomas Albright, May 13, 1971, Bruce Conner correspondence concerning *The Rose*, Bancroft Library; DeFeo, letter to Conner, October 27, 1972, Jay DeFeo papers, AAA.

93. Boswell makes a similar observation in "Theater of Light and Shadow," 74.

CODA

1. This paragraph's account of women artists in the 1940s and 1950s draws from Anne M. Wagner, *Three Artists (Three Women)* (Berkeley: University of California Press, 1996); Michael Leja, *Reframing Abstract Expressionism: Subjectivity and Painting in the 1940s* (New Haven: Yale University Press, 1997); and Ann Eden Gibson, *Abstract Expressionism: Other Politics* (New Haven: Yale University Press, 1999). DeFeo's art education is described in Richard Cándida Smith, *The Modern Moves West: California Artists and Democratic Culture in the Twentieth Century* (Philadelphia: University of Pennsylvania Press, 2009), 66, 127; and Dana Miller, "A Slow Curve," in *Jay DeFeo: A Retrospective*, ed. Dana Miller, exh. cat. (New York: Whitney Museum of American Art; New Haven: Yale University Press, 2012), 16.

2. Wagner, *Three Artists*, 4. For competing accounts of the origin of DeFeo's nickname, see Lucy Lippard, "Transplanting *The Rose*," in *Jay DeFeo and "The Rose,"* ed. Jane Green and Leah Levy (Berkeley: University of California Press, 2003), 57; Rebecca Solnit, *Secret Exhibition: Six California Artists of the Cold War Era* (San Francisco: City Lights, 1990), 51; and Miller, "Slow Curve," 49n11.

3. Notable instances of DeFeo's incorporation into feminist art history include Lippard's essay "Transplanting *The Rose*" and the inclusion of works by DeFeo in the exhibition *WACK! Feminist Art and Revolution*, which opened at the Museum of Contemporary Art, Los Angeles, in 2007. DeFeo's ambivalence toward the feminist art movement is discussed in Lippard, "Transplanting *The Rose*," 56; Cándida Smith, *Modern Moves West*, 127; Jason Goldman, "Open Secrets: Publicity, Privacy, and U.S. Artistic Practice in the Sixties" (Ph.D. diss., University of Southern California, 2011), 79; and Corrina Peipon, "Jay DeFeo," in *WACK! Art and the Feminist Revolution*, ed. Cornelia Butler and Lisa Gabrielle Mark, exh. cat. (Los Angeles: Museum of Contemporary Art; Cambridge, Mass.: MIT Press, 2007), 227. Feminist artist Judy Chicago confirmed these assessments, recalling that both DeFeo and Joan Brown "weren't really receptive" to her attempts to "get to know them"; Judy Chicago, interviewed by Jane Collings for the Center for Oral History, University of California, Los Angeles, Library, October 10, 2003, http://digital2.library.ucla.edu/viewFile.do?contentFileId=2384484. I would like to thank Catherine Spencer for bringing this passage to my attention.

4. Helen Molesworth, "Painting with Ambivalence," in Butler and Mark, *WACK!*, 430–31.

5. Gibson, *Other Politics*, 17; Anne M. Wagner, "Krasner's Fictions," in *Three Artists*, 105–90.

6. Molesworth, "Painting with Ambivalence," 433.

7. Kenneth Price and Henry Hopkins quoted in Anastasia Aukeman, *Welcome to Painterland: Bruce Conner and the Rat Bastard Protective Association* (Berkeley: University of California Press, 2016), 196, 197. For insight into the male-dominated nature of Los Angeles's postwar art world, see Cécile Whiting, *Pop L.A.: Art and the City in the 1960s* (Berkeley: University of California Press, 2006), 63–71; *The Cool School: How L.A. Learned to Love Modern Art*, dir. Morgan Neville (2008); and Thomas Crow, "The Nearest Faraway Place: Billy Al Bengston and Pop Life in Los Angeles," in *The Long March of Pop: Art, Music, and Design, 1930–1995* (New Haven: Yale University Press, 2014), 206–31.

8. Joyce Johnson, *Minor Characters: A Beat Memoir* (New York: Penguin, 1999); Ronna C. Johnson, "Mapping Women Beat Writers," in *Breaking the Rule of Cool: Interviewing and Reading Women Beat Writers*, ed. Nancy M. Grace and Ronna C. Johnson (Jackson: University Press of Mississippi, 2004), 5; Maggie Nelson, *Women, the New York School, and Other True Abstractions* (Iowa City: University of Iowa Press, 2007), 8–9.

9. Lippard, "Transplanting *The Rose*," 57. Scholars who have made some version of this argument include Solnit, *Secret Exhibition*, 51; Richard Cándida Smith, "Part II: Mythopoesis and Self-Narration," in *Utopia and Dissent: Art, Poetry, and Politics in California* (Berkeley: University of California Press, 1995), 143–298; Rebecca Schoenthal, "North Beach to Haight-Ashbury: Underground Artists and Community in 1950s San Francisco" (Ph.D. diss., University of Virginia, 2005), 230–31; Aukeman, *Welcome to Painterland*, 197–98; and Susan Landauer, "The Advantages of Obscurity: Women Abstract Expressionists in

San Francisco," in *Women of Abstract Expressionism*, ed. Joan Marter, exh. cat. (Denver: Denver Art Museum; New Haven: Yale University Press, 2016), 42–57.

10. Landauer, "Advantages of Obscurity," 49; Jay DeFeo quoted in Rebecca Solnit, "Heretical Constellations: Notes on California, 1946–61," in *Beat Culture and the New America, 1950–1965*, ed. Lisa Phillips, exh. cat. (New York: Whitney Museum of American Art, 1995), 82; DeFeo cited in Landauer, "Advantages of Obscurity," 42.

11. Jane Green and Leah Levy, "Introduction," in Green and Levy, *Jay DeFeo and "The Rose,"* 2.

12. Oral history interview with Jay DeFeo, June 3, 1975–January 23, 1976, Archives of American Art (AAA), Smithsonian Institution, Washington, D.C.

13. Michael McClure, interview with the author, July 26, 2015, Oakland, Calif.

14. Simone de Beauvoir, *The Second Sex*, ed. and trans. H. M. Stryker Parshley (New York: Knopf, 1953), 253.

15. Wagner, *Three Artists*, 6.

16. Judith Butler, *Excitable Speech: A Politics of the Performative* (New York: Routledge 1997), 137.

17. Beauvoir, *Second Sex*, 253.

18. Beauvoir, *Second Sex*, 253, 260.

19. Beauvoir paraphrased in Diane Richardson, "Conceptualizing Gender," in *Introducing Gender and Women's Studies*, ed. Victoria Robinson and Diane Richardson (Basingstoke, U.K: Palgrave Macmillan, 2015), 6; Judith Butler, *Gender Trouble: Feminism and the Subversion of Identity* (New York: Routledge, 2006).

20. Nelson, *Other True Abstractions*, 10.

21. Sharon Marcus, *Between Women: Friendship, Desire, and Marriage in Victorian England* (Princeton, N.J.: Princeton University Press, 2007), 26; Cándida Smith, "Part II: Mythopoesis and Self-Narration"; Michael Davidson, *Guys Like Us: Citing Masculinity in Cold War Poetics* (Chicago: University of Chicago Press, 2003).

22. Jay DeFeo, collaged letter to Wallace Berman, 1965, Jay DeFeo papers, circa 1940s–1970s, AAA.

23. Miller similarly uses the quote to describe DeFeo's "corpus" as "a curveball that defies the traditional narratives of twentieth-century art"; Miller, "Slow Curve," 47.

24. Marcus, *Between Women*, 26.

25. Judith Butler, *Bodies That Matter: On the Discursive Limits of Sex* (New York: Routledge, 1993); quote from Judith Butler, interview with Liz Kotz, "The Body You Want: Liz Kotz Interviews Judith Butler," *Artforum* 31, no. 3 (November 1992), https://www.artforum.com/print/previews/199209.

26. Wagner, *Three Artists*.

Index

Page numbers in *italics* indicate illustrations.

llustration Credits

:l works by Jay DeFeo © 2021 The Jay DeFeo Foundation/Artists Rights Society (ARS), New York; by /allace Berman © The Estate of Wallace Berman and Kohn Gallery, Los Angeles; by Wally Hedrick ɔ The Estate of Wally Hedrick; by Bruce Conner © 2020 Conner Family Trust, San Francisco/Artist Rights Society (ARS), New York (except figs. 65–68).

Photographs provided by Dennis Hearne/© The Estate of Jerry Burchard. Used with permission (figs. 1, 42–45)
Image courtesy of The Jay DeFeo Foundation, Berkeley, Calif. (figs. 2, 61, 63, 79, 84)
© 1991 Hans Namuth Estate, Courtesy Center for Creative Photography (fig. 3)
© Steve Schapiro/Corbis Premium Historical via Getty Images (fig. 4)
Digital Image © 2020 Museum Associates/LACMA/Licensed by Art Resource, New York (fig. 5)
Digital Image © The Museum of Modern Art/Licensed by SCALA/Art Resource, New York (figs. 6, 21, 27, 38, 52)
Digital Image © Whitney Museum of American/Art Licensed by SCALA/Art Resource, New York (figs. 8, 13–20, 47, 62)
Photo: Moss Photography (fig. 11)
Photo: Charles Brittin (fig. 22)
© Ernst Haas/Ernst Haas via Getty Images/© Burt Glinn/Magnum Photos (fig. 23)
© Gordon Parks/The LIFE Picture Collection via Getty Images/© 1957 The Picture Collection Inc. All rights reserved. Reprinted/Translated from LIFE and published with permission of The Picture Collection Inc. Reproduction in any manner in any language in whole or in part without written permission is prohibited (fig. 24)
© Gordon Parks/The LIFE Picture Collection via Getty Images/© Loomis Dean/The LIFE Picture Collection via Getty Images/© 1957 The Picture Collection Inc. All rights reserved. Reprinted/Translated from LIFE and published with permission of The Picture Collection Inc. Reproduction in any manner in any language in whole or in part without written permission is prohibited (fig. 25)
© J. Paul Getty Trust (fig. 26)
Photo: White Images/Scala/Art Resource, NY (figs. 30, 31)
Photo: J. W. White/Phocasso (fig. 36)
Photo: Lee Fatherree (fig. 37)
Photo: bpk Bildagentur/Sprengel Museum/Wilhelm Redemann/Art Resource, New York/Artwork © 2020 Artists Rights Society (ARS), New York/VG Bild-Kunst, Bonn (fig. 48)
Photo: Lawrence Fox/Artwork © Lawrence Fox/Artwork © The Estate of Wally Hedrick (fig. 54)
© Larry Keenan (figs. 55, 60)
Photo: James Oliver Mitchell/Grizzly Peak Press, Kensington, Calif./Liquid Pictures, Berkeley, Calif./ Artwork © James Oliver Mitchell (fig. 56)
Photo: Peter Paul Geoffrion (fig. 57)
© WNET (fig. 58)
Photo © Tate/Artwork © Hans Haacke/Artists Rights Society (ARS), New York/VG Bild-Kunst, Bonn (fig. 59)
Photo: With permission of New Directions Publishing Corp. (fig. 60)
Photo: Ben Blackwell (figs. 61, 80, 82–86, 89)
Photo © mumok—Museum moderner Kunst Stiftung Ludwig Wien (fig. 64)
© Conner Family Trust, San Francisco (figs. 65–68)
Photo: Brian Lucas (fig. 69)
Photo: Paul Hester (fig. 72)
Photo: Don Ross (fig. 76)
Photo: Courtesy of Michael Rosenfeld Gallery, LLC, New York (fig. 78)
© 2020 Conner Family Trust, San Francisco/Artist Rights Society (ARS), New York, and Edmund Shea Trust (figs. 80–81)